A History of Libraries in the Western World

by

Elmer D. Johnson

The Scarecrow Press, Inc.

New York and London   1965

CONTENTS

Introduction

The present work is an attempt to trace the history of libraries in the Western World: to indicate how libraries developed and how they influenced the social and cultural history of our civilization. The book is intended for the student of library science or of cultural history and for the general reader interested in the development of Western civilization. Much has been omitted concerning libraries and librarians that could have been included; conversely, it is quite possible that some facts have been included that could have been omitted without seriously detracting from the story as a whole. However, what has been included is here because it illustrates how library history developed; it points out the high spots and indicates trends without necessarily filling in all the details.

To aid the interested reader in filling in the details, additional readings are included at the end of each chapter. These listings are representative rather than comprehensive. The better-known works have been included, along with some rarer and less-known but still valuable ones. Some types of information that could well be useful to students of library history have generally been omitted. These include library directories and guidebooks, library reports and reports of state or national library agencies, most periodical material on library history, and all unpublished theses and dissertations on the subject. Also omitted are most biographies of librarians and most descriptive pamphlets on individual libraries.

This work is offered to the reader with the hope that it will be useful. It is the cumulative result of some 20 years of studying and teaching both the history of libraries and the history of Western civilization.

Thanks and heartfelt appreciation are due many people for

kindnesses that helped to make this book possible: to the students who listened to me patiently, sometimes even after the bell had rung; to the librarians, particularly those in charge of inter-library loans who made long-sought volumes available to me; to my friends, both historians and librarians, who encouraged me greatly; and finally, to my wife, who aided immensely in every way -- from keeping my notes in order, to proofreading my early efforts, and who always kept a full coffee cup and a dictionary handy!

Elmer D. Johnson

1.

The Origin of Libraries

The origin of libraries, like the origin of speech and of writing, is lost in the early history of man. Unlike speech and writing, however, the beginning of libraries came after the end of the prehistoric era, since the preservation of written records is considered to have begun the historic age. Conceivably, it should be possible to decide just when and where the first library existed, but such is not the case. Instead, all we know is that at certain times, and in certain locations early libraries existed. Before that, collections of graphic materials approaching the form of libraries undoubtedly existed, but facts as to when, where, and what are more difficult to pin down. One of the purposes for the development of writing was to preserve human communication -- to extend its duration beyond the sound of the human voice and beyond the memory of mortal man. Hence, it is quite probable that written communications were kept almost from the beginning of writing. Early written forms were often considered sacred, and this constituted another reason for their careful preservation. If these early records were kept in an orderly manner, suitable for future use when needed, they then had all the earmarks of a proto-library or archive.

Perhaps a good place to begin a discussion of the history of libraries would be with a definition for the term library. What is a library? What distinguishes it from a collection of graphic materials or from an archive? For the purposes of this work it is assumed that a library is a collection of graphic materials arranged for relatively easy use, cared for by an individual or individuals familiar with that arrangement, and available for use by at least a limited number of persons. That this definition would include early religious and governmental archives is readily admitted. The distinction between a library and an archive is a rela-

7

tively modern one, and for historical purposes the two can be considered together (although where they diverge distinctively, only the
library proper will be considered). The distinction, when it
emerges, will indicate that a library is an organized collection of
general information and literature, while an archive is an organized collection of records of a specific agency, whether government,
business, or church.

Although early libraries were commonly associated with religious edifices, it cannot be assumed that the temple library was
the only or even the most important early form of library. In
fact, there seem to have been at least three, if not four, types of
graphic collections that contributed to the general development of
early library form. The first of these was the temple collection;
the second the governmental archive; the third the business record;
and the possible fourth, the collection of family or genealogical
records. Where religious and temporal rule were in the same
hands the first two types of collections sometimes merged into one;
the second two were also close when family and business records
came together. In either case, the written records contained facts
or information that were meant to be preserved for future use, and
for such use a logical order of arrangement was necessary wherever a dozen or more individual items were kept.

The temple collection might be considered first, since this
is the form usually given as an example of the protolibrary. A
temple or any religious edifice of an advanced type presupposes a
formalized method of worship, a priesthood, and a hierarchy of
gods to be worshiped. Usually, there was also a story of creation
and a genealogy of the gods to be remembered. For generations,
possibly for centuries, such a religious literature could be handed
down orally from parents to children; but eventually it would become necessary to stabilize this story and to provide for an established, orthodox form of religious worship. This need might
have been brought about through political change, migration, the
threat posed by other religions, or simply by the growing complex-
ity of the religious literature itself. Perhaps the development of
writing made such a religious stabilization possible, or perhaps

the need for such a stabilization of religious practices helped to
bring about the development of writing. In either case, the temple
collection began with copies of the sacred laws, rituals, songs,
creation stories, biographies of the gods, and later the commentaries of religious authorities on all of these. The basic scriptures
might be carved on stone, inscribed on leather, or embossed on
clay to be baked into imperishable bricks. Less important religious writings might be on the common writing materials of a given
time and place -- papyrus, parchment, or whatever.

In any event, the theological collection was kept in a sacred
place and presided over by a priest. Only the most important of
the temple officials would have access to this library, and probably
only a few of them could read. In fact, in most early societies
the scribe, or the trained individual who could read and write, was
a most important person, and often only a few of the temple personnel belonged to this select group. The temple library may have
been of the few, and by the few, and for the few; but it did preserve the most important literature of a given religion, and as
such it was a basic cultural heritage for the religious group. In
Egypt, Palestine, Babylon, Greece, and Rome, the temple collection certainly was among the earliest and most important forms of
the protolibrary.

Next in importance were the government record collections,
or archives. To support the government, taxes, or tributes, were
necessary, and to make these sources of income reasonably accurate and honest, property ownership had to be guaranteed and tax
records compiled and kept. Deeds and property transactions had
to be recorded and a graphic representation of their legality filed
in some government office. On a larger scale, agreements,
treaties, and understandings between rulers had to be put down in
some permanent form. Partnerships between kings and princes
were made and broken, tribute was exacted from defeated powers,
satellite governors made their reports and pleas for aid in times
of need. Some of the earliest records of which we have knowledge
are such quasi-diplomatic bits of correspondence between chief
rulers and their subordinates. These were all official government

records, and when they were preserved and arranged for future use,
they became government archives.   However, when codifications of
laws, accounts of military campaigns, genealogies of rulers, and
other materials were added to these archival collections, the latter
took on the aspect of a library, and examples of such collections
are known.   Moreover, rulers sometimes commissioned histories
of their reigns to be compiled and preserved, and since these often
included more fiction than fact, they added an element of literature
to an otherwise staid collection of graphic facts.

At any rate, governmental archives are prominent among the
early library forms.   They existed as clay tablets in Babylonia, as
papyrus rolls in Egypt, and as both papyrus and parchment in
Rome; whatever their format, they preserved an account of the major activities of governing powers, and as such formed a basis for
future cultural and political histories.

The civilization that was advanced enough to have government
and temple libraries was also more than likely to have a rather advanced state of business and commerce.   Centers of government or
of religious worship were usually in relatively densely populated
areas.   Such urban or semiurban areas developed along rivers, on
harbors, or at junctures of overland trade routes.   Advanced civilizations required something beyond mere barter and exchange of
goods, and hence money or some other stable medium of exchange
became a necessity.   As business went beyond the barter stage,
records had to be kept.   Records of property, inventories, purchase and sales prices, taxes and tributes had to be preserved and
arranged for ready use.   Reports from and instructions to employees or agents in distant towns had to be recorded and kept.
Such records, of course, formed a business archive, but eventually
the nature of the information included might be broadened.   Accounts of ocean voyages or land explorations in search of trade,
military and political events effecting trade, natural disasters,
manufacturing methods, or of trade formulas -- all these might
well enter into the business archive, and if so, the latter took on
more of the nature of a library.   Whether archive or library, such
collections were familiar in the great trading houses of Egypt,

Phoenicia, Babylonia, and later in Alexandria, Athens, and Rome. The commercial origin of the library is possibly not so tangible as that of the temple or palace archive, but it must not be completely overlooked.

The relationship between the family manuscript collection and the development of libraries may also be tenuous, but it did have a direct connection with the development of private libraries, and as such is a part of library history. Some of the earliest-known examples of the written record relate to private matters. Property ownership and inheritance are important factors in any organized society; hence wills, deeds, sales forms, inventories of cattle and even of slaves form some of the earliest surviving records. Genealogies indicating family lineages and relationships were often kept for several generations. Marriages often involved dowries, and hence marriage contracts were vital records. Letters to and from distant relatives and friends also entered into the family collection of documents. Not infrequently, recipes for favorite dishes or formulas for making household products (such as dyes and oils) were kept. Even plans for simple, homemade tools have been found in the family "libraries" of Babylonia. If the family was wealthy or of the noble class, literature of a nonpersonal and non-economic nature, such as religious scriptures and rituals or perhaps works of astrology and divination might be added to the collection. Collections of omens seem to have been a favorite family item in Babylonia. Perhaps a list of kings, a historical chronology, or even the works of a local poet or storyteller might be added. Finally, the family collection might become a genuine private library with the addition of religious commentaries, "classical" writings, and other literature of historical or current content. The family archive is thus the ancestor of the private library; and by the days of the Romans, if not earlier, the well-established private library was a definite element in the library world.

One other factor in the early development of libraries was the official, or "copyright," collection of manuscripts. As literary works were produced and copies widely made, assurance of the accuracy, or purity, of the copied text was required. Historical texts might vary slightly from copy to copy, so long as the actual facts were unchanged; but in the text of a poem or a play, the author's original words were all-important to its literary value. For this reason, in ancient Athens in the days of Sophocles and Euripides, official copies of plays were placed in a public collection as a means of guaranteeing that any person might have access to the correct texts. Because plays and other literary works could be pirated with ease, corrupted texts often circulated as readily as the original wording of the author. When correct texts were always available in an official library, all other texts could be checked against the official one at any time and question as to authenticity could always be answered. Something similar to this was done in Egypt and possibly elsewhere in connection with religious scriptures. The official, or standardized, scriptures would be kept in a sacred place as a guarantee of the authenticity or authority of their contents. Where such "copyright" collections were arranged and available for use, they became early forms of public libraries.

Another important factor in the origin and early development of libraries was the form of the graphic materials contained in them. In the course of man's history, it is apparent that he has experimented at one time or other with almost every type of known material in his attempts to find the most suitable writing instruments and the most satisfactory writing surface. In his early history, Western man has tried wood, stone, several metals, many types of hides, leaves, bark, cloth, and clay as writing surfaces, and he succeeded fairly well on almost all of them. For writing implements, he has tried chisels, many types of brushes, sticks, wooden and metal styluses, bird feathers and quills, pointed objects of almost every kind, along with various substances such as paints or inks. In fact, the ingenuity of early man was equalled only by the variety of materials at hand.

Generally speaking, however, three major forms of writing materials were used in the ancient world, and these three constituted the great majority of the graphic records kept in early libraries. The first of these, and the most widely used in terms of time and geographic area, was papyrus. The papyrus reed grew

widely along the lower Nile and was also found in other locations
throughout the Mediterranean area. To prepare a writing surface
from the reed, the outer bark was removed, and the inner, softer
pith was then sliced into thin, narrow strips. When these strips
were placed in two layers, the top layer perpendicular to the lower
one, and pressed or pounded lightly while moist, a sheet of rough
paperlike material was produced. This sheet was then dried and
polished with pumice stone to form a writing surface that would
readily take ink and still withstand ordinary handling. Papyrus of
various grades was produced, with the grade depending upon the
quality of the reed, the care with which it was made, and the sizes
of the sheets. Some seven or eight grades were denoted by different names, ranging from the hieratica, used for most important
documents, down to the emporetica, used only for wrapping paper.
Once the sheets were finished, they could be used singly for letters,
short poems, or documents; for longer works, they could be glued
side to side to form a long strip. Since the original sheets usually
varied in height from 6 to 10 inches, the completed strip would
ordinarily form a roll of that height and from 10 to 30 feet in
length. Some rolls were, of course, higher and longer. The
Harris Papyri, for example, is some 133 feet long by 17 inches
high. For a completed manuscript, the end of the roll would be
glued to a cylindrical stick of wood, metal, or ivory, and the entire roll encased in a larger cylinder of the same substances, or
of leather or baked clay. A note on the contents of the roll and
perhaps the seal of the owner could be attached to the roll on a tab
of wood, metal, or ivory. Such rolls could be very ornate or
quite plain, but the roll in this form constituted the usual "book" of
the ancient Greek, Egyptian, and Roman libraries.

Very different in substance and appearance, but similar in
form, was the parchment roll. Parchment, or vellum, its close
relative, was the cured hide of a young sheep or goat. The hide
was scraped clean of hair and fat and then cured or tanned to a
thin, almost translucent whiteness. The completed parchment was
trimmed to page size and also glued into long rolls. Ordinary
leather made from various animal hides was also widely used in

roll form, especially for important religious works and ceremonial scrolls. The parchment roll had an advantage over papyrus in that it was more durable in ordinary usage, and it could also be more easily used for writing on both sides. Papyrus was more porous and the ink would ordinarily show through, making it difficult to use both sides for writing; but this was sometimes done, particularly on the better grades of papyrus.

The liquid used for a writing ink varied from time to time and from place to place, but usually took one of two forms. The first and most widely used was a black ink made by mixing lamp black in water with a thin solution of gum. The second was a red ink made by mixing a red ocher or iron oxide in water, with or without the gum solution. In either case, the ink was usually kept in a dried form and mixed with water just before use. The usual method of applying the ink to the writing surface was by means of a pencil-like wooden stick sharpened to a point, with the point then crushed into a brush-like condition. Quills made from fowl feathers were not employed until the Roman era, although hairbrushes, especially for finer, decorative work, were employed in Egypt at a very early date. The writing equipment of the Egyptian scribe, for example, included a rectangular palette with two shallow basins for the red and black inks, a deep bowl for water, and a tubular case for his writing brushes. For temporary work, the Egyptian student also used a writing board surfaced with gesso that could be wiped clean for reuse.

The other popular and widely used form of the book in ancient times was the clay tablet, used in the cuneiform writing of the Mesopotamian Valley and neighboring areas. In fact, the clay tablet was used from Persia to Egypt, from the fourth millenium B. C. on into several centuries of the Christian era. Essentially the clay tablet was just that -- a tablet of soft, pliable clay of a firm consistency, suitable for taking marks from a stylus of wood, bone, reed, or metal. The clay was kept soft until used, then kneaded into the required size and shape. If the writing took more than a short period of time or if additional writing was to be added at a later date, the clay had to be kept moist, and this was usually done by wrapping it in a dampened cloth. The usual clay tablet was pillow-shaped, about 2 or 3 inches wide by 3 or 4 inches long, and about 1 inch thick. Sometimes they were larger, reaching 8 by 12 inches. Not all of the tablets were rectangular; some were circular or triangular, while still others were cylindrical or cone-shaped. The writing instrument, something like a stylus with a square or triangular tip, was held at an angle to the table surface and was used to make an impression rather than a continuous stroke. This gave the writing the appearance of wedge-shaped dents with long tails; hence the name cuneiform, or wedge-shaped, for this style of writing. After the writing on the tablet was completed, it was left to dry; if it was to be kept permanently, it was baked in an oven. Sometimes an outer sheath of clay was placed around the baked and inscribed tablet, and in the case of legal documents, the text might be repeated on the outside tablet. If the outer envelope of clay was unbroken, the inner text could be considered intact and correct, thus giving a sort of insured carbon-copy to prevent tampering with texts.

The earliest writing on clay tablets was in vertical columns, beginning at the top of the right-hand side of the tablet and ending at the bottom of the left-hand side. Many centuries later, the method of writing changed; it was done in horizontal lines beginning at the top left-hand side and ending at the bottom right-hand side, as in the modern style. Works of some length might require several or even dozens of tablets. A series of tablets was kept together on shelves, in stacks, or even in baskets; each tablet was numbered separately, and a key word or text was prominently inscribed on the end of the tablet. However, a few lengthy texts were simply inscribed on larger tablets. One of the larger ones, containing the Annals of Sennacharib, was six-sided, about 1 foot high and 5 inches thick. It was found at Nineveh in 1830 and is now in the British Museum.

Since it is known that clay tablets were widely used in Egypt along with the papyrus roll, it is logical to assume that papyrus and parchment were also used in Babylonia, particularly in the later centuries B. C. Because the climate in Babylonia was

more moist, any papyrus or parchment would have decayed long
ago, but clay seals that were apparently originally attached to inscribed rolls have been found there. Moreover, there are also illustrations to be seen on the walls of excavated Babylonian palaces
depicting scribes reading from a roll. There are also illustrations
showing writers employing what was apparently a waxed wooden tablet for keeping temporary records. Further evidence that the Babylonians used materials other than clay has been shown by the discovery of several sheets of thin ivory, apparently originally hinged
together in the form of a book.

In the classic ages of Greece and Rome the roll was the
dominant form of written record. Papyrus was widely used, but
parchment also came into its own, particularly after the third century A. D., and it was used in Europe on occasion, especially in
legal documents, as late as the fifteenth century. It was replaced
in general usage, however, by the fifth century A. D. by a form
similar to the present-day book. This book-form was the codex,
taking its name from the Latin caudex, or trunk of a tree. The
earliest form or prototype of the codex was the diptych, that is,
two wooden or ivory leaves hinged together on one side. The inner
faces of these leaves were coated with wax so that they could be
written on with a sharp stylus. The wax could be easily smoothed
to make an erasure, and the surface was ready for another writing.
These wax diptychs developed from the single wax tablet; hinges
were simply added on the side. The diptych could be used for
sending letters, computing accounts, preparing lessons, or for
other writing that did not need to be preserved. Eventually, more
than two thin leaves of metal, wood, or ivory were hinged together,
and thus the codex form was approached. When parchment came into wide use as a writing material, larger sheets were folded or
creased in the middle, and thus a folio of two leaves and four
pages was formed. When other sheets of parchment were folded
and inserted and the resulting combined sheets were stitched along
the fold, then a codex in the form of a small pamphlet or single
signature was formed. Several of these signatures sewn, glued,
and bound together with leather or wooden covers virtually formed

a book in its modern form.

Although the codex is usually considered a product of the Christian era (the early Christians were among the first to adopt and use it widely instead of the usual roll), it is interesting to note that hinged, waxed tablets were used by the Assyrians in the eighth century B. C. In the ruins of Nimrud, 16 ivory tablets and several walnut tablets were found in 1953, each with evidence that they had been at one time hinged together. One set of 15 thin ivory leaves with heavier covers and gold hinges was found, indicating that 1 wax-tablet "book" had at least 30 pages. It may have been used as a student's workbook, or perhaps as an easier means of keeping current accounts. One palace wall-illustration shows a scribe using a similar tablet to record the number of dead after a battle.

Although they were perhaps not directly related to the early history of libraries, there are two other forms of ancient graphic records that should be mentioned. These are the cylinder seals and the large public inscriptions on brick or stone known as stele. The cylinder seal was a small stone or metal cylinder, embossed in relief with a small picture, with or without writing. In one form or other it was used in Egypt and Babylonia for several thousand years. The picture on the seal was often one with mystic or religious overtones, but sometimes it indicated the occupation of the owner. If there was an inscription, it might contain the owner's name or perhaps a prayer or invocation to the gods. For practical purposes, the seal was something of a signature stamp for the owner, and at times apparently every adult in Egypt or Babylonia, even women and slaves, had personal seals. The owner rolled the cylinder over soft clay or wax to impress his signature as a statement of approval or record of ownership. Later, the seals may have been inked lightly for use on papyrus or parchment documents, although for the most part they were used for "blind" impressions on clay or wax. In a sense, the cylinder seal was an early form of printing. As historical records, the seals sometimes reveal or confirm the names of important individuals, and the illustrations often tell something of the social, economic, and religious life of the era represented.

The stela (plural, stele), on the other hand, was a large public inscription, something of a monumental bulletin board. Long documents of importance to the public were inscribed on large stone or clay tablets and erected in a public square or at a palace gate for all to see. These stele might proclaim a victory of a king over some opponent, a treaty between two powers, or an important legal work. The Code of Hammurabi, for example, was inscribed on several such stele located throughout the Babylonian Empire, and one of them has survived in a fairly complete condition. This stela was found by French archaelogists in 1901 at Susa and was inscribed on a block of black diorite, some 7.5 feet high. It had been erected in a public square so that all citizens could read it, or have it read to them, and thus know what their legal rights were. The stela was thus a graphic form of communication and as such has a place in the history of books and libraries.

In summary, the library began as a collection of records -- government, temple, business, or private -- and it gradually grew into a library as other materials of a historical or literary nature were added and as its use grew beyond that of the immediate officials or priests who kept it. Organized collections of archival materials existed in both Egypt and Babylonia before 3000 B.C.; before 2000 B.C., there were institutions in both countries that closely resemble our best definition of a library. Libraries were developed as civilizations reached their peak, and then were scattered or destroyed as those civilizations fell before barbaric invaders. Whatever its fate, the development of the library had served a vital purpose as a communicative link in both time and space, and henceforth in the history of Western man no society would reach a highly organized level without the accompanying growth of literacy and libraries.

Additional Readings

(There are few works that treat directly with the origin of libraries, although many of the general works on history of libraries consider it briefly. On the other hand, there are a number of excellent works on the origin and development of writing, and information on early writing materials is also readily available. Hence, the readings for this chapter include some general histories of libraries, some on writing, and a few on the earliest libraries alone. Generally speaking, in these chapter bibliographies a work will be included only once, and then at the earliest period covered in the book.)

Bailly, Jean Louis Amand
    Notices historiques sur les bibliothèques anciennes et modernes. Paris, 1828. ii, 210 p.

Bushnell, George Herbert
    The world's earliest libraries. London, 1931. 58 p.

Clark, J. W.
    The care of books: an essay on the development of libraries and their fittings. New York, 1901. xviii, 330 p.

Dziatzko, Carl
    Bibliotheken. (In v. 3, pp. 406-423 of Paulys Real-Encyclopedie der Classischen Altertumswissenschaft, ed. by Georg Wissowa. Stuttgart, 1899.)

Guppy, Henry
    "Human records, a survey of their history from the geginnings," John Rylands Library Bulletin, XXVII (1942), 182-222.

Hessel, Alfred
    History of libraries, translated with supplementary material by Reuben Peiss. Washington, 1950. 198p. (Originally: Geschichte der Bibliotheken. Göttingen, 1925. vii, 147 p.)

Hogben, Lancelot
    From cave painting to comic strip: a kaleidoscope of human communication. New York, 1949. 286 p.

Holliday, Carl
    The dawn of literature. New York, 1931. x, 367 p.

Irwin, Keith G.
    The romance of writing from the Egyptian hieroglyphics to modern letters. New York, 1956. 160 p.

Kirchner, Joachim, ed.
    Lexikon des Buchwesens. Stuttgart, 1952-1956. 4 vols. (Original edition ed. by K. Loeffler and J. Kirchner, Leipzig, 1935-37, 3 v.)

Koops, Mathias
    Historical account of the substances which have been used to describe events, and to convey ideas, from the earliest date to the invention of paper. London, 1800. 91p. (2nd. ed., London, 1801. 273 p.)

Martis, Wilson
   A palavra escrita; historia do livro, da imprensa, e da biblio-
      teca. São Paulo, 1957. 549 p.

Milkau, Fritz
   Handbuch der Bibliothekswissenschaft. v. 3. Leipzig, 1940.
      xxiii, 1051 p.

Mummendey, Richard
   Von Büchern und Bibliotheken. Bonn, 1950. 348 p.

Presser, Helmut
   Das Buch vom Buch. Bremen, 1962. 497 p.

Richardson, Ernest Cushing
   The beginnings of libraries. Princeton, 1914. 176p.
      (Reprinted, Shoestring Press, 1963. x, 176 p.)

Schottenloher, Karl
   Bücher bewegten die Welt: eine Kulturgeschichte des Buches.
      Stuttgart, 1951. 278 p.

Teggart, Frederick John
   Contributions toward a bibliography of ancient libraries.
      New York, 1899. 13 p.

Thornton, John L.
   The chronology of librarianship: an introduction to the history
      of libraries and book-collecting. London, 1941. 266 p.

Vleeschauwer, Herman Jean de
   Encyclopedia of library history. Pretoria, 1956. 2v.
      (Mousaion, no. 2-3).
   Survey of library history. Pretoria, 1963. (Mousaion, no.
      63-66).

Vorstius, Joris
   Grundzuge der Bibliotheksgeschichte. Leipzig, 4th ed., 1948.
      114 p. ; 5th ed., 1953, 138 p.

Wyss, Wilhelm V.
   "The libraries of antiquity," Living Age, CCCXVI (Jan. 27,
      1923), 217-249. (Taken from Die Bibliotheken des Altertums
      und ihre Aufgabe. Zurich, 1923. 34 p.)

2.

Babylonian and Assyrian Libraries

It is difficult to say whether the first library in the Western World was located in Egypt or in Mesopotamia, but it is certain that in the civilizations emerging in those two areas in the fourth and third millenia before Christ, writing produced "books," and these were preserved in sufficient numbers to form a library. In the Mesopotamian Valley, inhabited successively by Sumerians, Babylonians, and Assyrians, the process that gave rise to libraries was certainly well under way during those periods. Writing in a pictographic form had developed there possibly as early as 4000 B. C., and by 3600 B. C. the Sumerians in the lower valley were developing a cuneiform script from the pictographs. By 3000 B. C., the use of cuneiform writing on clay tablets was common, and by 2700 B. C. libraries, or at least extensive archives, had been established. Thanks to the durable qualities of baked clay, we know of these libraries through their remains. Tens of thousands of clay tablets have been unearthed in the ruins of Mesopotamian towns, and since the cuneiform script has been deciphered, we can not only read the tablets, but we can also tell quite a bit about how they were collected and arranged into libraries.

The Sumerians in the lower valley were a non-Semitic people, but the upper reaches of the Tigris and Euphrates Rivers were inhabited about 3000 B. C. by a Semitic people known as Akkadians. About 2600 B. C., a Semitic leader, Sargon I, united the whole valley into the old Babylonian Empire and built a powerful state that extended from the Persian Gulf to the Mediterranean. With many ups and downs this Babylonian civilization lasted nearly 2,000 years, reaching a high point under the rule of Hammurabi (ca. 1950 B. C.), whose enlightened reign is remembered for important public works and the famous Code of laws. About 728 B. C., Babylonia was conquered by an Assyrian king, and the valley remained under Assyrian rule for about a century. The Assyrians, long-time neighbors to the north, were somewhat less advanced culturally than the Babylonians, but they were more militarily powerful. In their relatively short control of the whole valley, the Assyrians borrowed readily from the culture of their predecessors and brought literature and libraries to a high degree of development. After the defeat of the Assyrians about 625 B. C. , a new Babylonian state arose, the Chaldean Empire; but it too was short-lived, and the valley fell first to the Persians and then to the Greeks.

However, while the Sumerian-Babylonian-Assyrian civilization existed, the Mesopotamian Valley was one of the most enlightened and progressive areas in the world. As the many ancient townsites of the valley have been excavated and studied, the clay tablet collections have unfolded a long and virtually continuous story of library development. One of the earliest finds in clay tablets comes from the Red Temple at Uruk. Uruk, or Erech, was in the lower valley near the Euphrates, and this collection, dated before 3000 B. C. , is in a pictographic script. In another collection from the same area, but dated some 200 years later, the script is more advanced and appears to be partly pictographic and partly cuneiform. At Jemdet Nasr, near the site of the later Babylon, another more-advanced script has been found dating from about 2700 B. C. From Tello, near Lagash, a collection of almost thirty thousand tablets, all in cuneiform, have been dated at about 2350 B. C. , while many more thousands have been found at Nippur, 100 miles south of modern Baghdad, and dating from around 2000 B. C.

About the time of Hammurabi (ca. 1950 B. C.), an attempt was made to bring together an up-to-date history of the Babylonians. Chronologies of the reigns of kings were compiled, and the history of all wars and international disputes was written down. Another religious history was also composed, giving the story of the various gods, their temples and priests, half mythological and half historical. To compile these works, the Babylonians must have had at their disposal thousands of tablets of recorded history, well organized and cataloged into usable libraries. Unfortunately, both of these histories have failed to survive, but remnants of the political history, in the form of lists of kings, were copied by the later Assyrians, along with the story of how the histories were compiled. These king-lists, purporting to cover all rulers in the valley from before the Flood to Hammurabi, are questioned by modern historians, but they still form a basis for the study of early Mesopotamian history. Hammurabi's reign is also remembered, of course, for the codification of laws known by his name. This work also called for well-arranged legal collections as sources for the laws and presupposes what must have been an excellent legal archive or law library. From the viewpoint of library history, the important thing is that in order to compile such histories or codes of laws the writers must have had thousands of clay tablets to draw on, and those tablets must have been well arranged and organized for use.

There may be some question as to how well organized the tablet collections of the Babylonians and Sumerians were. There is no doubt that the Assyrians had true libraries, in the modern sense of the word after 1000 B. C. These were not only large and well organized but were also open to the public and were used. Particularly under Sargon II, who died about 705 B. C., the Assyrians developed a palace library at Khorsabad that was a notable beginning. Ruins of this library have been excavated; in it, among hundreds of other tablets, was a king-list dating from the twenty-third century B. C. down to Sargon himself. Sargon's immediate successors increased the size of the palace library, but it was his great-grandson, Ashurbanipal, who developed the library into the greatest of the ancient world. Ashurbanipal moved the royal capital to Nineveh and there in his palace accumulated a library of over 30,000 tablets. Under his personal direction, agents were sent to all parts of the Assyrian kingdom and even to foreign lands to collect written records of all kinds and on all subjects. Ashurbanipal had his scribes taught to read early Sumerian and Akkadian texts in order to translate the ancient records into Assyrian. He was particularly interested in religious texts, incantations, and verbal charms, but his agents were instructed to bring back every-

thing in writing. He is reported to have asked Nabu, the Assyrian
god of writing, to bless his library and to grant him the grace to
erect it. Like the Alexandrian Library a few centuries later, the
library of Ashurbanipal was open to scholars, both official and un-
official. In fact, many scribes and scholars were employed by the
King to revise, compile, and edit the thousands of texts brought together in his library.

Ashurbanipal's library was kept in many rooms in his palace, and apparently there was some subject arrangement by rooms.
One room, for example, was filled with tablets relating to history,
including records and biographies of former kings, both of Assyria
and neighboring countries, along with the king-lists. In this room
there were also copies of treaties, letters to the king's ambassadors in other lands, and orders to generals and military officials.
Another division of the library seems to have been given over to
geography, with descriptions of towns and countries, rivers and
mountains, and lists of commercial products available from each
area. One division concerned laws and legal decisions, while still
another was given over to records of commercial transactions,
records of contracts, deeds, bills of sale, and the like. Tax lists
together with accounts of tribute due from the nobility made up another division. One important room was given over to clay tablets
containing legends and mythology, the basis of the religion of Assyria. Included were the accounts of the Flood, the lists of the
gods, their various accomplishments and attributes, and the hymns
of praise dedicated to them. Rituals, prayers, and incantations
made up an important subdivision of this group. Still other divisions of Ashurbanipal's library were made up of works in the sciences and pseudosciences -- astronomy and astrology, biology,
mathematics, natural history, and medicine. It should be pointed
out that much of the library's contents consisted of copies and
translations of non-Assyrian works, drawn from their predecessors
in the valley and from their neighbors on all sides.

The clay tablets inside the rooms of Ashurbanipal's library
were kept in earthen jars, and the jars in turn were kept in orderly rows on shelves. Each tablet bore an identification tag, indicat-

ing the jar, shelf, and room in which it was to be found. On the walls of the room, beside the door, was a list of the works to be found in each room. This would correspond to a rough shelf list of the room's contents. Moreover, something on the order of a catalog, or a descriptive bibliography, has been found on tablets that may have also been kept near the door in each room. These tablets include entries giving titles of works, the number of tablets, the number of lines, opening words, important subdivisions, and the location or classification symbol. Just how this cataloging system worked is not fully understood, but there seems to be no doubt that the tablets were arranged for quick consultation, and the worn condition of some of the "catalog" tablets indicates that they were well used.

Ashurbanipal took pride in his library and in having collected it from all parts of the then-known world. His official seal is an example of this pride. On it, after invoking the aid of his favorite god, Nabu, he says: "I have collected these tablets, I have had them copied, I have marked them with my name, and I have deposited them in my palace." It is well for history that he did compile such a wonderful collection of literature, for it is through this collection that much of what is known of earlier Mesopotamian history has been learned. The Epic of Gilgamesh, for example, was preserved through a copy in Ashurbanipal's library, as was a Babylonian tale of creation on seven tablets, and many other legends, epics, and hero-tales. The remarkable thing is that the library survived as nearly intact as it did, and the reason for its survival is, oddly enough, probably due to a disaster. When Nineveh was destroyed in 612 B.C., the invading Chaldeans and Scythians apparently cared little for the clay tablets and simply destroyed the palaces containing them by pushing in the walls with battering rams. The collapsing walls buried the tablet libraries beneath them and helped preserve them for centuries until they were unearthed by archaeologists in the nineteenth and twentieth centuries.

Although Ashurbanipal's library was possibly the most spectacular of the Mesopotamian libraries, it was far from being the only major one.   In fact, from the many excavations in the area, evidence of many more palace and temple libraries has been found, with their approximate dating ranging from 2000 to 500 B. C.   Evidence is available that wealthy private families in several cities of the valley also had libraries, and collections of business archives have been found.   However, it is in the ruins of palaces and government buildings that some of the best clay tablet collections have been found.   In ancient Babylon itself, a municipal archive was discovered, containing several thousand tablets concerned with everyday city business -- taxes, deeds, contracts, marriage records, and court decisions.   A collection of over 30, 000 tablets was uncovered at Lagash, apparently also a government record library. One of the most interesting of the valley libraries was one found at the city of Mari on the upper Euphrates in what is now Syria. This collection was also partly archival in nature, but it took on the nature of a library in that it also contained historical and geographical works.   In the excavation of a palace at Nimrud, it was found that almost a whole wing of the building had been given over to the storage of records, including quantities of tablets concerning taxation and trade, agricultural and administrative reports.   Another room in the palace contained a series of treaties made by the Assyrian king with princes of neighboring countries.   In the ruins of Ur, a "Great House of Tablets" was uncovered; this was a whole building devoted to housing records.   It seems to have been a legal archive or law library and it was well organized.   The collection contained a code of laws, which apparently antedated Hammurabi's Code by several hundred years, and the records of a national court for over a century.

As for the temple libraries, they were quite different in nature and use from the government libraries.   In content they included histories of the gods, texts of formal rituals, incantations, invocations, and prayers, as well as the sacred epics and scriptures.   In addition, since Babylonian religion was closely connected with science, or pseudoscience, the temple libraries also contained works on agriculture, biology, mathematics, astronomy, and medicine.   Near the above-mentioned palace at Nimrud, there was also a temple library with tablets containing hymns, incantations, omens, and medical texts. Ashurbanipal also had a temple library apart from his main palace library, and this too was entirely religious and pseudo-scientific in nature.

Schools for scribes were often attached to the temple libraries. The writing of cuneiform was a difficult process, and long years of study were necessary before one could become proficient in the art. Tablets of practice work have been found, indicating how the pupil progressed from the simpler cuneiform symbols to the more complex ones and then on to the writing of complete tablets. There were textbook tablets to show the student how to write and dictionaries of foreign languages translated into Babylonian for the scribe who was corresponding with people who spoke other languages or who was translating ancient works. There were even interlinear translations of important works in other languages. There was a school for scribes in the temple at Nippur, and in its "school library" there were textbooks, dictionaries, grammars, and examples of business forms and letters.

Physically, the Babylonian and Assyrian libraries were quite different from anything resembling a modern library, but this difference was largely due to the nature of the "books" -- the clay tablets. Many of the tablet collections have been discovered in ruins, and it is difficult to tell how they were originally arranged. In a few cases, as in Ashurbanipal's library, it is possible to tell at least what rooms or areas they were originally in, but sometimes they were so badly scattered that even this is impossible. However, a few generalizations can be made from the numerous collections that have been found. It is apparent that, whether in temple or palace, the tablets were kept in a designated area, properly arranged, and supervised by experienced personnel. In some cases a few tablets have been found in other offices, as if they were being consulted by an official in his working quarters or as if they constituted a small "reference" collection housed there. Inside the record rooms, the tablets have been found, at different times and places, to be housed in various ways. Some were on narrow shelves, some in shallow bins, some in a pigeonhole arrangement, while still others were kept in baskets or clay jars.

When several tablets were needed to contain one single work, they were numbered consecutively and kept together by means of a running "title" made up of the first word or words of the text. For example, the account of the creation found in Ashurbanipal's library begins with the words "Formerly that which is above ...;" so the several tablets containing the story are labelled "Formerly that which is above, No. 1," "Formerly that which was above, No. 2," and so on for seven tablets. The tablets were apparently shelved by a fixed location system, but there was some attention paid to subject, since works of similar subject materials were usually found together. Finding aids were usually available adjacent to the stored materials, sometimes as simple shelf lists and at other times in the form of fairly efficient descriptive catalogs. One catalog of a collection at Agene, which for the most part included works on astronomy and astrology, advised the would-be reader to write down the number of the tablet he needed and present it to the librarian who would find it for him. Apparently there were no "open shelves" for the Babylonian reader!

The librarian, or "keeper of the books," was of necessity a well-trained person. First of all, he had to be a graduate of the school for scribes, and then he had to be thoroughly trained in the literature or type of records that he was to keep. After this, he served an apprenticeship for a number of years, learning the trade of librarian and several languages all at the same time. That the librarians must have been polylingual is indicated by the numerous cases of works in several languages found in the same collections. In addition to serving as librarian, he was often called on to edit, transcribe, and translate works needed by higher government or religious officials. He was variously titled "Man of the Written Tablets," "Keeper of the Tablets," or "Master of the Books." One of the earliest Babylonian librarians known by name was Amit Anu, who was the "Tablet Keeper" in the royal library at Ur nearly 2,000 years before Christ. In the temple libraries the librarian-scribe was a priest, often a high-ranking one, while in the palace libraries he was often an important official. In either case, he was usually of the upper classes, often the younger son of a noble family.

The cuneiform script and the clay tablet were used for some 4,000 years in the Mesopotamian Valley, and it was also widely employed by peoples and civilizations outside that area. One of these civilizations was that of the Hittites, which flourished to the north and west of Babylonia in what is now Turkey. The remains of several libraries or archives have been found in the Hittite cities, particularly one at Boghaz Keui, the Hittite capital. The Hurrians, another non-Semitic people who lived in an area that is now a part of Syria, also employed clay tablets as a writing material. The Hurrians may have used Babylonian as a diplomatic language, since at Nuzi, one of their main cities, a collection of tablets has been found that were apparently written by Hurrian scribes in Babylonian with many Hurrian words interspersed. Aside from these neighbors of the Babylonians, various peoples resident in the area of what is now modern Palestine used clay tablets; in fact, the Egyptians did so at times, especially for diplomatic purposes. Even on the island of Crete, the Minoan civilization made some use of clay tablets. Thus, it seems that the clay tablet and cuneiform script were used for business and diplomatic correspondence throughout the eastern Mediterranean. From the standpoint of the archaeologist and historian, it is fortunate that this was so, since they were far more durable than any other ordinarily used writing materials.

Whatever their other contributions to Western civilization -- and they were many -- the chief claim of the Sumerian-Babylonian -- Assyrian peoples to permanent fame lies in their contributions to the realm of communications. They developed a method of writing; an economical, readily available, and relatively permanent writing material; and a system of arranging and using this recorded information in archives and libraries. All of these, in the long run, probably contributed more to Western civilization than Hammurabi's Code of laws or the Assyrian war chariot. With the exception of Hellenic Alexandria in the last three centuries before Christ, or perhaps Rome in the first three centuries after Christ, no region in the Western World had such well-developed libraries as those of Babylonia and Assyria. It can well be argued that the continuity of Sumerian-Babylonian-Assyrian civilization for three thousand years, despite many wars and conquests, can be largely attributed to its method of writing and its system of libraries and archives. Moreover, it is also quite obvious that without the remains of those libraries and archives we would know virtually nothing today of that three thousand years of history in the Mesopotamian Valley. Few periods in the history of Western man so well demonstrate the cultural role of the graphic arts of communication and the practical value of well-organized archives and libraries.

Additional Readings

(Much of our information on ancient libraries comes from the archeologist, and so it is to works in this field as well as to writings on the history of libraries and culture in general that we must turn for knowledge of the Babylonian and Assyrian libraries. In addition to the following selected titles, there are a number of studies on individual "finds" and collections of cuneiform tablets. Journals of archaeology, ancient history, and linguistic studies often contain important articles on libraries in the Mesopotamian area.)

Castellani, Carlo
    Le biblioteche nell' antichita. Bologna, 1884. 84 p.

Chiera, Edward
    They wrote on clay: the Babylonian tablets speak today.
        Chicago, 1938. 235 p.

Dahl, Svend
    History of the book. New York, 1958. 279p. (Original edition: Haandbog i Bibliotekskundskab. Copenhagen, 1924.)

Dougherty, R. P.
    "Writing upon parchment and papyrus among the Babylonians and Assyrians," Journal of the American Oriental Society, XLVIII (1928), 109-1935.

Dziatzko, Carl
    Antikes Buchwesen: Untersuchungen uber ausgewahlte Kapitel des antiken Buchwesens . . . Leipzig, 1900. iv, 206 p.

Kramer, Samuel N.
    From the tablets of Sumer. Indian Hills, Colorado, 1956.
        xxv, 293 p.

Laessoe, Jorgen
Peoples of ancient Assyria, their inscriptions and correspondence. New York, 1963. 169 p.

Maspero, Gaston
Life in ancient Egypt and Assyria. New York, 1912. 376 p.

Menant, Joachim
Bibliothèque du palais de Ninive. Paris, 1880. viii, 162 p.

Milkau, Fritz
Geschichte der Bibliotheken im alten Orient. Leipzig, 1935. 58 p.

Rinaldi, Giovanni
Storia delle letterature dell' antica Mesopotamia. Milan, 1957. 314 p.

Rogers, R. W.
History of Babylonia and Assyria. New York, 1915. 2 vols.

Sayce, Archibald Henry
The archaeology of the cuneiform inscriptions. New York, 1907. 220 p.
The religions of ancient Egypt and Babylonia. Edinburgh, 1902. vii, 509 p.

Smith, George
Ancient history from the monuments: Assyria. London, 1875. 191 p.
Ancient history from the monuments: Babylonia. London, 1895. 183 p.

Telloni, Bruto
Libri, documenti e bibliotheche nell' antica Mesopotamia. Florence, 1890.

Thompson, James Westfall
Ancient libraries. Berkeley, University of California Press, 1940. 120 p.

Weitemeyer, Mogens
Babylonske og Assyriske Biblioteker. Copenhagen, 1955. 104 p.

Weitzmann, Kurt
Illustrations in roll and codex; a study of the origin and method of text illustration. Princeton, 1947. 219 p.

3.

Egyptian Libraries

The earliest-known libraries in Egypt were connected with palaces and temples, just as they were in Babylonia. Recorded history in Egypt is thought to go back at least to 3200 B.C., or roughly about the same time that writing and records began in Babylonia. The earliest form of writing by the Egyptians was pictographic, and many surviving examples of this writing have been found on inscribed monuments. Since this early pictographic writing was carved on stones, it is known by the Greek term hieroglyphic, which means sacred stone-writing. As other materials, such as leather and papyrus, came to be used for writing and more writing was done, the formalized hieroglyphic characters were gradually replaced by stylized representations of the former pictures, often bearing only a slight resemblance to the originals. This more cursive form of writing was called hieratic. Still a third means was later employed to write the Egyptian language, and this was demotic script, a kind of shorthand developed from hieratic script. The demotic became the script generally used in business and commerce, particularly after about 1500 B.C. In time, the stylized hieratic characters developed to the point where they could be used as a syllabary or even for separate sounds and letters, but they were used in this manner only in reproducing foreign names and words, and the writing of Egyptian continued with each complete word usually represented by one hieratic character. Thus, the Egyptians came close to producing a phonetic syllabary and even an alphabet, but never quite made it.

As soon as writing was relatively well developed in Egypt, records began to be kept. In both temples and palaces, special rooms were designated for the preservation of official manuscripts. Undoubtedly the archive preceded the library, and records of law, church, or business were kept in orderly arrangement probably for

32

centuries before the addition of histories, literature, or theological commentaries brought the earliest real library into existence. As in Babylonia, the early archives and libraries were under the direction of specially trained scribes, and as early as 3000 B.C. such titles as "Controller of the Library" or "Keeper of the Scrolls" can be found on the tombs of men who were apparently highly honored officials. Both the temple and palace libraries were almost certainly maintained only for official use, and the concept of a "public library" was unknown. However, there is evidence of the existence of business libraries or archives and of private libraries in the homes of wealthy merchants and noblemen.

Although we have reliable evidence that libraries did exist in ancient Egypt, the archaeological evidence for specific collections is much less available than in Babylonia. Instead of the thousands of tablets found in the Mesopotamian ruins, we have only fragments of texts, tomb illustrations, and wall inscriptions to rely on for the history of Egyptian libraries. There is, for example, evidence that Khufu, a monarch of the Fourth Dynasty (ca. 2600 B.C.), had a library of considerable size, as did also Khafra, one of his successors, who built the second great pyramid. It is known that King Akhenaton, who lived about 1350 B.C., had a library, but virtually nothing is known of its contents. King Ramesses II (ca. 1300 B.C.; also known as Ozymandias) had a library of some size in his palace at Thebes. His library is reported to have been called "The Dispensary of the Soul" or "The Healing Place of the Soul;" so it was apparently a religious or philosophical library rather than merely a government archive. Incidentally, at least one of Ramesses' librarians is known by name -- a worthy called Amen-em-hant, whose bibliographic profession was noted on his elaborate tomb. At various times, palace libraries are reported to have existed at other cities in Egypt, such as Memphis, Edfu, and Philae, but little is known of their actual condition or contents.

The palace library about which most is known was that at Tell-el Amarna. Here the remains of a library have been found in a room designated as the "Place of the Records of the Palace of the King." This library consisted of clay tablets -- or at least all

that has survived are the clay tablets -- written in Babylonian
cuneiform characters.   As already noted, cuneiform was something
of an international diplomatic language at various times in the ancient world, and collection of tablets at Tell-el-Amarna consisted
mainly of correspondence between King Amenophis III (ca. 1400
B. C.) and various rulers in Asia Minor.   It is quite probable that
this library contained other literature and government records on
papyrus or leather that have failed to survive.   In the ruins of palaces elsewhere in Egypt, there are rooms that could well have
been archives or libraries; the tombs of many scribes who were
designated as "Keepers of the Books" have also been found, so that
it is logical to assume that many other palace libraries existed during the three thousand years of ancient Egypt.

     Evidences of Egyptian temple libraries are somewhat more
plentiful than for the palace collections, although it should be
pointed out that in some cases the temple and the palace were the
same structure or wings of the same building.   Just as the palace
library began as a collection of government records, so the temple
library began as a collection of sacred scriptures.   The Book of
Thoth, attributed to the Egyptian god of learning, was possibly the
nucleus around which such a collection began.   In time there grew
up around this book a collection of writings of exposition and com-
ment that became a small library in itself, something of an encyclopedia of both religion and science.   In addition to the sacred
writings, there were books of ritual with instruction on how certain
religious rites were to be performed.   There were even sacred
dramas, such as the Drama of Osiris, a kind of passion play dating
from about 1800 B. C., of which only a fraction has been discovered.
Gradually, however, the temple libraries came to include much
secular literature, especially science, since as in Babylonia, medicine and astronomy were closely connected with Egyptian religion.
Hence, the Egyptian temple library was much more than an archive
of the church; it came to be a library in the fullest sense of the
word.

     Some temples, such as that at Abu Simbel on the upper
Nile, were communities in themselves.   In addition to the fairly

large staff of priests, the temple community included farmers, tradesmen, skilled craftsmen, and a host of minor officials and clerks, all engaged in the maintainance of the temple and its lands and properties. To keep up with all this communal activity, a number of scribes kept records, taught school, and served as "keepers of the books" in libraries that contained not only theological works but also technical works, literary writings, historical annals, and practical texts in various fields. In some of the temples there were two libraries, one a general library for the use of all who could read, and another inner library of theological works for the exclusive use of a select circle of high priests. In one temple there was a special group of priests and scholars called the "House of Life" whose duties were to preserve the religious traditions, compile the annals of the kings and temples, and record scientific discoveries and technical advances. This group had its own library, a kind of copyright collection of authentic religious texts kept separately to guarantee their validity and authenticity.

As in Babylonia, the temple was the scene of schools for the training of scribes. In fact, most education, or at least most formal education in writing and the literary arts, was carried on in the temples, and these schools for scribes had libraries of reference works and texts. To become a scribe, the Egyptian boy began serious study at an early age and then served many years of apprenticeship before he finally became a full-fledged scribe. He had to learn as many as 700 different hieroglyphic characters in order to become proficient, and many of those characters had two or more meanings, while many words could be written by two or more characters. In addition to texts and grammars, histories and business forms, the libraries also had books on ethics and moral life as well as examples of general literature for use by the students.

Some of the Egyptian temples were particularly known as centers of healing, and their library rooms contained collections that might easily be considered medical libraries. In the "Hall of Rolls" in Heliopolis, long works with lists of diseases and their cures were found. In the temple of Ptah, remnants of books of medical prescriptions were discovered, and in that at Edfu there were tracts on "the turning aside of the cause of disease." Six medical works were found in the temple at Hermopolis. Keepers of these medical books were given such titles as "Scribe of the Double House of Life" and "Learned Men of the Magic Library." One of the largest papyrus rolls ever found is on medicine. This is the Ebers Papyrus, consisting of 110 pages and thought to have been written about 1500 B. C. Of all the medical collections, probably the most complete and best organized was that of the temple of Thoth, where, in addition to the priest who was "Keeper of the Sacred Books," there was an assistant, an early woman librarian who had the title of "Lady of Letters, Mistress of the House of Books."

In addition to temple and palace libraries, the several thousand years of Egyptian culture also saw the growth of private libraries, ranging from a roll or two and a few pages of papyrus to fairly large collections in the homes of wealthy merchants or noblemen. The collection, as indicated by fragments that have survived and a few cases where charred remains of a whole collection have been found, varied to suit the taste of the collector. It might for the most part consist of family history and genealogy, or business records, or the popular literature of the period, including fiction and travel tales. Again, it might be a fairly general collection, representative of wide interests and tastes. The wealthier collector might have a scribe to copy books for him, or he might purchase them from public scribes and copyists. His "library" might be housed in a separate small room or closet equipped with special cupboards pigeonholed for rolls of papyrus. In other, less wealthy homes, the rolls might be kept in jars, and the jars themselves kept on shelves. In still other cases where the family owned only two or three rolls, these might be kept together in a leather case. The site of El-Lahun, excavated by Flanders Petrie, revealed many private homes of a higher class, and remains of papyrus were found in nearly every one of them, indicating a high degree of literacy and literary interests in this social group at least. Not only were personal business files, family correspondence, legal papers, and wills found in some quantity, but there were also many examples of literature, history, theology, and even medical and veterinary works. One particularly fine papyrus, almost complete and in good condition, turned out after translation to be only the equivalent of a grocery list for a large household for a period of about 12 days.

Although it is generally assumed that only the upper classes could read and write with any degree of ease, it is interesting to note the results of the excavation of a "workers' town" from the period of Ramesses II, when the village of Der El-Medina was constructed for workers who were building a large project, probably a monument to the King. The homes of these workmen and their families revealed large numbers of papyrus scraps and even more "ostraka," that is, scraps of limestone and broken pottery used for writing. On these odd bits of written records were found bills, records of trades, payment of wages, contracts, law suits, work reports, letters, memoranda of all kinds, and many bits of literature and religious and magic writings. Although such miscellaneous collections of scraps could not be called a library (in fact, in none of the individual homes were there enough scraps to indicate anything like a private collection), they nevertheless present as a whole a wonderful picture of the economic and social life of lower-class Egypt. If not libraries, they represent the material from which books and libraries are made.

Closely related to Egyptian libraries were those of the neighboring area of Palestine. In an area from which the Bible came, one would naturally suppose a long history of preserved information that preceded and formed the foundation for such a scriptural text. Such is probably the case, but for long periods of time that combination of history, literature, and mythology was undoubtedly preserved through memory and repeated orally from generation to generation. However, there is evidence in the Bible itself for the existence of collections of holy writings, similar to the Egyptian temple writings, going back at least to the days of Solomon. In the Hebrew Temple in Jerusalem, the Books of the Law, the writings of Moses, and those of the Prophets were preserved in a most secret place open only to a few priests. The Book of Joshua was added to this collection, and later other sermons and exhortations of the Prophets were added. All of this was preserved in and for the use of the Temple; it was also preserved for posterity. Much if not all of it was destroyed during the period of the Babylonian captivity. After the Hebrews returned from Babylon, Nehemiah reassembled the Books of Moses and those of the Kings and Prophets to re-form the sacred library. He was aided in this task by Esdras, who some believe first edited the Pentateuch. This library was probably burned when Antiochus captured Jerusalem in the second century before Christ, and may have been re-established a third time by Judas Maccabeus. There are various references in the Old Testament to such a collection. For example, Jeremiah speaks of the "book of the records of the fathers" that was kept in the Temple, and Ezra speaks of rolls being kept in the "scribe's chamber." In Second Kings, there is a note on a scribe being sent for the "Book of the Law," which was kept in the House of the Lord. In later pre-Christian years, there were probably small collections of Scriptures in all synagogues, and libraries were maintained for the use of the students in the schools for priests in the larger ones. By tradition, the Hebrew Scriptures were usually preserved on leather rolls when they were written down. Internal evidence in the Old Testament indicates that many of the Books were compiled from older written sources as well as from oral tradition.

Some early writers thought there was a "city of books" in ancient Palestine, because that is a possible translation of the place-name Kirjath-sepher. On this basis it was assumed that one town either contained a number of libraries, or at least was a center of the book trade. However, more modern research indicates that this was not the case.

As for actual archaeological discoveries from the Palestine area, only a few ostraka discovered in the ruins of Lachish and a few other miscellaneous inscriptions have been found. None of these points to an actual collection that could be called a library or an archive. The Lachish ostraka, dating from about the sixth century B.C., are apparently remnants of a military correspondence relating to one of the several sieges undergone by that hill town.

However, in the ruins of a city close to Palestine, Ugarit (modern
Ras-Shamrah) on the Mediterranean coast, a temple collection has
been uncovered that has all the earmarks of a library. Actually,
there were apparently two libraries, one in the home of a high
priest and the other in a royal palace. The Ugaritic city-society
flourished about the thirteenth century B. C. and seems to have had
close relations with both the Hittites and with Minoan Crete. Clay
tablets were found in the palace library representing diplomatic correspondence, treaties, and laws. In addition, there was some history (including a military campaign), some commercial texts, and
a dictionary of Ugaritic and Sumerian. Apparently this was the official library of a King named Nigmed, and although it was on clay
tablets and in a cuneiform script, it was in the Ugaritic language.

The library of the high priest was for the most part a theological collection with most of its works relating to the religion and
mythology of the Ugaritic people; but there were also some epic
poems, magic lore, and history, with a few items that could be
called scientific or medical. There were also wordlists, or dictionaries, including bilingual ones. It is interesting to note that
among the religious texts were portions similar in style and content
to parts of the Old Testament, and also long genealogical lists of
kings and priests. The Ugarits apparently had borrowed from both
the Babylonians and Egyptians in their writing materials and used
both the cylinder seal and the stamp seal.

At Alalakh, 40 miles north of Ugarit, a similar palace-
temple combination was excavated, and again remnants of two collections were unearthed. Here, however, the collections were
largely religious and diplomatic, respectively, with little evidence
of literature or historical works as such. There were wordlists
that indicated a wider use of the written language, similar to the
Ugaritic, but the lists consisted mainly of commercial or religious
terms.

The physical nature of the Egyptian libraries is a subject on
which very little is known. For example, it is known from excavations and from illustrations found in tombs and on walls that the
rolls were apparently kept in rooms on shelves or pigeonholed

walls. But the method of arrangement, if any, is unknown. The
individual papyrus rolls were kept in cloth or leather covers, and
one or more of them might be kept in a clay jar-like container
with a cover. More valuable ones were kept in metal containers,
often inlaid with jewels. They were arranged in some manner, it
seems fairly certain, because the "keeper of the books" was supposed to be able to supply the demand for a book on request. Just
how they were arranged, however, is unknown. In some cases, as
in Babylonia, a list of the books in the library room was written or
inscribed on the wall, and such inscriptions have been found on excavated temple walls. In other cases, it is probable that books of
a similar nature were kept in individual book chests.

    Although papyrus seems to have been widely used over a
long period of time, other materials were used for writing in ancient Egypt. Clay tablets have already been mentioned, but it
should also be pointed out that leather was used before papyrus and
continued to be used for important documents. Wax tablets, or
simple wooden leaves with a coating of wax, were also used for
lessons, letters, and accounts. Beyond this, virtually anything
that would take in -- flat stones, broken pottery pieces, and even
uncoated wood -- was used for writing purposes in everyday practice.

    The Egyptian librarian was a highly educated person, at
least if we can assume that title for the many "keepers of the
books" and "masters of the rolls" whose names have been found. He
was often of high political position or trained in other professions
besides that of scribe. We know much of some of these scribes
from the "funeral literature," the laudatory biographies that were
frequently buried with the Egyptian dead. The various titles of the
deceased and the accounts of his activities often indicate that the
"keeper of the books" was also an editor as well, if not an author.
He corrected, translated, amended, and criticized the material that
passed through his hands-- and probably censored it, too. "Scribe
of the Sacred Writings," "Inspector of Scribes," "Overseer of
Scribes," "Scribe and Judge," and "Scribe and Priest" are a few of
the titles given to scribes in Egyptian funeral literature. Some

others were "Keeper of the King's Document Case," "Scribe of the King's Decrees," "Scribe of the King's Archives," and simply "King's Scribe" or "Royal Scribe." Whatever his title, the Egyptian librarian was a credit to his profession if he was even half as important as his funerary biography made him out to be.

Although not libraries in even the widest sense of the word, there are several other types of graphic information that have come down to us from ancient Egypt, and they deserve mention as a part of our total heritage from Egyptian culture. The funerary inscription and the scattered fragments known as ostraka have already been mentioned. Besides these, there are the engraved writings on monuments and stele. These are fairly numerous and are often quite long and informative. They may be anything from a simple name and title to long accounts of battles, military campaigns, royal decrees, and laudatory biographies. Sometimes these inscriptions are in the nature of chronologies or king-lists, with genealogies of several generations, and as such they are very important in establishing dates for various portions of Egyptian history. Still another minor form of graphic information is the seal. Both the cylinder type and the scarab, a peculiarly Egyptian form of seal, have been found in numbers, and they often contain valuable bits of information concerning the name, religion, or occupation of the owner.

Two other sources of papyrus -- in roll, sheet, or fragment -- should be mentioned. In the Egyptian tombs, papyrus has been found in at least three different forms. One of these is the funerary biography and another is the so-called "Book of the Dead." The latter is one of the most common Egyptian papyri known, and has been found in almost every opened tomb. Contrary to popular opinion, the "Book of the Dead" was not a single work but varied according to the person for whom it was intended. It was supposed to serve as a guidebook for the deceased to lead him safely to the life after death. The texts varied in length and ornateness according to the importance and wealth of the individual, and often included hymns, prayers and magical formulas to add to its value. Sometimes literary works, perhaps favorite books of the

deceased, were also buried intact with the corpse. The third form
in which papyrus has been found in the tombs was strictly utilitarian. Rolls of papyrus were used as pillows for the head of the
corpse, while other papyrus sheets were used as wrappings for the
corpse and even as stuffing for the eviscerated mummies. In each
case where papyrus was used as wrapping or bulk, the writing on
the papyrus was, of course, not considered important; but for this
very reason much of it has proven most interesting. Generally,
such writing consisted of various badly worn texts or wastepaper
of a routine nature, but occasionally genuine "finds" of historical or
literary value have been discovered in just this form.

Another form of accidental or incidental preservation of
papyrus records has been in the junk piles or garbage heaps surrounding ancient Egyptian towns. Where the papyrus was covered
with dry sand and separated from other organic matter, it has often been well preserved, but usually it is in fragmentary or badly
torn form. However, from this source have come some of the
most important pieces of information that we have on economic and
social life of ancient Egypt. Prices, taxes, wages, bits of local
history and customs, even love letters and suicide notes have been
found in this accidentally preserved form. The task of piecing the
information together is often tedious, but it is nevertheless reward-
ing.

Whatever its forms, the written material that has come down
to us from ancient Egypt is only a fraction, probably less than 1
per cent, of the literature that flourished there before 500 B. C.
Unlike Babylonia, where a more-or-less complete library was discovered in Ashurbanipal's clay tablets, or Greece and Rome, where
much of the classic literature was preserved, there was no continuing stream of civilization in Egypt to preserve its literature
and libraries down through the ages. Instead, after developing and
surviving for some three thousand years, much of Egypt's civilization was destroyed in a series of conquests. First the Assyrians
(about 670 B.C.) and then the Persians (about 525 B.C.) overran
Egypt, virtually destroying all of the country. Nobles, priests, and
scribes were killed or carried away as slaves, while temples and

palaces were ransacked and razed. Whatever survived in the way of recorded information was either entombed or indestructible. The glory that was ancient Egypt was effectively destroyed, and although the Nile Delta flourished again a century or two later under the Ptolemies, this was primarily a Greek, or Hellenic, culture rather than an Egyptian one.

Additional Readings

(There are numerous works on the history and culture of ancient Egypt, and almost all of them touch on the subject of Egyptian papyri. However, information on Egyptian libraries as such is scattered and must be gleaned from many sources. General works on ancient civilization, such as the Pauly-Wissowa Real-Encyclopedie der Classischen Altertumswissenschaft, are also very valuable.)

Baikie, James
    The Amarna age: a study of crisis in the ancient world. New
        York, 1926. xvii, 464 p. (A study largely based on the
        Tell-el-Amarna library of cuneiform tablets.)
    Egyptian papyri and papyrus hunting. London, 1925. 324 p.

Blau, Ludwig
    Studies zum althebraischen Buchwesen und zur biblischen Littera-
        tur und Textgeschichte. Strasburg, 1902. iv, 203 p.

Breasted, James H.
    The ancient records of Egypt: historical documents from the
        earliest times to the Persian conquest. Chicago, 1927. 5 v.
    Development of religion and thought in ancient Egypt. New
        York, 1959. 379 p.

Budge, Ernest A. W.
    The literature of the ancient Egyptians. London, 1914. 285 p.

Cerny, Jaroslav
    Paper and books in ancient Egypt. London, 1952. 36 p.

Cross, F. M.
    The ancient library of Qumran and modern biblical studies.
        New York, 1958. 196 p.

Davies, Nina M.
    Picture writing in ancient Egypt. New York, 1958. 56 p.

Egger, Emile
    Histoire du livre depuis ses origines jusqu'à nos jours.

Paris, 1880. xi, 323p.

Gardthausen, Victor
Handbuch der wissenschaftlichen Bibliothekskunde.   Leipzig,
1920.   2 v.

Nichols, Charles L.
The library of Ramesses the Great and some of its books.
Boston, 1909.   43 p.

Petit-Radel, Louis Charles François
Recherches sur les bibliothèques anciennes et modernes jusqu'à
la fondation de la Bibliothèque Mazarine . . . Paris, 1819.
viii, 439 p.

Pinner, H. L.
The world of books in classical antiquity.   Leiden, 1948. 64 p.

Porter, Bertha
Topographical bibliography of ancient Egyptian hieroglyphic texts,
reliefs and paintings.   Oxford, 1927-   . 6 v.

Richardson, Ernest Cushing
Biblical libraries: a sketch of library history from 3400 B. C.
to A. D. 150.   Princeton, 1914.   xvi, 252 p.   (Reprinted,
Shoestring Press, 1963).
Some old Egyptian libraries.   New York, 1911.   93 p.

Sayce, Archibald Henry
Aramaic papyri discovered at Assuan.   London, 1906. 79 p.

Schottenloher, Karl
Das alte Buch.   Berlin, 1921. 432 p.

Wilson, John Albert
The culture of ancient Egypt.   Chicago, 1951.   344 p.

4.

Greek Libraries

In considering Greek libraries it is usual to begin with those
of classical Greece, from the sixth century B. C. onward. However, it is known now that there was a literate civilization in
Greece and the Aegean Islands almost a thousand years earlier,
and that there were archives or collections of writings at Pylos and
Mycenae on the mainland and at Knossos on Crete. This knowledge
has come largely from the twentieth-century excavations at those
points and in the decipherment since 1950 of some of the inscriptions and tablets found there.

Since the late nineteenth century, clay tablets and inscribed
stones have been collected in the vicinity of Knossos on the island
of Crete. These inscriptions fell into two types that came to be
known as "Linear A" and "Linear B" scripts. These tablets were
associated with the excavations of ruins dated in the Minoan period
of the island's history, from about 1400 to 1100 B. C. Later, in
the twentieth century, tablets were found on the mainland at Mycenae and later at Pylos, inscribed with the same type of writing
as Linear B. For many years undeciphered, this Linear B was
finally translated in the early 1950's by Michael Ventris, who discovered it to be an early form of Greek. Linear A remained undeciphered.

With this discovery, the Linear B texts took on new meaning, and hundreds of them have been studied. This type of writing
seems to have been used almost exclusively for business purposes,
or at least all of the surviving texts are on business and economic
subjects. Tablets have been discovered concerning land tenure, ra-
tions for soldiers, ritual offerings, inventories, and the like, but
much social and economic history can be gathered from them. The
absence of literature, or even of much in the way of historical
writings, is notable. Several possible explanations have been ad-

45

vanced for this absence. The first is that there was simply no
literature at that period, or that all literature was then oral. However, this does not explain the scarcity of historical or legal inscriptions. Another possible reason is that the Linear B script
was employed only for business purposes -- it has been called a
"palace code" of writing -- and that the literature of the era is all
in the Linear A script that is yet to be deciphered. The argument
against this is that the Linear A script seems to have been more
widely used by the common people than the B, and it seems doubtful that a well-developed literature could have been achieved in
such a script. Still another explanation suggests that the literary
and historical materials might have been kept in other places,
either completely destroyed or yet to be discovered. Finally, the
most logical reason yet advanced is that the literary compositions
of the Minoans and Mycenaeans were written on materials other than
clay tablets (for example, on papyrus) that have decayed with time,
whereas the cheaper clay material was used for business transactions and has survived.

Both at Mycenae and at Pylos, rooms have been found in the
palaces with large numbers of clay tablets in them, some of them
in jars neatly arranged on shelves. At Knossos many tablets were
found, but they were so scattered that it was difficult to ascertain
in what room or rooms they had originally been kept. Apparently
the clay tablets in this civilization were not baked but simply dried,
and they were stored in jars, baskets, or even in wooden boxes.
At Pylos one room contained census records and military statistics;
apparently it was an official governmental archive. Elsewhere, the
Linear B collections contained similar business and governmental
information, ranging from the purely archival to the more usable
"ready-reference" type of information in the form of commodity
prices, sources of various goods, and even information on ship
sailings and cargoes.

It is interesting to note that on a smaller scale similar collections of tablets have been found in the ruins of private homes,
particularly at Pylos. Here, in what were apparently the homes of
wealthy merchants, many scattered clay tablets have been found,

indicating a highly literate business society. One of the homes
seems to have been that of an oil merchant, and the tablets found
there dealt with accounts and inventories of trade in oil and other
goods, along with some business contracts and official papers.

These two relatively contemporary civilizations had been
overrun by less-civilized peoples from the north by the twelfth century B. C. , and their literary culture disappeared. There seems to
have followed several centuries in which the peoples of Greece and
the nearby islands had no written language. This period includes
the era of Homer, when the Iliad and the Odyssey were composed
and handed down as oral epics for many generations before they
were finally written down. By the seventh century, however, a
literate society had emerged, and once again a written literature
began to be followed in due time by libraries.

Actually the libraries of classical Greece, which we might
date from the sixth century B. C. through the third century A. D. ,
have left us little in the way of physical remains. Instead, we
must rely upon references in ancient Greek and Roman literature
for information concerning them. That literature in itself is relatively plentiful, but references to libraries are few and scattered.
What is more, these references are sometimes contradictory. For
example, there are at least two accounts of the ultimate fate of
Aristotle's library.

Sometime prior to the seventh century B. C. , and probably
as early as the ninth, the Greeks obtained the alphabet from the
Phoenicians and adapted it to their own language. The first known
Greek writers of note, with the exception of the semi-legendary
Homer, lived in the sixth century B. C. , and some of their writings
have come down to us. Poetry, philosophy, and science, as represented by Sappho, Thales, and Anaximander, existed in this era.
In order for libraries of any size to exist at all, there must be an
accumulation of records or imaginative writings in the language
generally spoken, and there must be a reading population great
enough to use it. Also, the economy of the city or area must be
such that leisure time, both for the writing and the reading of
books, must be available. Contact with other peoples via trade and

travel also helps to contribute the material from which libraries are
formed.   Hence, Greece by the sixth century B. C. was in most
respects ready for the appearance of libraries.

If we are to believe the writer Aulus Gellius, Athens did
have a public library after 560 B. C.   Gellius says that the tyrant
Pisistratus (605 - 527 B. C.) collected a large library of books and
later gave it to the city of Athens, where it was opened to the public.   He also says that the people themselves added to the library
and took care of it for many years, until the Persian conqueror
Xerxes confiscated it when he captured Athens in 480 B. C.   Continuing with Gellius's account, we learn that long after Xerxes had
carried the library to Persia, that country was conquered in turn
by King Seleucus, who returned the books to Athens.   This makes
an engaging story, but one for which there is little corroboration
elsewhere and which is generally doubted.   However, the story may,
like many ancient tales, contain an element of truth embedded in
its web of fiction.   From other sources we learn that Pisistratus
was a builder of temples, a lover of music and art, and that he
ordered a critical edition of the works of Homer to be compiled
during his period as ruler of Athens.   That he could and did compile a collection of books is not difficult to believe, but what happened to them is not known, and it is certainly very doubtful that
they ever constituted a "public" library.

During the fifth century B. C., the library history of Greece
remains vague, but it can be deduced that some types of book collections existed.   For example, there were schools, and although
much of the teaching was still done orally, with no textbooks or
written lessons, it is logical to assume that the teachers did have
books to aid their excellent memories.   Plato (427 - 348 B. C.), the
great philosopher and teacher of Aristotle, must have had a private
library of considerable size, although here again we have little direct evidence to prove it.   Plato was widely traveled and read,
and he must have had access to many volumes to become as well
educated as he was.   One source says that his library was based
on books bought from one Philolaus of Tarentum, with others purchased at the Greek colony of Syracuse in Sicily.   Plato is re-

ported to have paid Philolaus a small fortune for books. Whether
any of his library was left to Aristotle is not known, but Aristotle
is supposed to have purchased some of Plato's books that had been
left to Speusippus. At any rate, Aristotle went on to collect one
of the largest of ancient private libraries.

Aristotle (384 - 321 B. C.) founded a school of philosophy or
lyceum known as the Peripatetic school. He taught his followers,
or pupils, while walking about in the grove of the hero Lycus.
Aristotle's library of several hundred volumes was probably also
used by his students and friends. Upon his death, this library was
inherited by his successor, Theophrastus of Lesbos. Theophrastus
in turn increased the library and later bequeathed it to his nephew
Neleus. Neleus was not a successful teacher, and in his later
years he moved with his books to Scepsis in Asia Minor. His descendants, apparently unlettered, saved his books but allowed them
to become mildewed and worm-eaten through storage in a dank,
dark place for many years, according to the geographer Strabo.
At the time the Attalid Kings of Pergamum were building up their
famous library, the descendants of Neleus are supposed to have
buried their books to save them from the agents of the Attalids.
Finally, about 100 B. C. the surviving remnants of Aristotle's library were sold to Apellicon of Teos, a minor Athenian military
leader and book collector who tried to restore the damaged books.
His diligence resulted in some additional damage, in that he made
incorrect "corrections" for missing fragments of pages and otherwise edited the works. After Apellicon died, Athens was captured
by the Roman general Sulla, who carried Apellicon's library off to
Rome. There it eventually became a part of Tyrannion's library.
Another account has it that Ptolemy II (285 - 246 B. C.) acquired
Aristotle's library directly from Neleus and brought it to Egypt to
become a part of the great Alexandrian Library. It is possible
that both stories are in part correct, and that part of Aristotle's
books eventually went to both Alexandria and Rome. At any rate,
Aristotle goes down in history as the creator and owner of an important private library of considerable size for its period.

The actual size and content of Aristotle's library remain a

mystery. It is logical to suppose that it contained many of the
sources that he used in his own writings, and that would in itself
make a sizable collection. Also, it probably contained most if not
all of his own writings, estimated to have been at least 400 rolls.
Since it is known that Aristotle's friends and followers often sent
him botanical and geological specimens from their travels outside
Greece, it is also possible that they sent him copies of their manuscripts on science and history, so that his library would be as
well-rounded in subject fields as his own multifaceted writings.

Among other early Greek collectors of books who might have
acquired collections important enough to be called private libraries,
a few might be mentioned. Polycrates (d. 522 B. C.), a ruler of
the island of Samos, is reported to have amassed a useful library
at his palace and to have invited scholars there to study and use it.
Euripedes (480-406 B. C.), the poet and dramatist, was also a book
collector. His plays show that he was well read, and it is logical
to assume that he owned many of the books he used as background
for his dramas. Clearchus (d. 353 B. C.), tyrant or ruler of Hera-
clea, is reported to have founded a library in Bithynia about 364
B. C. Demosthenes, the political leader and orator, had a small
but well-selected library, many volumes of which he had copied in
his own handwriting.

Other private libraries mentioned in the literature of ancient
Greece include those of Nicocrates of Cyprus, Euthydemus, Euclid,
and Isocrates. Euthydemus is recorded as a collector of poetry and
as the owner of a complete set of Homer's works. Larensis is
supposed to have had the largest private library of the fourth century B. C. and to have had it well arranged and classified. Other
libraries mentioned include ones at Patrae in Greece, at Smyrna,
Ephesus and Antioch in Asia Minor, and at Syracuse in Sicily.
Still others were reported at Delphi, Corinth, and Helicarnassus.

Besides the library on Samos, other Aegean islands with reported libraries were Cos, Rhodes, and Cnidos. Excavations on
the island of Cos have uncovered an inscription on the wall of a library enumerating donors of money and books. Frequent mentions
of "100 drachmas and 100 books" indicate fairly wealthy donors.

Also, it is apparent that "drives" were staged to collect books and funds for the libraries, with the inscription on the wall to honor the donors. Portions of a similar inscription have been found on the island of Rhodes, indicating a similar practice there. Still another inscription from Rhodes, and possibly from the same library, seems to be a catalog of a small library or possibly a list of the books in some gift collection.

An interesting story is told of the formation of a public library in Athens in the fourth century B. C. This collection was formed because of the popularity of the plays of Aeschylus, Sophocles, and Euripides. When some groups of players began performing the plays of these authors with additions and corrections to the accepted texts, other playgoers objected. In order to make sure that only authentic versions of the plays were produced, official copies were deposited in a public collection. These could not be removed, but anyone could read them and copy them. Thus in one location we have an early "copyright office" and a public library.

The most famous Greek library of all, indeed the most famous of all antiquity, was not in Greece but in Egypt. When Alexander the Great had conquered most of the known world during his brief reign (337 - 323 B. C.), the glory of Greece was spread far from the borders of the land itself. Alexander's Empire broke up after his death, but his various successors established Hellenism, as Greek culture is called, in Asia Minor and Egypt especially. During the reign of the Ptolemies, beginning in 305 B. C., with their capital in Alexandria, lower Egypt because a nation that was strongly Greek in population and culture. Here Ptolemy I (Soter) built magnificent buildings and attracted scholars and scientists from all over the Greek world, despite the fact that he was rather a despotic ruler.

One of the scholars who was attracted to Alexandria was Demetrius of Phalerum, who was driven from Athens in 307 B. C. and turned up at the court of Ptolemy about 297, where he soon became a court favorite. Apparently he suggested to Ptolemy that in addition to buildings and monuments, a school, or "museum," with a well-stocked library might add to the glory of his regime and make

his memory more palatable for generations to come.   The term
museum was used to indicate a "house of the muses" (that is to say,
of the arts and sciences), and Demetrius hoped to emulate or surpass the schools then in vogue in Athens.   The results of his efforts was the establishment of the Museum, or Brucheion, in
Alexandria as an institution that was something like a loosely organized university of scholars.   There was a group of buildings to
make up the Museum, and all were connected by covered walks, or
porticoes.   Included in the group of structures were lecture halls,
study rooms, dining rooms, cloisters, gardens, an astronomical
observatory, and a library, all in the midst of grounds replete
with statuary and pools.   The whole of the Museum was dedicated
to the gods of learning, and the director was technically a priest,
but usually a scholar as well.   In fact, the scholars who made up
the staff of the Museum seem to have worked much on their own.
Some of them were scientists, including mathematicians, astrono-
mers, geographers, and physicians, while others were historians,
literary students, writers, and editors.   In fact, one of the major
functions of the scholarly group seems to have been that of revis-
ing or editing the works of earlier writers, beginning with Homer.
All of these scholars were paid from the royal treasury and most
of them were Greeks; some scholars were invited from neighboring
countries, particularly if they could translate from their native languages into Greek.   Research, editing, and experimentation rather
than teaching seem to have been the functions of the scholars, and
although there may have been many apprentices, there seem to have
been no classes as such.

The library connected with the Museum was housed in a
separate building.   Demetrius apparently directed the early acquisitions for the collection.   He had known the library of Aristotle in
Athens and had been a student of Theophrastus.   Later other scholars took up the task of building the library, and especially after the
accession of Ptolemy II (Philadelphus), there were many men assigned to the task of acquiring and arranging books.   In fact,
Philadelphus was so active in enlarging the library and its group of
scholars that he is sometimes called its founder.   He did, however,

establish a smaller library, that at the Serapeum, or Temple of
Serapis, in the Egyptian section of Alexandria. This smaller collection, sometimes called the daughter library, never became as
large as the Brucheion library, but it may have been more of a
public collection, used by ordinary students and citizens.

To enlarge the Museum library, copies of all known books in
the city of Alexandria were added to the collection, and then efforts were extended to all parts of the known world. Ships arriving
in the harbor of Alexandria were forced to lend any books they
might have to be copied. Agents were sent to other lands to buy
books or borrow them to be copied. Sometimes deposits were left
for borrowed books until they could be copied and returned, and according to some stories the deposits were sometimes forfeited and
the books never returned.

An important feature of the history of the Alexandrian Library is the list of outstanding figures who served it as librarians,
or who were at least connected with it as scholars. There is some
confusion as to which of the scholars whose names are associated
with the Library were actually librarians, but the following names
are worth considering, along with their approximate and estimated
dates of activities with the Library:

Demetrios of Phaleron	290 - 282 B. C.
Zenodotus of Ephesus	282 - 260 B. C.
Callimachus of Cyrene	260 - 240 B. C.
Apollonius of Rhodes	240 - 230 B. C.
Eratosthenes of Cyrene	230 - 195 B. C.
Aristophanes of Byzantium	195 - 180 B. C.
Apollonius the Eidograph	180 - 160 B . C.
Aristarchus of Samothrace	160 - 131 B. C.
Onesander of Cyprus	100 - 89 B. C.
Chaeremon of Alexandria	50 - 70 A. D.
Dionysius, son of Glaucus	100 - 120 A. D.
Caius Julius Vasinus	120 - 130 A. D.

It is not known whether these men were "head librarians," but their
names are associated with the library during the periods indicated.
Whatever their capacity, surely no other library in Western history
has ever had such a distinguished list of men connected with it.
Of these men, all noted scholars, Callimachus and Apollonius of
Rhodes were poets; while Zenodotus, Aristophanes, and Aristarchus

were critics, editors, and Homeric authorities. Eratosthenes was a geographer and astronomer who taught that the earth was round. Callimachus was probably the most important, at least from the point of view of library history, since he is supposed to have compiled a catalog of the famous Library. At any rate, to him is ascribed a work, of which only a few fragments remain, entitled "Tables of those who were outstanding in every phase of culture, and their writings." This work itself is thought to have originally been made up of 120 rolls, but whether it was a catalog of the Library or merely a bibliography of all known literature is uncertain. Certainly it was something more than a mere bibliography, since the extant fragments give something of each author's life, his works, and even the number of lines of text in each work. Callimachus' catalog is usually called "Pinakes," from a word originally meaning tablets, but later coming to mean a list of works. Callimachus is also credited with devising the system of dividing longer works into "books," or parts, in order to make the rolls more even in size and more easily handled and stored. That Callimachus was also a classifier as well as a cataloger can be deduced from his division of his work into eight major subject categories: Oratory, History, Laws, Philosophy, Medicine, Lyric Poetry, Tragedy, and Miscellany. Unfortunately for Callimachus and his unfinished catalog, he did not find favor with Ptolemy II and was exiled to upper Egypt where he died.

The Alexandrian Library flourished for several hundred years, and for at least 200 years it was of tremendous importance in the cultural development of the Hellenic world. It brought scholars from great distances and from almost all fields of knowledge. Hundreds, probably thousands, of books were compiled or written from its sources. Thousands upon thousands of rolls were bought, copied, stolen, and compiled for its shelves until the Library contained, according to some estimates, over 700,000 rolls. It must be pointed out that this figure may well be an exaggerated estimate, that many works were most probably present in many editions or copies, and that one roll was probably only about one-seventh of an average modern book. With all these factors considered, the

Alexandrian Library was still a tremendous collection, and it must
have contained most if not all of the extant literature of the period.
Not only works in Greek, but also translations of Egyptian, Hebrew,
and Chaldean literature were included, and later Latin and other
languages as well.   Manethos, the Egyptian scholar, was employed
to translate Egyptian works and to compile a chronology of Egyptian history; 70 Hebrew scholars were supposed to have translated
the Old Testament into Greek (the Septuagint) at the Alexandrian
Library.

Some scholars think that the Alexandrian Library may have
had a stultifying effect on Hellenic literature.   That is, they believe that little or no really new literature appeared from its influence; instead, the effort of its scholars was to collect everything
of importance that had ever been written and to preserve it in the
Library.   Once the literature had been collected, then scholarship
took the form of editing, compiling, and criticizing, rather than
originating or composing new literature.   Certain it is that many
compilations came out of the Library.   A philologist named Didymus
is supposed to have compiled 3,500 rolls of commentaries on famous works of literature in the Library.   Athenaeus, in the second
century A.D., said he studied 1,500 volumes in the Library at
Alexandria in order to compile his Deipnosophistae in 15 volumes.

Unfortunately, the flowering of Alexandria as a cultural center was not to last forever.   After several Ptolemies who were
friends to literature and learning, Ptolemy VIII (Cacergetes) came
to the throne.   He was definitely not a friend to the Museum, and
after having been forced to leave Alexandria by his enemies, he
returned in the course of a civil war (88 B.C.) and burned much
of the city.   The students and fellows of the Museum were at least
temporarily scattered, and Athenaeus reports that "great numbers
of grammarians, philosophers, geographers, and physicians [were
roaming] the entire world, forced to earn their living by teaching."
Though never again at its former greatness, the Museum was reconstituted and survived for several hundred years longer.

Wars and civil strife continued to plague Alexandria and its
libraries.   To bring the story of the Library to its conclusion, it

is necessary to go beyond the Hellenic era and into several centuries of Roman domination in Egypt. Even then, the end of the Library is even more uncertain than its beginning. The Museum and
its library were in decline by 100 B. C. , and in 47 B. C. , when
Julius Caesar was conquering Egypt, the Library is thought to have
been at least partially destroyed. This story is doubted since it
hinges on the translation of a passage from the historian Dios Cas-
sius, but it is possible that some volumes that had been stored in
a warehouse were burned during a dock area fire. At any rate,
Anthony is supposed to have given Cleopatra some 200, 000 rolls
taken from the library at Pergamum to replace those burned by
Caesar. The Alexandrian Library did decline further in its influence after the beginning of the Christian Era, and since later
writers mention only one library in Alexandria and do not distin-
guish between the Brucheion and the Serapion, it is possible that
only the latter survived. In A. D. 273 the Roman Emperor Aurelian,
conquering Egypt once again, burned much of Alexandria, including
the Library, although it is thought that afterwards a library and
museum were rebuilt on a smaller scale. Any schools or libraries
would have most likely suffered again in the Egyptian campaigns of
the Emperor Diocletian in A. D. 296. Again, in A. D. 391, the
Temple of Serapis, being a pagan church, was destroyed by the
Christian under Emperor Theodosius I, and it is most probable that
any library remaining there would have been destroyed at that time.
Finally, if anything was left of the library or libraries, it was supposed to have been finally destroyed by the Moslem conqueror Omar
in A. D. 645. However, little is heard of the Alexandrian Library
after A. D. 200, and it is very doubtful that anything was left to be
destroyed by Omar. If he did burn a library, it may have been a
Christian library established in a church of monastery on the original site of the Serapeum.

      The two great libraries of Alexandria were by no means the
only libraries in Ptolemaic Egypt. A library called the Sebasteum,
was located in the Temple of Augustus and there were others attached to temples and schools during the Greek and Roman periods.
Private libraries were also known in this era, for in the ruins of

a home identified as that of Zenon of Philadelphia, both business and personal records were found along with fragments of literary and music manuscripts. Something of a professional or technical library can be presumed from the scraps of papyrus found in what were apparently the offices of engineers assigned to reclamation work being done in the Fayum area of Egypt. Other papyri found in the Fayum are remnants of business, family, and local government records. Apparently all government agencies under the Ptolemies kept extensive records not only of laws but also of taxes, finances, and diplomatic affairs, if scraps of records found in the provincial townsites can be believed. Hence, Alexandria itself must have had several government archives in addition to its various libraries.

Turning from Egypt to other areas under Greek influence during the post-Alexandrian epoch, the libraries at Pergamum, Antioch, and Ephesus should be mentioned. That at Pergamum in particular was probably the second greatest library of the Hellenic world, if reports concerning it are true. Attalus I, King of Pergamum, is probably responsible for the beginning of a library in his city, but it was his son, Eumenes II (197-159 B.C.), who brought it to its highest point. Eumenes strove to match the library at Alexandria and is even accused of trying to get a librarian, Aristophanes of Byzantium, to come to Pergamum from Egypt. The library at Pergamum was also something of a school, or group of scholars, similar to that at Alexandria, and the scholar Crates of Malos headed it for a while under Eumenes II. The library was located in the Temple of Athena. Crates was probably responsible for the early growth of the library, but Athenodorus of Tarsus was also its head for a while, and he was invited by Cato to visit Rome and advise on the construction of libraries there.

Related to the library at Pergamum is the story of the origin of parchment. The Egyptians are supposed to have cut off the supply of papyrus being sent to Pergamum to prevent its library from growing as large as that in Alexandria. The librarians at Pergamum then developed a new writing material, parchment (from the Latin Pergamene) as a substitute for papyrus. This is probably an exaggerated tradition, since tanned and cured skins were used for writing in Egypt and Palestine for hundreds of years before Pergamum existed. It is probable, however, that Pergamum made greater use of parchment or even developed a finer, whiter type of parchment that became famous throughout the Mediterranean world; hence the story. It is also most probable that the great majority of the rolls in the library at Pergamum were of papyrus.

Attalus II (159 - 138 B. C.) continued to develop the library at Pergamum, and it flourished for some time, but after his death it declined, and in 133 B. C. Pergamum fell to the Romans. The library probably suffered some loss to the captors, but it must have remained of considerable size if we are to believe the story of Antony seizing 200, 000 rolls from it in 43 B. C. as a gift for Cleopatra. This story is also most probably exaggerated, if not completely untrue.

The ruins of the Temple of Athena in Pergamum have been excavated, and from them we have our best example of an Hellenic library. The plan of the library may have been adopted from that of Aristotle's in Athens, with the library rooms located off a colonnade, in this case the north colonnade of the Temple. The largest library room, some 42 by 50 feet in area, had a narrow platform or bench around three sides with holes, apparently for shelf-brackets, on the walls behind them. The bench could have been used as a means of reaching the higher shelves or possibly as a barrier to keep the public away from the shelves. In the middle of this room was the large statue of Athena for which the Temple was noted. From Pergamum the idea of the temple-colonnade library was probably carried to Rome either by Crates, who visited there about 157 B. C. , or by Athenodorus.

Antiochus the Great (224 - 181 B. C.), founder of Antioch in Syria, built a theater, art museum, and library in his capital city. In 200 B. C. this library was under the direction of the epic poet Euphorion of Chalcis. Either this library or another one was located in the Temple of the Muses in Antioch in 69 B. C. , and there is also evidence of a library or archive there even before Antiochus. Also in Syria, in the town of Apamea, there was re-

ported to be a notable library of 20,000 volumes at the time the
Romans conquered the country, although its fate after that is unknown. Other libraries in Asia Minor were those at temples in
Ephesus, Tarsus, and Smyrna, although these flourished more under the Romans than under the Greeks.

Returning to Greece proper, as distinguished from the Hellenic world that grew out of Alexander's conquests, it is interesting
to note that by the end of the third century B. C. libraries were
common in all parts of the peninsula. Public libraries became common not only in the larger towns and cities, but also in the smaller
ones and in the inland areas. Apparently there was more than one
in Athens, as well as many private libraries. Polybius says that
there were so many libraries in Athens that one scholar, Timaeus,
the Sicilian historian, spent 50 years doing research in them.
Polybius also reported that research could be carried on by any
citizen in any one of Greece's major cities. A gymnasium, or high
school, the Ptolemaion in Athens, flourished for some two centuries prior to about 100 B. C., and it must have developed a considerable library. It was the custom of the students of this school
to present 100 volumes annually to the school library as a gradu-
ating gift. Such school libraries must have been fairly common in
all the cities of the Hellenic world, since fragments of textbooks
and lesson sheets have been found in Egypt, on the island of
Rhodes, and elsewhere. Private libraries also became common
among the wealthier Greeks, and Vitruvius says that in their man-
sions it was always considered correct to have the library rooms
on the east side in order to have the best light for reading. Aside
from its libraries, Athens also had its official archives, kept in
the Metroon, or Temple of the Mother of the Gods. Book collectors, of whom Appellicon of Teos has already been mentioned, became common, and books themselves were plentiful. More than
1,100 authors are known to have written during the classical period
of Greek literature, and the collection of Greek writers alone would
have been a major occupation. The Macedonian King Perseus had
a large library that was captured by the Romans in 167 B. C. and
carried off to Rome as spoils of war.

In addition to public and private libraries there were also
special, particularly medical, libraries in ancient Greece. Near
Epidauros was one of the great medical schools, the Asklepieion,
which flourished for some six or seven hundred years, or from approximately 500 B. C. to later than A. D. 100. It was a combined
school and temple, with many buildings, accommodations for
teachers, students, officials and visitors, ceremonial halls and
baths, and a library. The library was dedicated to Apollo Maleates
and to Asklepios, the god of healing. Other medical schools are
known to have existed at Cos, Cnidos, Rhodes, Cyrene, and Alexandria; each of these is thought to have had a medical library.
According to one tradition, the library on Cnidos was burned at the
order of Hippocrates because its students refused to follow his
teachings.

In physical terms, the library in classical Greece was usually located in a temple, with special rooms off colonnaded approaches to the temple itself. Inside the library rooms, the rolls were
kept in pigeonholes or on shelves on the walls. Usually there was
a counter or desk from which the librarians could dispense their
wares. The rolls were arranged according to major divisions of
literature, and booklists or catalogs were compiled, usually on
separate rolls, but sometimes on the walls of the library. Individual rolls, especially the more valuable ones, were wrapped in
cloth or some other protective covering, and a tag was left hanging
out to identify the contents. Librarians during this period were for
the most part outstanding scholars, although it is quite possible
that the names of literary figures who are associated with the
great libraries acted as administrators or advisors rather than as
librarians. Be that as it may, the role of the library and the librarian was high in Hellenic society, and it has seldom been higher
in all of Western history.

In studying the history of libraries it is worthwhile to ask
a question at this point: Why do we know so little about Greek libraries when such a relatively large amount of classic Greek literature has been preserved? Why did not more of the writers, historians, and compilers mention libraries if libraries were common?

Why do we have only fragmentary, incidental references to libraries
in all of the pages of Greek literature? The answer seems to be
that, although much Greek literature has been preserved, the
amount actually brought down to modern times is probably less
than 10 percent of all that was written. It is quite possible that
histories of libraries were written and later lost, and that histories
of towns, temples, and of education in general that might have
given more attention to libraries have also been lost. But a more
probable answer is that libraries were considered so natural, so
necessary to a well-ordered society, that writers did not consider
it of importance to mention them. They could well have thought
that libraries had always existed and would always exist. The
writer Athenaeus, writing ca. A.D. 200 about the great library at
Alexandria, said: "And concerning the number of books, the establishment of libraries, and the collection in the Hall of Muses, why
need I even speak, since they are in all men's memories?"

          More important to library history is the very fact that so
much Greek literature was preserved, since that preservation took
place in libraries, public and private. Also, it was from libraries,
both public and private, that much of that literature was compiled
and written. Many of the Greek authors were name-droppers; they
frequently mention earlier writers whose works they had studied or
read. If Western library history begins with the Egyptians and
Babylonians, it has its first "golden age" in classic Greece. All
the heritage that the Western World has from ancient Greece, with
the possible exception of sculpture and architecture, has been preserved for us in books and libraries - and still reaches us in the
same manner. Surely in no period of history has the role of the
library in a civilization been better evidenced than in the era of
classic Greece.

Additional Readings

(In the Hellenic era of ancient history, roughly from 500 B.C. to
A.D. 100, the information from archaeological studies is supplemented by passages about libraries in the surviving classical texts.
However, this information is scattered and often contradictory. The
general works already mentioned in the previous bibliographies are

also valuable for the Greek and Roman eras; some of them, in fact, are better than the more specific titles below.)

Birt, Theodor
    Das antike Buchwesen in seinem Verhältniss zur Litteratur.
        Berlin, 1882. viii, 518 p.
    Die Buchrolle in der Kunst. Leipzig, 1907. ix, 352 p.

Busch, Wilhelm
    Die bibliothecariis Alexandrinis qui feruntur primis . . .
        Leipzig, 1884. 56 p.

Conze, Alexander C. L.
    Über die pergamische Bibliothek. (In Sitzungsberichten der
        Berliner Academie, II [1884], 1259-1270).

Dunlap, Leslie W.
    Alexandria, the capital of memory. Emporia, Kansas, 1962.
        25 p.

Gardthausen, Victor E.
    Das Buchwesen in Altertum and im Byzantischen Mittelalter . . .
        Leipzig, 1911. (v. 1 of his Griechische Paleographie).
    Die alexandrinische Bibliothek. Leipzig, 1922. 31 p.

Heitz, Johann H. E.
    Die verlorenen Schriften des Aristoteles. Leipzig, 1865. 312 p.

Irwin, Raymond
    The origins of the English library. London, 1957. 272p.

Kenyon, Frederick G.
    Ancient books and modern discoveries. Chicago, 1927. 83 p.
    Books and readers in ancient Greece and Rome. Oxford,
        1932. 136 p.

Krehl, Ludolf
    Über die Sage von der Verbrennung der Alexandrinischen
        Bibliothek durch die Araber. Florence, 1880. 24 p.

Parsons, Edward A.
    The Alexandrian Library, glory of the Hellenic world: its rise,
        antiquities and destructions. Amsterdam, 1952. 468 p.

Sarton, George
    Hellenistic science and culture in the last three centuries B. C.
        Cambridge, Mass., 1959. 554 p.

Schmitz, Wilhelm
    Schriftsteller und Buchhändler in Athen. Heidelberg, 1876.
        58 p.

Schubart, Wilhelm
  Das Buch bei den Griechen und Römern. Berlin, 1907. 59 p.

Tarn, William W.
  Hellenistic civilization. London, 1952. 372 p.

Westermann, William L.
  The library of ancient Alexandria. Alexandria, Egypt, 1954.
    16 p.

5.
Roman Libraries

The libraries of ancient Rome were a direct inheritance from those of Greece, in types, organization, and contents. In fact, many of the actual manuscripts from the Greek libraries found their way into Roman collections. This cultural inheritance was a part of the general succession of the Roman world over that of classical Greece. From about 200 B. C. onward, the Roman Republic gradually spread its military influence eastward and southward across the Mediterranean until by the beginning of the Roman Empire, about 30 B. C., the Roman world extended throughout Asia Minor, much of Egypt and North Africa, the southern Balkans, and of course Sicily and Italy. The conquering Roman legions sometimes destroyed the cultures they overran, but more often they took over at least the physical effects of those cultures. Sculptures and manuscripts, architectural ideas and educated slaves were carried back to Rome, along with more immediately valuable gold and jewels. Thus it was that Rome's first major libraries probably were acquired as spoils of war from Greece and Asia Minor.

The earliest archives of Rome were probably the collections of chronologies, such as the Annales Pontificum that were supposed to have been brought together in 80 volumes about 120 B. C. These were strictly annals, brief accounts of major happenings in the Roman Republic, and were apparently kept in the official residence of the Pontifex Maximus, or chief priest. Even earlier than this, according to legend, the Twelve Tables of Roman law were engraved on bronze and exhibited to the public about 450 B. C. Another early collection of public records was the Libri Magistratum, or Books of the Magistrates, recording their names and official actions over a long period of time. Some of these were recorded on linen, known as the libri lintei, and were preserved in the Temple of the goddess of memory, Moneta, on Capitol Hill. Just as in Egypt and

64

Babylonia, the early Roman temples had their schools for priests and most probably collections of books as well as copies of the formal religious works kept in the temple sanctuary.   Beyond these, there are also a few references to private libraries in the second century B. C., but little concise information.

Probably the first notable Roman library of which we have recorded information was that of Paulus Aemilius.   This Roman worthy, a general as well as something of a scholar, defeated King Perseus of Macedonia in 168 B. C.   While his victorious soldiers ransacked the palace of everything of value, Aemilius himself claimed only the library, saying that he would rather have it than gold for the benefit of his sons.   A few years later Crates of Mallus, then librarian at Pergamum, came to Rome as an envoy to the Roman Senate.   While in Rome he lectured and taught, and it is quite possible that he aroused interest in the building of libraries and also in the temples that would house them.   At any rate, it is interesting to note that a few years later when the Porticus Metelli was built to enclose a temple, the result looked surprisingly like the Temple of Athena at Pergamum, although there is no evidence that it contained a library.

After Aemilius it became common for the Roman conquerors to bring home books as spoils of war.   One particularly notable collection was that acquired by Cornelius Sulla, the Roman general who took Athens in 86 B. C., and along with it the library of Apellicon of Teos.   This is the private collection that was thought to contain some of Aristotle's library.   Sulla passed it on to his son Faustus, in whose home Cicero saw the library in 55 B. C., but its later history is unknown.   Lucius Lucullus, in 67 B. C., returned from campaigns in Asia Minor with great quantities of books, including the library of the King of Pontus, and set them up in his private library in Rome.   Tyrannion served as librarian for Sulla's collection, and Andronicus of Rhodes is supposed to have studied Aristotle's works there.   Apparently Sulla opened the library to his scholarly friends and became something of a literary lion in his later years, just as he had been a military genius in his earlier ones.   There were libraries in Carthage, in North Africa, before

it was conquered by Rome's Scipio Aemilianus in 146 B. C. , but
they were destroyed or scattered and only a few volumes were carried to Rome.

As of 50 B. C. , private libraries were becoming common
among the wealthy families in Rome, but the only public collections
were the temple and government archives.   However, Julius Caesar
had the idea of founding a public library to equal or better that of
Alexandria, and to this end he appointed Terentius Varro (116-27
B. C.), a renowned scholar and book collector, to gather together
a collection of the best-known literature for a Roman public library.
Unfortunately, Caesar was assassinated (44 B. C.) before his library
aims could be accomplished.   Instead, the first public library in
Rome, like so many of the private ones, came into being as the
result of spoils of war.   C. Asinius Pollio, who had amassed a
fortune in his conquests of Dalmatia, used his wealth to bring together several collections already made, including those of Varro,
possibly some of the remnants of Sulla's library, and others to
form a library in the Temple of Liberty (Atrium Liberatatis) on the
Aventine Hill.   Public archives had already been housed there, but
Pollio reorganized the collection, added the libraries he had acquired, and opened the whole to the public about 39 B. C. , making
it the first-known public library in Rome.

Beginning with Augustus, the Roman emperors took over the
task of building libraries in Rome.   Actually Augustus founded not
one but two public libraries.   The first, founded in 33 B. C. , was
in the Porticus Octaviae, a magnificent structure built in honor of
Octavia, Augustus' sister.   The lower part of the portico served
as a promenade, while the library was in chambers above.   Caius
Melissus was the first librarian, and this library survived more
than a century, until it was destroyed by fire in the reign of Titus,
about A. D. 80.   The second Augustan library was the Palatine collection in the Temple of Apollo, founded about 28 B. C.   This library, as many later Roman ones, was divided into two separate
compartments, one for Greek books and one for Latin.   Pompeius
Macer was the first librarian, and Julius Hyginus, a noted gram-
marian, was a later one.   Later enlarged by the Emperor Tiberi-

us, and also by Caligula, the Palatine library was burned during
the reign of Vespasian, rebuilt by Domitian, and survived until well
into the fifth century.

The successors of Augustus maintained the tradition of founding public libraries in Rome. Tiberius established one in his palace on the Palatine Hill about A. D. 20, and this collection remained in existence until at least the third century. Tiberius is
also credited with establishing a library in the Temple of Augustus,
but there may be come confusion here with the library Augustus established in the Temple of Apollo or with Tiberius' own palace library. The Emperor Vespasian established the fifth public library
in Rome in A. D. 71, decorating it with the spoils captured in Jerusalem. This was in the Temple of Peace, or the Forum Pacis.
It was burned in A. D. 191, but was restored by Severus, and was
still in existence as late as the fourth century. Domitian (A. D. 81-
96) restored the libraries and other public buildings damaged in
the fires of Nero's reign; he is also credited with founding a library on the Capitoline Hill. Hadrian is also given credit for
founding this library, and little else is known about it.

Probably the greatest of the Roman libraries was the Ulpian
Library, first begun by Trajan in A. D. 113 in his Forum. Like
most of the other Roman libraries, this had two divisions, Greek
and Latin, but it also contained the government archives that had
survived the various fires. In the fourth century this library was
transferred to the Baths of Diocletian. There was a theater and
lecture room along with the Baths, so that it was more of a gentlemen's club than a public bathhouse. Trajan's Library was still in
existence in A. D. 455 when a bust of Apollonarius was placed there
by the Emperor Avitus. The custom of founding public libraries
continued while Rome's power both waxed and waned, and there
were reported to be no less than 29 established in the city before
the fourth century. The fate of most of them is unknown; just how
many existed at any one time, or even their names, is also lost in
history. Most of them were probably in temples, although possibly
some were in wealthy private residences. These latter were still
considered public because of the generosity of their owners.

The Emperor Hadrian is also remembered for his own private
library, which was modeled on a Greek library, at his palatial residence outside of Rome in Tibur.   Also during his reign, a magnificent library was built in Athens, which was then under Roman control.   The remains of this Athenian library have been excavated,
and from the ruins it appears to have been a most elegant building.
It was built in the shape of a square enclosed by a colonnade of
120 columns, with spacious rooms inside sparkling with alabaster
and gold and filled with paintings and statuary.   About its book collection we know little, but we do know that in addition to rooms for
books, there were reading rooms adorned with statues, lecture
rooms, and a central area from which books may have been de-
livered to borrowers in a proper "circulation desk" atmosphere.
Another library in Athens during the same era had a sign on the
wall giving the library hours from 7 a.m. to noon and noting that
no books could be taken out of the library because "we have sworn
an oath to that effect."   Hadrian is also credited with having revived or established libraries at Ephesus and Pergamum.

The public libraries were by no means the only sources of
literature available to the wealthier Romans, since private libraries
were common for several hundred years at the height of the Roman
era.   That most of the Roman writers had libraries is apparent
from their writings, but it is also verified by references in their
correspondence and other records.   Also, there is evidence that
other Romans, including physicians and lawyers, collected books
and built up sizable libraries.   The writings of Cicero frequently
mention his own library and those of his friends.   About 56 B.C.
he wrote to his friend Atticus:

> Mind you don't promise your library to anybody, however
> keen a collector you may find for it, for I am hoarding up
> all my little savings to get it as a resource for my old age.
> If I succeed I shall be richer than Crassus and look down
> on any man's manors and meadows.

In his own library, Cicero at one time employed Tyrannion as librarian, and he praised him highly for the work done in arranging
the books and in attaching title slips to them.   Titus Pomponius
Atticus was a book collector in his own right, and also a book-

dealer who supplied Cicero and others with rare volumes.   Atticus
also built up his own library to some 20,000 rolls, but this was
small compared to the physician Sammonicus whose library, some
three centuries later, contained over 60,000 rolls.   This latter collection, incidentally, came into the hands of Emperor Gordian II
(238-244) and was opened by him as a public library.

Epaphroditus, a Greek secretary to the Emperor Nero, had
a library of 30,000 rolls.   The two Plinys -- Pliny the Elder, the
great naturalist, and his nephew Pliny the Younger, whose letters
have been preserved -- both had large libraries.   Pliny the Younger
also gave a public library to the temple in the town of Comum,
dedicating it to the young men of the community in the hope that it
would turn them to literature instead of sports and gaming.   Pliny
may have aided in the founding of a library in Milan, although evidence of this is indefinite.   Cicero called his library "the soul" of
his house, while Terentius Varro wrote a book, now lost, on libraries (De bibliothecis).   Aulus Persius Flaccus, a poet of A.D.
34-62, had a relatively small library of only 700 rolls, but it was
well selected.   He left it in his will to his friend Cornutus.   Silius
Italicus, another poet who died in A.D. 101, was reported by Pliny
the Younger to have become so wealthy from his writings that he
had several villas, all furnished with large collections of books,
statues, and portraits.   Herrenius Severus, a person of distinguished learning, asked Pliny to obtain for him pictures of his favorite authors to adorn his private library walls.   Livius Larensis,
a priest during the reign of Marcus Aurelius, had a noted library
of theological works.

Other private libraries must have been common, since Sene-
ca says that they had become as necessary in the homes of the
rich as baths with hot and cold water.   He deplored the buying of
books by those who were not scholars, and asked: "What is the
use of having countless books and libraries, whose titles their
owners can scarcely read through in a whole lifetime? . . . It is
better to surrender yourself to a few authors than to wander through
many."   A later author, Lucian, wrote an essay on "The Ignorant
Book Collector" and asked: "For what expectation do you base upon

your books that you are always unrolling them and rolling them up,
glueing them, trimming them, smearing them with saffron and oil
of cedar, putting slip covers on them, and fitting them with knobs,
just as if you were going to derive some profit from them?" Even
Petronius in one of his satires introduces a character, Trimalchio,
who boasts of his Greek and Latin library but who displays ignorance as to its contents. Martial, however, was slightly more
charitable toward the private library, and dedicated one of his poems by saying: "O library of a dainty country house . . . thou
mayest put in a niche, though it be the lowest one, these seven
little books which I have sent thee --."

The capital city of Rome was by no means the only city in
the Roman Empire to be graced with one or more libraries. In
fact, although early Rome profited from thousands of rolls brought
in from elsewhere, later imperial and Christian Rome served as a
distributing center from which thousands of books were dispersed
throughout the empire. Moreover, philanthropists from Rome provided the means to establish libraries in many cities and towns.
Augustus, having set the example by founding two libraries in Rome,
encouraged wealthy Romans to use their funds to endow temples,
libraries, and schools throughout the Empire. Other libraries were
founded by the imperial government, possibly in attempts to Latin-
ize the inhabitants of newly conquered territories. In Tibur (modern Tivoli), just a few miles from Rome, there was a celebrated
library in the Temple of Hercules. Also, there were libraries at
Comum (Como), Tortona, and Milan in Italy, and probably many
others whose names have failed to come down to us. In Greece
the Romans established libraries at least in Athens, Corinth, Delphi, and Patrasso. There were Roman libraries in Durazzo on the
Adriatic and at Soli on the island of Cyprus. In Asia Minor there
were Roman libraries at Ephesus, Halicarnassus, Antioch, Smyrna,
and later at Jerusalem. In Africa, there were libraries at Carthage and Timgad, while in the western Mediterranean there were
those at Massila (Marseilles) in France and at Cordova in Spain.

The library at Antioch was originally established by a merchant, Maron, about 100 B. C. in the Shrine of the Muses there.

Maron had grown wealthy in the shipping trade and wished to ex-
press his appreciation to the people of Antioch. This library, or
possibly another one established later, was burned in A.D. 24, but
was replaced by the Romans. In the second century A.D., the
Roman Titus Giulio Aquila founded a library in Ephesus in honor of
his father. In Athens, a prominent business man, Pantainos, built
a library in A.D. 100 and dedicated it to the city of Athens and to
the Emperor Trajan. It was in a magnificent building whose ruins
were excavated in 1933. An inscription slab was uncovered, and
from the message on it we learn that Pantainos had "erected from
his own means the outer stoa, the peristyle, the library with its
books, and all the decorations in the building."

At Timgad (Thamugadi) in North Africa, one Rogatinus left
funds for the building of a library, and a magnificent structure was
erected. Here again the remains of this building have been excavated, and thus we know something of one provincial Roman library. It was about 81 feet square with a forecourt surrounded by
white limestone columns. A central circular court had niches in
the walls, apparently for cases holding the rolls, and rooms on
each side could have served as reading rooms.

One interesting private library has been found in Egypt at a
site some 120 miles south of Cairo. It was founded by a Roman
colony that is believed to have existed there from about A.D. 200
to 500. This collection, known as the Oxyrhynchus papyri, most
probably belonged to the library of a Christian who perished during
the persecutions under the Emperor Diocletian. His books were
probably thrown away into a sandy trash heap where the dryness
preserved them some 1500 years, or until they were discovered in
1897. The collection contained some 125 papyrus rolls, 70 papyrus
codices, and 36 parchment codices. The contents included a variety of materials ranging from personal letters and business letters
and contracts, to fragments of classical literature and excerpts
from the New Testament and early Christian writings.

Another Roman library of note, and in fact about the only
one of papyrus and parchment rolls that has been uncovered in its
original location, is that discovered in the ruins of the city of

Herculaneum. This city was covered by ashes and lava from an
eruption of Vesuvius in the year A.D. 79; it was excavated in the
eighteenth century. From one private library some 350 rolls have
been disinterred, most of them in Greek but a few in Latin. The
rolls were of papyrus encased in wooden boxes. Additional fragments seem to indicate an original collection of some 3,000 rolls,
and although charred, some of them have been unrolled and deciphered. The collection appears to be largely of philosophy, although some of the works were of medicine, literary criticism,
and general literature. Since most of the philosophic works were
of the Sophist school, and particularly by the philosopher Philo-
demus, it is conjectured that this was either the home of Philo-
demus himself or one of his disciples. The Herculaneum papyri
were first unrolled and deciphered by Sir Humphrey Davy in 1821.

Contemporary with the Romans in Palestine was a religious
group thought to have been the Essenes, a Hebrew congregation
dating from about 125 B.C. to A.D. 70. The remains of a library
maintained by this group were found in 1947 and later, in an area
to the west of the Dead Sea known as the Khirbet Qumran. Many
rolls of papyrus and several of thin sheet copper were found in
several caves. Remnants of more than 600 rolls have been identified in these "Dead Sea Scrolls," most of them of a religious nature. Included were some books of the Old Testament, a collection of hymns, a manual of discipline, and other religious works.
Apparently the collection was a type of master library maintained
with a scriptorium where scribes made copies of the religious
texts for individuals or outlying groups of the congregation. Many
similarities have been noted between the general religious philosophy of this Qumran group and that of the early Christians.

The later era of the Roman Empire saw a decline of the
great libraries of the ancient world, but it also saw the beginnings
of Christian libraries. The early Christians felt the need for preserving and disseminating their scriptural literature and hence
made good use of books and libraries. The sayings of Jesus, the
letters of Paul, and the early gospels were kept by each congregation and guarded zealously at or near the altar of each church.

Bishop Alexander founded a Christian library in Jerusalem before
A. D. 250, and about the same time Origen (A. D. 182-251) was establishing his theological school and library nearby.   At Alexandria
in Egypt there was probably a Christian library as early as A. D.
200.   Alexandria became a capital of Christian scholarship in the
third century, and Clement of Alexandria, who died in 217, quoted
from 348 authors in his works, indicating that he had access to a
fairly sizable library.   Origen had been a pupil of Clement, and he
in turn passed on his books to a pupil, Pamphilus, who lived,
studied, and taught at Caesarea near Jerusalem.   In 303 the Emperor Diocletian made a conserted effort to destroy all Christian
libraries, and many perished, but that at Caesarea survived.   Eu-
sebius, writing in A. D. 330, says he used this library in writing
his history of the Christian Church.   Jerome used this library in
the fourth century and Euthalius in the fifth century; in fact, it may
have survived until the Persians captured Palestine in 614, when all
Christian records were destroyed.

   With the recognition of Christianity by the Roman Emperor
Constantine in 325, the situation in the Christian churches improved considerably, and the remainder of the fourth century saw
the rapid spread of Christian churches and the establishment of
many Christian libraries.   Jerome studied at Caesarea, later went
to Rome as secretary to Pope Damasus, and then retired to Bethlehem in his old age.   He is probably responsible for starting a
papal library in Rome, and he also built up a large private library
that he moved to Bethlehem.   He described his personal library in
a letter written in 397, indicating that it had many secular works
as well as theological books.   George, Bishop of Alexandria, built
up a library in that city containing history and philosophy as well as
theology.   When he was murdered in 361 by an anti-Christian mob,
the Emperor Julian secured his library and had it carried to Antioch and placed in a temple.   Unfortunately, it was burned a few
years later during the reign of the Emperor Jovian.

   There were also libraries in the Christian churches of North
Africa.   One is known to have existed at Cirta as early as 300.
Augustine, Bishop of Hippo, had access to books in his early years

and built up a private library that he left to his church at his
death.   In his will he gave specific directions for the organization
and use of the library, which contained both religious and secular
literature.   There were Christian libraries in France (Gaul) in the
fourth century, especially at Lyons, Treves, and later at Arles.

In the early Christian churches, the small collection of
Scriptures and related books were kept to the right of the altar,
while the sacred vessels of the church were kept to the left.   It is
also interesting to note that the early Christians were among the
first to use the parchment codex instead of the papyrus roll as a
book form.   For instance, when the papyrus rolls that made up the
library of Pamphilus in Caesarea became worn in the fourth century,
Jerome ordered them recopied onto parchment codices.   This was
accomplished over a number of years by two dedicated priests,
Acacius and Euzoius.

Turning from consideration of specific libraries and types of
libraries, it will be worthwhile to look briefly at the physical nature of the Roman library, both public and private.   As we have
seen, most of the publicly owned libraries were connected with
temples, even though they contained public archives and general literature rather than religious works.   The temple libraries, in
whatever part of the Empire, usually followed the same general
plan, being adjacent to or over a colonnade leading to the main
structure of the temple.   There were often two divisions of the library, Greek and Latin, with sometimes a third division for archives.   There were rooms for the storage of books and also rooms
for reading, although the colonnades lent themselves to reading or
discussing books while walking.   Some of the libraries were associated with meeting rooms where public readings of an author's
works could be given.   Quite often there was a statue connected
with the library, as for example that of Apollo, some 50 feet high
and made of bronze, in the Temple of Apollo in Rome, or that of
Athena in the library at Pergamum.   Inside the libraries, counters
or benches often stood in front of the shelves or niches where the
rolls were stored.   On the walls above the books were paintings,
semi-reliefs, or sculptures of famous writers.   Originally the

rolls were kept in niches or pigeonholes on the walls, but later in
Rome some of the better or more expensive rolls were kept in
chests known as armaria. These were made of fine woods, sometimes inlaid with ivory, and often were tall and exquisitely carved.
As the codex took the place of the roll, this new book-form was
kept almost exclusively in the armaria, and the custom continued
well down into the later Middle Ages.

Books from the public libraries apparently circulated to influential people, if not to the ordinary borrower, since there are
several references in the literature of the era to such borrowings.
Marcus Aurelius, for example, writing to his friend Fronto about
A. D. 145 tells him that there is no need for him to send to the libraries of Apollo for certain volumes since he, Aurelius, already
has them out. Instead he suggests that Fronto try Tiberius's library, although he may have to bribe the librarian there in order
to be permitted to take them. Owners of private libraries were
apparently equally ready to lend their volumes to their friends,
since there are also references to such loans in the letters of both
Cicero and Pliny.

Libraries in private homes varied in physical accommodations according to the wealth of the owner and the size of the collection. If only a few rolls were owned, they might be kept in a
container of wood or lead similar to a modern hatbox. A larger
collection would be kept in its own armarium. As the collection
became even larger, it would be kept in a special room or apartment with armaria, desks, and works of art. A typical library in
a rich private home would have been about 15 by 23 feet with several armaria in it. The armarium would have been about 3 feet
high by 5 feet wide, and a medallion above it would indicate the
author whose works it contained, or perhaps merely a favorite author of the owner. Such a library room has been unearthed in
Rome and a similar one in Herculaneum.

The average Roman papyrus roll was about 20 to 30 feet
long, and about 9 to 11 inches high. The roll was usually wrapped
in a linen cloth, particularly if it was treasured, and tied with a
string. More valuable rolls might be kept in envelopes or jackets

made of parchment or leather, sometimes dyed in bright colors.
The armaria were divided into nests (nida) by both horizontal and
vertical shelves for rolls, or by horizontal shelves only for codices.   Sometimes the armaria were built into the walls of a room,
while usually they were separate, movable pieces of furniture.
Pliny notes that he had an armarium built into the walls of his bed-
room.

The early Roman librarian was often a highly educated
slave or a prisoner of war from Greece or Asia Minor.   Many
early teachers and scholars reached Rome in just this manner.
Later on in Roman history, the librarian was a native scholar, often an author as well.   Still later, however, the position became
more that of a civil servant.   Tyrannion, one of the early librarians in Roman history, was taken prisoner by Lucullus on the island of Rhodes and brought to Rome about 72 B. C.   He soon obtained his freedom, however, and set himself up as a teacher of
Greek.   Later he became wealthy, probably from his trade in
books, and was a friend and confidant of both scholars and politi-
cians.   He advised both Sulla and Cicero on the building up of their
libraries and helped Cicero at least in the cataloging of his collection.   Terentius Varro was a man of great learning, a writer of
history, satire, and poems.   He served as librarian, or at least
as book collector for Julius Caesar.

Under the Emperors, the several libraries in Rome seem to
have been administered by a central library administrator known as
the Procurator Bibliothecarum.   From Nero to Trajan this position
was held by Dionysius, an Alexandrian rhetorician, and under Hadrian it was held by C. Julius Vesinus, a former tutor who later became administrator of the Museum in Alexandria.   Beneath this
general library administrator there were individual librarians for
each of the city's libraries.   Generally speaking, the librarians of
Rome did not equal in importance those of Alexandria or Pergamum
in their more prosperous days.   Instead, the administrative positions became just that, something of a political civil-service job,
whereas the actual library work was done by well-educated but
less-important assistants and even by slaves.   The work in the li-

braries became highly specialized, with copyist, binder, and librarian all sharing in the work to be done.   Closely allied with the
libraries were the booksellers, who often made their wares available to the libraries and even selected or built up the collections,
especially in private libraries.

That the books within the Roman libraries were arranged
according to general subjects is known, but just what those subject
"headings" were is uncertain.   Certainly they were divided into
Greek and Latin, and apparently all the works of a single author
were kept together under his major subject.   Schools of philosophy
were divided, as were the works by or about various religious
groups.   Catalogs of two types were known and sometimes one,
sometimes both were used.   The first type was the classified catalog, or shelf list, arranged just as the rolls themselves were arranged.   The second was a bibliographical catalog, arranged by author but giving titles or first lines, lengths of the works in number
of lines, and sometimes biographical information about the author.

Although it is quite probable that censorship had reared its
ugly head in libraries earlier than the Roman era, our first direct
evidence of this deterrent to free libraries comes during this period.   The Emperor Augustus was a builder of libraries, but he also
disliked the poet Ovid and his works and ordered them removed
from the public libraries in Rome.   Ovid was subsequently banished
to the Black Sea area.   The writings of the Christians were suppressed by most of the Emperors before Constantine, but later,
when Christian bishops came into power in various areas, they in
turn suppressed non-Christian writings.   In doing so, they destroyed many works of classical authors now unknown to us.   For
example, while the Emperor Diocletian had attempted to suppress
all Christian libraries in A. D. 303, the Emperor Theodosius I in
391 attempted to destroy all "heathen" libraries.   Under his direction the Temple of Serapis in Alexandria was reported to have been
destroyed along with most if not all of its books.   A Christian
church replaced it with a small library of Christian works.   The
Emperor Justinian in 529 confiscated the library of the Platonic
Academy in Athens and forbade the teaching of Greek philosophy

there. In the same century, Pope Gregory I is reported to have
suppressed the works of Cicero and Livy, not because of their
contents, but because young men were reading them when they
should have been reading the Bible. Gregory is also accused of
having ordered the burning of the Palatine Library, but this is generally discredited. At any rate, between the activities of the
Christian bookburners and the later censorship of the Moslems in
the Mediterranean world, many works of classical authors were
suppressed and destroyed that otherwise might have survived.

The great libraries of the classical world were, one and all,
destined not to survive. Some of them were destroyed in accidental
fires or natural disasters, such as those of Rome and Herculaneum.
Many more were destroyed in wars and barbarian raids. However,
just as many simply died of neglect. The northern hordes who
swept down on Rome and Greece in the fifth and sixth centuries had
little or no respect for learning, and books were just so much
papyrus or parchment to them. Athens' last great library, the
Academy established there by Marcus Aurelius, was destroyed in
529. Just when the last classical library in Rome was destroyed
is difficult to say. There is some evidence that at least a part of
the Palatine Library survived into the sixth century. But it is also evident that there were more active libraries in France and
Spain in the sixth and seventh centuries than in Italy.

Some of the rolls and codices in the Roman libraries passed
into private hands, survived the barbarian wars, and eventually
turned up in monastery libraries. Others went with their owners
to Constantinople or other havens in the Eastern Empire when the
west was overrun. But the great majority of them were lost forever. Ammianus Marcellinus, writing about A. D. 378, reported
that the libraries of Rome were even then like tombs, closed forever. This was probably a somewhat premature judgment, for
some of them are known to have been open after that, but in general he was right. The days when Rome's libraries were open and
used were over. The great period of Roman literature and learning had passed; the classical era was over, and the Dark Ages had
begun.

Additional Readings

(Most of the readings already mentioned contain information on libraries of the Roman era, and these may be supplemented by the numerous excellent studies on Roman archaeology, literature, and culture, many of which have references to Roman libraries. References to libraries are fairly frequent in Latin literature. The following titles refer more specifically to Roman libraries and to the use of books in the Roman Empire.)

Barker, Ethel Ross
Buried Herculaneum. London, 1908. 253 p.

Bell, Harold I.
Egypt from Alexander the Great to the Arab conquest. Oxford, 1948. 168 p.

Boak, Arthur E. R.
The archive of Aurelius Isidorus in the Egyptian Museum . . . Ann Arbor, 1959. xix, 478 p.

Boyd, Clarence Eugene
Public libraries and literary culture in ancient Rome. Chicago, 1915. vii, 77 p.

Cagnat, René L. V.
Bibliothèques municipales dans l'Empire Romain. Paris, 1906. 26 p.

Clement, Paul
Études sur les droits des auteurs . . . chez les Grecs et chez les Romains. Grenoble, 1867. 152 p.

Clift, Evelyn H.
Latin pseudipigraphia: a study in literary attributions. Baltimore, 1945. 158 p.

Garbelli, Filippo
Le biblioteche in Italia all' epoca romana, con un' appendice sulle antiche biblioteche di Ninive et Allessandria. Milan, 1894. vi, 232 p.

Geraud, Hercule
Essai sur les livres dans l'antiquité, particulièrement chez les Romains. Paris, 1840. xiv, 232 p.

Glover, Terrot R.
"Cicero among his books," in pp. 131-159 of his: Springs of Hellas and other essays. Cambridge, 1946. 225 p.

Haenny, Louis
Schriftsteller und Buchhändler im alten Rom. Leipzig, 1885. 117 p.

Lanciani, Rudolfo
Ancient Rome in the light of recent discoveries. London, 1888.
(Chapter 7, pp. 178-205, is on Libraries).

Langie, André
Les bibliothèques publiques dans l'Ancienne Rome et dans
L'Empire Romain. Fribourg, 1908. 172 p.

Luersen, Sylvester
De templo et bibliotheca Apollinis Palatini . . . Frankfurt,
1719. 301 p.

Nash, Ernest
Pictorial dictionary of ancient Rome. New York, 1961-1962.
2 v.

Reichmann, Felix: "The book trade at the time of the Roman
Empire," Library Quarterly, VII (January, 1938), 40-76.

Stobart, John C.
The grandeur that was Rome. New York, 1962. 4th ed. xxvi,
322 p.

Vleeschauwer, Hans Jean de
Jules César et l'origine de la bibliothèque dans le Rome
antique. Pretoria, 1958. 70 p. (Mousaion, no. 28)

6.

Byzantine and Moslem Libraries

Of all the libraries of antiquity, the ones that came nearest to surviving through the Middle Ages were those in Constantinople. In particular, the Imperial Library, founded by Constantine the Great in the early fourth century, varied in size and importance with the fortunes of the Byzantine Empire, but in one for or other it did survive down to the capture of the city by the Turks in 1453.

The background of Byzantine history is both Greek and Roman. Its location on the Straits of the Bosporus, the connecting link between the Mediterranean and the Black Sea, was known to the Greeks as Byzantium. After the Emperor Constantine had won control over both the Eastern and Western Roman Empires about A.D. 325, he established his capital at this spot and renamed it Constantinople. In the course of time the Western Roman Empire declined and was overrun by barbarians from the North, but the Eastern Empire continued to exist, at times powerful and at other times weak, but culturally effective for more than a thousand years. Essentially, however, the Byzantine culture was Greek rather than Roman and more Eastern than Western. Its role in Western civilization is due to its effect on the Balkans and Russia and to its preservation in libraries and monasteries of many of the Greek and Latin classics. Of course more Greek writings than Latin were preserved in Constantinople, and although many were lost in battles and fires, large numbers were saved. A thousand years later, in the fourteenth and fifteenth centuries, copies of these manuscripts found their way to Italy and western Europe, and the Renaissance was the result. It is interesting to note that the same Emperor who founded Constantinople was also the first Emperor who adopted Christianity.

The Imperial Library founded by Constantine at Constantinople was begun about A.D. 330 or shortly thereafter. The Em-

81

peror had agents search for Christian books throughout the Empire,
and these were brought together in his library. He also permitted
the writings of the Greek and Latin secular writers in the collection, but its growth was slow, and there were only about 7,000
rolls in the library at Constantine's death in 337. A generation
later, the Emperor Julian tried to overthrow Christianity, and he
may have destroyed some Christian works in the library, but Julian
did add greatly to the Greek classical literature there. Under succeeding emperors, the library grew steadily until it contained over
100,000 rolls by about A.D. 475. In 477, under the Emperor
Zeno, it suffered great losses in a fire. Zeno began rebuilding it
immediately, and in a few years it was again in a flourishing state.

The fifth century brought another notable library to the scene
in Constantinople. This was the library of the Academy, a university or school of philosophy begun in the reign of Theodosius II
(408-450). This school flourished for several centuries, particularly under the Emperor Justinian (527-565). Under Leo the
Isaurian (717-741) the greater part of the library was reported
burned in an attempt to drive out all anti-Christian influences in
his realm, but this is doubted. After the decline of the Academy,
a new institution of learning, the University of Constantinople, was
begun about 850. This soon became a leading university in the
Near East, and its library grew steadily, playing a large part in
the Byzantine renaissance of the eleventh century.

The Emperor Justinian is noted in library history for two
other reasons. First, it was he who closed the last surviving
classical school, that of Athens, in 529. He did so because he
considered that the philosophy it was teaching was anti-Christian.
But a more positive accomplishment under Justinian was the codification of Roman law. This work was done by a commission of
scholars appointed by Justinian, and it involved the study and con-
densation of some 2,000 volumes of legal works, going back nearly
a thousand years in Roman history. The Justinian Code, with its
Digests and supplementary works, form the Corpus Iuris Civilis,
the basis of all civil law in western Europe through the Middle
Ages and on into the modern era. Around this work there grew up

in Constantinople a school of law that flourished for centuries. To
compile such a code there must have been available a considerable
library of legal sources, and such a library must have been maintained for the law students, but no direct knowledge is available
about the location or contents of this "law library." Too much
emphasis cannot be placed on this legal work of Justinian's era and
its effect on the legal and juristic history of the Western World.
Under Justinian the Byzantine world reached its high point, governing under one rule the entire Mediterranean from Gibraltar to the
Euphrates and from the upper Nile to the Alps. Literature flourished during this reign, including particularly the important historians Procopius and Menander. The works of each of these
writers show familiarity with many earlier historical writings and
give evidence of heavy use of the libraries of the city. A number
of religious works, books on the saints, and some poetry survive
from this period. After Justinian, however, Constantinople went
into a period of literary decline that lasted until the middle of the
ninth century.

Aside from the libraries of the Emperor and the university,
there was usually a third major library in Constantinople. This was
the library of the patriarch, the head of the Eastern Church. Constantine is reported to have also started this library with a gift of
50 volumes, elegantly inscribed on parchment, but little is known
of its later history. There was a patriarchal school, particularly
after the seventh century, for the training of nonecclesiastical
leaders. These schools probably had libraries, as did also those
of the monasteries where the clergy were trained. The Byzantine
monasteries usually followed the rules for monastic life laid down
by Pachomius of Egypt. These rules encouraged study but did not
insist on the formation of libraries. About 825 at Studium, a
monastery near Constantinople, the Abbot Theodore produced a new
set of monastic regulations that emphasized the scriptorium and the
library and outlined the duties of the librarian. There were many
monasteries formed under the Byzantines in Asia Minor and
Greece, and each of them was encouraged to form a library of its
own. The monastic libraries on the Greek peninsula of Mt. Athos

are particularly noted for the fact that their libraries have survived down to the modern era.   Religious works were the texts usually preserved in the monasteries, but many secular works were
also found there.   An example of one of the most important texts
found in this area is of course the Codex Sinaiticus, one of the
earliest extant manuscripts of the Bible, now in the British Museum
but originally found at the monastery of St. Catherine on Mt. Sinai.

The period from 850 to 1200 was again a notable era in
Byzantine learning and literature.   It produced a number of important authors, although their works for the most part consisted of
compends, or encyclopedias, rather than original productions.   In
the ninth century Photius compiled his Bibliotheca (or Myrobiblion),
which was a summary or digest of some 280 earlier works, many
of them now lost.   Whether he had all of the works he included in
his own library or whether he borrowed them from other libraries
is unknown, but he must have had access to a considerable library
somewhere.   Included in his works were many theological titles,
but also Greek history and literature, with some works in the arts
and sciences.   Photius had a student and follower, Arethas, whose
private library is better known.   In fact, some volumes from the
library of Arethas have survived, and one now in the Bodleian Library at Oxford has a note in it indicating that it was originally
purchased in the year 888 for the equivalent of about $60.   Em-
peror Constantine Porphyrogenitus (913-959), re-established or enlarged the library in the imperial palace, and also established several schools and libraries for the public in the city.   Eustatius,
Archbishop of Thessalonica in A. D. 1175, was a historian and
scholar originally from Constantinople.   In his works he quoted
from more than 400 earlier writings, indicating a familiarity with
and access to a considerable library.   On the other hand, when
Michael Acominatus became Archbishop of Athens in 1175, he found
that city to be completely devoid of libraries.   He noted that his
own library, two chests of books, was the largest collection of literature in the city.

Private libraries also flourished at various times under the
Byzantines.   In 620, for example, a teacher in Constantinople by

the name of Tychicus was reported to have owned a large library,
a fact recorded because of the envy of a government official who
may have wanted the books for himself.   The Emperor Valens in
the fifth century hired both Greek and Latin scribes to produce a
library for himself and his children.   In the same century, the
Academy at Constantinople was reported to have 28 professors,
most of whom were reported to own professional libraries. Caesar
Bardas, who reopened the University after 850, owned a considerable collection of books, and probably helped restock the University library from his own possessions.   Kyrillos, who was librarian
of the Patriarchal Library in St. Sophia in the early tenth century,
also had a private library of his own.   Moses of Bergamo, a poet
of the twelfth century, owned a library of classic Greek manuscripts that was destroyed in a fire.   St. Christodulus, who died
in the late twelfth century, bequeathed his library to the monastery
at Patmos.   In 1201 this monastery had 330 volumes, 267 on parchment and 63 on paper.   Some science and history were included
along with theology in this collection.   It is interesting to note that
the Patmos collection in 1382 contained only 300 volumes, with
some of the same titles as those listed in the 1201 catalog, but
with many different items.

      At various times during its long history, Byzantine influence
extended from Ceylon to Paris and from Spain to Moscow.   Charlemagne, for example, obtained books from the Imperial Library at
Constantinople for his palace library at Aachen.   Monasteries in
Armenia borrowed books from Constantinople, and copies of them
are still preserved in the Miasnikian State Public Library in Ere-
van.   Byzantine influence was strong in southern Italy, where there
was a Greek monastery before 1100.   The library at this monastery
included works of Aristotle, Aristophanes, and other Greek authors
who were virtually unknown at that time in the remainder of western Europe.   The Serbian Empress Elizabeth in the thirteen century had a Greek library obtained from Constantinople, and Basil
Lapu, Prince of Moldavia in the next century also had a library
containing classical Greek works.   Thus it can be seen that the
classics, particularly those from ancient Greece, were never ex-

actly lost to the Western World.   They were always available to
those areas in diplomatic and cultural contact with Constantinople.
However, during most of the Middle Ages these contacts were few
and tenuous, so that for all general purposes they were insignifi-
cant.

Unfortunately, the glory of Byzantium that had withstood
wars both external and civil for many centuries gradually came to
an end after 1200.   Norman invasions of the Greek peninsula in the
late twelfth century presaged the end, and when those powerful
forces captured Thessalonica in 1185, they destroyed many palaces
and homes filled with works of art and ancient manuscripts.   Some
of the invaders realized that the writings had value, and so collected large groups of them and sold them to the Italians.   A few
years later the push of the Norman Crusaders brought them to
Constantinople itself, and that city was almost completely destroyed.
It is estimated that more destruction of libraries and works of art
was accomplished by these Christians in 1204 than by the Turks in
1453.

After the fall of Constantinople, the capital of Byzantium
was removed to Nicaea, where Emperor John III (1222-54) established a library.   Nicaea became a center of culture in the thirteenth century, with schools, churches, monasteries, and hospitals
the equal of any in the Western World.   From Nicaea the Byzantines began a return to power, capturing Salonika from the Nor-
mans in 1246 and returning to Constantinople in 1261.   There Michael Paleologus reinstated the imperial library in a wing of the
palace.

The significance of Constantinople in Western civilization is
great, not because of its own art and literature, but because it
preserved so much of classical culture through the Middle Ages
when it was lost in the West.   Roman law, Greek literature, history and philosophy, even some of the early Christian literature,
were saved by the libraries of Constantinople.   Even before 1200,
the flow of manuscripts to the West had begun, but after that date
the parchment codex became a major commodity in the trade from
the East to Italy and Europe.   These manuscripts were probably

more important than any other single factor in bringing about the
Renaissance. In this sense, it was Byzantium in its decline that
provided the impetus which brought about the end of the Middle Ages
in Europe and gave birth to the modern era.

Constantinople was not the only center of culture in the
Eastern Mediterranean during the Middle Ages. Close neighbors
and long-time enemies of the Christian Byzantines were the Moslems who sprang into prominence in the seventh century. In the
century after A. D. 622, when the Moslem era began, the religion
of Islam swept most of the Arabic world from Persia to Morocco.
The Moslems came close to Constantinople on several occasions,
but never succeeded in overthrowing that city until 1453. Under the
impetus of the Islamic religion, the Arabs developed both a military power and a literary culture that was to flourish for some
eight hundred years.

Before the coming of the Prophet Mohammed, however,
there was little literature among the Arabic peoples. In fact, there
was little literacy. Instead, there was an oral literature of tales
and poetry handed down from generation to generation, much as in
Homeric Greece. The first major item of written literature among
the Moslems was the Koran itself. This collection of sayings of
the Prophet brought together by his followers came to comprise
both the "Bible" and the philosophic base of Mohammedanism. To
know the Koran and its teachings became the duty of all Moslems,
and hence literacy became all important and schools began to be
organized. To teach the Koran, scholars and priests were necessary and higher institutions of education were started, many of
them connected with the churches or mosques. The result of all
this was a stabilized Arabic language that was suitable for a secular as well as a religious literature. Another fortunate development occurred to aid in the expansion of literature and learning.
This was the coming of paper as a writing material, much cheaper
and more available than parchment or papyrus. An economical
writing material meant that more copies of literary works could be
produced and that reading material of all kinds could reach a wider
audience. The technique of manufacturing paper came to the eastern

Moslems from China by way of central Asia about A. D. 800, and
the knowledge of the process spread gradually through the Moslem
world, reaching Spain about 950.

Although Mohammedanism spread through the strength of its
military power, and some Moslem military leaders were supposed
to have held that no book was necessary except the Koran, the
world of Islam was actually a book-loving society. Seldom in the
history of the world have books been held in such high esteem, at
least among the upper classes. Along with studying the Koran,
the devout Moslem was dutybound to copy it and make it available
to others, so the craft of the scribe became a popular one in the
Arab world, and thousands of copies of the Koran were produced,
many of them in beautiful scripts and bindings.

The first center of the Moslem world was Damascus, where
the Umayyid dynasty ruled from A. D. 661 to 750. These rulers
promoted learning and established a royal library that also included the archives of the church and state. In A. D. 689 the archives were separated from the literary and religious works, with
the latter forming an open public library and the former being rele-
gated to the House of Archives. Manuscripts were bought, borrowed, or otherwise obtained from all parts of the known world,
and copies were made for the Damascus library. Works of alchemy, medicine, and astrology were collected, as well as literature, history, and philosophy, and of course works on the Moslem
religion.

A footnote to early Moslem culture concerns the Nestorian
Christians who were driven from Syria by the Emperor Zeno about
485. These Christians fled to Persia, where at Nisibis they built
up a strong center of Greek culture, complete with libraries of
Greek classics. They attracted scholars from Greece, including
some of the faculty of the school at Athens that was closed by
Justinian in 529. Thus the Moslems found, deep in the heart of
Persia, a treasure house of Greek science and philosophy that they
soon had translated into Arabic. In fact, most of the surviving
Greek literature had been translated into Arabic by 750, and Aristotle, for example, became so widely studied that literally hun-

dreds of books were written about him by Arabic scholars. The
Moslems also obtained Greek works from Constantinople through
regular trade channels and captured others in libraries of Syria and
Palestine.

The great period of Moslem literature and learning came under the Abbasid rulers, or Caliphate, from 750 to 1100. These
Caliphs moved the capital of the Moslem world to Baghdad, and by
750 this world extended from Persia around the south shore of the
Mediterranean to Spain and even southern France. Actually Spain
and Morocco did not recognize the rule of the Abbasids, and other
parts of the empire broke away from time to time, but culturally
speaking, whatever the ruling government, the area that accepted
Islam became something of a unit. The early Abbasid Caliphs, including Harun al-Rashid (785-809) of Arabian Nights fame, were
great lovers of learning, and at Baghdad a great university and library were developed. Particularly under the reign of al-Mamun
the great (813-833) the university, or "House of Learning" grew into prominence, with laboratories, subsidized scholars, a translating
service, and even an astronomical observatory. The study of science was stressed by the scholars under al-Mamun, and libraries
from India to Spain were culled to find new sources of information
for the Baghdad shelves. The library was open to scholars from
all over the world, whether their specialties were religion or science, poetry or medicine. Scholarly relations with the Western
World were maintained to some extent, particularly during the periods of peace with Constantinople, and it is quite possible that for
the great part of the period before 1200 the Arabs received more
from the West than the West did from Islam.

By 900 Baghdad had served as a model for schools and libraries throughout Islam. It was said that in 891 Baghdad alone
had over 100 booksellers, and that at the height of its cultural
glory before it was destroyed by the Mongols in 1236, it had 30
public libraries. Other university and public libraries in the Moslem world ranged from Bokhara and Merv, deep in the heart of
Asia on the land route to China, through Basra and Damascus,
Cairo and Algiers, to Morocco and Spain in the west. A geogra-

pher, Yakut al-Hamawi, who visited Merv in 1228 found no less
than 12 libraries there available to the public.   Ten were endowed
libraries and two were in mosques.   One had 12,000 bound volumes,
and another had been in existence since A.D. 494.   Yakut noted
that the lending policies of the libraries in Merv were so liberal
that he was able to have over 200 volumes to work with in his
rooms at one time.   The philosopher Avicenna in the early eleventh
century found in Bokhara a sultan's library consisting of many
rooms filled with bookcases, all arranged for easy use and all
available to serious scholars.   In Moslem Persia there were libraries at Nishapur, Ispahan, Ghasnah, Basrah, Shriaz, and Mosul.
In Ispahan a rich landowner had given the city a public library in
885, and in Nishapur a similar gift was received in 965.

In Egypt the Fatimid Caliphs during the ninth and tenth centuries built up a center of culture in Cairo that was to rival Baghdad and Damascus.   The Caliph al-Aziz (975-996) protected poets
and scholars and collected a large library for their use.   Catalogs
of the various libraries in Cairo were compiled, and subject bibliographies of the known branches of learning were made.   It was
reported, although probably an exaggeration, that the libraries of
Cairo in the early eleventh century contained over 1,200,000 volumes.   One of them had around 100,000 volumes, including 2,400
copies of the Koran, under the Caliph al-Hakim around 1005.   This
library had its own staff of librarians, administrators, binders,
calligraphers, and guards, and was supported by rentals from property with which it had been endowed.   Further west there was a library in the mosque in Tripoli, which was destroyed by Christian
crusaders in 1109.

Another place in which Moslem scholarship and learning
reached high levels was Spain, where the followers of Mohammed
prevailed for several centuries.   The Moslems entered Spain after
A.D. 711, and in Cordoba, Seville, Toledo, and other cities built
up an advanced civilization that outshone anything Europe had to offer during the same period.   At Cordoba, for example, there was
a noted Moslem university and several large libraries including one
reputed to have over 400,000 volumes.   Its catalog alone consisted

of 44 volumes.   Under al-Hakim II, this library was reported to
have given employment to over 500 people, including many agents
sent to all parts of the world to buy books.   Elsewhere in Moslem
Spain there were a total of 70 libraries in the tenth century, with
Toledo having several.   Sicily also came under Muslim influence
during the ninth and tenth centuries, and so did Sardinia and Cor-
sica.   Generally speaking, although the Moslem world was split into factions, often warring with each other or with outsiders from
India to France, there were developed in all the major Islamic
cities and in many smaller towns as well, libraries of major importance.   Libraries were connected with schools, mosques, and
palaces, and many fine ones were in the homes of private citizens.

Probably at few times in history of the world have private
libraries reached such size and elegance as under the Moslems.
The wealth brought on by conquest, tribute, and trade developed an
elite and highly literate upper class among the Arabic peoples.
Since bigamy was practiced, and even encouraged for those who
could afford it, large families were the rule among the nobility,
and among them there were thousands who pursued learning and
scholarship as a career.   In fact, next to war and conquest, these
became the most revered professions, and the collecting of libraries, both for use and for show, became common among the
wealthy.   Many of these private libraries reached remarkable size,
according to the notes we have referring to them in the works of
historians and biographers.   The library of one Baghdad scholar of
the tenth century was reported to be so large that it took   400
camel loads to move it when he took his family from one residence
to another.   Abu al-Mutriff, who died in 1011, owned a library of
rare books and masterpieces of fine binding and calligraphy.   He
considered his books so valuable that he would neither use them nor
allow them to be used for anything except display.   The historian
Omar al-Waquidi possessed 120 camel-loads of books.   Another
tenth century resident of Baghdad left his sons in his will no less
than 600 boxes of books.   Ibn al-Alkami, vizier of Baghdad in 1258,
had a library of 10,000 volumes.   Ibn al-Amid, vizier of Rayy in
971, employed a full-time librarian to care for his collection of 100

camel-loads of books. In Cairo about 1170 there were four private
libraries large enough to be noted by a visiting scholar. One of
these belonged to a prince, one to a doctor, and two to Jewish
merchants. In Syria in the twelfth century a minor noble owned a
library of 4,000 volumes that was destroyed by Christian crusaders.
So prevalent were the private libraries of the Moslems that one
writer has estimated that, as of 1200, there were more books in
private hands in the Moslem world than in all libraries, public and
private, of western Europe.

        One interesting thing about the Moslem libraries is the wide
variety of subject matter they contained. With the exception of religious works of other faiths, the Moslems gathered, copied, and
translated everything they could, in all subjects, of all times, and
in all available languages. Greek and Latin classics, Sanskrit
philosophy, Egyptian history, Hindu epics, and medieval French
love-poems -- all were to be found somewhere in the Moslem libraries, along with biography, science, and pseudoscience from all
times and places. Though most of these libraries were subsequently destroyed, from surviving catalogs and isolated volumes we find
evidence of all these subjects and others as well. For example,
the library at Fez in Morocco contained the works of the Roman
Livy and the Greek Galen, among others. The library at Damascus
contained all the known works of Aristotle. A library at Gaza, between Egypt and Palestine, contained many Egyptian papyri, some
in hieroglyphics. The Justinian Code of Laws was present in many
Moslem collections, indicating the respect that was felt among the
Arabs for this basic legal collection, even though it differed sub-
stantially from that in vogue among themselves.

        Of course, the major holdings of most Arabic libraries, par-
ticularly those in the mosques, related to the Moslem religion.
Copies of the Koran were numerous in all collections, and commentaries on it filled thousands of other volumes. Many other volumes
contained biographies of early Moslem rulers and military leaders.
Every member of Mohammed's family, both his immediate ancestors
and descendants, were subjects of biographies, many of them somewhat more fanciful than accurate. Next to religious topics came

poetry, and thousands of volumes were filled with this major literary form among the Moslems. Fiction, as represented by such
tales as those of the Arabian Nights, was also popular. Geogra-
phies and histories were favorites, particularly tales of exploration
and accounts of the reigns of the various Caliphs and their wars.
Works in science, particularly medicine, and philosophy were fairly
plentiful, along with the pseudosciences of astrology and alchemy.
In addition, particularly in the more popular libraries, there were
more mundane volumes such as dictionaries and grammars, textbooks, and writing copybooks, or calligraphies. Books on the keeping of accounts were popular in the trading centers, which included
almost all Moslem cities, and tables for the conversion of foreign
moneys into those of local usage were popular. Something akin to
a travel guide was widely found, indicating that travel, at least
within the general confines of the Moslem world, was rather frequent.

About the physical conditions in the Moslem libraries, unfortunately we have little accurate knowledge. The usual book-form
was the codex, either of parchment or some other animal skin, or
of paper. However, rolls were by no means unknown, particularly
in the earlier centuries, both on parchment and papyrus, and in the
eastern Moslem areas the exotic Asiatic accordion-shaped volumes
and even the Hindu palm-leaf olas were occasionally seen. As for
library arrangement, there are frequent references to the custom
of placing books on different subjects in different rooms in the
larger libraries, and even of having "subject specialists" in charge
of them. In other places there are references to the books being
kept in chests, with a list of the contents on the outside. Staffs in
the larger libraries often ran into the hundreds, when copyists,
binders, illuminators, and guards were added to those whom we
would usually consider as librarians. The latter were often scholars, often writers or poets more or less pensioned by patronizing
rulers or nobles. However, library administrators are also mentioned, indicating that the management of these large enterprises
often called for more of a business man than a scholar. At any
rate, the position of librarian was an honored one, and one to

which many of the younger sons of the nobility often aspired.

The larger libraries seem to have been cataloged as a matter of normal procedure, and the catalogs took the form of manuscript volumes.   References are found to libraries cataloged in 10, 20 and even 40 volumes.   Apparently the arrangement was by subject, but within the subject by acquisition rather than by author or title.   Since shelving was by subject in room or chest, the catalog was thus something of a classified accession list, but it apparently served its purpose and was widely used.   It is interesting to note that many of the Moslem public libraries included not only rooms for reading but also rooms for meetings and smaller rooms for discussion and debate.

Particularly in the wealthy private libraries, but also in some of the public ones, the arts of illuminating and binding reached a high level among the Moslems.   Calligraphy itself was an art, and the cursive Arabic script lent itself to beautiful productions.   The use of fine vellums, often dyed into exotic colors, and of different colored inks, together with ornate, heavily tooled and embossed leather bindings, produced some of the most beautiful books the world has ever known.   Such fine works were of course exceptions, but the book itself was thoroughly appreciated and widely used.   The general policy in most Moslem libraries seems to have been rather liberal toward the use and even the circulation of books, particularly to known students and scholars.   Although only a few libraries were public in our sense of the word, most of them, even large private ones, were available to serious scholars.   In fact, some of the endowed libraries subsidized scholars and provided them with the services of copyists and translators.

Some of the results of the scholarship in these libraries and schools can be seen in the writings of the great authors of the Moslem era.   In 987 Muhammad al-Nadim produced a multivolumed "Index of the Sciences," a bibliography of books in Arabic on all branches of knowledge, with biographical notes on the authors. Some idea of the great loss to world culture in the destruction of Arabic libraries can be obtained when it is noted that not one in a thousand of the books al-Nadim described is presently known to ex-

ist. Another tenth century writer, Muhammad al-Tabari, wrote a
history of the world in 150 volumes, saying that he had consulted
over 10,000 other volumes in writing them. The Egyptian scholar
and astronomer Ibn al-Haytham, of the early eleventh century, wrote
over 100 volumes on mathematics, astronomy, philosophy, and medicine. Even greater writers, although not so prolific, were the
Arabic authors who became best known to the medieval European
world. Averroes (Ibn Rushd), who lived in Spain in the twelfth century, brought the works of Aristotle back to western Europe with
his text and commentaries which were translated into Latin and
French. Avicenna (Ibn Sina), born in Bokhara toward the end of
the tenth century, was encyclopedic in his interests and knowledge,
but is best known in western Europe for his texts on medicine,
which were used as late as the seventeenth century. Avempace (Ibn
Bajja) was another Spanish Moslem who exercised considerable influence in Europe through his free-thinking philosophy. Finally, we
might mention Ibn al-Arabi, whose mystical theology so closely re-
sembles Dante's Divine Comedy that it would seem to be a source.

Unfortunately, the story of Islamic libraries is too similar
to those of their predecessors in the Mediterranean world, for they
too ended in wholesale destruction. Many Moslem libraries suffered
in civil wars and in the decline of interest in learning under various rulers at different times. For example, when Saladin conquered Egypt in 1175, many of the more valuable books in the libraries there were seized and distributed among his friends and
followers. After 1100, reactionaries gained control in most of the
eastern Moslem world, and literature and libraries declined considerably. Learning continued to flourish in North Africa and Spain
for two more centuries, but there too there was a noticeable decline after 1300.

Not the least important in the destruction of Islamic libraries
were the depredations of the Christian crusaders from the eleventh
to the thirteenth centuries. In Syria, Palestine, and parts of North
Africa, the Christians destroyed libraries as enthusiastically as the
barbarians in Italy a few hundred years earlier. When Spain was
reconquered from the Arabs, the great Islamic libraries at Seville,

Cordova, and Granada were destroyed or were carried away by their retreating owners. When in the sixteenth century, less than a hundred years after the last Moslem had been driven from Spain, the Escorial Library was founded by Philip II, virtually no Arabic manuscripts could be found in the whole of Spain. Instead Philip obtained some 4,000 Arabic manuscripts relating to Spain from the libraries of neighboring Morocco. As if human causes were not enough, at least one great Moslem library was destroyed by fire. This was the library at Medina, burned after being struck by lightning in 1257.

The great destruction of Moslem libraries came, however, from the raids of the Mongols in the thirteenth century. From out of the mountains and steppes of central Asia came the hordes of Genghis Khan, conquering and destroying everything before them. In the first great sweep to the Caspian Sea and northern Persia, the cities of Bokhara, Samarkand, and Merv were destroyed along with many smaller towns. Samarkand had been a Moslem city for over 500 years, and its schools and libraries were well endowed and well used. Merv's libraries were justly famous, but all were destroyed along with many of the scholars who were using them. These depredations took place about 1218 to 1220, and after that the Mongols retired. In 1258, however, they returned in greater force, under new commanders, and this time they reached and destroyed Baghdad. In one week libraries and their treasures that had been accumulated over hundreds of years were burned or otherwise destroyed. Leather bindings were used for the repairing of Mongol shoes, and illuminated manuscripts were employed to start camp fires. Students and scholars were considered particularly useless to the victors, and they were killed by the hundreds. The Mongols also destroyed at this time one of the strangest libraries in history. This was one built up by the sect known as Assassins at Alamut and reputed to contain much in the way of magic and murder, but also some fine works in philosophy and science. After destroying 36 public libraries and hundreds of private ones in Baghdad, the Mongols under Hulagu swept on through Syria, virtually wiping out the ancient city of Damascus. Finally, the Moslems of Egypt were able to stop the Mongols in 1260, and they gradually fell back to central Asia.   Although they did not long maintain their hold over eastern Islam, the Mongols left such losses in wealth, books, and lives that the glory of Islam was forever dimmed.   There was a comeback in the early fourteenth century in Baghdad, but this was again set back by the invasion of Tamerlane in 1393.   Between foreign invaders and bickering native leaders, the Arabic peoples for the most part sank back into a state of widespread illiteracy that continued down to the twentieth century.   Before that happened, however, there had flourished for nearly a thousand years one of the world's truly great civilizations.

But what was the effect of that Moslem civilization on the Western World and particularly on the libraries of the Western World?   Since much of the literature itself was lost, it can be safely stated that the effect was not as much as it might have been if the libraries could have been preserved.   However, it is apparent that the Islamic libraries, possibly even more than those of Constantinople, were the connecting link between the learning of classical Greece and the Renaissance of western Europe.   One point of contact in particular was Spain.   As early as 953 John of Gorce was sent to Cordova by the German Emperor Otto the Great. He learned to read Arabic and returned to Germany with his saddlebags filled with Arabic manuscripts, including some translations from Aristotle and some Arabic works of science.   When the Christians captured Toledo in 1085 they found a wealth of Arabic books, and although many were destroyed others were translated into western European languages.   Even before this, in 1070, Daniel of Morley, an English scholar, had visited Toledo and returned to England with copies of Arabic scientific works.   Gerard of Cremona, who died in 1187, spent most of his life in Toledo and translated over 70 scientific works from Arabic into Latin.   Alfonso X of Castile had been taught by Arabic teachers, and when he founded the University of Salamanca in the thirteenth century it was largely modeled on the Moslem universities, even using translations of the same textbooks.   Thus even before 1250, much of Arabic science and translations and commentaries on the Greek classics had reached western Europe either through Spain or through Sicily and southern Italy.   The early medical schools, such as those at Bologna, Padua, Naples, and Paris, taught medicine almost entirely from texts borrowed from the Arabs.

Although the Crusades resulted in the destruction of some Islamic libraries, they did result in contact, even if military, between western Europe and the eastern Mediterranean, and through that area with the whole of the exotic East from Arabia to China. This contact resulted in an expansion of trade and in the development of new tastes in western Europe, both culinary and literary. With the trade in fine fabrics, rare metals, and tasty spices came the trade in manuscripts that flourished at least 200 years.   Both from Constantinople and from the Moslem libraries and bookdealers came the books, and with them the ideas that touched off the Renaissance.   In any study of western library development, it is necessary to remember that for almost a thousand years much of the best in our literary heritage was preserved in the East -- in the libraries of Islam and Byzantium.

Additional Readings

(The best source of material on Byzantine and Moslem libraries is to be found in publications in Greek, Russian, and the Middle Eastern languages.   Material in English is particularly scarce, except in the case of a few excellent translations.   The following readings, mostly general, will give the student a good foundation for the subject.)

Brehier, Louis
     Le monde Byzantine.   Paris, 1947-1950.   3 v.

Buksh, S. Khuda
     "The Islamic libraries," Nineteenth Century, LII (1902), 125-
          139.

Byron, Robert
     The Byzantine achievement, an historical perspective.   London,
          1929.   xii, 345 p.

Chauvin, Victor C.
     Le livre dans le monde arabe.   Brussels, 1911.

Fuchs, Friederich
Die höheren Schulen von Konstantinopel im Mittelalter. Leipzig,
1926. vi, 79 p.

Gibb, H. A. R.
Arabic literature, an introduction. London, 1926. 128 p.

Grohmann, Adolf
Bibliotheken und Bibliophilen im islamischen Orient.
(In Vienna. Nationalbibliothek. Festschrift, 1926).

Hussey, Joan M.
The church and learning in the Byzantine Empire, 867-1165.
London, 1937. ix, 250 p.

Jacobs, Emil
Untersuchungen zur Geschichte der Bibliothek im Serai zu Konstantinopel. Heidelberg, 1919, 2 v.

Kremer, Alfred von
Kulturgeschichte des Orients under den Chalifen. Vienna, 1877.
(Partially translated as: The Orient under the Caliphs.
Calcutta, 1920. xii, 463 p.)

Krumbacher, Karl
Geschichte der byzantinischen Literatur von Justinian bis zum
Ende des Oströmischen Reiches (527-1453). Munich, 1897.
xx, 1196 p.

Lampros, Spyridon P.
Die Bibliotheken der Kloster des Athos. Bonn, 1881. 32 p.

Mackensen, Ruth S.
"Arabic books and libraries in the Umaiyad period," American
Journal of Semitic Languages and Literatures, LII (1935-36),
245-253; LIII (1936-37), 239-250; LIV (1937), 41-61.

"Background of the history of Moslem libraries," ibid., LI
(1934-35), 114-125; LII (1935-36), 22-33, 104-110.

"Four great libraries of medieval Baghdad," Library Quarterly,
II (1932), 279-299.

Mez, Adam
The renaissance of Islam. London, 1937. 538 p.

Nicholson, Reynold A.
A literary history of the Arabs. Cambridge, 1930. xxvi, 560 p.

Pinto, O.
"Libraries of the Arabs during the time of the Abbasides,"
Pakistan Library Review, II (March, 1959), 44-72.

Ribera y Tarrago, Julian
  Bibliofilos y bibliotecas en la España Musulmans.   Saragossa,
      1896.   67 p.

Runciman, Steven
  Byzantine civilization.   New York, 1956.   255 p.

Southern, Richard W.
  Western views of Islam in the middle ages.   Cambridge, Mass.,
      1962.   114 p.

Volk, Otto
  Die byzantinischen Klösterbibliotheken von Konstantinopel,
      Thessalonike und Kleinasien.   Munich, 1955. vi, 205 p.

Von Grunebaum, Gustave E.
  Medieval Islam: a study in cultural orientation.   Chicago,
      1953.   vii, 378 p.

Monastic and Cathedral Libraries

With the fall of the ancient world, the great libraries of antiquity were gone forever. For nearly a thousand years the typical European library was to be the small collection of manuscripts, laboriously copied and jealously guarded, in the many monasteries scattered from Greece to Iceland. Instead of the magnificent temple library, with its thousands upon thousands of rolls in vaulted marble rooms, the library of the Middle Ages was more often a collection of a few hundred codices kept in a bookchest or two in the corner of a monastery chapel. This decline in books and libraries was typical of the general cultural decline that took place after the fall of Rome.

Fortunately for Western civilization, even before the end of the old order there was a definite beginning of the new, or at least of the institution that was to preserve a part of ancient culture through the dark ages and until it could be revived again during the Renaissance. That institution was, of course, the medieval monastery. Monasteries were already being established in Egypt, in Palestine, and possibly in neighboring areas during the second and third centuries after Christ, and the idea of the monastery library was already in vogue in those places. Also, the earliest Christian churches, as already mentioned, were virtually built around their small collections of Scriptures, epistles and commentaries. Christianity and its early development were closely connected with the use and preservation of written materials.

The exact origins of monasticism are obscure. The earliest known Christian monasteries seem to have been in Egypt, although the idea did not originate there, as indicated by the recent discoveries in the Qumran caves. The monastery may well have begun around the hermit, the Christian who fled the populated areas in order to live alone in the desert to meditate on his sins and to avoid committing more. Despite their desire to be alone, these sincere hermits attracted followers and gradually these devoted Christian groups became monasteries. In order to promote their beliefs, they soon acquired copies of the early Christian texts, and the monastery library was under way.

In 1931 a collection of papyri was discovered in Egypt that apparently represents the remains of an early monastery library. These papyri, known as the Chester Beatty Papyri, date from the second to the fourth centuries A.D., and include, among other Christian writings, parts of both the Old and New Testaments. Oddly enough, all of these papyri were in codex form rather than in rolls, indicating the early preference of the Christians for this book form. One reason why they preferred the codex can be seen in one of the Beatty Papyri codices that contains the four Gospels plus the Book of Acts. In roll form this amount of text would have required at least five rolls.

One early Egyptian monastery of which we have some record was that founded by St. Pachomius (A.D. 292-345) at Tabennisi in Upper Egypt. St. Pachomius had only a small collection of religious works, and so he guarded them zealously. In the rules that he formulated for his monastic group there were several relating to the use of books. They were to be kept in a cupboard built into the monastery chapel wall, and all were to be locked up each night. During the daytime, each monk was allowed to use one book at a time, but it had to be used in the chapel area only and could not be taken to any other part of the monastery. From Pelusium, another Egyptian monastery that flourished around A.D. 400, we have the letters of the monk Isidore. These indicate that the monks there were acquainted with Greek and Latin literature as well as with the religious texts. The remains of still another early Christian library were found in 1935 in excavating some ruins in the Negev Desert. The exact dates of this church or monastery is not known, but an important settlement is known to have existed there from the second to the sixth centuries. This collection also included both Greek and Latin, Christian and secular writings, with a Latin-Greek glossary to aid in the use of the materials.

Just as the origin of Christian monasticism is obscure, it is also difficult to say just what the connection was between Egyptian monasteries and those that were founded in Italy in the fifth century. Certainly their existence and purpose were known, and as the civilized world began to crumble under the raids of the northern barbarians, the monastic idea took hold in southern Italy. A few small groups of devoted Christians withdrew into remote mountain areas and formed monastic communities. One of the earliest and best known of these is the monastery founded by Magnus Aurelius Cassiodorus in A. D. 540. Cassiodorus had been secretary to Theodoric, the Ostrogoth ruler of Rome from 489 to 526, and had hoped to found a university in Rome similar to the Museum in Alexandria. He failed at this because of the uncertain conditions of the time, but when he at last retired from public office he used the wealth he had acquired to begin a monastery at Vivarium in Benevento. His own private library became the nucleus of the monastery book collection, and he spent the remainder of his long life in study and devotion. Cassiodorus had a strong respect for learning and a reverence for books in general, so he added to his religious texts many works of classical Latin authors and a few Greek. Not content with merely collecting and copying other writers, he also did some effective writing on his own. His most important writing, the Institutiones, included an annotated bibliography that was either a catalog of his library or of the library he hoped to build. At any rate, it is a well-selected list of books suitable for the monastery library, and as such it served as a standard book-selection list for monastic collections for several centuries. Cassiodorus is also credited with having introduced the idea of intellectual labor into the duties of the monastic societies, and hence is the spiritual ancestor of both the scriptorium and the monastery library. Under his direction a few Greek works were obtained and translated into Latin, and he along with his contemporary Boethius is responsible for much of the relatively small amount of classical learning available in western Europe from the sixth through the tenth centuries.

Also contemporary with Cassiodorus was the work being done at Monte Cassino by St. Benedict and his followers. This

monastery, founded in 529, was the parent house for the Benedictine order, and from it monks went out to establish other monasteries throughout Europe.   Along with them went the "Rule of St.
Benedict" for the daily life of the monks, which included strong
orders for the production and reading of books.   The copying of
books was made a part of the regular labor of the Benedictine
monks, and hence as the order spread each monastery soon came
to have a library of the best-available texts.   Especially during
Lent each monk was assigned a book that he was to read from beginning to end.   Another monastic library in southern Italy during
the sixth century was that at St. Severinus, although little is known
of its contents.

Still another sixth-century scholar was the martyred writer
Boethius.   Like Cassiodorus, Anicius Manlius Boethius (480-524)
had served under Theodoric; but unlike him, Boethius lost favor,
was imprisoned, and eventually executed.   He had become a
learned man through access to the library of Symmachus the Orator,
and he had once hoped to translate all the available works of Plato
and Aristotle into Latin.   He succeeded only in part, but it was
through those translations that western Europe knew the Greek philosophers until the eleventh century.   Though a Christian, Boethius
is best remembered for his Consolation of Philosophy, which he
wrote while he was in prison.   This work, which has been called
the "swan-song of classical philosophy" was virtually a textbook for
European scholars for nearly a thousand years.   Incidentally, in it
Boethius describes his memories of a library in which he had once
studied, picturing it as having walls of ivory lined with rows of
beautifully bound books.

The monastic idea spread gradually throughout Europe, but
oddly enough, many of those in northern Europe and even in northern Italy were established not by monks from Vivarium or Monte
Cassino but by monks from Ireland.   To understand this it is necessary to look into the history of Christian Britain and the era of
Roman domination of those islands.   The Romans had conquered
the southern part of England after 40 B.C., and that area remained
under Roman domination for some 400 years.   Although England

proper was never converted to Christianity under the Romans, the natives of Ireland became Christians under the teaching of St. Patrick in the fifth century. From Ireland monks went out to England, Scotland, France, and other parts of Europe, preaching Christianity and founding monasteries. One of these monks, St. Columban (543-615), established a series of monasteries at Luxeuil in Burgundy, at St. Gall in Switzerland, at Würzburg and Salzburg in Germany, and at Tarantum and Bobbio in Italy. In each of these monasteries the importance of libraries was stressed and the inclusion of nonreligious works was permitted.

The monastery and its library first came to England through the efforts of St. Augustine, who was sent there as a missionary by Pope Gregory about A.D. 597. Augustine brought with him a small collection of Christian texts, and other books were later obtained from Italy, along with the library rules of St. Benedict. With these a small library was begun at Canterbury, made up almost entirely of Scriptures and religious texts. Later in the seventh century Benedict Biscop founded a monastery at Wearmouth and endowed it with a small library. During his lifetime Biscop is credited with making at least six trips to Rome, in each case obtaining books for the library at Wearmouth and for another that he founded at Jarrow. He also obtained books from the monasteries at Vienne, the capital of Gaul. The Venerable Bede (673-735), sometimes called the "Father of English literature," made good use of these libraries in writing his Ecclesiastical History of England. Biscop's successor, Coelfried, continued to build up the library at Wearmouth, while one of his students, Egbert, founded a library at the cathedral school at York.

In France a monastery of great importance was that at Corbie, established about 660 by monks from Luxeuil. A celebrated school was attached to this monastery, and its library and scriptorium became one of the best in western Europe. Bobbio, near Pavia in northern Italy, was another monastery that became famous for its manuscript collections in the seventh and eighth centuries. In Germany, St. Boniface, an English monk, was establishing monasteries in the eighth century, including those at Fulda, Heiden-

heim, and Fritzlar.   Libraries at each of these monasteries are
known to have existed in the eighth century, and a catalog compiled
at Fulda between 744 and 749 still exists.   On the whole, however,
the period from the sixth to the ninth centuries was an unproductive
one from the library point of view, and the period between Cassiodorus and Alcuin has been described as the darkest era of the Dark
Ages.

One bright cultural spot in the seventh century was Christian Spain.   Despite the fact that much of the population was illiter-
ate, there were cultural centers in several cities, and a number of
religious groups that served as schools or training corps for
priests.   One of the foremost Spanish scholars of this era was Isidore, Bishop of Seville from 600 to 636, who not only collected a
library of the best-known literature of his day but also culled from
it to form an early version of an encyclopedia.   Just how many
books he owned is uncertain, but they must have numbered several
hundred, since he kept them in fourteen bookcases, or armaria.
Each case was dedicated to a particular author, although it may
have held other works as well.   Seven cases were inscribed with
the names of religious writers, such as the Sts. Augustine, Am-
brose, and Jerome, while others were dedicated to literary figures,
historians, and writers of sacred and secular law.   Over each case
there was a poem to the author, and for the whole collection there
was a descriptive poem that included the following passage:

> Here sacred books with worldly books combine;
> If poets please you, read them; they are thine.
> My meads are full of thorns, but flowers are there;
> If thorns displease, let roses be your share.
> Here both the Laws in tomes revered behold;
> Here what is new is stored, and what is old . . .
>
> A reader and a talker can't agree;
> Hence, idle chatterer; 'tis no place for thee!

(The last two lines would still make a good motto for a modern
library.)

The late eighth and early ninth centuries saw the development in western Europe of what is known as the Carolingian Renaissance under the rule of the Emperor Charlemagne (768-814).
This revival of learning brought with it the creation of schools,

churches, and libraries, particularly after the arrival in France of the English scholar Alcuin. Alcuin (735-804), who had been educated at the cathedral school at York, was brought to Charlemagne's capital at Tours in 782 and placed in charge of a school there. He sent back to England for books to be copied and set up a scriptorium and library at Tours. Later, as Bishop of Tours, Alcuin planned the establishment of schools and monasteries throughout Charlemagne's Empire, which then included most of western Europe. Many such institutions were established, and for a few years literature and learning flourished. Charlemagne himself had at least two libraries in his palaces, one at the Isle-Barbe, near Lyons, and later one at his palace at Aachen. He is reported to have had his volumes richly bound and to have exchanged gifts of books with the Emperor at Constantinople.

The library Alcuin had used at York was probably the best in northern Europe in its day, and it flourished from the seventh to the middle of the ninth century. The Danish and Viking invasions, which had begun in the late eighth century and continued for almost 200 years, effectively destroyed many monasteries and libraries in England, including those at York. There was a modest revival in the mid-tenth century, but as late as 1066 there were only 48 monasteries and 12 convents in all of England. Elsewhere in northern and western Europe the story was much the same. Beginning in the latter half of the ninth century, the raiding Norsemen put an end to the Carolingian Renaissance and once again plunged the area into feudalism. About the same time, the Huns were invading Europe from the east and the Moslems from the South. Amidst these troubles many monasteries were destroyed, others lapsed into uneasy stagnation, while a few prospered and even some new ones were established. Their libraries suffered as well, but through donations, copying, and borrowing, they managed to survive in all but a few cases.

Looking at monastic libraries in general it is easy to see that most of them were small. In the ninth century St. Gall had only 300 volumes, while Reichenau in Germany had only 413. After almost three centuries of existence the justly famous collection at

Bobbio had only 650 volumes, and that at Cluny only 570. It is
estimated that, despite the continued work of the copyists, there
were actually fewer books in the libraries of western Europe in
1200 than there were in 900, thanks to wars and raids and to the
ensuing decline of interest in learning.

The various orders of monks had different ideas concerning
books, libraries, and literary labors. The Rule of the Benedictines has already been noted, and it was among the foremost in the
development of monastery libraries throughout the Middle Ages.
Among the other orders the Carthusians and Cistercians also
adopted library and reading rules, although they were not as interested in nonreligious works as were the Benedictines. The Au-
gustinians generally collected only a few books but prized them
highly, while the Franciscans at first would own no books at all.
Later, in the thirteen century, the Franciscans began to collect
books for their libraries, and the parent house at Assisi developed
a comparatively large library within a few years. Of whatever order, the monastery was generally accepted as a center of learning,
and the saying was common that "A monastery without a library is
like a castle without walls." Incidentally, convents for nuns were
also active in collecting and preserving both religious and secular
literature, and several nuns became well known in literary fields.
St. Paula was a scholar in Hebrew and Greek as well as Latin,
and St. Aura lectured on the Bible to both men and women students.
Gertrude, Abbess of Nivelle, was active in building up the library
in that abbey, and St. Hroswitha (d. 997) not only collected a library at her convent at Gandersheim in Germany, but also wrote
religious poetry and dramas.

Throughout the early Middle Ages Rome remained a literary
center or at least a source of supply for copies of books. The
headquarters of the Church, the Vatican, maintained a library with
varying degrees of success. Although legend has it that St. Peter
founded the Vatican Library, or that St. Clement did in A. D. 93, it
is not known exactly when the first collection of books was brought
together. Since most of the early Christian churches maintained
collections of Scriptures, and since these collections were often

augmented by religious commentaries, lives of the martyrs, congregational records, and accounts of missionary activities, it is most probable that a central collection of Christian literature existed in Rome even before Christianity was officially adopted.   However, nothing definite is known of such a collection, and the first-known library for the church at Rome was that of Pope Damasus in the late fourth century.   Damasus is reported to have built a structure to house the library near the theater of Pompey in the Campus Martius and to have modeled it after the Temple of Apollo.   An inscribed stone has been found that reads: "I have erected this structure for the archives of the Roman Church; I have surrounded it with porticoes on either side; and I have given it my name which I hope will be remembered for centuries."   The archives and books in the library were open to scholars for studying and copying.

Pope Hilary (461-468) is credited with establishing two small libraries for the use of laymen and pilgrims, placing in them approved copies of the Scriptures and other religious works.   Pope Agepetus, about 535, is reported to have established a school of theology and literature at Rome with the help of Cassiodorus. Agapetus endowed it with a library for the use of scholars, although there is some doubt that this library ever materialized. Later in the sixth century, Pope Gregory was active in building up the Church Library and loaned volumes to be copied in churches and monasteries as far away as Spain and Constantinople.   In the seventh century the Vatican Library was moved to the Lateran Palace, where the Pope resided, and when the Church Council of 640 met, the library there was so well organized that the librarian was congratulated by the Council for being able to find any book at any time it was wanted by the members of the Council.   It was also noted that this librarian could translate Greek into Latin at sight, apparently an unusual scholarly ability at that time.   In the tenth century, during civil wars on the Italian Peninsula, the Vatican Library was moved again, this time to a specially built tower, the Turris Cartelaria, where apparently it was little used.   Pope Honorius III, who died in 1227, is the last Pope to mention this original Vatican collection, and it is likely that nothing of importance in the way of a Vatican Livrary was known from then until its re-establishment in the fifteenth century by Pope Nicholas V.

Closely akin to the monastery libraries were those developed in connection with the medieval cathedrals. Actually, the cathedrals, which were the headquarters churches for bishops or archbishops, were far more than merely large churches. Instead they were something in the way of religious universities, where training for the priesthood took place and often secular training at a lower level as well. In some cases, the cathedrals were in the direct charge of some monastic order, as in England where seven cathedrals were in the hands of the Benedictines. In other cases they were directly under the Church, in charge of bishops appointed by the Pope; and in a few cases they were more secular schools than religious, and offered little or no religious services or training. In almost all cases their income came from the proceeds of church-owned lands or from gifts of wealthy patrons. Some of them date from the eighth or ninth centuries, or at least had their beginnings at that time, but most of them came into importance in the twelfth century or later.

The cathedral library often differed from the monastery library in several ways. It was later in developing and hence had access to more books; it was usually more heavily endowed or had more funds for the acquisition of books; it was usually larger; and it contained more secular books than the average monastery library. Some of the better-known cathedral libraries were those at York, Durham, and Canterbury in England; at Notre Dame and Rouen in France; at Bamberg and Hildesheim in Germany; and at Toledo and Barcelona in Spain. The cathedral at Rouen had in 1150 almost one-third of its library in classic authors, and by 1425 its collection was large enough to require a separate building. Durham's cathedral library in 1200 consisted of only some 600 volumes, but included among them were some medical works. Canterbury, one of the largest of the cathedral libraries, had about 5,000 books in 1300, but this was exceptional. Not as numerous as the monastery libraries nor in general as important in the cultural history of western Europe, the cathedral libraries did serve

a purpose in bridging the gap between the monasteries and the universities, and also in bringing together the material wealth and cultural resources that only they could afford.

The monastery and even the cathedral library of the early
Middle Ages, up to the thirteen century, was usually only a small
collection of books kept in a bookchest or two in the monastery
cloister rather than in a specific library room or building.   The
library was often connected with or near to the scriptorium, or
workroom, where the monks copied texts as a part of their regular
duties.   A common word for library in the monasteries was armarium, which was literally the bookchest or press where books were
kept.   Naturally the librarian, or person who supervised the books,
was known as the "armarius."   Other terms for the librarian were
"bibliothecarius" and "custos librorum," or keeper of the books.
Early Benedictine monasteries strove to have at least a collection
large enough for one book per monk, but once this ratio was
achieved, their collections grew but slowly.   Accessions came from
copies made of borrowed books, or by monks who went to other libraries to copy important works, and by gifts.   Most of the libraries received books as gifts from entering monks, visiting digni-
taries, wealthy patrons, neighboring scholars, and from religious
leaders.   Many gifts came as bequests upon the death of their
owners.   In considering the size of the monastery collection, it
should be pointed out that the average "volume" was usually a codex
of folio size, containing the equivalent of 20 or 30 classical rolls.
Also, many of the volumes were made up of "florilegia," or selections from many authors, giving a wide range of literature in a
relatively small library.

As for its specific contents, the average monastery library
contained largely religious volumes.   The core of the collection
was the Bible, often in large script and in many volumes.   Next
in importance were the works of the early Church Fathers with
later commentaries on them, the lives of the saints, and the service books of the church.   Finally there would be Latin textbooks
and grammars, a few of the Latin classics, and perhaps a few
works on local history or by local authors.   Greek authors were

unknown, excepting possibly a few in Latin translation. By 1200,
the monastery library's contents would have broadened somewhat.
All of the former works would still be present, but in addition there
would be more and better editions of the Latin classics, some civil
and canon law, works of the medieval writers from Boethius to
Peter Lombard, and even some science, poetry, and drama of the
later writers. Local writers would be more prominent in each collection, and works in the local language would be added to the majority in Latin. In format, the books of the twelfth century were
almost entirely parchment codices. Papyrus had gone out of use
and paper had not yet reached most of Europe.

Inter-library lending was not unknown in the Middle Ages.
Books were lent to be copied and also apparently just for reading.
Usually such lending was between neighboring collections, but sometimes it was between libraries as far apart as France and Greece
or England and Austria. One English library, of the Priory of
Henton, lent no less than 20 volumes in 1343. Books were also
rented and pawned. Ordinarily, of course, the books were to be
lent only to the residents of the monastic community, and then only
one at a time. In some monasteries the books could be used only
in the daytime and in the vicinity of the bookpresses. In others
they were lent for as long as a year at a time and could be taken
to the reader's living quarters. In some cases books were lent to
outsiders, usually neighboring church leaders or rulers, but then
some collateral was usually required, either a book or books of
equal value, or a deposit of money.

Books were classified roughly by subject in the monastic libraries, and secondarily by size or acquisition number. Theological works were kept separate from secular ones, Latin works from
those in other languages, and textbooks from more serious tomes.
In some libraries the divisions or classes were designated by letters and those letters were prominently inscribed on the bookchests. Such a division of books into broad subject groups apparently sufficed as long as the collections were relatively small,
although more complicated schemes of classification were planned,
if not actually used. Catalogs of the collections were made almost

from the earliest days of the monastery libraries. These catalogs were in reality more nearly lists of books, some arranged by author, some by title, and others by a catchword from the title or first line; almost none of these were in alphabetical order. Such lists are known from the eighth century on, and from the twelfth century a number have survived, particularly from French libraries. Some of these catalogs were originally kept on strips of parchment tacked on the side of the book-chest. Other longer ones were in codex form and more carefully prepared, with some logic in the arrangement.

The librarian, or custodian of the library, was usually one of the monks designated for the task. Sometimes the work rotated; at other times an older or incapacitated monk would be given the task of caring for the books. However, since the task was usually a simple one, owing to the small number of books and smaller circulations, the position of librarian was usually combined with some other duty. In English church libraries, the position of keeper of the books was often combined with that of the cantor or sub-cantor (precentor or succentor). Rules for one of these libraries read:

> Let not a book be given to anyone without a proper and sufficient voucher, and let this be entered on the roll.

The same rules reminded the librarian that he should know his wares:

> Thou must have full knowledge of what is given to thy charge. The first duty of a librarian is to strive, in his time, as far as possible, to increase the library committed to him. Let him beware that the library does not diminish, that the books in his charge do not in any way get lost or perish. Let him repair by binding books that are damaged by age. Let him know the names of the authors.

Some librarians were held personally responsible for the safety of the books in their charge and had to replace any that were lost or damaged.

Toward the end of the Middle Ages there were of course many changes in the physical make-up of the monastic and cathedral libraries. The number of books increased in most cases,

with collections being numbered in thousands of volumes instead of
hundreds. Armaria or book-cases gave way to reading desks with
shelves above, and library rooms by the fifteenth century tended to
become separate library buildings. The library collection tended
to become divided into two parts -- a public collection for general
use, and a private or reference collection that could be used only
under restricted conditions. These two collections were sometimes
designated as the "bibliotheca publica" and the "bibliotheca secreta."
Books constantly in use were the ones that first came to be chained
to the desks, rather than the more valuable ones as usually supposed. Later, after the coming of the printed book, most of the
manuscript volumes were chained simply for protection. Various
devices were employed to make the books more readily available,
such as the book wheel and the circular desk. The book wheel was
just that, something like a water wheel with a number of books arranged on it so that a reader standing in one position could consult
as many as a dozen different volumes in succession without moving
from his original position. The circular, hexagonal, or octagonal
desk was a similar arrangement on a horizontal plane. Here the
reader usually had to walk around a desk to consult the several
books arranged on its top, but in a few cases these desk tops were
also attached to axles so that the books could be rotated into a
single position in front of the reader.

Monasticism flourished and declined at various times and
places in western Europe, but generally speaking its libraries represented the heart of learning for over a thousand years. Then,
as the cathedral libraries grew and as the universities developed
and emerged as full-blown educational centers, the monasteries declined and their cultural significance faded. Their importance
lasted for varying times in different countries, but for the most
part they had disappeared by the seventeenth century. Where they
remained in operation, their libraries became of little significance
outside the monastery walls.

In England, for example, the monasteries were closed under
Henry VIII in the sixteenth century, and their libraries were scattered. It is estimated that the 900 or more monasteries in Eng-

land must have contained at least 300,000 volumes at the time of
the confiscation of the monastery properties. Of these only some
3,600, or a little more than 1 percent, are known to have survived.
Some of the finer manuscripts that were taken from the monastery
libraries eventually ended up in booksellers' hands, but many of the
ordinary ones were used for candle lighters, pot cleaners and even
for scrubbing boots. Similarly in Germany, peasant uprisings in
1524-25 resulted in great losses to monastic libraries, and the
French libraries suffered in the religious wars in that country a
century later. In the eighteenth century it was the libraries of
Austria and Scandinavia that suffered, to be followed by others all
over Europe in the French Revolutionary and Napoleonic wars. Besides these trials, many individual monasteries suffered from fires
and natural disasters. Others suffered from neglect or even aban-
donment as the fortunes of various orders and individual monasteries
declined. Where the contents of the monastery libraries were not
lost or destroyed, they were often transferred to other libraries --
church, municipal, or university, -- and it is usually these that
have survived. The library of the Abbey of Cluny, justly famous
for its books in the early Middle Ages, had declined to just a few
manuscripts in the town hall by the eighteenth century, but in the
nineteenth these now priceless relics were turned over to the National Library in Paris.

Some idea of the ups and downs of an individual monastery
library can be gathered by considering the history of Corbie in
northern France. It was founded about 660 by a colony of monks
from Luxeuil. It grew rapidly, enjoying the favor of both religious
and royal leaders, and its school and library became famous
throughout Europe. It went through periods of decline in the tenth
century, prosperity in the twelfth, neglect in the fourteenth, revival in the fifteenth, and again decline in the sixteenth. In 1636,
during a French war with Spain, Corbie suffered a loss of several
hundred volumes that were eventually returned to the French National Library. Finally, in 1791, during the French Revolution,
the remainder of Corbie's books were taken, some to the National
Library in Paris, and others, after devious travels, to the Russian

Imperial Library in St. Petersburg.

Even if the monasteries had not declined physically and in-
tellectually, the coming of printing would have effectively ended
their cultural significance on the larger scale.   The ready availability of books by the hundreds and thousands meant that many
types of libraries and other educational institutions would become
available.   But whatever its fate, the role of the monastery library
in the preservation of Western culture cannot be denied.   For
more or less a thousand years, it was the intellectual heart of
Europe, and without it western civilization would have been a far
different world.   Of the monastic book-copyists and libraries it can
be truly said that never has so much been owed by so many to so
few.

Additional Readings

(Material on medieval libraries is relatively plentiful, particularly
in Latin and German.   Catalogs of a number of libraries, particularly monastery collections, have been preserved.   Many of the
titles listed below concern libraries other than monastic, and many
of them cover the history of libraries later than 1500.   Thus it is
more of a list of readings for the history of libraries during the
medieval and Renaissance periods rather than merely for the monastic and cathedral libraries.)

Bayerri, Enrique
    Los codices medievales de la catedral de Tortosa.   Barcelona,
        1962.   698 p.

Becker, Gustav H.
    Catalogi bibliothecarum antiqui collegit . . . I.   Catalogi
        saeculo XIII vetustiores.   II.   Catalogus catalogorum
        posterioris aetatis.   Bonn, 1885.   334 p. (Reprinted 1962).

Beddi, J. S.
    Libraries in the twelfth century: their catalogs and contents.
        Boston, 1929.   23 p.

Bischoff, Bernhard
    Die süddeutschen Schreibschulen und Bibliotheken in der
        Karolingerzeit.   Leipzig, 1940.   280 p.

Cassiodorus Senator.
    An introduction to divine and human reading, ed. by L. W.
        Jones.   New York, 1946.   xvii,   283 p.

Clark, John W.
  Libraries in the medieval and renaissance periods.   Cambridge,
    1894.   61 p.

Delisle, Léopold
  Recherches sur l'ancienne bibliothèque de Corbie.   (Mémoires
    de l'Academie des Inscriptiones, XXIV (1860), 266-342.)

Ehrle, Francisci
  Historia bibliothecae Romanorum Pontificum tum Bonifatianae
    tum Avenionensis . . .   Rome, 1890.   xvi, 786 p.

Falk, Franz
  Die ehemalige Dombibliothek zu Mains . . . Leipzig, 1897.
    iv, 175 p.

  Beiträge zur Rekonstruktion der alten Bibliotheca Fuldensis
    und Bibliotheca Laureshimensis.   Leipzig, 1902. 112 p.

Faucon, Maurice
  La librarie des papes d'Avignon: sa formation, sa composition,
    ses catalogues, 1316-1420.   Paris, 1886-1887. 2 vols.

Gasquet, Francis Aidan
  Some notes on medieval monastic libraries.   London, 1891.
    (Included in his The Old English Bible and Other Essays.)

Gottlieb, Theodor
  Über mittelalterliche Bibliotheken.   Leipzig, 1890. 520 p.
    (Rep. 1955).

Hughes, H. D.
  A history of Durham Cathedral Library.   Durham, 1925.
    xiii, 134 p.

Humphries, K. W.
  Book provisions of the medieval Friars.   Amsterdam, 1964.
    150 p.

Hunter, Joseph
  English monastic libraries.   London, 1831.   xii, 30 p.

James, Montague Rhodes
  The ancient libraries of Canterbury and Dover.   Cambridge.
    1903.   cv, 552 p.

  On the abbey of St. Edmund at Bury.   I.   The library.
    Cambridge, 1895.   vii, 220 p.

Ker, Neil Ripley, ed.
  Medieval libraries of Great Britain: a list of surviving books.
    London, 1941.   169 p.

Lehmann, Paul
　　Die Bibliotheksraume der deutschen Kloster im Mittelalter.
　　　　Berlin, 1957. 50 p.

　　Die mittelalterliche Dombibliothek zu Speyrer.   Berlin, 1934.
　　　　64 p.

Lesne, Emil
　　Les livres, scriptoria, et bibliothèques du commencement du
　　　　VIIIe à la fin du XIe siècle.   Lille, 1938.

Loeffler, Klemens
　　Deutsche Klosterbibliotheken.   Bonn, 1922.   310 p.

Meinsma, Koenraad O.
　　Middeleeuwsche bibliotheken.   Zutphen, 1903. vii, 317 p.

Merryweather, Frederick Somner
　　Bibliomania in the middle ages . . . with anecdotes illustrating
　　　　the history of the monastic libraries of Great Britain in
　　　　the olden time.   London, 1849.   iv, 218 p. (Rev. and enl.
　　　　edition, London, 1933, 288 p.)

Ogilvy, Jack David Angus
　　Books known to Anglo-Latin writers from Aldhelm to Alcuin
　　　　(670-804).   Cambridge, Mass., 1936.   xix, 108 p.

Pelzer, Augustus
　　Addenda et emendanda ad Francisci Ehrle historiae bibliothecae
　　　　Romanorum Pontificum tum Bonifatianae tum Avenionensis.
　　　　Rome, Vatican, 1947.   vii, 184 p.

Phillips, David Rhys
　　The romantic history of the monastic libraries of Wales from
　　　　the fifth to the sixteenth centuries . . .   Swansea, 1912.
　　　　62 p.

Rand, Edward K.
　　Founders of the middle ages.   New York, 1928. 365 p.

Roth, F. W. E.
　　Geschichte . . . der Klosterbibliotheken Nassaus.   Frankfurt-
　　　　am-Main, 1886.   32 p.

Savage, Ernest A.
　　Old English libraries: the making, collection and use of books
　　　　during the middle ages.   London, 1911. xv, 298 p.

　　Notes on the early monastic libraries of Scotland . . . Edin-
　　　　burgh,   1928.   46 p.

Steffenhagen, Emil
Die Klosterbibliothek zu Bordesholm und die Gottorfer-Biblio-
thek. Kiel, 1884. 232 p.

Streeter, Bennett H.
The chained library: a survey of four centuries in the evolution of the English library. London, 1931. xxi, 368 p.

Thompson, James W.
The medieval library. Chicago, 1939. 694 p. (Rep. 1957).

Weidman, Franz
Geschichte der Bibliothek von St. Gallen, seit ihrer Gründung
um das Jahr 830 bis auf 1841. N. p., 1841. iv, 493 p.

Williams, Thomas Webb
Somerset medieval libraries. Bristol, 1897. 199 p.

Wormald, Francis
The English library before 1700, studies in its history.
London, 1958. 273 p.

8.

Early University Libraries

In the long drama of Western civilization, the role of the monastic libraries, and even of the libraries of Constantinople and Islam, can be largely considered to have been that of preserving the cultural remains of the classic era. The monastery libraries were largely concerned with theology and saved secular works almost incidentally, but they did collect and preserve in addition much of the works of the medieval writers. The Byzantine libraries were used as sources by commentators, encyclopedists, codifiers, and compilers of epitomes and summaries, but not very much as sources for original works. The Moslem libraries were somewhat better employed, and particularly in the sciences their scholars improved upon the Greeks and turned over to western Europe works far advanced in mathematics, medicine, and astronomy. But for libraries to be a great cultural influence, they must be used; their doors must be open to large numbers of scholars and students, so that the information contained in their volumes can be disseminated to the largest possible proportion of the population. Though the cathedrals with their attendant schools did to a certain extent put their libraries to work, it remained for the coming of the medieval university to bring libraries that would not only preserve the heritage of the past, but that would also open it up to general use.

Although there were a few places where schools that could be called institutions of higher learning existed in the early Middle Ages, it was not until the thirteenth century that the university as such emerged. However, long before there was anything like an organized institution, there were groups of students who gathered around a teacher to learn what he had to teach. The best teachers attracted the most students, and gradually the teachers and students came to organize into something like guilds. For many years there was no curriculum nor any specific courses of degrees; students

120

attended lectures as and when they wished. Gradually, however,
the teachers united into faculties, university charters were obtained
from king or pope, and formal institutions were recognized. The
students, too, organized, according to their home areas, into "nations." The early term for the universities was "studium generale," while the word university came from the Latin universitas,
which at first meant any organized guild or corporation.

It is quite probable that the inspiration for the early universities in Italy, France, and England came from the already established centers of learning in Moslem Spain. Christian students had
attended the Moslem universities in Spain long before any were established in the rest of Europe. Some of them were from Christian Spain, but others were from France, Italy, and probably from
other parts of Europe. By the early twelfth century there were
schools of medicine at Salerno and Bologna in Italy, with the teaching at both schools heavily influenced by Moslem learning. Also, at
Paris there was the beginning of a university long before 1200.
From cathedral schools there developed at least three strong theological schools, those at Notre Dame, Saint-Victor and Sainte-
Geneviève. At Salerno no university as such developed, but at
Bologna in 1158 the group of teachers and students was officially
recognized by Emperor Frederic as a university. By 1150 the
theological schools at Paris were approaching university status, and
in 1167 a group of English students there withdrew to form their
own school in England -- a school that was the beginning of Oxford
University. In 1179 the schools at Paris set up requirements for
the title of master, along with a regular organization of chancellor,
masters, and students, with a system of lectures and examinations.
It was thus to all intents and purposes a university, but that status
came officially in 1200 when Emperor Philip August granted a
charter. By 1300, there were other universities established at
Naples, Padua, and Reggio in Italy; at Salamanca and Seville in
Spain; at Angers, Toulouse, Montpelier, and Orléans in France;
at Cambridge in England; and at Lisbon in Portugal.

For many years the universities did not have libraries as
such. The teachers or masters had small book collections of their

own, and these were sometimes lent to favored students. The students copied the lectures and thus secured textbooks, or bought or rented them from booksellers. The position of bookseller in the vicinity of a university was an important one, and great care was taken to insure that the texts of books sold or rented to students were authentic. Probably the earliest "libraries," other than the stocks of the booksellers, that formed around the universities were those of the student groups, or "nations." These groups sometimes lived together or at least had headquarters where books were communally owned and used. Sometimes fees were collected to pay for the purchase or copying of texts for the library, and of course there were often gifts from alumni and interested patrons. On the continent the "nations" continued to be something like boarding groups or fraternities, but at Oxford and Cambridge they gradually developed into the "colleges," each with its own faculty, curriculum, and later its own library. At Bologna, the libraries of the nations had student librarians with the title of "conservateur des libres," and it is quite probable that similar practices existed at the other universities. Whatever their nature, the early book collections at the universities, like those at contemporary monasteries and cathedrals, were small.

The growth of the libraries at the University of Paris and at Oxford will perhaps give a representative picture of early university library development. At Paris the earliest definite information we have as to a library comes in 1250 with the endowment of a college there by Robert de Sorbonne. As a part of his endowment, Sorbonne gave his own personal library to the school, along with funds to provide for its upkeep. Other gifts of books came to this collection, and its catalog of 1289 listed over 1,000 titles. Along with this catalog there is a physical description of the Sorbonne Library, and this should give a general idea as to the nature of the early university libraries in general. The library room itself was long and narrow, 12 by 40 feet, and lighted by 19 small windows on each side. There were 28 desks in the room. The more valuable books were chained to the shelves, but the chains were long enough to reach to a nearby desk. According to the catalog, the books in the library were arranged into 10 major divisions, including theology, medicine, law, and the seven major divisions of the medieval liberal arts curriculum known as the "trivium" and the "quadrivium." The trivium included grammar, rhetoric, and logic, while the quadrivium was made up of arithmetic, geometry, astronomy, and music. In each of the 10 divisions the works were arranged alphabetically by authors, with the first few words of the text following each title in the catalog. Of 1,017 titles then in the Sorbonne Library, only four were in French while the remainder were in Latin. Another catalog compiled in 1338 listed some 1,700 titles in the Sorbonne Library, and 400 years later there were still only about 30,000 volumes there.

Rules for the use of the Sorbonne Library in the early fourteenth century are enlightening. Books were to be used only in the building in which the library was housed, and if taken from the library room, they had to be returned before the end of the day. If anyone other than the students or teachers took a book from the library, he had to leave a deposit of equal value. Somewhat later, the library was divided into two parts, one of permanent reference that remained chained to the shelves or desks, and one of second copies and works of less value that could be circulated. The chained works were known as the small library or reference library, while the circulating collection was known as the great library or common library.

In the fourteenth century and after, other colleges at the University of Paris formed libraries of their own, including one for the Faculty of Medicine, formed in 1391. Many of them were originally begun with donations of private libraries, including some given by former faculty members. Over the years more than 50 different colleges and schools connected with the University formed their individual libraries, but it was not until the nineteenth century that the University as such formed a central library, and when this was done it was formed with the Sorbonne Library as a nucleus.

At Oxford, although many of the colleges making up the University date from the thirteenth century, their libraries were usu-

ally not begun until the fourteenth century or later.   For example,
Merton College dates from 1264, but its library was not formally
begun until 1377; University College may have had a collection of
books for the use of its students as early as 1280, but an organized library is not noted there until 1440; and for Balliol College
the similar dates are 1282 and 1431.   Oriel College was founded
in 1324, and as late as 1375 owned only 100 volumes.   However,
in 1444 this College removed its books from their ancient chests
in the chapel hall and housed them in an entirely separate library
building.   New College, founded in 1380, was the first Oxford College to begin with a library of its own, and after that date most of
the colleges as formed began with their own libraries.

The New College Library is one for which we have some
early information.   The founder of the College, William, Bishop of
Winchester, gave 62 volumes for the chapel library, and 312 for a
common or circulating collection.   Of this latter group, an early
inventory showed 136 volumes of theology, 34 of philosophy, 52 of
medicine, 53 of canon law, and the remainder of civil law.   Every
fellow at New College could borrow two books at a time and keep
them for periods up to a year.   He also had a key to the library
so that he could use other books there during the day.   The books
for general reference use were chained, and an inventory was taken
of all books once a year.

At the Priory of Durham, which was really something of a
Benedictine monastery loosely associated with the University at Oxford, a library was begun in 1345 with books donated by Richard
de Bury, Bishop of Durham and noted bibliophile.   Five Benedictine monks were placed in charge of the library, and all monks
were to have the right of borrowing books for perusal in their own
rooms.   Duplicate copies of books could be borrowed by anyone in
the university community, providing that a deposit was left in its
place.   Unfortunately, this library did not long survive and its
books were scattered.

The general university library at Oxford had an involved
early history, and really did not emerge as an effective collection
until the fifteenth century.   About 1320 Thomas Cobham, Bishop of

Worcester, erected a building at Oxford with a lower floor to be
used as a church and an upper floor to be used at least partly for
a general library. Unfortunately, Bishop Cobham died before his
library could be effectively begun, and his books ended up in the
Oriel College library. In 1367, Bishop Cobham's books, having
been forcibly removed from Oriel by the university chancellor,
were placed for general use in a room above St. Mary's Congregation hall. Some of the books were sold to obtain funds for the
care of the remainder by the chaplain. The small collection drift-
ed until 1411 when a new Chancellor, Richard Courtenay, took the
library under his supervision and guaranteed pay for a chaplain to
act as librarian and to keep the library open five hours each week-
day. With this stimulus the collection grew, and with many gifts
from Humphrey, Duke of Gloucester, and others, the general library in 1480 moved into a new location. This was in the new Divinity School Building, and the library there was known as "Duke Humphrey's Library" in honor of its chief donor. Duke Humphrey's
gifts to the library were noted for their Greek and Latin classics,
for relatively contemporary French and Italian works, and for the
usual works found in medieval libraries.

      At Cambridge University the library history was somewhat
similar to that at Oxford, with most of the college libraries small
in numbers of volumes before the sixteenth century. The library
of Pembroke College was begun there in 1347, that of University
College in 1350, and that of King's College in 1441. University
College Library had 122 volumes in 1424 and only 330 in 1473,
while King's College had only 174 volumes a quarter century after
its beginning. Peterhouse College Library in 1418 had only 380
volumes, with 220 of them chained for reference and the remainder
available for circulation to its fellows. The main university library
is considered to date from about 1415, but its growth was slow until about 1480 when Thomas Rotherham, Archbishop of York, aided
it with gifts of books and a building.

      Elsewhere in Europe more than 70 universities were estab-
lished before 1500, ranging from Seville in Spain to Uppsala in
Sweden and from Catania in Sicily to Aberdeen in Scotland. All

followed in general the organizational pattern of Paris and Oxford, and libraries of more-or-less importance were found in all.   On the continent, however, the formation of central university libraries was often delayed for several hundred years after the formation of separate college or institute libraries, and in fact the central library is still not a major consideration in many European universities.   At Prague, the Collegium Carol, founded in 1348, had a library soon after its founding; in addition, the College of the Bohemian Nation there also had a notable library.   At Orléans in France, at Coimbra in Portugal, or at Cracow in Poland, the early universities began their libraries before 1400, and elsewhere the number of universities increased rapidly in the fifteenth century. The universities in Germany, particularly at Heidelberg, added a different type of library in the faculty collection, as distinct from the college or student libraries and the common or university collections.

Unlike the monastery libraries, where acquisitions were gained by copying, the early college libraries grew largely through donations.   Numerous instances can be cited of gifts to the colleges of books from kings, nobles, bishops, and merchant collectors. Aside from the gifts already mentioned, notable examples would include gifts in 1336 of books to Balliol and Marton Colleges at Oxford from Bishop Stephen Gravesend; gifts of 80 books in 1350 to Trinity College, Cambridge, by Bishop William Bateman; and gifts of 250 volumes to New College, Oxford, in 1387 by Henry Whitefield.   On the continent, university libraries received similar gifts, as when Bishop Matthias of Worms gave 90 books to Heidelberg in 1410, and Johannes Sindel bequeathed 200 volumes on medicine and mathematics to Prague University in 1450.   Endowment funds were also used to purchase books in many of the university libraries, and there is also some evidence that fees were collected in some of the colleges for the benefit of the library funds.   Generally speaking, however, the university collections remained relatively small until the late fifteenth and sixteenth centuries when printed volumes began to become available.

The physical condition of the early university libraries strong-

ly resembled the contemporary monastery collections. The manuscript codices were kept in bookchests in the twelfth and thirteenth
centuries. By the late thirteenth and early fourteenth centuries,
they came out of the armaria onto desk-bookcases, called pulpitum
in many cases. Each of these desks would hold about 18 to 20
books, all chained but all removable to a lower desk-shelf, usually
slanted. At Queens College, Cambridge, there were 192 volumes
on 10 desks and 4 half-desks. In another library there were 988
books chained to 50 desks. By the fifteenth century, separate library buildings were being erected -- usually long, narrow rooms
lighted by many tall windows. The shape of the room was probably governed by the necessity of making as much use of natural
light as possible, and also owing to the fact that prior to placing
libraries in separate buildings they had often been housed in rooms
over arcades or open corridors. Inside the library rooms, the
bookdesks were located between the windows, so that the light fell
directly on the reading shelf. This system grew into the book-
stalls or carrells of the sixteenth century, where tall bookcases
held four to six shelves of books plus a slanted desk or reading
shelf beneath. This system held many more books in the same
space, and particularly as the printed book replaced the manuscript
folio, it completely supplanted the older desks.

Early university library catalogs were little more than manuscript shelf lists or finding lists. Books were shelved roughly by
subject in the various desks or stalls, and the end of the desk often contained a list of the books shelved within. The catalogs or
booklists were arranged alphabetically, but sometimes indiscrimi-
nately by author, title, or catchword. Location symbols referred
to stall, desk, and shelf number. Circulation rules varied considerably from time to time and from place to place, but in general followed precedents set by monastery libraries. In some
cases students could take out the circulating books for a year; in
others all books had to be used in the library only. Some books
could be taken out if a deposit was left. Duplicates were sometimes sold, and on a few occasions valuable books of little direct
value to the students were sold so that more usable titles could be

bought. Library books were sometimes even pawned or taken for debts owed by the college or its masters. As for availability of the libraries there is again a wide range of regulations. In some cases the chained volumes, those in most demand, were available at all times to the students and masters. In other cases, more valuable books were kept under triple locks, with the keys in the hands of three different officials, so that all three had to be present before the book could be seen.

Librarians as a professional class did not emerge in the early universities. Instead, the keeper of the books was usually a minor faculty member or even a student. Where the colleges were connected with religious orders, the books were in charge of one or more monks. At Oxford and probably elsewhere, they were left to the care of the chaplain. Sometimes the librarian was a scholar well-versed in the contents of most of the volumes he guarded, but at other times he was little more than a "keeper of the books" charged more with the care of their physical condition than with knowledge of their contents. In some cases the library caretaker was personally responsible for every book in his charge and liable for their costs if any were lost or damaged. Inventories were usually made annually and were often carried out in the presence of a high college or university official.

The early university library was, generally speaking, a direct outgrowth of the monastery library and resembled it in many ways. However, it varied in at least one aspect, and that was in the fact that it was a working library. There are frequent references to heavily used volumes in the early university and college libraries, to books that were badly worn and frequently mended, and to the need for replacements. The emphasis of the libraries was on maintenance of the books for use and not on the keeping of volumes for rarity alone. In this sense, the medieval university library might be called the earliest modern library. In the use of these libraries, in the education of the thousands of students who flocked to the early universities, the medieval world was given a new society of learned men. These "graduates" for the most part did not remain secluded in monasteries or dedicated to theology, but were trained in civil and canon law, in medicine and philosophy, and they went out into the world and made their knowledge known to others. From the universities and their modest book collections came the learning that was to pave the way for the Renaissance in western Europe. If it was the monastery libraries that preserved knowledge for a thousand years, it was the university libraries that put that knowledge to use, and in doing so ushered in the modern era and put an end to the Middle Ages.

Additional Readings

(Many of the works listed in the preceding bibliography include material on the early university libraries, as do also the previously mentioned general works on the history of libraries. Most of the European universities have well-written histories that include information on the development of their libraries, and many of them have specific library histories as well. Two periodicals stand out for their coverage of European library history. These are the Zentralblatt fur Bibliothekswesen, published in Leipzig, and The Library published in London. Many other articles on libraries may be found in the various journals of medieval history.)

Alker, Hugo
    Die Universitätsbibliothek Wien: Geschichte, Organization, Benützung. Wien, 1957. 83 p.

Bourmont, Amédée de
    La bibliothèque de la Université de Caen au 15e siècle. Paris, 1884. 16 p.

Danielewicz, Maria
    The libraries of Poland. St. Andrews, Scotland, 1943. 63 p. (Good account of the early library of the Jagellonian University at Cracow).

Franklin, Alfred
    Les anciens bibliothèques de Paris. Paris, 1867. 3 v.

Garrod, H. W.
    "The library regulations of a medieval college," The Library, VIII (1927), 312-335.

Haskins, Charles H.
    The rise of the universities. New York, 1923. ix, 134 p.

Macray, William D.
    Annals of the Bodleian Library, Oxford, with a notice of the earlier library of the university . . . Oxford, 1890. 2nd ed.

Rait, R. S.
Life in the medieval university. Cambridge, 1912. viii, 164 p.

Rashdall, Hastings
The universities of Europe in the middle ages. Oxford, 1936.
New ed. 3 v.

Sayle, Charles Edward
Annals of Cambridge University Library, 1278-1900. Cambridge, 1916. vii, 155 p.

Schachner, Nathan
The medieval university. New York, 1938. 388 p.

Schmidt, Charles G. A.
Zur Geschichte der altesten Bibliotheken und der ersten Buch-
drucker zu Strassburg. Strassburg, 1882. 200 p.

Serrurier, Cornelia
Bibliothèques de France, description de leurs fonds et histoire
de leur formation. The Hague, 1946. 346 p.

Vleeschauwer, Herman Jean de
Libraria magna et libraria parva dans la bibliothèque universi-
taire du XIIIe siècle. Pretoria, 1956. 60 p.

Wilken, Friedrich
Geschichte der Bildung, Beraubung und Vernichtung der alten
Heidelbergischen Büchersammlungen. Heidelberg, 1817.

9

Medieval Private Libraries

Although the monastery, cathedral, and university libraries were the most significant centers of learning during the Middle Ages, there were also private libraries worthy of mention. These libraries were of importance for several reasons. First, they added materially to the amount of literature available at any given time and place, supplementing the institutional libraries. Second, by means of gifts and bequests, they frequently became parts of the institutional libraries. Finally, in the case of the private libraries of the feudal nobility, they often formed the nuclei of future municipal, state, or national libraries. In any case they were often more finely bound, more handsomely written, less used, and better preserved than their counterparts in the more public collections.

The fate of the many Roman private libraries that existed prior to A. D. 500 is a topic worth consideration, since it would seem logical that at least some of the thousands of manuscripts in the villas of the classical nobility would have survived. The probability is that a very few of them did survive in monastic and church collections and in the isolated private family libraries of Italy and southern France. Certainly a good percentage of the extant Latin literature did survive in the West. Early manuscripts were of course worn out, and those that have come down to us are copies of copies, so that textual examination, comparison, and criticism are necessary in order to obtain anything close to the correct original. But though some of the contents of the great Roman private libraries may have survived, the fact is that most of them were destroyed as definitely and finally as those of the Roman temples themselves.

Though they were few and far between, or at least modern evidence of them is scarce, there were private libraries existing in western Europe even in the darkest periods of the Middle Ages. In

Southern France in the fifth century, we have a description of a
private library of secular literature, including most of the Latin
classics, from the writings of Rusticus, Bishop of Narbonne from
430 to 461. He describes what was obviously a Roman villa with
bookcases adorned with portraits of orators and poets. Appolonius
Sidonius, writing at Toulouse in the fifth century, apparently had
access to a considerable library. The private library of Isidore of
Seville, accumulated in the sixth century, has already been mentioned. Eberhard, Margrave of Friuli, left a fairly large library
when he died in 864. He had corresponded widely with other scholars during his lifetime. During both the ninth and tenth centuries
the Dukes of Naples were book collectors and owners of libraries
in both Latin and Greek, although the latter language was almost if
not entirely unknown in the remainder of western Europe. Duke
William V of Aquitaine in southern France (993-1030) was also a
book collector and scholar. Gerbert of Gaul, a tenth-century
schoolmaster, collected a library that included scientific texts.
Particularly in southern Italy and Sicily from the ninth to the
twelfth centuries there was an atmosphere of learning that encouraged private book collections and individual scholarship. This is
true despite the fact that there was constant strife with and between
the Byzantines and Moslems there, and because of these contacts
with the east, this area was a meeting ground of Greek, Latin,
Arab, and Jewish cultures.

Thus, at no time in the Middle Ages is it possible to say
that the private library as such had disappeared, but there were
times when noteworthy ones were few. In addition to actual private
collections, it should be pointed out that many of the monastery
and cathedral libraries were often the achievements of only one or
two serious book collectors. Besides collecting theology for their
institutional libraries, many medieval Church officials also amassed
private libraries of their own, but these usually ended up in the
public collections.

Servatus Lupus, Bishop of the monastery at Fulda in the
ninth century, was such a collector, and from his letters we learn
that he included in his library the works of Cicero, Suetonius,

Virgil, and other Latin writers, as well as the customary theological writings.   Count Heccard, a Burgundian nobleman who died
in 875, left a library that included works on law, agriculture, and
military science, in addition to theology.   Some of his books had
been purchased, but many of them were obtained by borrowing and
copying.   The Bishop of Passau in the tenth century prized his library, which included only 56 books.   Magister Moses of Bergamo
in Italy in the early twelfth century collected Greek works while
living for some years in Constantinople, and returned to his home
with a small library.   Indeed, although Italy lagged behind France
and Germany in the development of monastery libraries between the
ninth and thirteenth centuries, many private libraries were formed
there.   They were usually small but representative of the best literature available at the time.   This was true in both north and
south Italy, with the southern private libraries containing some
Greek works, while the northern ones were theological and almost
entirely in Latin.

Many of the Roman Catholic archbishops and cardinals were
especially avid book collectors.   Cardinal Gualo Bicchieri in the
early thirteenth century left a fairly large library, almost 100 volumes, all theological.   Gilbert of Rheims, later Pope Sylvester II,
had a large personal library, including besides theology some Latin classics but no Greek.   He lived in the tenth century.   Philip
d'Harcourt, Bishop of Cayeux, gave over 100 volumes from his personal collection to the cathedral library at Bec in Normandy in the
twelfth century.   These volumes included theological, classical,
and contemporary works.   Similarly, John of Salisbury willed his
library at his death in 1180 to the cathedral at Chartres.   Richard
Gravesend, Bishop of London, 1280-1303, owned eight volumes, including three Bibles, the Church Fathers, canon law, and some
works of secular history.   Roger de Thoris, Archdeacon of Exeter,
gave his library to the Greyfriars at Exeter in 1266.   Even parish
priests found it possible to own a few books, and Geoffrey de La-
wath, of St. Magnus in London, had a library of 49 books in the
thirteenth century, including several Latin grammars and some
medical works.   Simon, Abbot of St. Albans who died in 1180,

left a small library locked in three chests. Peter of Nemours,
Bishop of Paris in the same century, owned a Bible in 22 volumes
that he bequeathed to the Abbey of St. Victor. Usually the books
owned by religious figures were theological, but evidence of interests in literature and practical subjects were often noticeable.

Some of the women of the Middle Ages, or at least some of
the women of the nobility, were well educated and became scholars
and book collectors. This is noticeable particularly after the
twelfth century. Clemence of Hungary, wife of Louis X of France,
had a library of her own in the early fourteenth century. Jeanne
d'Evreux, wife of Charles the Fair (1322-28) owned a library,
largely religious but containing some secular works in French.
Jeanne of Burgundy and Blanche of Navarre, both wives of Philip
VI (1328-50) brought books of their own to be added to Philip's library. Queen Isabel, wife of Charles VI (1380-1422) had so many
books that one of her ladies-in-waiting had to serve as her personal librarian. Gabrielle de la Tour, Countess of Montpensier in
France, owned over 200 volumes in 1474; and Yoland, daughter of
Charles VII and wife of Amadeo of Savoy, owned a large library at
the time of her marriage. Marie Payenne, a Flemish lady of
twelfth-century Tournai, left her library to a convent. One of the
largest of medieval libraries belonging to women was that of Marie
of Austria who in 1530 left her books to the Ducal Library of Burgundy, and the number was so large that it almost doubled the
size of that library. Margaret of York, English wife of Charles,
Duke of Burgundy, brought a small library of English writings
with her in 1468 and joined with her husband in building up his library thereafter. She commissioned William Caxton to print the
Historie of Troye in Bruges in 1475, probably the first printed
book in English. She also commissioned the translation of
Boethius's Consolation of Philosophy into French. There were also several nuns who were noted for their literary activities, both
the collecting of books and the writing of religious and inspirational
works. The subject interests of women book collectors in general
were similar to those of contemporary men -- heavily theological,
but ranging widely into philosophy, history, and literature, both

classical and contemporary.

It is interesting to note that the Jewish minority in western
Europe produced many scholars and book collectors. Under the
Moslems in Spain and Sicily, the Jews flourished in a tolerant atmosphere, and many scholars, lawyers, and physicians emerged
among them. The Jewish Bible, together with the core of literature built up around it, formed the basis of many Jewish book collections, but others went far beyond this theological center and
built up large libraries of secular literature. David d'Estella, a
Jewish physician of fourteenth-century France, left a library including medical works in Greek and Latin and other titles in literature
and science. Leo Mosconi, a contemporary Jewish doctor on the
island of Majorca, included in his library works of medicine, theology, philosophy, music, and literature. Jewish libraries were often dispersed in the persecution of Jews, and in 1223 when the
Palestinian physician Abraham ben Hillel was arrested and forced
to leave his home, his fine library was sold at auction. It contained many rare medical works in Arabic and Greek.

Jews in the north of Europe were not so wealthy as those in
the Mediterranean areas, so that they were often hard-pressed to
acquire even the necessary books for their synagogues. However,
one French Jew, Juda ibn Tibbon of the twelfth century, left a library notable for content if not for great size. Tibbon left his
books to his son with concise instructions on how to handle them:

> Arrange them all in good order, so that thou weary not
> in looking for a book when thou needest it. . . Write
> down the titles of the books in each row of the cases in
> a separate notebook and place each in its row, in order
> that thou mayest be able to see exactly in which row any
> particular book is without mixing up the others. Do the
> same with the cases. Look continually into the catalog
> in order to remember what books thou hast. When thou
> lendest a book, record its title before it leaves the house;
> and when it is brought back draw thy pen through the
> memorandum . . .

Tibbon (1120-70) was a philosopher and scholar who translated
books from Arabic into Latin. His motive in building his library
was to make it so complete that he would never again have to borrow a book.

In addition to the nobility and clergy, the professional man of the Middle Ages was sometimes a collector of books. Also, some of the skilled craftsmen, particularly those connected with books and monasteries, were readers and owned a few books. The physicians were particularly interested in books and often went beyond their medical treatises in their collecting. Johannes Sindell, physician to Emperor Frederick III, left 200 books at his death in 1450. In Austria, Dr. Johannes Polzmacher in 1453 gave his library to a monastery near Vienna. It was strong in both civil and canon law plus many classics. Herman Scheidel (1410-85) a Nuremberg physician, began collecting books in Greek, Latin, Italian, and German, and on his death his cousin, Hartman Scheidel, also a physician, took over the library and broadened its contents to include art and archaeology to build up a large and valuable collection. Later passing into the hands of the Fugger family, the Scheidel library eventually became a part of the Royal Library in Munich. Other professions also collected books, as evidenced by the gift of a library, in 1456, to Greifswald University by Heinrich Rubenow, lawyer and burgomaster. The merchant Johannes Reichlin left his library to the city of Pforzheim. In England, the fifteenth-century family of Pastons built up a large and continuing library, while Sir John Fastolf divided his library into French and English on one side and Latin on the other. John Carpenter, town clerk of London, left a small collection of 26 volumes when he died in 1442. Members of the profession of law, whether canon or civil, usually had at least small collections of books so necessary in the conduct of their duties.

The famous medieval book collectors left us works concerning their collecting activities, or at least describing books they owned or wanted to own. One of these was Richard de Fournival, Chancellor of Amiens in France who wrote his Biblionomia in the thirteenth century, describing a "garden of literature" in which different tables were covered with manuscripts on different subjects. His largest subject area was philosophy, but medicine, law, and theology were also included in his "garden." There is some doubt as to whether the work describes an actual book collection or or whether it is merely an imaginary one. Also, there is some doubt that it was actually written by Fournival, although it is usually ascribed to him. At any rate, it is an excellent account of literary interests of the period, and many of the manuscripts described are known to exist or to have existed at one time.

Another bibliophile was Richard de Bury (1287-1345), teacher, officeholder, and later Bishop of Durham. He was an ardent book collector from his earlier years, and when he later became a diplomat in the service of Edward III, he visited libraries, booksellers, and scriptoria in many parts of Europe. He bought many books, but others were given to him, particularly after he became a bishop. He respected and would accept books in almost any form and on almost any subject. His Philobiblion (or Love of Books) was completed about 1344, but it was not printed until 1473, and since that date has gone through many editions. Generally speaking, it is a book in praise of books, but it also tells how the author collected his books, and thus gives an elaborate picture of the book world of his day. Some of his chapter titles were: "That the treasure of wisdom is chiefly contained in books," "Of the numerous opportunities we have had of collecting a store of books," "That it is meritorious to write new books and to renew the old," and finally, "That we have collected so great store of books for the common benefit of scholars and not only for our own pleasure." De Bury notes that books are the storehouse of wisdom, and he says of it: "There everyone who asks receiveth thee, and everyone who seeks finds thee, and to everyone that knocketh boldly it is speedily opened." One other notable quote from the Philobiblion shows the author's basic belief: "All the glory of the world would be buried in oblivion, unless God had provided mortals with the remedy of books." De Bury's books were supposed to have been given to the Priory of Durham at Oxford, but the general belief is that most if not all of them were sold to pay the bishop's debts.

Probably the most important private libraries in the Western World prior to 1500 were the libraries of the Italian scholars that ushered in the Renaissance. From the fourteenth century on

through the sixteenth, Italian merchants, princes, and religious
leaders either in collaboration or competition succeeded in bringing
to light the majority of the Greek and Latin classics now known to
the world.   Some of these classics were discovered in Italy itself
in monasteries, church libraries, or in private hands.   Still others
were found or refound in the by then neglected monastery libraries
of France, Switzerland, and central Europe.   But of most importance were the volumes brought to Italy from Constantinople and
the Moslem countries.   These had been for centuries lost to the
Western World and would in all probability have been lost forever
if they had not been rescued at the time they were.

Petrarch (1304-74) was one of the earliest of these Italian
book collectors.   He collected manuscripts from all parts of Europe
and devoted himself particularly to the classic Latin authors.   He
could not read Greek but knew Homer in Latin translation.   His
library also contained the major religious writings, and although it
contained only about 200 volumes, it was one of the most complete
and well-rounded of his era.   Unfortunately, this library was
scattered after Petrarch's death.   His contemporary and follower
Boccaccio (1313-75) also collected a library, searching out missing
manuscripts with all the diligence of a literary detective.   His library was bequeathed at his death to the monastery at San Spirito.

By 1400 the movement to collect books from the East was
well under way, and many Venetian, Florentine, and Genoese ships
considered manuscripts to be valuable cargo for their return trips
from the eastern Mediterranean.   In 1408, Guarino of Verona returned from a visit to the East with a collection of 50 Greek manuscripts for which he found a ready sale.   The Sicilian book collector Aurispa brought in over 200 Greek manuscripts in the year
1423 alone.   Filelfo, who went to Constantinople in 1420 as a member of the Venetian legation there, brought home with him about 40
Greek volumes, many of which were unknown in Latin translation
before that date.   The quest for manuscripts led not only to works
in Greek but to Hebrew as well.   Pico della Mirandola, a Christian Hebrew scholar, owned more than 100 Hebrew works, while
his student and friend Reuchlin acquired 36 more in the same lan-

guage.

It is noteworthy that much of this collecting activity was due to individual effort rather than to universities, church, or governmental agencies. Many of the individuals were merchants or religious personnel, but the greatest collecting activity was done by the Italian princes and their agents. Several men became famous for their ability to locate and obtain manuscripts for pay. Janus Lascaris, for example, obtained many manuscripts from the East, first for Louis XII of France and later for the Medici family in Italy. Many of these came from the monasteries on Mount Athos in Greece, and in 1492 he brought back over 200 manuscripts on one trip. Vespasiano da Bisticci was another of the book agents, noted for obtaining originals or copies of hundreds of manuscripts for several collectors.

One noted religious collector was Cardinal Bessarion, himself a Greek by birth, but a long-time resident of Italy. He tried to build up the largest Greek library in the world and sent agents to all parts of Greece and Asia Minor in search of manuscripts. He was responsible for rescuing several hundred manuscripts, most of which eventually went with his library to the Biblioteca Marciana in Venice.

Probably the most important Italian collectors were the members of the Medici family. Cosimo de Medici (1434-64) hired Vespasiano de Bisticci to collect books for him. At one time Vespasiano employed 45 copyists and in 22 months produced 200 books, all elegantly bound, for the Medici library. Cosimo's library contained the Bible in several copies, religious commentaries, works of the Church Fathers, the medieval writers, and also many classical works in philosophy, history, poetry, and grammar. In addition to the works he obtained himself, Cosimo also acquired a library of 800 volumes collected by Niccolo di Niccoli of Florence. From his collections, Cosimo began several more-or-less public libraries, including one in the Convent of San Marco at Florence and one at Fiesole. Tomaso Parentucceli, later Pope Nicholas V, was at one time Cosimo's librarian. Cosimo was himself something of a scholar who read Latin well and who had some knowledge of Greek, Hebrew, and Arabic.

Cosimo's grandson, Lorenzo de Medici, carried on the work
of building up the Medici library. He was one of the first of the
Italian princes to collect printed works or even to allow them in
his library. After his death the Medici family library was kept together, and eventually it was housed in the Biblioteca Laurentiana,
designed specifically for it by Michelangelo.

Federigo, Duke of Urbino (1444-82), was another of the ardent fifteenth-century Italian collectors. He had a series of rooms
in his palace filled with books and invited artists, scholars, and
writers to use them. He loved the classics, but also added to his
library the standard church literature and contemporary authors.
For many years he had a staff of 30 copyists, and Vespasiano da
Bisticci also served him for a time as librarian and bookbuyer.

Domenico Malatesta Novello built up a personal library in
Cesena in northern Italy in 1452, and then opened it to the public
at the Convent of San Francisco. Two citizens of the town were
associated with the Friars in controlling the library. It was
housed in a separate building designed by Matteo Nuzio, a celebrated architect of the period. In 1473 this same library received
a gift of another important private collection. This was the medical library of Giovanni di Marco, and it included many scientific
manuscripts dating from the thirteenth century onward in Latin,
Greek, and Hebrew.

The D'Este princes of Modena began collecting a library in
the fourteenth century. Nicolo III (1384-1436) began the collection,
and by the time of his death it was quite large, housed in a palace
tower, and divided by language rather than subject. There were
165 volumes of Latin, largely classical, plus 20 in Italian and 56
in French. Only a very few of them were of a religious nature.
Leonello (1436-1450) enlarged the D'Este library and added many
volumes of literature and drama, while Duke Ercole (1471-1505)
found the collection large enough to require the services of a librarian, and hired Pellegrino Prisciano for this purpose. When
the palace library had virtually become a public one, he and his
wife, Eleanor of Aragon, began collecting another private library

in their own palace apartment.

The Gonzaga family at Mantua also built up a large library over several generations, beginning in the fourteenth century. In 1407 it contained 400 manuscripts, including many in French and Italian. The library remained in the family for over 300 years, only to be dispersed in the early eighteenth century. Another noble family, the Visconti Sforza's of Pavia, amassed a library of almost 1,000 volumes by 1400, including some of Petrarch's personal manuscripts. This collection was enlarged in the fifteenth century, only to end up as spoils of war in the royal French library of Louis XII at Blois. In the late fifteenth century Bartolomeo Calco was librarian of the Sforza library, and he was responsible for organizing and cataloging it.

The development of the Vatican Library in Rome during the late Middle Ages can be considered along with private libraries because it was largely the result of the activities of a few individuals. Pope Nicholas V (1447-55) who, as Tomaso Parentucelli, had been librarian to Cosimo de Medici, was responsible for a rebirth of the Vatican Library. When he became Pope, he found some 350 manuscripts in various states of repair in the library, and to this he added his own private library. Then he proceeded to add to it with all the resources at his command and with his own wide knowledge of the book world. He sent papal agents all over Europe seeking manuscripts as gifts or for copying. The papal librarian Tortelli helped to build the collection and translated Greek works into Latin. By the time of his death, Nicholas had built the Vatican Library to over 1,200 volumes and had made it one of the finest in all of Italy. Pope Sixtus IV (1471-84) continued to build up the library, so that by 1475 it contained about 2,500 volumes, with about one-third of them Greek. By 1484 an inventory showed 3,650 volumes divided into four collections: the public Greek library, the public Latin library, the rare books collection, and the Pope's private library. The humanist scholar Bartolomeo Platina was librarian in the Vatican after 1475. He cataloged and classified the library, keeping strict records of all use, and opening it to all serious scholars, but particularly to those interested in the

history of the Church.   It is interesting to note, however, that after Nicholas VI, the Vatican Library contained classical and secular works as well as religious literature.

Though many of the libraries of the Italian collectors ended
up in public or semi-public collections, a few of them, and of
their contemporaries in other parts of Europe, were the fortunate
beginnings of future national libraries.   The kings of Naples, beginning with Charles I (1220-85), built up a notable library in that
city.   This royal collection grew in size and usefulness for some
200 years.   In 1485, however, when the French captured Naples,
most of the library was carried away as spoils of war to join other
collections in forming the French royal library.   More specifically,
however, the French national library began with Charles V, who
took a small collection left by his father and installed it with many
additions in the Chateau du Louvre in 1367.   With Gilles Malet as
librarian, the French royal library grew to nearly a thousand volumes scattered through three rooms of the palace.   Though largely
theological, the library also contained much on other subjects, including history, law, contemporary French literature, and astronomy.   There were even some works translated from the Arabic.
Actually, earlier kings of France had collected libraries since the
days of Pepin the Short, but most of these works were dispersed
or lost after the death of the collector.   In the wars with the English in the fifteen century, much of the royal French library was
lost, with the major part going to England with the Duke of Bed-
ford.   When Louis XI regained the throne in 1461, he re-established
a library in the Louvre.   In 1472 the library of the Duke de Berry
was added to this collection, and still later the collection of the
Dukes of Burgundy.   A library built up at Blois by the Dukes of
Orleans was even larger than the collection in the Louvre, so
King Louis XII moved the entire collection to Blois about 1500 and
added to it the libraries he had captured in Italy.   The Royal library grew gradually, but in the sixteenth century it was merged
with still another collection at Fontainebleau and finally in 1595 returned to Paris to a more-or-less permanent home there.

In England the kings had also been haphazard collectors of

books at various times, but no royal library as such emerged before the end of the Middle Ages. Several German principalities began their libraries with the collections of their rulers before the sixteenth century, including that founded by the Emperor Maximilian I in Vienna in 1493. Local nobility gave their private collections to form town libraries, as in Nuremberg in 1429, Schlettstadt (Alsace) in 1430, Mainz in 1477, and Frankfort in 1484. Probably the most famous of the central European royal libraries was that of King Matthias Corvinus of Hungary (1440-90). Matthias had agents all over Europe buying and borrowing volumes for his library. In that library, which occupied a wing of his palace at Buda, he had some 20 or more copyists, illuminators, and bookbinders producing beautiful volumes in Latin, Greek, Arabic, and Hebrew for him. In 1476 he married Beatrice of Aragon, herself an ardent book collector, and between them they gathered a library that was for its time unusually large and beautiful. Various reports maintain that he had up to 50,000 volumes, but it is generally supposed that he could not have had over a tenth of that number. Even so, it was one of the finest in Europe for its time. Unfortunately, the Corvinus library was scattered after the King's death, and it is doubtful that many were left for the Turks to capture when they took Buda in 1526. Many individual items from the Corvinus library have survived, however, and they now form some of the most treasured items in modern European manuscript collections.

All told, the fifteenth century was a remarkable one from the standpoint of library development, and much of this progress came through the efforts of individuals rather than organizations. Many of the greatest libraries of Europe had their beginnings in this century. Also, it should be pointed out that the custom of constructing separate library buildings can for the most part be dated from this era. From Spain to England libraries began to mean distinct architectural entities rather than merely rooms or wings of larger buildings. The library that Domenico Malatesta Novella built at Cesena in 1452 was a long, narrow building, 34 by 133 feet. Inside it contained 3 rows of bookcases, with 29 in each

row.   Each bookcase was really something of a lectern with shelves
below and a seat opposite.   The books were chained to the shelves
but stood upright, and the chains were long enough to reach the
sloping lectern.   The library that the Medicis gave to the Dominican Convent of St. Mark at Florence was similarly built, about 34
by 148 feet, containing 64 separate book-shelf desks, each holding
about 16 books.   This system of long, narrow buildings with high
windows was apparently designed to take advantage of as much day-
light as possible on each bookstall or desk.

Most of the late medieval libraries, whether institutional or
private, were to a large extent open to any serious scholar.   Records were kept of borrowers, and although terms were often leni-
ent enough to allow books to be taken from the library, particularly duplicates, there was usually some deposit required or other assurance that the book would be returned.   The Vatican Library
went so far as to invoke the power of the Pope to assure the safe
return of its volumes:

> Whoever writes his name here in acknowledgment of
> books received on loan out of the Pope's Library,
> will incur his anger and his curse unless he return
> them uninjured within a very brief period.

The endowed private library, more so than either the monastery
or unitversity library, came to have the scholar as librarian and
to be the home of the serious student.

Not only were the medieval private libraries notable for
collecting books, but they should be remembered for the work they
did in copying, repairing, restoring, and rebinding the works that
were collected.   Wealthy library owners kept binders, illuminators,
and copyists busy supplying their demands for more and more
books.   But beyond preserving books, many of the private library
owners put their collections to use.   Students, scholars, writers,
even poets and musicians were invited to use the collections of the
Italian merchants and princes, and such use often carried with it
food and lodging.   Under such use, the musty tomes gave up their
long-held ideas, their philosophies were rediscovered, reconsidered,
and reinterpreted in the light of the fifteenth-century world.   Perhaps the Renaissance was not wholly due to the activities of the

book collectors, but certainly they made the resources available from which the scholars brought forth the "new learning." The combination of scholars, books, and students was vital to the Renaissance and helped to make it a permanent epoch in the history of Western man. Surely the cultural strength of the library was never more effective than in the fourteenth and fifteenth centuries, and it is worthwhile to note that it was the private library as much as the institutional libraries that played a major role in this cultural drama.

Additional Readings

(Many of the private libraries of note during the Middle Ages later became parts of public, university, and national libraries; so their histories are recorded along with those of the larger libraries. Moreover, the fourteenth- and fifteenth-century private libraries of Italy and France are a part of and often recorded with the history of the Renaissance. Hence the readings specifically concerned with medieval private libraries are relatively few, and the following are noteworthy examples.)

Berkovitz, Ilona
    Bilderhandschriften aus der Bibliothek des Konigs Matthias Corvinus. Wiesbaden (?), 1963. 200 p.

Delisle, Léopold
    Recherches sur la librarie de Charles V . . . Paris, 1907. 2 v.

De Marinis, T.
    La biblioteca Napolitana dei Re d'Aragona. Verona, 1947-52. 4 vols.

Elsdon, James H.
    The library of the Counts of Benavente. Annapolis, 1955. 41 p.

Geisenhof, Georg
    Bibliotheca Corviniana; eine bibliographische Studie. Brunswick, 1900. (Reprint: Nieuwkoop, 1963. 223 p.)

Gonzalez, Juan
    El maestro Juan de Segovia y su biblioteca. Madrid, 1944. 213 p.

Holzknecht, Karl J.
    Literary patronage in the Middle Ages. Philadelphia, 1923. v, 258 p.

Kibre, Pearl
    The library of Pico della Mirandola. New York, 1936. xiv,
       330 p.

    The intellectual interests reflected in libraries of the 14th and
      15th centuries. New York, 1946. 40 p.

Lehmann, Paul
    Eine Geschichte der alten Fugger-Bibliotheken. Tübingen,
      1956-60. 2 v.

Muntz, Eugène
    La bibliothèque du Vatican au XVe siècle. Paris, 1887. 388 p.

Pellegrin, Elisabeth
    La bibliothèque des Visconti et des Sforza, ducs de Milan, au
      XVe siècle. Paris, 1955. vii, 491 p.

Pitteri, D.
    La biblioteca Marciana. Venice, 1893. 92 p.

10.

European National Libraries Since 1500

The growth of libraries in Europe since 1500 has been stupendous as compared with the pitifully small collections available during the Middle Ages. The primary cause of this remarkable growth was, of course, the development of printing, which produced more books and cheaper books than could have been imagined a century earlier. But more books meant a higher rate of literacy; a higher rate of learning meant more scholars to write more books. Hence there were not only more books printed, there were more books to be printed, more books written, and more books used. Before 1500 a great book might be read possibly by a few hundred people; after that date its readers could be numbered in thousands or even hundreds of thousands. The power of the printed word increased a hundredfold the power of the written word, and never again was Europe and the Western World to suffer from a lack of graphic communication in the conveyance of facts or philosophies.

Of all the libraries of modern Europe the most outstanding have been the national libraries, those rapidly growing collections of "one of everything" that developed in the national capitals. Sometimes these national collections developed at the expense of other libraries, but they have generally aimed at an impossible goal of completeness, at least within the publications of their own country. They may not always have been as influential as some other libraries, notably those of the great universities, but they benefited from the spirit of nationalism and often survived and even flourished while other libraries suffered in wars or depressions. Generally speaking, they had permanency and economic security if not generous budgets and well-trained staffs. Their collective success and survival have meant much to the total history of libraries in the Western World.

The French national library in Paris, the Bibliothèque Nationale, is an outstanding example of European national libraries. Its development through a series of royal family libraries down through the sixteenth century has already been traced. During the reign of Henry IV (1589-1610) the royal library was moved into Paris. For some years it was housed in the College of Clermont, on the rue St. Jacques, but in 1622 it was installed in the rue de la Harpe. In that same year its first printed catalog was issued, listing some 6,000 titles. This catalog was divided into two main divisions, manuscript and print, and each of these divisions was subdivided by language. Under Louis XIV (1643-1715), and particularly under his Prime Minister, Colbert, the royal library grew rapidly. With Nicholas Clement as librarian, the collection was reclassified and a new catalog was issued in 1688. This catalog, of the printed works alone, was in 10 printed volumes, with 6 volumes arranged alphabetically by author or main entry and 4 volumes alphabetically by subject. In 1690, a catalog of the manuscripts in the collection was published in eight volumes. In 1714 the library contained no less than 70,000 volumes, and in 1719, when it was forced for lack of space to move into new quarters on the rue Richelieu, it contained 80,000 printed volumes and 16,000 manuscripts. These quarters, in what was formerly the Hotel de Nevers, have been enlarged, extended, remodeled, and virtually rebuilt over the years, but the site has remained the same down to the twentieth century.

Throughout its history the Bibliothèque Nationale has been favored by the accession of thousands of major works, including many whole libraries. Some of these have been purchased, others were donated, and still others have been acquired by more direct means. One of the earliest collections was that of Catherine de Medici, obtained under the librarianship of J. A. de Thou in the early seventeenth century. In 1662 the library of Raphael Trichet du Fresne, containing some 1,200 volumes, was purchased. Later in the same century came the libraries of Jacques Mentel, several thousand volumes, and that of the former librarian De Thou himself. In 1728 the greater part of the library of Minister Colbert was purchased, and about the same time a large collection of med-

ieval manuscripts was donated by Archbishop Roger de Gaigneres.
But in addition to large gifts, the library also benefited from selective purchasing, with bookdealers throughout Europe sending choice
items for consideration and French diplomats and missionaries obtaining books and manuscripts from all over the world.

The late eighteenth century saw the Bibliothèque Nationale
growing at the expense of other libraries. In 1763, for example,
when the Jesuits were expelled from Paris, their libraries were
seized and the more valuable works added to the royal library.
The French Revolution, which overturned much that was established
in French society, also served in the long run to benefit the national library. After some early difficulties and a shortage of
funds in the early days of the Revolution, the Library became officially known as the Bibliothèque Nationale rather than as the "Bibliothèque Royale," and thousands of volumes from the seized libraries of the fleeing nobility were added to it. Later on libraries
belonging to the church, to other nobles, and to "counterrevolution-
aries" were seized, and all books that were not duplicates were
placed in the national library. The unwanted volumes were distributed to public libraries throughout France. Although many
books were lost or destroyed during the Revolutionary period, the
ideas and ideals of national bibliographies, national library planning,
and library service for all the people were introduced into the
French cultural scene. Still later, the French armies of both the
Revolution and the Empire under Napoleon seized libraries in other
parts of Europe and added choice volumes to their national library.

Thus, in the nineteenth century the Bibliothèque Nationale
was one of the foremost libraries in the world. By 1818 it contained nearly one million volumes; by 1860, a million and a half.
By 1908 there were more than 3,000,000 printed volumes, and by
1960 well over 5,000,000, not counting the thousands upon thousands of manuscripts, maps, pictures, and engravings. Along with
the growth in size came an almost continuous problem of reorganization to keep up with that growth. In 1739 the librarian, Abbé
Bignon, had divided the library into four main collections: theology, canon law, civil law, and belles lettres. In 1840 a new clas-

sification was begun, and in that year the author catalog alone totaled 89 volumes. In the 1850's the library building was virtually
rebuilt under the architectural guidance of Henri Labrouste. The
late nineteenth century found the library under the able direction of
Léopold Delisle (1874-1907), and although he was a medievalist at
heart and strongly interested in manuscripts and paleographical
studies, he did much to modernize the library and make it available
to scholars from all over the world. In the 1890's a new catalog
was begun, but acquisitions have usually come in more rapidly than
they could be cataloged, so that there are still literally hundreds of
thousands of uncataloged items in the vast collections of the library.

In the twentieth century the Bibliothèque Nationale has been
faced with numerous problems but has grown steadily and continues
to be one of the world's great libraries. Crowded conditions have
resulted in the addition of new bookstacks wherever possible, in the
opening of four new reading rooms, and in the storage of bulky and
little-used materials in an annex at Versailles. During the two
world wars the library suffered considerably, but in each case the
post-war period brought new and rapid growth. Rare and valuable
items were sent to rural areas for storage during World War II, so
that actual war damage was slight. The Bibliothèque Mazarine was
added to the national library in 1930, at least for administrative
purposes, and the catalog of printed books was almost completed
before the World War II began. Since 1945 the library has sought
to enlarge its services and its position in the cultural world by becoming a national bibliographical center as well as the national library.

Close to the Bibliothèque Nationale in international importance is the British Museum, which is the national library of Great
Britain. This library is not as old as that of France, since the
early royal libraries of England were usually dispersed upon the
deaths of their compilers; but it has grown more rapidly so that it
is now one of the two greatest libraries in the English-speaking
world. Although based in part on royal collections, the British
Museum has been largely the result of the amalgamation of many
large private libraries. Beginning in 1700, the valuable manuscript

library of Sir Henry Cotton was acquired for the government by
King William III, but it was not until half a century later that a
move was made to organize a truly national library. Sir Hans
Sloane, royal physician and a notable book collector in his own
right, was the chief instigator of the movement. At this death in
1753, he directed in his will that his library be sold for a modest
amount to the British government on condition that it be suitably
housed and maintained. After much debate in Parliament, the collection was purchased and a sum set aside for a building.

Along with some 50,000 printed volumes and 2,000 manuscripts acquired from Sloane, the British government purchased the
Robert Harley manuscript collection and added the already owned
Cottonian collection. King George II added his private library in
1757, and with the purchase of the large, rambling building known
as the Montagu House, the British Museum found its first home and
was opened to the public in 1759. Since the Sloane collection had
contained a wide variety of museum material, in the form of geological and scientific specimens, the title of British Museum was
appropriate, but the library portion has far surpassed the museum
in general significance over the years.

Although several minor collections were added to the Museum in the eighteenth century, the book collection as a whole grew
only slowly until after the Napoleonic wars. In 1817 a major accession came in the purchase of the Charles Burney library of some
13,000 volumes and 500 early Greek and Latin manuscripts. Most
important in the Burney library, however, were the files of seven-
teenth- and eighteenth-century British newspapers, bound chronologi-
cally and indexed by Burney himself. In 1823 the library of George
III was added to the Museum, literally doubling the size of its
printed collection. Plans for a new building were begun, and a
first wing of this permanent structure was completed in 1828.
Planned originally as a huge quadrangle of buildings surrounding an
open court, the Museum in the 1850's was converted into a solid
square by making the center court into a bookstack surrounding a
circular reading area. Other major gifts in the nineteenth century
include the Joseph Banks library and herbarium in 1820, with some

16,000 choice scientific volumes; the Thomas Grenville library of
some 20,000 rare books in 1846; and the Arundel collection of
manuscripts transferred from the archives of the Royal Society in
1830.   Aside from the major accessions, the British Museum has
steadily acquired thousands of volumes through individual purchase,
exchange, and by legal copyright deposit from the printers of the
Empire.

The British Museum has had many outstanding librarians and
directors, but probably the most outstanding was Sir Anthony Pan-
izzi who came to the staff as assistant librarian in 1831.   His energy and interest led him to the position of Keeper of the Printed
Books in 1837, and under his administration the library became
modernized both in arrangement and in housing.   He supervised the
move into the new building in 1838, the building of the central
reading room and stacks in the 1850's, the first complete catalog
and the accompanying catalog rules, the enforcement of the deposit
law, the obtaining of special funds from Parliament for the enlarge-
ment of the collection, and the beginning of the printed catalog.
Finally, in 1856 he was rewarded with the title of Principal Librarian, and he filled this position until his retirement in 1868.
His influence in libraries and librarianship was felt around the
world, and he undoubtedly goes down in history as one of the world's
greatest librarians.

In the twentieth century the British Museum ranks as one of
the great cultural resources of the world.   In addition to being the
national library for Great Britain and the Commonwealth, it houses
in its immense collections whole libraries on almost any and all
phases of world history and culture.   Whether it is Egyptian papyri
or Babylonian cuneiform tablets; Sanskrit manuscripts or early
Chinese printings; material on the French Revolution or the Russian
Revolution; history of science or history of travel; or any of a
hundred other subjects, the British Museum contains virtually definitive collections on the subject.   In addition to its many other holdings, it contained in 1960 over 6,500,000 printed volumes.   Many
of its rarer possessions were stored outside of London during
World War II, and its newspaper collection, the largest in the

world, has been permanently stored in a London suburb.

In addition to the British Museum, there are also national libraries in Scotland and Wales. The National Library of Scotland, which has had that title since 1925, was formerly the Advocate's Library founded in Edinburgh in 1682. Originally a legal library, it began at an early date to specialize in Scottish literature and history. In 1709 it was granted depository rights for all books published in Great Britain, and under the librarianship of the historian David Hume in the mid-eighteenth century, it grew to be a collection of some 30,000 volumes. In the nineteenth century gifts of books and funds brought slow but steady growth, and by 1900 it contained nearly a half-million volumes. Today its holdings are close to the 2,000,000 mark. The National Library of Wales, at Aberystwyth, was founded in 1873. Based on two large private libraries, those of Sir John Williams, a Welsh surgeon, and Edward Owen, a Welsh language scholar, and on the library of the University College of Wales, the library concentrates on Welsh language and literature. It contains virtually everything published in Welsh or about Wales since the invention of printing. In a building of its own since 1916, the Welsh National Library also serves as the library for the University of Wales and as a regional library for Wales in the National Library System. It contained well over a million volumes in 1960, in addition to some 10,000 manuscripts and over 150,000 government documents.

Possibly the largest single library in the world today is the national library of Soviet Russia, the Saltykov-Shchedrin State Library in Leningrad, formerly the Imperial Russian Library of St. Petersburg. The Russian national library owes its beginnings to a much later period than the western European libraries. In fact, it was not until the late eighteenth century that the Empress Catherine the Great took a captured Polish library and used it as a basis for the St. Petersburg collection. The Polish library had been built up by the Counts Andreas and Joseph Zaluski in the years before 1740. It was largely western European in language and origin, but it did contain a few Russian works and virtually everything printed in Polish. In 1740, the Zaluski library was formally

turned over to the Polish government, and in 1748 it was opened
as the Polish National Library.   When Warsaw was captured by the
Russians in 1794 and Poland was divided among Russia, Prussia,
and Austria, the national library went to the Russians as spoils of
war, with its 250,000 books and 10,000 manuscripts.   Unfortunately for the library, the Empress Catherine died in 1796 and very
little was done to get the library organized and opened in St. Petersburg.   Count Alexander Stroganoff was appointed director of the library in 1800 and began to get it in order, adding to the Polish
collection the various small libraries owned by the government; in
1805 he acquired the Dubrovsky collection of manuscripts.   These
valuable medieval papers were obtained by a Russian agent in Paris
during the French Revolution, and most of them had originally
come from the Abbey of St. Germain.   At Stroganoff's death in
1811, A. N. Olenin became director of the imperial library, and
under his guidance the library was finally arranged and officially
opened.   He compiled two catalogs, one alphabetically by author and
the other by a classified subject arrangement.   Since the original
Polish collection had contained only a few books in Russian, this
defect was remedied in 1810 by a legal deposit law that gave the library two copies of every book published in Russia.   With a relatively meager budget, Olenin greatly increased the size of the library through exchanges, purchases, and gifts, and at his death in
1843 he left a scholarly collection that was really a national library.

Count M. A. Korf, librarian of the Russian Imperial Library
from 1849 to 1861, was responsible for the next period of growth
for the collection.   During his administration he added some
350,000 printed volumes and 11,000 manuscripts, as well as large
numbers of prints, photographs, musical scores, and maps.   He
also remodeled the library building and completely reorganized the
book collection, dividing it into departments on the general plan of
the British Museum.   Among major accessions in the mid-nineteenth century were the Tischendorf manuscripts, collected in the
Near East by the German biblical scholar Constantine Tischendorf,
and including the famous Bible manuscript, the Codex Sinaiticus.
More important for the library, Korf advertised it and brought it to

public attention, so that it not only grew in size but in use and public esteem, and by 1860 it was second only to the Bibliothèque Nationale in all the libraries of Europe.   Growth was steady, if not spectacular, throughout the remainder of the nineteenth century, and a new building was completed in 1901.   In 1913 an inventory of the Library disclosed holdings of 2, 800, 000 printed books and 45, 000 manuscripts.   In the latter field it was especially strong, having been enriched by the gift and purchase of several other strong manuscript collections after those of Count Tischendorf.

The Russian Revolution, like the French of a century earlier, resulted in the long run in the improvement of the national library.   After a few months of disorganization, the former imperial library was proclaimed a national collection, and its holdings were enriched by many libraries confiscated from the Russian nobility, from various monasteries, and even from the libraries in the various palaces of the former royal family.   Under the Communist government the growth and effectiveness of libraries in general have been strongly encouraged, and the Saltykov-Shchedrin State Library in Leningrad had reached some 5 million volumes by 1930, and over 13 million by 1963.   Its importance has grown with its size, and its activities in all phases of library, bibliographic, and documentary services have increased in proportion.

Although the State Library in Leningrad may be called the Russian national library by virtue of its descent from the former imperial library, the Lenin State Library in Moscow also has all the earmarks of a national library and is even larger in bookstock. Developed largely since 1917 from the former Rumyantsev Museum Library, this collection was renamed for Lenin in 1925 and has since grown phenomenally.   In 1963 it contained almost 22 million cataloged items, including over 14 million books plus pamphlets, periodicals, and other library materials.   It includes books in 173 different languages and serves as a public library for the city of Moscow as well as a national bibliographic center.   In addition to these superlibraries, there are also "national" libraries in each of the constituent parts of the Union of Socialist Soviet Republics. Many of these libraries are quite large and important with that of

the Ukraine at Kiev having over 6 million volumes, and even the
Moldavian State Library at Kishinev having over 2 million volumes.
It should be pointed out that Russian library statistics seem in-
flated from the Western point of view, in that they include all copies of each individual work (and some popular titles are owned in
hundreds of copies), all pamphlets or leaflets above eight pages,
and all issues of periodicals rather than volumes.   Nevertheless,
the Russian libraries are still enormous and effective.

Another late comer in the national library field in Europe
was the German imperial library in Berlin.   In 1661, the private
library of Frederick William, the Great Elector of Prussia, was
opened to the public, but it was housed in an almost publicly inac-
cessible wing of the palace and was not very large at that.   Before
his death, Frederick William had built this collection to more than
20,000 volumes, all catalogued and classified by its librarian,
Christoph Hendreich.   In 1699 the legal deposit system was adopted,
and this aided somewhat in the growth of the collection as far as
German-printed works were concerned.   Under Frederick William I
of Prussia the library grew to about 75,000 volumes by 1740, and
under Frederick the Great to about 150,000 volumes by 1790.   The
library was moved into a new building in 1780, and after that date
the book collection grew fairly rapidly through the purchase and
gift of several major private libraries.

In 1810 the library was placed under the Prussian Department of Culture, and thus divorced from the direct control of the
King.   Growth of the collection was henceforth more systematic,
and for a while the national library served also as the library of
the University of Berlin, but this connection was severed in 1831.
In 1817 Frederich Wilken became head librarian, and his administration, which lasted until 1840, was one of remarkable growth for
the library, bringing the book count to over 300,000 volumes.   The
political unification of Germany in the 1870's brought new importance to the former Prussian National Library, and made of it instead the Imperial German Library.   Since there were other and
larger libraries in the new Germany, such as the former national
libraries of Bavaria, Saxony, and Hanover, the Imperial Library

concentrated on building up its collections of foreign publications from all parts of the world. By 1890 the collection numbered 800,000 volumes; and by 1909, when the Library moved into a new building, it had over 1,250,000 volumes, including one of the finest collections of incunabula in the world, and over 33,000 manuscripts. After World War I, the title of the Berlin library reverted to that of Prussian State Library, but its collection grew to more than 2,500,000, by 1930, with 55,000 manuscripts and over 400,000 maps. At that time it was receiving regularly some 20,000 periodicals and cooperating closely with other major libraries in Berlin and with other university libraries in Prussia. Among its many strong points were an almost unequalled collection on music and music history and a collection on the history of World War I containing over 100,000 items alone. Under such librarians as Adolph von Harnack, Fritz Milkau, and Hugo Anders Kruess, the influence of the Berlin library was felt throughout the library world.

During World War II the holdings of the Prussian State Library were evacuated from Berlin, some parts going to various smaller towns where it was felt they would be safer. After the end of the War and the division of Germany into East Germany and West Germany, the holdings located in West Germany were brought together into the library of the University of Marburg. Under the name of the West German Library, this collection contained some 1,700,000 volumes by 1950, and a new building was under construction to house up to 8,000,000 volumes. However, another major West German library has been developed at Frankfurt, where the German Library (Deutsche Bibliothek) opened in 1959 with some 300,000 volumes. Designed more for preservation than for immediate use, this library will serve West Germany as a national bibliographic center.

There are other state libraries in Germany that in many respects are also "national" libraries. In particular, the Bavarian State Library at Munich has a longer history and at times has been larger than the Prussian State Library. Many monastic and church libraries in Bavaria were taken into the Bavarian State Library in the nineteenth century, making it one of the treasure houses of

Europe in consideration of its manuscripts and incunabula.   There
are also strong state libraries in Bremen, Darmstadt, Hamburg,
and Stuttgart.   In East Germany, the remainder of the former Prussian State Library is housed in East Berlin, while at Leipzig the
former Deutsche Bucherei continues to function as a second national library and bibliographic center for the Soviet zone.

The Austrian National Library in Vienna also has a long and
interesting history.   Although the "Hofbibliothek" was founded as
such in 1493, it later added two collections that were even older.
These were the libraries of the University of Vienna, begun in
1364, and the Vienna town library that dates from 1466.   The Emperor Maximilian I was largely responsible for the opening of the
national library in 1493, but the royal family continued to build up
and maintain private libraries as well.   In the eighteenth century,
during the reign of Maria Theresa, some of the royal collections
came into the National Library, adding to those already given by
Emperor Leopold in 1665.   Little is known of the early housing of
the collection, but around 1600 it was located in the monastery of
the Minorite Order in Vienna.   In 1623 it was transferred to the
Hofberg Castle, where it occupied a wing of eight rooms.   Under
Charles VI, in 1726, a new building for the library was erected,
and though soon inadequate it served with new wings and additions
until it was completely rebuilt in the early twentieth century.

The Austrian National Library has been favored with a long
line of illustrious librarians and directors, with the result that its
collections have grown tremendously over the years.   In the sixteenth century many important manuscripts were obtained from Austrian monasteries, and also a portion of the library of King Matthias Corvinus of Hungary.   Hugo Blotius, as librarian under Maximilian II, greatly enlarged the collection, cataloged it for the first
time, and secured the law of legal deposit to gain for the national
library a copy of each book published in the Holy Roman Empire.
In the seventeenth century the valuable Fugger family library was
purchased, adding at one time over 15,000 volumes.   About the
same time the library of the scientist and astronomer Tycho Brahe
was acquired.   The eighteenth century saw the coming of a new in-

flux of books and manuscripts from monastery libraries, especially
when the Society of Jesus (Jesuits) was dissolved in central Europe
in 1775. The French Revolution and the Napoleonic era threatened
Austria's libraries, and treasures from the national library were
removed from Vienna several times to avoid capture by the French.
The nineteenth century saw a relative decline in rate of growth for
the library, at least partly due to lack of space in which to operate,
but it did see a better organization of the collections and a greater
use and appreciation by the public.   Johann Karabacek, director of
the library from 1899 to 1917, saw the library through the rebuilding period and into the new quarters, as well as completely reorganizing and modernizing the routines of the library.   After World
War I, the Imperial Library was renamed the National Library, and
although post-war Austria was considerably smaller than the old
Austro-Hungarian Empire, it still remains one of the great libraries of Europe.   It is especially strong in source materials on the
Balkans and the Near East.   Its collection includes over a million
and a half printed volumes, plus some 35,000 manuscripts, thousands of maps, prints, music scores, autographs, and pictures.

Another former part of the Austro-Hungarian Empire that
emerged from World War I as a free nation was Czechoslovakia.
Here the Public and University Library of Prague serves as the
National Library, and this collection goes back at least as early as
1366.   Prior to 1773 there were actually three libraries, the University Library, a Jesuit library that was semi-public, and a library of law and medicine separate from the University.   The suppression of the Jesuits in the eighteenth century led to the joining
of that library with the University collection, and later the professional libraries were added as well.   During the nineteenth century,
growth was only moderate, but after World War I and its recognition as the national library of the new Republic of Czechoslovakia,
a period of rapid growth ensued.   Several entire private libraries
were purchased, and the bookstock grew from about 250,000 volumes before 1914 to nearly a million in the 1930's.   From 1622 to
World War II the library was housed continuously in the same building, with of course many alterations and additions.   Its major hold-

ings include strong collections on the history and culture of the various nationality groups of central Europe. Since World War II and the domination of the nation by the Communists, the Czech national library has been made the head of a nation-wide system of public research libraries, and its facilities have been coordinated with those of other research and reference libraries both in the capital city, Prague, and in the entire nation.

Italy, like Germany, has several national libraries, including two with the title of National Central Library at Rome and Florence. The national library in Florence, although not the oldest, largest, or most famous library even in its own city, is still worthy of mention. It originated in 1747, with its main book collection coming from the library of Antonio Magliabecchi, a bibliophile who bequeathed his library in 1714 for the good of the "poor people of Florence." During the latter half of the eighteenth century, books from several suppressed monasteries were added to the collection, and during the nineteenth it received other major gifts and bequests. By 1859, there were nearly 100,000 volumes and over 3,000 manuscripts, but the nature of the collection was more that of a rare reference collection than that of a public library. After the formation of the Kingdom of Italy in 1861, the Florence library was united with the Palatina Library formed by the Grand Duke of Tuscany, and the complete collection became the National Library. Growth was rapid after this date, and by 1930 it contained over 2,000,000 printed works, 22,000 manuscripts, and many thousands of letters, music scores, maps, and other ephemerata. Its holdings include over 3,500 incunabula and exhaustive collections on Dante and Savonarola, with the largest collection of works printed by Aldus Manutius in existence. The library moved into a modern building of its own in the 1890's, and unlike most other European national libraries, into a completely new building in the 1930's. It is thus one of the most efficiently housed of all Europe's major libraries.

The Victor Emmanuel Library at Rome is also designated a National Central Library, and there are six other national libraries in Italy located at Bari, Milan, Naples, Palermo, Turin, and Ven-

ice. The library in Rome dates only from 1875, and it also benefited from the libraries of monasteries and religious houses suppressed in 1873. It contained close to a million volumes by 1930
and had strong collections on the history of Rome and on Italian
and other European literatures. A new building is under construction in the 1960's to hold eventually as many as 6,000,000 volumes.
It will have three independent wings, one for offices, one for reading rooms, and one for stacks.

The National Library at Milan dates from 1763 when a private library of Count Carlo Pertusati was purchased by the government and placed at the service of the public. It enjoyed the sponsorship of Empress Maria Theresa of Austria and received several
large gifts through her interest. In the nineteenth century it grew
steadily, concentrating its acquisitions in the fields of Italian drama
and the history of Lombardy. By the 1930's, it had over half million printed works and about 2,000 important manuscripts. The National Library in Venice is the famous Biblioteca Marciana, originally begun with the collection donated by Cardinal Bessarion in
1468. Although it contains only about a half million printed volumes, its manuscript collection of some 13,000 volumes is invaluable and contains some of the rarest early medieval codices in existence. The National Library at Turin is one of the most recent
to be so designated, having been formerly the Biblioteca Civica
founded in 1868. It is housed in an eighteenth-century palace remodeled for library purposes. Considering them collectively, the
national libraries of Italy from both a cultural heritage and asset
that will rank with the national libraries of any of the Western nations.

In Spain and Portugal the national libraries are also of relatively modern growth. That of Spain dates from the Royal Library
of Philip V, founded in 1712. The King himself gave 8,000 volumes to start the collection. It grew but slowly at first, having
but 30,000 volumes by 1750; but in the late eighteenth and early
nineteenth centuries it received many important gifts, including
some complete libraries, and by 1874 it had over 300,000 volumes.
In the 1880's the Spanish government purchased the library of the

Duke of Osuna, including 32,000 books and 2,700 manuscripts for the National Library. By the 1930's it had over 1,500,000 volumes, over 30,000 manuscripts, and thousands of prints, maps, and letters. Its strength lies in its holdings on Spain and Portugal, together with large collections on Arabic history and literature. It suffered from the fighting in Madrid during the Spanish Civil War of 1936-1939, but of course was not involved in the fighting of World War II as so many European libraries were. Since the 1930's it has been considerably modernized, and today its facilities are among the best of any large research library on the continent. In Lisbon, the National Library of Portugal was founded in 1796, largely from the contents of suppressed monasteries. For this reason its collection even in the twentieth century is heavily theological, although it is also strong in Portuguese history and literature. By the 1930's it contained some 600,000 volumes, with over 13,000 manuscripts.

Of the smaller nations of northern Europe, probably the most interesting national library is that of Belgium. This collection, parts of which go back to the fifteenth-century Dukes of Burgundy, was officially created in 1837 after Belgium became an independent nation. This "Bibliothèque Royale" was made up of three older libraries, including a private library compiled by Charles van Hulthem of Ghent, bought by the Belgian government in 1836; the remnants of the library of the House of Burgundy; and the Public Library of the city of Brussels. In the fifteenth and sixteenth centuries the various Dukes of Burgundy had built up a considerable family library, and this together with other "royal" libraries in the Low Countries were brought together in one Royal Library at Brussels in 1599. There were at this time 958 volumes of manuscript and 683 of print. After a flurry of interest at this time the library was neglected for nearly a century, and in fact was largely destroyed in a fire in 1731. The remaining volumes were stored for many years, and although a royal library was again constituted on paper in 1754, very little came of it. In 1772, under the guidance of a literary society, the collection was made public, and the library was augmented with many gifts and arranged for use. The

French Revolution saw much of the library taken by French troops as spoils of war, but at least some of the volumes were later returned. The closing of monasteries brought thousands of books into the Royal Library during the Napoleonic era, and by 1810 it was larger than ever before. By the time the new national library was created in 1837, the collections brought together totaled over 200,000 volumes with 3,000 manuscripts.

In the later nineteenth century a series of good administrators brought rapid growth to the Belgian Royal Library, with additions to the original building to house the new acquisitions. World War I saw the library closed temporarily by the conquering German armies, but it was later reopened and suffered little material damage. Complete reorganization and modernization came after the war, and by the 1930's the Library contained over a million volumes and some 30,000 manuscripts. Again in World War II the Belgian national library was fortunate in escaping material damage, and since 1945 it has moved into a new building and greatly expanded its bibliographic and library services.

The National Library of the Netherlands dates from the French Revolutionary period, when the private library of the ruler, William V, was taken over by the French-dominated government and opened to the public in 1798. After several moves and different names, the library again became a Royal Library under the new King William I in 1819, and it was housed in a wing of the former palace, although it was now a public library. As it grew it took over all of the palace building, and then in the later nineteenth century added wings to form a solid block of buildings. It has been increased by many gifts and purchases of large collections, so that by the end of World War I it had over a million volumes and 6,000 manuscripts. It has always been a library for use, rather than preservation, and it forms a part of a nation-wide system of public libraries that is probably one of the most effective in Europe.

In Switzerland, a small nation with many fine libraries, the national library was created only in 1893. By 1934, however, when it moved into a new and modern building, it had over half million volumes and 1,500 manuscripts. It concentrates on collecting ma-

terial on the history and literature of Switzerland, particularly since
the 1890's. It cooperates very closely with other reference and
university libraries throughout the nation, both in selection and in
usage of books.

In the Scandinavian countries, the national libraries vary
considerably in age, size, and function. The Danish Royal Library
came into existence in the 1660's, when King Frederick III acquired three private libraries and installed them in a separate library building. Containing only about 20,000 volumes at this time,
the library grew rapidly through gifts and purchases until by 1750
it had over 70,000 books. Under some rulers and some library
directors, it was neglected, but in general it continued to grow.
In the nineteenth century it tended to limit its acquisitions to the
humanities, while the Royal University Library collected books in
the sciences. It also has a large collection on the history of Denmark and one of the largest collections on Iceland and in the Icelandic language in existence. It was moved into a new building in
1906, and by the 1930's its collection numbered some one million
volumes plus about 30,000 manuscripts.

The Royal Swedish Library in Stockholm owes its beginning
to the book-collecting activities of King Gustavus Vasa in the mid-
sixteenth century. Many books were added when monastery libraries were closed in the same century. Since 1661 the library has
enjoyed the right of legal deposit for all books published in Sweden,
and in many years these accessions were about all obtained by the
library. However, in the eighteenth century the private libraries
amassed by the Kings of Sweden (including 15,000 volumes from
Gustavus III and 7,500 volumes from Gustavus IV) were added to
the library, and its size and importance increased steadily. Several other private libraries were added in the nineteenth century, and
by 1878, when it was moved out of the royal palace and into its
own building, it numbered over 200,000 volumes. Since then its
holdings in printed volumes have grown to nearly a million, while
its collection of manuscripts numbers some 12,000 and its printed
miscellanea numbers over 1,500,000. Like the Danish Royal Library it concentrates largely on the humanities and social sciences,

leaving the physical sciences to the special and university libraries.

Norway has no royal library as such, but the library of the Royal Frederick University at Oslo, founded in 1811, serves as one in most respects. Housed at first in the former home of a noble, the University Library moved into its own building on the campus in 1850, and when this was outgrown, into a new one in 1914. In addition to serving the needs of the University, the library collects everything possible on the history and literature of Norway, and through purchases and exchanges, obtains as much as possible of the modern literature of other nations. Its holdings were well over a million volumes in the 1930's, and although it lacks much of the medieval manuscripts and early printed works present in other European national libraries, its holdings in literature since 1800 are among the best in Europe.

The smaller and newer nations of Europe present a variety of aspects to the international library scene, but for the most part they have all grown considerably since 1920. In the Balkan countries the national libraries often contain treasures in manuscripts obtained from ancient monasteries, but these libraries are smaller and more poorly financed than those in the larger countries. After World War I some library progress was made in such countries as Poland, Finland, Bulgaria, and Rumania, only to be set back in one way or the other during World War II. The Yugoslav national library in Belgrade was, for example, destroyed in military action. However, since 1945, with most of these countries under Communist domination, the emphasis on books and libraries has been remarkable, and the national libraries have grown accordingly. The Bulgarian National Library in Sofia, founded in 1879, had about 750,000 volumes in the early 1960's. In Yugoslavia, each of the six states has a state library in its capital. In Finland the library of the University of Helsinki serves as the national library. Whatever the situation, the national library in each country tends to serve as a bibliographic center for the nation, and its cultural importance is if anything stronger now than ever before.

To summarize, then, the national libraries of Europe present together a magnificent cultural heritage in graphic form. They have

grown over the centuries by many means -- gifts, bequests, confis-
cations, military conquest, legal deposit, and purchase -- and have
preserved their collections poorly or well at various times and
places, but they have preserved them. Today they are often poorly
housed, imperfectly cataloged, and sometimes difficult to use.
They are faced with a multitude of problems: inadequate funds,
housing, and staffs; inability to obtain and control the volume of
graphic materials being produced; difficulty in keeping up with the
new methods brought on by the revolutions in science and technology; and often additional difficulties brought on by national and international political developments. Yet, despite these problems,
they are on the whole forging ahead, individually and collectively,
and attempting to maintain their positions as cultural centers.
Their history is by no means all behind them, and their position
today in the Western World is stronger than ever.

Additional Readings

(Published material on the history of the European national libraries is plentiful. Almost all of the national libraries and the state
libraries of Germany have not one but several published histories.
The literature on the national libraries in periodicals and pamphlets
is also generous.)

Assmann, Kurt
  Sachsische Landesbibliothek Dresden, 1556-1956. Leipzig, 1956.
    304 p.

Barwick, George F.
  The reading room of the British Museum. London, 1929. 174 p.

Brummel, L.
  Geschiedenis der Koninklijke Bibliotheek. Leiden, 1939.
    x, 215 p.

Burton, Margaret
  Famous libraries of the world: their history, collections, and
    administration. London, 1937. xix, 458 p.

Cain, Julien
  Les transformations de la Bibliothèque Nationale de 1936 à 1959.
    Paris, 1959. 74 p.

Carini Dainotti, V.
La biblioteca nazionale 'Vittorio Emanuele' al Collegio Romano.
Florence, 1956. 217 p.

Davis, W. L.
The National Library of Wales: A survey of its history.
Aberystwyth, 1937. 236 p.

Délisle, Leopold
La Bibliothèque Nationale en 1875. Nogent-Le-Totrou, 1875.
52 p.

Deutsche Staatsbibliothek, Berlin.
Deutsche Staatsbibliothek, 1661-1962. Pt. 1, Geschichte und
Gegenwart. Berlin, 1962. xii, 469 p.

Edwards, Edward
Lives of the founders of the British Museum, with notices of its
chief benefactors . . . London, 1870. 780 p.

Esdaile, Arundell
National libraries of the world. London, 1934. xii, 386 p.

Fabritius, Albert
Det Kongelige Biblioteks embedsmaend og funktioneerer, 1653-
1943. Copenhagen, 1943. 216 p.

Fava, Domenico
La Biblioteca Nazionale Centrale di Firenze e le sue insigni
recolte. Milan, 1939. xix, 242 p.

Franklin, Alfred
Histoire de la Bibliothèque Mazarine et du Palais de l'Institute.
2nd ed. Paris, 1901. xxxii, 401 p.

Godet, Marcel
La Bibliothèque Nationale Suisse, son histoire, ses collections,
son nouvel édifice. Berne, 1932. 46 p.

Gorrini, Giovanni
L'Incendio della Biblioteca Nazionale di Torino.
Turin, 1904. 292 p.

Halm, Hans
Die Schicksale der Bayerischen Staatsbibliothek während des
Zweiten Weltkrieges. Munich, 1949. 70 p.

Hamburg. Staats-und-Universitäts-Bibliothek.
Der Wiederaufbau der Staats- und Universitäts-Bibliothek, 1951-
1954. Hamburg, 1954. 84 p.

Hopf, W.
Die Landesbibliothek Kassel, 1580-1930. Leipzig, 1930. 254 p.

Klevenskii, M. M.
   Geschichte der Staatlichen Lenin-Bibliothek der USSR. Leipzig,
      1955. 158 p.

Koch, Theodore W.
   The Imperial Public Library at St. Petersburg. New York,
      1915. 35 p.

La Serna Santander, Charles Antoine de
   Mémoire historique sur la Bibliothèque dite de Bourgogne.
      Brussels, 1809. iv, 216 p.

Le Prince, Nicolas T.
   Essai bibliographique sur la bibliothèque du Roi . . . Paris,
      1856. v, 466 p. (Originally published in 1782).

Lomeier, Johannes
   De bibliothecis . . . Zutphen, 1669. (Chapter 10, on Euro-
      pean libraries, translated and edited by J. W. Montgomery
      as A seventeenth century view of European libraries,
      Berkeley, 1962. 181 p.)

Lundstedt, Bernhard
   Om Kunglige Biblioteket i Stockholm. Stockholm, 1879. 16 p.

Netherlands. Royal Library.
   Koninklijke Bibliotheek Gedenkboek, 1798-1948. The Hague,
      1948. 240 p.

Partridge, R. C. Barrington
   The history of the legal deposit of books throughout the British
      Empire. London, 1938. 364 p.

Rawlings, Gertrude B.
   The British Museum Library. London, Grafton, 1916. 231 p.

Shelley, H. C.
   The British Museum: its history and treasures . . . Boston,
      1911. xii, 355 p.

Switzerland. National Library.
   La Bibliothèque Nationale Suisse: un demi-siècle d'activité,
      1895-1945. Bern, 1945. ix, 188 p.

UNESCO
   National libraries, their problems and prospects, symposium on
      national libraries in Europe. Paris, 1960. 125 p.

Weber, Ulrich
   Wilhelm Brambach und die Reorganization der Grossherzoglich
      Badischen Hof- und Landsbibliothek in Karlsruhe, 1874-
      1904. Cologne, 1954. 73 p.

Yugoslavia.   Narodna Biblioteka.
  Istorija Narodne Biblioteke u Beogradu.   Belgrade, 1960.
    264 p.

Zwiedineck-Südenhorst, Hans von
  Die Steiermärkische Landes-Bibliothek.   Graz, 1893. 24 p.

11.

European University Libraries Since 1500

By 1500 the university was a well-established institution on the European scene. Although they differed widely in organization from country to country and even from institution to institution, the universities were on the whole a powerful cultural influence that had few competitors in the era that changed the Western World from medieval to modern. Some of the universities were strongly theological in emphasis, while others turned more toward the professional schools of law and medicine. In either case the liberal arts were more often considered mere handmaidens to the professions and not ends in themselves. In the same manner, libraries differed considerably from university to university. In some there were major central or university libraries; in others the college libraries were all important, with little or no central collection. In still others the emphasis was on faculty or departmental libraries. In any case the university communities depended heavily on the "stationers," or booksellers and renters, who gathered around every campus.

Two factors combined to bring about a relatively large increase in the number of books in the university libraries after 1500. One of these was the invention of printing, which made available large numbers of books at a comparatively low cost. The printing press to some extent also relieved the libraries of some responsibilities in that the students were able to buy and keep their own books rather than depending so heavily upon the library texts. The other factor resulted from the political suppression of the monasteries. From the sixteenth century through the nineteenth, in various parts of Europe at different times, monasteries were closed and in many cases their books and manuscripts eventually reached the shelves of university libraries. Other libraries also benefited from this situation, but particularly in central Europe it was most often the universities and colleges.

170

At the University of Paris the most important and the largest of the many college libraries was that of the Sorbonne. From about 2,500 volumes, mostly manuscript, at the end of the fifteenth century, the Sorbonne collection grew slowly through periods of successive prosperity and decline with the fortunes of the University as a whole. By the time of the French Revolution it contained only about 25,000 volumes and some 2,000 manuscripts. At the beginning of the Revolution, the Committee of Public Instruction ordered the Sorbonne Library opened to the public at large, and although this was done for two days per week for a while, the arrangement did not satisfy the Revolutionary authorities, and it was completely closed in 1792 along with the remainder of the University. The Sorbonne Library remained intact, however, until it was seized and divided in 1795. The printed volumes were distributed to the public libraries of Paris, while the manuscripts were taken to the Bibliothèque Nationale. When the University of Paris was reopened after the Napoleonic era, a new Bibliothèque de la Sorbonne was established, and in 1861 the name was changed to Bibliothèque de la Université. Since then its growth has been steady, so that by 1900 it was approaching a million volumes in all of its departments. In 1897 the Sorbonne Library was moved into new quarters with a reading room seating 300 persons and two stack rooms of five floors each.

In all, the University of Paris has five major libraries and a number of smaller departmental and institute collections. Besides the Sorbonne, which now serves as the library of the college of arts and sciences, there are the libraries of the colleges of law, medicine and pharmacy, and the Bibliothèque Ste. Geneviève. The library of the Faculty of Medicine dates from the late fourteenth century, and its holdings by 1500 numbered only about 1,100 volumes. In 1509 the system of chaining the most used volumes to the reading desks was adopted and this system was used for nearly three hundred years. During the French Revolution the medical library profited to some extent in that it was combined with the library of the Royal Society of Medicine, and the entire collection moved into a new building to serve the medical college. By 1900

it contained about 180,000 volumes and was one of the best medical
libraries in Europe.   The library of the Faculty of Law was formed
in 1772 and included some 80,000 volumes by 1900, while that of
the Faculty of Pharmacy was not begun until about 1882 but owned
50,000 volumes by 1900.

The fifth library of the University, that of Ste. Geneviève,
is probably the oldest of the five, dating from the twelfth century.
Originally the library of the Abbaye of Ste. Geneviève, it remained
small until the sixteenth century, when the printing press and many
gifts increased its size considerably.   Numbering some 40,000 volumes by 1710, it was then a semipublic library, noted as being
open to "all honest men who requested admittance."   Apparently the
librarian at that time had staff problems much as modern librarians do, since he reported that a gift of books received seventeen
years earlier had still not been cataloged.   Though it lost some of
its rarer manuscripts during the French Revolution, it survived as
a whole, and by 1860 claimed 160,000 printed books and 5,000
manuscripts.   By 1900 its holdings had grown to 350,000 volumes,
and in its strong collections of literature on the history of France
and Europe in general it was one of the most valuable libraries in
Paris.   After years of separate administration as a government-
owned library, the Bibliothèque Ste. Geneviève was placed under
the administration of the University of Paris in the 1930's.

Elsewhere in Paris there are some 30 other major college
and university libraries, and of course several hundred throughout
France.   Some of them that might be mentioned include the library
of the Catholic Institute of Paris, with a half million volumes; that
of the University of Montpelier with 800,000 volumes; University
of Aix-Marseilles (600,000 volumes in the two libraries); University of Besançon (200,000 volumes); University of Bordeaux
(450,000 volumes in the central library and the library of the
Faculty of Medicine); University of Caen (600,000 volumes); University of Grenoble (375,000 volumes); University of Lyons
(325,000 volumes); University of Nancy (nearly 1,000,000 volumes);
University of Poitiers (300,000 volumes); University of Rennes
(350,000 volumes); and the University of Strasbourg (nearly

3,000,000 volumes). Aside from these, there are over a hundred specialized colleges and institutes, many of them in Paris, but others scattered throughout France, with libraries ranging from 5,000 to 100,000 volumes, according to their needs and age. Especially since World War II, the number of specialized scientific institutions has grown considerably.

Generally speaking, the universities founded in France before 1500 reached a high point in the fourteenth and fifteenth centuries and declined in size and importance from that time to the Revolution. Virtually no new institutions were established between 1500 and 1800, and the Revolution saw the disruption, if not the end, for many of them, especially those with strong church connections. Education was "nationalized" during and after the Revolution, but some church colleges were allowed to recommence in the later nineteenth century. The late nineteenth and early twentieth century has seen the establishment of a number of new colleges and institutes. Some of them rely heavily on established libraries for their students and faculty, but most of them have developed strong libraries of their own. World War I saw the destruction of some university libraries in northeastern France, particularly that of the University of Nancy, but in most cases these were rebuilt in the 1920's and considerably enlarged. In World War II the University of Caen saw most of its buildings, including the library, destroyed by bombing, and some other college and university libraries were damaged in the invasion area of northern France. Since World War II the libraries of France's institutions of higher education have been faced with the usual problems of crowded conditions and a shortage of staff members, but they are meeting their problems to some extent with new methods and inter-library cooperation. Although many of them have difficulty in keeping up with the great influx of contemporary publications, their holdings in manuscripts, incunabula, and other historical research materials make them of almost unlimited value to scholars in the social sciences and humanities.

Down to the nineteenth century, the universities of England were in reality only two -- Oxford and Cambridge. The libraries

of these two venerable institutions were already centuries old by
1500, but the religious troubles of the following century severely
crippled them.   When Henry VIII ordered the dissolution of the
monasteries and religious orders in 1537, it marked the beginning
of one of the most tragic destructions of books in history.   Thousands of invaluable and irreplaceable books and manuscripts were
wantonly destroyed.   At first the university libraries benefited to
some extent, with acquisitions from some of the closed monastery
collections, but later they too were forced to have their contents
"censored" and almost decimated in numbers.   Many books were
seized by agents of the king and sold as wastepaper, although some
volumes found their way to collectors on the continent and a few
were saved by zealous collectors in England.   The Universities'
turn came in the 1550's when Royal Commissioners almost completely destroyed the remainder of the Cambridge and Oxford libraries.   For several decades both universities were almost completely devoid of libraries, even in the colleges.   About the only libraries left in England were those at the older cathedrals.   A contemporary writer, John Bale, approved the end of the monastic
orders but deplored the destruction of the books:

> If there had been in every shire but one single library,
> to the preservation of those noble works, it had been
> well.   But to destroy all without consideration is and
> will be unto England forever a most horrible infamy.

The central library at Oxford found its rebirth in 1602 when
the activities of Sir Thomas Bodley resulted in the reforming of the
library there with the gift of his own private collection and the purchase of many volumes in Europe.   He himself had travelled on the
continent many times, both as a private citizen and as a government envoy, and he knew the best sources of books and manuscripts.
Thomas James was selected as the first librarian of the new library that was to become known as the "Bodleian."   James issued
the first printed catalog of the library, numbering about 2,000
titles, in 1605.   When Bodley died in 1613, he further endowed the
library, and its growth since that date has been continuous.   In addition to the University library, the various college libraries at Oxford were reconstituted in the late sixteenth and early seventeenth

centuries, and as new colleges were formed, each of them began a library of its own. Wadham College, Oxford, was founded in 1612, with a library beginning the following year. Pembroke College, founded in 1624, was fortunate in having a library from the beginning. The Bodleian Library moved into a new, separate library building in 1612, and several of the college libraries also moved into their own buildings, as distinct from being rooms or halls in other structures. By 1620 the Bodleian claimed 16,000 volumes, and by 1700 nearly 30,000. During the seventeenth century it had obtained two important gifts, a collection of 1,300 manuscripts given by Archbishop Laud and a library of 8,000 volumes donated by a lawyer, John Selden. In 1714 a physician, John Radcliffe endowed a library of science and medicine at Oxford with a building of its own. In the mid-nineteenth century this library and building were given to the trustees of the Bodleian and thus became a part of the main libraries. By 1900 the Oxford University libraries contained over 800,000 volumes and 41,000 manuscripts.

After the disturbances of the sixteenth century, the library at Cambridge University had only a few volumes, and so slow was its growth that by 1650 it still had only about 1,000 books and 400 manuscripts. After the Restoration of King Charles II, Cambridge received some royal attention, and in addition the library gained several large bequests of books and manuscripts. Henry Lucas left a collection of 4,000 volumes to Cambridge in 1666, and Bishop Tobias Rustat presented an endowment of L1000, the proceeds of which were to be used for the purchase of books. In 1715, King George I gave to the University the library of Bishop Moore, numbering some 30,000 volumes and very strong in early English history and literature. In 1755, Cambridge moved its library into a new building, and by 1900 its holdings had reached a million volumes.

Although Oxford and Cambridge were for centuries the only universities in England, other universities were established in Scotland and Ireland. The University of Glasgow, founded in 1453, had a notable library almost from the beginning, while St. Andrews University, also in Scotland, has a library dating from 1610. The

library at the University of Edinburgh was founded in 1583, largely
with funds and books donated by Clement Little, a wealthy merchant-
lawyer. A fourth Scottish university, at Aberdeen, was in operation by 1634, but never equalled the others in size or importance.
In Ireland, the library of Trinity College in Dublin was begun with
a gift of books by the English Army after a victory over the Irish
in the Battle of Kinsale, 1601. By 1604 this collection had 4,000
volumes, and it grew steadily after that to become the most important library in Ireland. James Usher, later primate of Ireland,
directed the early growth of the collection, and on his death in
1655, willed his own library of 7,000 volumes and 600 manuscripts
to it.

Elsewhere in England and Scotland several new universities
and colleges emerged in the nineteenth and twentieth centuries, and
some of these have built up imposing libraries. Among those that
might be mentioned are the University of Durham, begun in 1832;
the University of London (1837); Victoria University at Manchester
(1851); and the University of Liverpool (1882). By mid-century
each of these universities had libraries ranging from 100,000 to
500,000 in their main collections, not counting the books and periodicals in their institute and departmental collections. Many of
these subsidiary libraries are quite large, as evidenced by the situation at the University of London. There in 1960 all library units
related to the University taken together owned over three million
volumes. The 1930's brought new buildings to several British universities, including Cambridge (1934), Leeds (1936), Swansea
(1937), and London (1937). The new building at Cambridge was designed by Sir Giles Scott in a modern, functional design and with
an attached book-tower.

The library situation at Oxford in the 1950's, although not
typical, is illustrative of the height of university library organization. The Bodleian Library, usually considered the main University library, is actually only one of several libraries known as the
Bodleian group that includes the Radcliffe Camera, which contains
supplementary reading rooms; the Radcliffe Science Library; the
Library of Rhodes House; and the library of the Indian Institute.

In addition to these there are literally dozens of other libraries at Oxford, including the college libraries, many of which are of major size and importance; and libraries of research institutes, museums, and clubs. Some of these are loosely joined together into larger units, while others are strictly independent. Altogether they represent easily some five million volumes, forming one of the most important research centers in the world.

Although university libraries began later in Germany than in France, England, and Italy, they early assumed an important role in the cultural history of the German states, and by the eighteenth century they were taking a lead in higher education in Europe. In many respects, the German universities may be said to have developed the first modern universities, as distinct from the medieval type, and to have taken the lead in the development of research on the university level. By 1500, German universities had been established at Cologne, Erfurt, Freiburg, Greisswald, Heidelberg, Leipzig, Munich, Rostock, and Tübingen. In the sixteenth century came those at Marburg, Würzburg, Königsberg, Wittenberg, and Jena. Later German universities of importance include Giessen, established in 1607; Kiel (1665); Göttingen (1737); and Bonn (1777).

The German university libraries suffered much during the religious wars of the sixteenth century, but they also gained many valuable volumes when the monasteries were closed in some areas. In fact, some of the universities founded during this century began with libraries almost completely taken from nearby monasteries. The seventeenth century saw much of Germany involved in the Thirty Years' War, with the universities and their libraries again suffering in many cases; but the eighteenth century saw a definite revival of interest in higher learning. Leipzig University's library, for example, began in 1543 with books taken from a closed Dominican monastery, and by 1700 it still had only a few thousand volumes. However, its growth in the eighteenth and nineteenth centuries was such that by 1900 it contained over one-half million volumes. Göttingen University, on the other hand, was not begun until 1737, and in 30 years its library numbered 60,000 books. With steady growth, including many large gifts, it had 200,000 volumes by 1812 and 536,000 by 1900.

Although the French Revolution and the Napoleonic wars
brought more disruption to German universities, they soon over-
came these handicaps. Not only did the central collections increase in size in the nineteenth century, but the many separate college, faculty, and institute libraries grew accordingly. By 1875,
the German university libraries were individually and collectively
among the best research libraries in the world. Not only were
their book collections excellent, but their librarians were leaders
among the profession and provided a scholarly example for librarians of other places and later eras to follow. Many noted scholars
were librarians in Germany, including the dramatists Goethe and
Lessing and the philosopher Leibniz. Others noted mainly for their
librarianship were also scholars in other fields, as in the case of
Otto Hartwig, librarian at the University of Halle in the late nineteenth century and also an outstanding scholar in the field of medieval Italian history. New ideas of librarianship, down to 1875,
either originated in German libraries or were quickly adopted and
adapted to German needs.

The twentieth century has seen both great disasters and
great progress for German libraries of all types. Although university libraries were not physically damaged during World War I,
they suffered from a lack of staff, funds, and foreign publications.
The needs of science and industry, emphasized by the war, did encourage the growth of technical institutes and colleges, some connected with universities and some independent. The Hitler period
saw university libraries subjugated to the Nazi philosophy, but in
general they did not suffer from book purges and book burnings as
much as the public libraries. World War II brought tremendous
physical destruction in the Allied air raids on Germany. The university libraries at Bonn, Breslau, Frankfurt, Giessen, Göttingen,
Jena, Kiel, Munich, Münster, and Würzburg were either destroyed
or heavily damaged, with in many cases losses of staff lives. At
Jena, for example, 16 staff members were killed in one bombing
raid. At Hamburg over 700,000 volumes were lost -- almost the
entire collection of the combination State and University Library

there -- while at Frankfurt over 600, 000 volumes were destroyed, and at Würzburg over 350, 000.

After the war Germany was divided into East Germany and West Germany, with the former becoming a Communist state under the tutelage of Soviet Russia. Here the universities of Jena, Leipzig, and Rostock, for example, have been converted into centers of Communist learning, and the libraries have become instruments in the general state policy of Communist indoctrination. At first the libraries were severely purged of all pro-Nazi or anti-Communist literature; but then with the emphasis on books and learning that is an earmark of Communist countries, the empty shelves were quickly filled with proper Communist literature, and these universities have rapidly regained their position in the library world, at least in number of volumes. In 1960, the University of Jena library had some 1, 200, 000 volumes; that of Rostock, 850, 000; and Leipzig, more than 1, 700, 000.

In West Germany the postwar period has also seen remarkable recovery. One new university, the Free University of West Berlin, has already grown to nearly a million volumes, while the University of Frankfurt library, after having been almost destroyed, has come back to over 1, 200, 000 volumes. Major problems in West German university libraries since 1945 have been, besides rebuilding and recouping war losses, the acquisition of foreign publications missed during the Hitler and war years. The training of new staff members for the tasks brought on by crowded quarters, large numbers of students, great influxes of books and materials, and new methods of controlling that material, have also been major tasks. German libraries have traditionally been the workshops of scholars rather than the study halls or required reading rooms for undergraduates, hence a new outlook or philosophy of librarianship was needed for this new era. Then, too, the traditional problem of institute libraries connected with the universities remains unsolved. These libraries contain thousands, sometimes tens of thousands, of volumes, but the lack of a campus union catalog or of central planning of purchases results in much duplication and confusion in the use of the various collections. However, progress

is being made, and the German university libraries are rapidly re-
suming their former prominent position in world library circles.

In Italy, where the medieval universities began and flourished,
the period since 1500 has seen less progress than the auspicious
beginnings might have promised. By 1500 there were already
strong universities at Bologna, Camerino, Catania, Ferrara, Florence, Genoa, Modena, Naples, Padua, Parma, Pavia, Perugia,
Rome, Siena, and Turin. New ones in the sixteenth century included Messina, Sassari on Sardinia, and Urbino, with Cagliari
coming shortly after in 1606. After this, with the exceptions of
Palermo in 1779 and Trieste in 1877, no new Italian universities of
note were established until the twentieth century. In most cases
central libraries were not begun until long after the establishment
of the universities, and in a few cases central libraries have never
been established. Instead, institute and college libraries have always been prominent around Italian universities, and some of them
have large and valuable collections. Padua did not have a central
library until 1629, and Bologna not until 1712, although universities
established later, such as Messina and Sassari, had central libraries from the beginning. Major gifts have frequently been responsible for the largest growth of Italian libraries, as when Bartholomew Selvatico bequeathed his library of books and manuscripts to
Padua in 1630, or when Luigi Marsigli gave an important group of
Greek, Arabic, Turkish, and Persian manuscripts to Bologna in
1712.

Italian university libraries suffered less from wars in the
sixteenth and seventeenth centuries than those of northern Europe,
but at the same time they grew only slowly. Even by the nineteenth century collections usually numbered less than 100,000, and
in many cases these were valuable research materials; they were,
however, hardly suitable for current student use. Italian university libraries also suffered from lack of staff and poor organization. However, the unification of Italy in the late nineteenth century soon brought increased emphasis on the growth of universities
and their libraries, and most of them were taken over as state-
controlled institutions. In the twentieth century, new public univer-

sities have been established in Bari and Milan, and the Catholic
University of the Sacred Heart also began at Milan.   The Mussolini
period from 1924 to 1945 saw the Italian university libraries subjugated to the demands of Fascist politics, but not so much so as in
Hitlerian Germany.   During World War II there was some damage
to university libraries with the University of Naples probably suffering most.   Some 200,000 volumes were lost in a fire there in 1943.
Since World War II, Italian university libraries have grown tremendously, but much of the growth has been in the form of libraries for new institutions of higher education, particularly those of
scientific institutes and colleges for teacher education.   As of
1960, sizes of the university libraries vary considerably, with only
a few having over a million volumes.   The University of Florence,
in its various campus libraries, has over two million volumes,
while those at the University of Rome have close to a million.
Most other university libraries contain less than half that figure,
but it should be noted that many of them are in centers where other
large libraries are located, and the students and faculty take full
advantage of these.   Lack of coordination between central and pe-
ripheral libraries on the same campus is also a problem in Italy.

Universities in Spain and Portugal have also had long histories, but for the most part small libraries.   Although only three
university libraries in both countries established before 1500,
(those at Coimbra in Portugal, and Barcelona and Salamanca in
Spain), have survived into the twentieth century, five others were
established just after that date: Granada, Madrid, Santiago, Seville, and Valencia.   The University of Ovieta followed in 1604 and
La Laguna in 1701.   Modern Spanish universities include those at
Murica, established in 1915, and Comillas in 1890.   In Portugal,
universities were established at Oporto in 1803 and in Lisbon in
1911.   In 1803 the older church-related universities were for the
most part closed or continued as secular institutions, but at Salamanca a new Catholic university was reopened in 1940.   Hence,
today there are two universities descended from the original University of Salamanca, one Catholic and one public.   When the original university was closed, the libraries of its four colleges, with

many manuscripts and incunabula, were transferred to the Royal Library in Madrid, so that the present libraries of both institutions are relatively modern.

During the Spanish Civil War in the 1930's, the University of Madrid suffered when its campus was virtually a battlefield for some of the hardest fighting. Also, the University of Valencia library was severely damaged in a disastrous fire in 1932. Otherwise the twentieth-century history of Spanish and Portuguese libraries has been one of steady growth, with both central collections and subsidiary libraries increasing in size and importance. Today the libraries of the Universities of Madrid in Spain and Coimbra in Portugal are the largest in those countries, each numbering more than a million volumes in its campus collections. With the exception of the Catholic institutions, the universities are all publicly controlled. Like their Italian counterparts, they suffer from lack of organization and from a failure to consider the needs of the undergraduate student.

Quite another story in university libraries is that found in Russia. There universities were late in beginning and grew only slowly until the twentieth century. Since the Russian Revolution, however, the university libraries have grown tremendously, both in size and numbers, and they constitute today an important part of the over-all library program in the Soviet Union. The oldest university in Russia proper is the University of Moscow, founded by M. V. Lomonosov in 1755. Its library began at the same time with a gift of books by the founder. It was joined early in the nineteenth century by universities at St. Petersburg, Kazan, Kharkov, Kiev, Dorpat, and Odessa. University libraries were for the most part small in the early nineteenth century. Along with the central collections, popular student libraries as well as the typical professional libraries developed. Moscow University grew most rapidly, being favored with over a hundred major gifts of private collections. The University of Kazan Library was fortunate in having the mathematician Nikolai Lobachevski as librarian from 1825 to 1835, and he made of it the best-organized library in Russia, complete with a full catalog and his own classification system. In 1834 it moved

into its own new building, and shortly afterward it began a card
catalog.

Something of the development of Russian university libraries
in the late nineteenth century can be gathered from their bookstocks
in 1876.   At that time the University of Moscow had about 100,000
volumes; St. Petersburg, 50,000; Odessa, 40,000; Kiev, 135,000
with an additional 15,000 in student libraries; and Dorpat (now the
University of Tartu), 125,000 volumes.   In the generation just preceding the Russian Revolution, library growth was slow, but there
was an emphasis on collecting Russian history and literature and
securing scientific journals from the Western nations.   The Revolution itself saw great changes in both the universities and their libraries, and new universities were being established in the Com-
munist-held areas even before the Revolution was over.   The Ural
State University at Sverdlovsk was founded by Lenin himself, and
by 1925 there were universities in virtually every part of the Soviet Union.   The importance of the Soviet university libraries in the
period since 1925 can hardly be underestimated.   The Communist
effort to educate all the people to the highest degree of which they
are capable has brought an emphasis on education and libraries unsurpassed anywhere else in the world.   Although the libraries have
served a propaganda purpose and at times have been severely curtailed to keep out non-Communist ideas, they have undoubtedly
served to help bring the people of the Soviet Union from the Middle
Ages to the twentieth century in a little more than a generation.

During World War II, many university libraries in the
Ukraine, White Russia, and even in Moscow and Leningrad were
severely damaged if not completely destroyed.   The State University of Leningrad, for example, was almost completely destroyed
in the fighting for that city, but much of its library had already
been moved to Saratov, and after 1945 it was rebuilt even larger
than before.   Since World War II, more universities have been established in the Soviet Union, along with scores of technical and
scientific institutes.   Each of these is well equipped with a library,
particularly in scientific subjects.   The humanities and social sciences are often neglected in the library holdings, and are complete-

ly controlled in content. The Marxist-Leninist philosophy is of
course an exception, and many books in multiple copies represent
this subject, which is virtually a curriculum in itself in Soviet colleges. In 1960 the Moscow State University had over five million
volumes in its combined central and departmental collections, and
it received over 2, 000 foreign periodicals as well as all major Russian publications. It has a total of 45 separate reading rooms in
its various facilities, with a seating capacity in all of 1, 900. Its
budget for books and materials totals over a million rubles annually, and it circulates over five million books per year. This is one
of the largest of Russian university libraries, but there are many
others with over a million volumes each. All university libraries
are under the direction of the Higher Education Ministry which controls in all more than 765 universities, colleges, institutes, academies, and conservatories.

In territories acquired at the end of World War II, Russia
gained control over three universities even older than that at Moscow. These are the universities at Lvov, formerly in Poland,
dating back to 1661; Vilna, formerly in Lithuania, founded in 1579;
and Königsberg, formerly in East Prussia, founded in 1509. Each
of these is now thoroughly Sovietized and integrated into the general
Communist library system.

Poland's university libraries go back well into the fourteenth
century, when the University of Cracow was founded in 1364.
Called the Jagellonian University since it was reorganized in 1400
by Ladislas Jagellon, this university has played a prominent part
in the history of Poland. Copernicus studied there in the fifteenth
century. Although other early universities were established in Lvov
and Vilna, now in the Soviet Union, Cracow University remained
the major institution of higher education in Poland down to the nineteenth century. A university was established in Warsaw in 1808, a
and several others were added when Poland was re-created as an
independent state in 1918. During World War II, the University of
Warsaw was forced to go "underground" when the Germans occupied
Poland, and its campus and libraries were virtually destroyed in
the early fighting in 1939 and the uprising of the Poles against the

Germans in 1944. However, these hardships only served to stir
the students and faculty to higher efforts. Today an entirely new
university has been rebuilt, and it is playing a major role in the
development of postwar Poland. The Jagellonian University was
closed by the Germans in 1939 and later reopened with its library
increased by books confiscated from the estates of executed Poles
and Jews. In 1944 the loyal members of the library staff secretly
collected Polish underground publications. When the German Army
retreated, they carried away some of the treasures from the university library, together with literally hundreds of thousands of new
acquisitions, which are now housed in a new library building, one
of the most modern in Europe.

Since 1945 other universities have been established in Poland,
including the Marie Curie Sklodowska University in Lublin, whose
central library now totals over 250,000 volumes; the University of
Lodz; and numerous technical and industrial institutes. Two universities are located in areas reclaimed by the Poles from Germany in 1945. These are the universities of Wroclaw (Breslau),
originally founded in 1505, and the Copernicus University at Torun
in Pomerania. University libraries in Poland, as in other Communist countries, have a double role to play in that they are agencies
of both education and indoctrination. However, those in Poland
are showing more independence than those in other Soviet-controlled
areas and are taking a position of leadership in the cultural and
technical development of their nation.

Poland's neighbor Czechoslovakia is also a nation with one
major ancient university and a variety of modern new ones. Charles
University, founded in Prague in 1348, became a state university in
1791. During the nineteenth century it was almost literally two
universities, one German and one Czech. During the centuries under Austro-Hungarian domination, the Czech universities found it
difficult to promote their native language and culture, but the university library did manage to acquire and preserve an outstanding
collection of works in Czech and other central Slavic languages.
Today its library numbers over 1,600,000 volumes. Other Czech
universities, most of them dating from the independence of Czecho-

slovakia in 1919 and later include the Comenius University in Bratislava (750,000 volumes), the Palacky University in Olomouc (570,000 volumes), the Purkyne University in Brno (1,000,000 volumes), and the Technical University in Prague (500,000 volumes). This latter university can be traced back to an engineering school founded in 1707, but it grew only slowly until after World War I. Since 1945 it has become the central technical library for the entire nation and coordinates technical bibliography for all of Czechoslovakia. The University at Brno has since 1945 received many books from several church-related colleges that have been closed. The Charles University Library also serves as the national library of Czechoslovakia, and its collection is the general bibliographic center for all nontechnical publications.

Yugoslavia has major universities for each of its states, usually located in the state capitals. The University of Belgrade, the Serbian university, was founded in 1863 and in 1960 had a library of over 700,000 volumes. In 1960, a branch of the university at Novi Sad was given full status as a second Serbian state university. The University of Zagreb, founded in 1669, is the Croatian state university and serves virtually as the state library as well. Descended from an early Jesuit college, its library is well stocked with both literary treasures of the Middle Ages and modern technical publications. It contains over a half-million volumes, not counting those in departmental and institute collections. The University of Sarajevo (1946) serves the combined states of Bosnia and Herzegovina; as a relatively new institution, it is served largely by faculty libraries, but a central library was in the planning stage in 1960. The University of Skoplje (1949) serves as the Macedonian state university, and its library is also in early stages of development. Finally, the University of Ljubljana, the state university for Slovenia, goes back to a church college founded in 1595, but in reality is largely a modern school founded in 1919. It has a central general library plus large collections in medicine, law, economics, and engineering. There are several other smaller colleges and a number of technical and industrial institutes with libraries to suit their needs.

Bulgaria has only one major university, the State University at Sofia, established in 1888 and enlarged considerably since 1945. Its central library numbers 360,000 volumes, with another 200,000 in the specialized related libraries. In Bulgaria today the greater part of higher education is being carried on in subject institutes, of which there is at least one specializing in every major scientific field. In addition to these there are a number of teachers colleges, preparing educators for the elementary and secondary schools. Most of the teachers colleges have relatively small libraries. Rumania has three state universities, at Bucharest, Cluj, and Jassy, with the latter having a library of over a million volumes. There are also technical institutes located in the major cities of Bucharest, Jassy, Timisoara, and Cluj. Hungary has universities at Budapest, Debrecen, Pecs, and Szeged, with several technical universities and other professional and scientific institutes. The largest university library is that at Budapest, numbering nearly 2 million volumes in its central, faculty, and institute libraries. This university, like others in central Europe, can trace its development back to a Jesuit college founded in the sixteenth century. The University of Debrecen and its library were established in eastern Hungary in the nineteenth century. Today its library contains over one million volumes, making it the third largest library in Hungary. Since 1945 several libraries from church-related institutions have been added to its collection, and in 1960 it was suffering considerably from lack of space, shortage of trained personnel, and a large arrearage in cataloging. All Hungarian universities are under the control of the Ministry of Culture and are financed by the government.

Austria has universities at Graz, Vienna, and Innsbruck, and also has technical universities at the first two cities. The older universities date back to the fourteenth, sixteenth, and seventeenth centuries, respectively, and their central libraries are virtual treasure houses of early books and manuscripts, whereas their faculty and institute libraries are more modern in contents and arrangement. The two technical universities are more modern, and their libraries reflect this fact. The library at the University of

Vienna has over a million volumes, while those at Graz and Innsbruck have well over a half million volumes each.

Belgium has major universities at Brussels, Ghent, and
Liège, each with libraries of over a million volumes. Belgian universities suffered considerably both in World War I and World War
II, and in addition the University of Brussels Library was virtually
destroyed by fire in 1886. The Catholic University of Louvain,
however, is historically one of the most important in Belgium. It
was founded in 1425 and served as an academic home for Erasmus
in the sixteenth century. Suppressed during the French Revolution,
it was restored in 1834, only to be destroyed in military action during World War I. Rebuilt in the 1920's with aid from friends
around the world, Louvain was again virtually destroyed in World
War II. It now receives some aid from the Belgian government and
ranks as one of the major university libraries of all Europe. Its
central, departmental and institute libraries contain in all over a
million volumes. Belgium also has a polytechnic university at Mons
and several technical institutes in various parts of the country.

The Netherlands' four major state universities at Leyden,
Groningen, Utrecht, and Amsterdam were founded by the seventeenth
century or earlier, and each has a long and glorious history. The
University of Leyden library, for example, was in operation as
early as 1575, and by 1610 it had a library consisting of 22 bookcases of about 40 books each. There were six cases of theology,
five of law, four of history, two each of philosophy, literature, and
medicine, and one of mathematics and science. This was one of
the greatest universities in Europe in the seventeenth century, with
students from many other nations attracted by the excellence of its
faculty. By 1960 the Dutch universities had libraries ranging in
size from some 400,000 at Groningen to nearly 2,000,000 at Amsterdam, and these four libraries, together with the Royal Library,
constitute something of a scholarly cooperative that works closely
together at all times. They cooperate in shared union catalogs and
also to some extent in book selection, particularly in specialized
fields. Other colleges and institutes with special collections also
join in this national library network, as do also some libraries of

learned societies and museums. The resulting organizations, by means of inter-library loans, avoids duplication of expensive and little-used materials, but also makes everything available in any one collection easily obtainable by the reader in any one of the co-operating libraries. In addition to their general collections in all major European languages, the Dutch research libraries have very strong collections on the history and literature of the Low Countries and also on Indonesia, where Dutch colonial influence was strong for so many years. Cooperation between university and public libraries is also common in the Netherlands, and at least one university library, that at Amsterdam, also serves as the municipal public library. Though most higher education is public, there are two major private universities in Holland, the Catholic University of Nijmegen and the Free Reformed University in Amsterdam.

Scandinavian universities, like their neighbors in Germany and the Netherlands, are strong combinations of both the old and the new. Fortunately, however, their libraries have not suffered as much from wars as have the more exposed ones on the continent proper, and their growth has been more steady over the years. Probably the oldest university in this area is that at Uppsala in Sweden. The University of Uppsala was founded in 1477, and although there was no central university library before 1620, there were available the local cathedral library and the libraries of the university student groups, or "nations." There were eventually to be 13 of these student groups, one for each province of Sweden, and there was considerable competition between them in building up their libraries. The central library began with a gift from King Gustavus Adolphus of his private library. In the subsequent Thirty Years' War, the libraries of several German monasteries were captured by the Swedish armies and presented to the library at Uppsala. With the gift of a large private library, that of Count Magnus Delagardie, in the later seventeenth century, the library at Uppsala reached some 30,000 volumes. Most of the contents were in Latin, however, until after 1692, when copyright deposit privileges for all books published in Sweden were granted to the University. The student libraries continued to function down through the nineteenth century, and by 1900 they contained anywhere from 2,000 to 30,000 volumes each, greatly supplementing the central library. By 1960, the central library alone contained over 1,200,000 volumes.

Other Swedish universities are those at Goteborg, Lund, and Stockholm; technical universities are also located in Goteborg and Stockholm. Their libraries range in size from about 150,000 to over one million volumes. There are also several professional and technical colleges and institutes with libraries of their own. Swedish libraries cooperate very closely, whether public, university, or institute, and virtually any book available in any publicly owned institution can be borrowed by any citizen in person, by mail, or by inter-library loan.

In Norway, the major university library is that at Oslo, with its million and one-half volumes. This library also serves as the national library for Norway, and it dates from 1811. The Technical University at Trondheim was opened in 1910, and it had by 1960 a library of some 250,000 volumes. A third university, that at Bergen, was begun in 1948, and its library is rapidly taking its place as one of the major libraries in the nation. There are also Norwegian colleges of agriculture, economics, and business administration, dentistry, veterinary science, and teacher training. Denmark's major university is that of Copenhagen, founded in 1479 by King Christian I. Its library is in two divisions, one for general literature and reference and the other for science and medicine. The latter division moved into new quarters fn 1938, with a ten-story book tower. The two divisions together contain well over a million volumes. A second major Danish university was founded in 1928 at Aarhus, where the state library of a half-million volumes also serves as the university library. Several specialized institutes and professional colleges round out the higher education program in Denmark, including a Royal College of Librarianship established in Copenhagen in 1956.

Since 1500 the university libraries of Europe have borne more than their share of the task of preserving and extending the cultural heritage of the Western World. National libraries have contributed to this task, and in the past half century the public libraries have joined in. On the whole, however, it has been the university libraries that have served as the research centers in all fields -- scientific, literary, historical, and others. In some instances and some places the university library has curtailed the search for knowledge, limiting the acquisition and use of books according to some preconceived religious belief or political philosophy. But on the whole this has not been the case, and the university library has served as a treasure house of old ideas and a fountainhead of new ones. Whether it was the university of 1500 (with few teachers, few books, and unruly students) or that of 1960 (with millions of books, hundreds of teachers, and thousands of serious students), the basic story has been the same. The university has been a combination of teachers, students, and books that have together preserved, passed on, and increased man's knowledge of himself and his world.

Additional Readings

(Many of the works referred to in the readings for the chapter on medieval university libraries are also applicable to this chapter. Most of the great European universities and their libraries have printed histories and guidebooks. The titles noted here are simply examples of the many such volumes that are available.)

Anonymous.
    Une visite à la bibliothèque de l'Université de Bâle, par un
        bibliophile Lyonnais. Lyon, 1880. 45 p.

Bougy, Alfred de
    Histoire de la Bibliothèque Sainte-Geneviève. Paris, 1847. vi,
        427 p.

Bülck, Rudolf
    Geschichte der Kieler Universitäts-Bibliothek. Eutin, 1960.
        xv, 297 p.

Craster, H. H. E.
    A history of the Bodleian Library, 1845-1945. Oxford, 1952.
        xi, 372 p.

Cuthbertson, David
    The Edinburgh University Library: an account of its origin.
        Edinburgh, 1910. 45 p.

Gibson, Strickland
  Some Oxford libraries. Oxford, 1914. 119 p.

Hartmann, Karl J.
  Geschichte der Göttinger Universitäts-Bibliothek. Göttingen,
    1937. 331 p.

Hausmann, Sebastian
  Die Universitäts-und-Landesbibliothek Strassburg. Strassburg,
    1895. 51 p.

Heuser, Frederick W. J.
  German university and technical libraries: their organization,
    condition and needs. New York, 1951. 54 p.

Horecky, Paul L.
  Libraries and bibliographic centers in the Soviet Union.
    Bloomington, 1959. xviii, 287 p.

Jena. University. Library.
  Geschichte der Universitäts-Bibliothek Jena, 1549-1945.
    Weimar, 1958. 627 p.

Kuhnert, E.
  Geschichte der Staats- und Universitäts-Bibliothek zu Königs-
    berg. Königsberg, 1926. 330 p.

Macray, William D.
  Annals of the Bodleian Library, 1598-1867. London, 1868.
    372 p.

Newcombe, Luxmoore
  The university and college libraries of Great Britain and Ireland.
    London, 1927. 220 p.

Oslo. University. Library.
  A brief survey of the Oslo University Library, its history,
    collections and building. Oslo, 1947. 20 p.

Oxford. University.
  Library provision in Oxford, report and recommendations of the
    Commission appointed by the Congregation of the University.
    Oxford, 1931. 152 p.

Roloff, Heinrich
  Beiträge zur Geschichte der Universitäts-Bibliothek Rostock im
    19. Jahrhundert. Leipzig, 1955. 66 p.

Tinker, Robert
  The library of Trinity College, Cambridge. Cambridge, 1891.
    v, 136 p.

Wepsiec, Jan
   Polish institutions of higher learning. New York, 1959. 109 p.

Werner, Gunda
   Die Bibliotheken der Universität Altdorf. Leipzig, 1937. 142 p.

Zedler, Gottfried
   Geschichte der Universitätsbibliothek zu Marburg von 1527-1887.
      Marburg, 1896. 166 p.

12

European Public Libraries Since 1500

Before considering the development of public libraries in Europe since 1500, it is necessary first to define what we mean by "public library." Certainly the national libraries were publicly owned in the later centuries, although they may have begun as private libraries of kings or nobles. Also many of the universities, and almost all of them in later years, were owned by the governments, so they were public in ownership at least. On the other hand, many libraries not publicly owned were open to the public or at least to individual scholars. What we mean today by the public library is the general library that is not only publicly owned but which is also in general use by any citizen who desires to use it. More particularly, we generally mean by the public library the public circulating library. In this restricted sense, the public library as such does not appear on the European scene to any great extent until the nineteenth century, and in many respects it is a twentieth-century development. However, public reference libraries were available in most parts of Europe throughout the period covered, and no consideration of public library history in Europe can be complete without noticing them.

These public reference libraries began in many ways, but usually as a gift of a private library, the transfer of a monastery or cathedral library to public usage, or as a professional collection. No matter how established, the growth of such libraries for the centuries between 1500 and 1900 was usually slow. Where progress was made in times of peace and prosperity, collections were often destroyed or dispersed in times of war. The libraries were usually poorly housed (although a few of them were in architecturally elegant surroundings) and had inexperienced or disinterested "library keepers" rather than librarians in charge of them. Hours of opening were brief and the contents were of such a scholarly nature that few people bothered to use them. A few librarians emerged who saw in the public library something more than an antiquarian collection, but these were few and far between.

The history of public libraries in France is quite illustrative of this situation. In the sixteenth century a number of town libraries were established in the larger cities. Lyons, for example, had a town library in 1530, and Aix-la-Chappelle by 1556. These, and others like them, were largely monastery or church libraries taken over by municipal officials, ineffectively housed and little used. Paris, of course, had a number of semipublic libraries, such as the Mazarine Library, and others connected with churches and colleges, but before the French Revolution there was little in the way of public library service elsewhere in France.

The period from 1789 to 1815 saw a social and economic revolution in France, accompanying the political revolution and the Napoleonic era, and the effect on French libraries was tremendous. First, in 1789, shortly after the Revolution began, all religious libraries were declared national property and confiscated or closed. In 1792, this was followed with a general confiscation of books belonging to the nobility or other citizens who had fled France after the Revolution began. Perhaps as many as 8,000,000 volumes were confiscated and gathered into general book deposits at several points in France. Although many were lost or damaged in this process, several hundred thousand of the more valuable volumes ended up in the Bibliothèque Nationale, while the remainder were to be divided among new district libraries to be established throughout France. Most of these libraries were established, at least in name, but the books assigned to them often languished in warehouses for years, and even when opened the libraries were poorly organized and even more poorly used. In some cases the books were sold and the funds put to other uses. In the 1830's France experimented with the idea of public libraries for adults located in the public schools, but this idea did not catch on, and the majority of adults continued to read books that they purchased or obtained from lending libraries in the towns and cities. The subscription library, begun in England in the eighteenth century, had its counterpart in France, but it was never very successful outside of Paris

and a few other larger cities. After 1850 there were opened a few
"popular" libraries in Paris, small collections of circulating books,
mostly light reading. By 1908 there were some 80 of these in various parts of Paris. There was no central public library, but the
collections were centrally supervised. For the most part they had
only a few thousand volumes each; they were housed in rented
rooms or in odd areas of municipal buildings; and they were open
only a few hours each week.

In 1904 a new stimulus to public library service in France
came with the activities and writings of Eugène Morel, who attempted to introduce in France the American and English conception
of the public library. This resulted in some increase in the numbers and usage of the popular libraries, but they remained almost
completely directed toward recreational reading and for the use of
adults only. Shortly before World War I, a survey of public libraries in France was made, and its report stated that the library
situation in France was deplorable. Unfortunately, the war came
before anything could be done to correct this situation.

During World War I there was considerable destruction of
public libraries in northeastern France, including those at Rheims,
Arras, Lille, and Verdun, plus scores of smaller collections.
Many rare and valuable books were lost in the ruins of these libraries. After the war, American aid helped in the establishment
of model public libraries in Soissons and Paris. Recognition of the
public circulating library as distinct from the public research library became more common in France in the 1920's, and several
cities made efforts in reorganizing their public libraries in this direction. In 1929-30, a second nationwide library survey was made,
with much the same findings as that of a generation earlier. This
time, however, there were some results. In the 1930's, despite
the depression, experiments were made not only with public circulating collections but also with children's libraries, bookmobiles,
branch libraries, factory libraries, and even a barge library for
families living and working on the network of French rivers and
canals. Paris enlarged most of its popular libraries and placed
them in larger quarters or separate buildings. An Association for

Public Libraries was formed to promote libraries and library services. In 1937 two million francs were appropriated by the French Government for the purchase of books to be distributed to the public libraries throughout the nation. Some 300 public libraries shared in this distribution, all of them under the control and supervision of the Ministry of Public Instruction. They were divided into three types: those with large or valuable collections, supervised directly by the national library office; those of smaller size or less-important collections, requiring at least one trained librarian to direct; and those smaller libraries without professional staff but visited regularly by supervisors from the national library office. Despite this relative progress, the coming of World War II found France without a modern public library system and still generally under the impression that libraries should be for serious research only.

Owing to the fact that France capitulated to the Germans early in World War II, war damage to French libraries was relatively light. In 1944 and 1945 when the Allied invasion took place, there was some damage to libraries, but nothing to compare with that of World War I. However, during the German occupation many libraries were closed, some valuable manuscripts were seized by the Germans, and a few libraries suffered confiscation of materials judged to be anti-German or pro-Communist. Some Jewish librarians and others too active in the French underground were imprisoned or sent to concentration camps. The librarian of the Bibliothèque Nationale, Julian Cain, was one of these. After the war, the new French Government recognized the importance of public libraries by the establishment of a National Office of Public Libraries and Public Reading, but there are still too few real public libraries in France, and the service from those is often not up to Western standards. Few trained librarians and low salaries for those employed in libraries are two reasons for relatively poor public library service in France. In the towns where local government is in the hands of left-wing parties, there is a greater realization of the value of reading matter, and public libraries are often strongly supported, probably more for propaganda purposes than

for education.   However, the promotion of library service in these
towns stimulates other municipalities to similar action and arouses
the general public to the potential value of public libraries.

Across the Channel in Great Britain, the development of public libraries has proceeded in quite a different manner from that in
France.   The sixteenth century began with the great loss of libraries brought on by the closing of the monasteries and the dispersal of their libraries.   The seventeenth century saw the revival
of the university libraries and the re-establishment of several cathedral libraries, but there was little done in the direction of public library service.   Several municipally owned libraries were
founded in the seventeenth century, but these could hardly be called
public libraries in the modern sense of the word.   Most of them
were the results of books left to the towns upon the death of prominent citizens.   Norwich, for example, had a collection given to the
town in 1608, and some of the original volumes are still in existence in the Norwich Free Public Library.   In 1615 a city library
was opened in Bristol through gifts and efforts of Dr. Toby Matthew
and Robert Redwood.   Leicester dates its public library from 1632,
and the Chetham Library at Manchester was a gift of Sir Humphrey
Chetham in 1653.   The contents of these early libraries were
heavily classical and theological, were not allowed to circulate, and
hence were little used.   In some cases they were uncared for or
stored away for years at a time.   In the late seventeenth century
some parish churches also opened small gift collections for public
use, and the private grammar schools made primitive beginnings
toward library collections.

In the eighteenth century a few additional free public libraries were added, but the two major moves toward providing library service to the public were the parochial libraries and the
circulating libraries.   The first were largely the work of one man,
Dr. Thomas Bray, who late in the seventeenth century had taken
part in the formation of the Society for the Propagation of the Gospel in Foreign Parts.   This group was mainly interested in providing ministers for the English colonies in America, but Dr. Bray
went further and attempted to supply those ministers and their

parishes with books for religious training and inspirational reading.
Finding that the English parishes needed the same service, Dr.
Bray and his associates founded similar church libraries in some
60 parishes throughout England.   These parochial libraries were almost entirely theological in nature, but they did provide the ministers with professional reading and the interested public with some
rather heavy fare.

The commercial circulating libraries were of an entirely different nature.   They were established by booksellers, usually on a
purely commercial basis, or by groups of readers on a nonprofit
system.   There was one in Edinburgh as early as 1725, and in
London by 1740.   These "libraries" would be called rental collections today, but they did provide the general public or all who could
afford the small fees with popular reading matter.   By 1800 most of
the major towns in the British Isles had circulating rental libraries,
and some of them remained profitable down through the nineteenth
century.   Rental fees at these collections were usually about one
shilling per month.   William Lane of London was one of the most
enterprising of the circulating library founders.   He established
chains of bookstores with circulating collections in them, and then
published books, fiction and popular non-fiction, to fill them.
Charles Edward Mudie established Mudie's Circulating Libraries in
the nineteenth century, and had at one time over 25,000 subscribers
in London alone.   Paperbacks and public libraries have virtually replaced the commercial circulating libraries in the twentieth century.

The latter part of the eighteenth century saw the development of the subscription library.   Here a group of the more well-
to-do readers of a community would form a "lyceum" or "athenaeum"
society with a library for the use of members only.   Fees were by
the month or year, and the quality of the reading matter was much
better than that of the circulating libraries.   These subscription libraries were generally housed in rented halls or rooms with a
keeper on duty at certain hours.   Some of them grew to respectable
size, moved into their own buildings, and in the early nineteenth
century provided a large part of the "public" library service available, even though their number of users was limited by the sub-

scription fees.   Some of these subscription libraries include the
Liverpool Lyceum, founded in 1758; the Leeds Library, 1768; and
others before 1800 at Bradford, Hull, Birmingham, Leicester, New-
castle, York, and Liverpool.

For the benefit of the workers and small tradesmen who
could not afford the subscription libraries, benevolent individuals
and groups formed "mechanics' institutes" that included in their programs libraries of popular reading matter available at small rental
fees.   Probably the first of these was the Birmingtham Artisans'
Library, formed in 1795.   The Glasgow Mechanics' Institution,
formed in 1823, not only had a library but conducted classes and
later became a recognized college.   Other mechanics' libraries
were founded at Edinburgh, 1821; Perth and Liverpool, 1823; and
Aberdeen and London, 1924.   The idea spread to the smaller towns,
and by 1850 there were almost 400 such libraries in Britain, with
more to be established later.   Many of them eventually became local public libraries or their collections were given to local public
libraries after the passage of the Public Library Act.   The role of
the subscription libraries and the mechanics' institute libraries as
forerunners of the free public library cannot be overlooked.   Their
audience was limited, but it probably included a majority of those
who would have been able and interested in using a free public library, and it helped in providing a ready-made reading public when
free libraries were established.

Modern public library history begins in Great Britain in
1847.   In that year Parliament passed an act appointing a Committee on Public Libraries to consider the necessity of establishing libraries throughout the nation.   The Committee reported in 1849,
and noting the poor condition of library service then available,
recommended the establishment of free public libraries in all parts
of the country.   The Public Libraries Act, passed in 1850, allowed cities of over 10,000 population to levy taxes for the support
of public libraries, and subsequent laws extended the act to Scotland and Ireland and to smaller towns.   In 1870, the Public School
Law, which made communities responsible for the establishment
and maintenance of free public schools, increased the number of

readers and consequently the demand and need for free public library service.   By 1877 over 75 cities had taken advantage of the
Library Act to establish free public libraries, and by 1900 the number had passed 300.

Although public libraries in Great Britain were relatively
poorly supported until after World War I, they did meet a definite
need, and as generations of school children accustomed to public
library service grew up, both use and support of the public libraries
increased.   Fortunately, the growth of public libraries came at a
time when many large private libraries were being broken up, and
many of them were bought by or given to public libraries.   In this
manner some of the public libraries in the larger cities, although
founded late in the nineteenth century, came to have collections that
rival many of the older collections on the continent and compare
favorably with university and research libraries.

Disturbed by two world wars in the twentieth century and a
period of economic depression, England's public libraries have
nevertheless grown and extended their usefulness to all parts of the
country and to all walks of life.   In 1919 the County Library Act
removed the tax rate limitations previously imposed on local funds
for libraries, and thus increased the financial support of library
service considerably.   County libraries were started in the 1920's,
many of them with aid from the Carnegie United Kingdom Trust.
By 1926 there was countywide library service in all but five counties in England, Scotland, Wales, and Northern Ireland.   The depression years saw increased demands on public library services,
but decreased funds at the same time.   Nevertheless, the British
public libraries have pioneered in branch libraries, bookmobiles,
library service by mail, library service to hospitals and institutions, and in general library cooperation, so that they have taken a
lead in the library world and set examples of service for all to
follow.

One special element of British public library service that is
worthy of mention is that provided by the National Central Library
in London.   Founded in 1916 as the Central Library for Students to
provide books for adult education classes, it was enlarged in 1927

to provide a source for loans to students of all ages throughout
Great Britain.   In addition, it serves as a clearinghouse for inter-
library loans and as a center for cooperative library and bibliographic projects.   In 1933 it moved into a new building given by the
Carnegie Trust, but this was largely destroyed by bombing raids in
World War II.   Since 1945 it has been reconstructed, and with its
bibliographic tools and union catalogs it aids in making available to
all British citizens any book in any British library.   Connected
with it is the British National Book Centre, which controls exchange
and distribution of library duplicates.

Many public libraries suffered great losses during the air
raids of the war.   The British Museum lost a wing that housed
some 150,000 books and 30,000 volumes of bound newspapers, many
of them unique.   Public libraries in Manchester, Birmingham,
Bristol, Liverpool, Sheffield, and Portsmouth were also hard hit by
the enemy raids.   Numerous smaller libraries and branches also
suffered partial or complete destruction, and the total book loss of
the war in Britain, including libraries, bookstores, and publishers'
stocks has been estimated at over 20,000,000 volumes.   In the rebuilding, however, Britain has gained many modern library buildings, and library service has improved in proportion.   As of 1962,
there were 548 public library administrative units in Great Britain,
with over 40,000 separate distribution points.   These libraries contain over 75,000,000 volumes and circulated over 450,000,000 books
per year.   More than one-fourth of the population are regular library users, making Britain one of the most library-conscious nations in the world.   No account of the library service of modern
Britain should omit the work done by the Library Association,
founded in 1877 and now having well over 10,000 members.   In
promoting library education and research, improved library legislation, and the progress of library service in general, the Library
Association has taken an important role, and in so doing it has
greatly improved the status of libraries and librarians not only in
Great Britain but throughout the world.

Germany since 1500 has been the home of some of the
world's greatest libraries, but although many of them have been

owned by the government and open to limited public use, they have
not been public libraries in the modern sense of the word.   Probably one reason for this has been the fact that Germany was divided into a number of small kingdoms and principalities down to
1870, and each of these governmental units tended to promote one
large "national" library rather than several smaller public ones.
Also, library tradition in Germany has always been directed toward
the scholarly research library, whether university or public, and
the English-American idea of the popular circulating library has
been slow to win acceptance.

Municipally owned libraries however, did have an early beginning in Germany.   Several of these had already been established
before 1500, but after that date town libraries were established in
Ulm (1516), Magdeburg (1525), Lindau (1528), Hamburg (1529),
Augsburg (1537), Eisleben (1542), Luneberg (1555), Grimma (1569),
and Danzig (1580).   These "libraries" however, were usually small
collections of theological works, poorly cared for and little used.
Martin Luther in 1524 urged that public libraries should be established to encourage the spread of Protestantism, and many small
collections were instituted in churches and town halls.   In the seventeenth century there was little progress in German public libraries, and those already established were often neglected.   The
Thirty Years' War caused great losses of life and property, and
many libraries changed hands, but the small public collections were
hardly worth taking as spoils of war.   Several royal libraries were
established in the German states during this century, including ones
at Bamberg (1611), Salzburg (1617), and Gotha (1647), which joined
those previously established at Cassel in 1580 and at Münster in
1588.   These royal libraries began as essentially private collections, but in almost every case they were eventually opened for public use or combined with already established public collections.

Eighteenth-century Germany saw the development of what
were then the greatest libraries in the world in the national or
court libraries and in the universities.   Concentrating on scholarly
materials, these libraries secured and preserved from all sources
books, pamphlets, and manuscripts on all subjects.   As monasteries

declined and were closed or lost interest in their libraries, the
books and priceless manuscripts were in many cases obtained by
the scholarly libraries and thus preserved for future generations.
Many private collections were also bequeathed or given to the court
and university libraries.   The scholarly reference library became
the standard in Germany during this century, but popular libraries
for the general reading public were never seriously attempted, and
the small municipal libraries remained small and little used.

In the nineteenth century a beginning toward popular circulating libraries was made.   The town of Grossenhain, for example,
opened a library for the circulation of popular books in 1828, and
about the same time a system of village libraries was begun in
Saxony and a similar one in Würtemburg.   In the 1840's an attempt
was made to open popular libraries (Volksbibliotheken) in Prussia,
and by 1850 four such libraries were opened in Berlin.   By 1900
there were 28 popular libraries in and near Berlin, ranging in size
from three to ten thousand volumes, and appealing largely to the
working classes.   Shortly after this a public lending library was
opened in Kiel, but the idea of popular libraries did not find much
support in other German cities.   In 1907 the Berlin Municipal Library was formed to act as a central library for the many popular
libraries in the city, and it grew rapidly until the coming of World
War I.   Little attention was paid to public library service for children, although there was one public children's library in Berlin.
Elsewhere in Germany before 1914, small public libraries were
made available to the general reader by educational societies and
local charitable organizations, but it was difficult to obtain any
municipal support for them.   Where city-owned libraries had grown,
as in Hamburg with its Stadtsbibliothek of 600,000 volumes in 1900,
they were largely reference collections with many rare books and
manuscripts rather than public libraries in the modern sense of the
term.

World War I did not seriously affect the physical condition of
German public libraries, but it did slow down library service in
general.   After the war the new Republic of Germany paid more
attention to the need for popular library service, and town libraries

became more common, particularly in northern and eastern Germany. By 1926 there were 356 <u>Volksbibliotheken</u>, but their size was usually small, and since the name implied that they were for the use of the poorer classes, they were neither well used nor adequately supported. In the same year, there were 273 research libraries in Germany with holdings of more than 34,000,000 volumes. The gulf between research libraries and popular libraries seemed to be as wide as ever. However, there was a government agency established to promote library service and assist the smaller libraries in selecting and obtaining books. The Society for Library Service in the Frontier States helped provide popular libraries in the eastern states. Among the larger cities, Berlin and Hamburg took a lead in providing library service for the people, and a few of the smaller towns revised their libraries along western lines with circulating and juvenile collections. In Berlin the Municipal Library was given quarters in the former royal stables, and in these quarters it contained over 260,000 volumes by 1930. A systematic build-up of all Berlin's library services was begun, with the public, special, and university libraries cooperating to provide the best possible arrangement, but this progress was slowed in the depression years following 1929.

When the Nazis came into power in 1933, the development of libraries in Germany was seriously curtailed except for a few favored institutions. All public libraries were placed under strict government control, and censorship over their contents was rigidly enforced. Books by Jewish or Communist authors were removed from circulation and often publicly burned. Acquisition of books from other countries was virtually stopped. Libraries were made a part of the propaganda system, and all efforts were directed toward the development of a strong German nationalism. In the Slavic areas of eastern Germany, books and libraries were employed to make good German citizens out of the former Poles and Czechs. Not only was the freedom of the press curtailed, but the Nazis tried to control the minds of the people as well, and the public library was considered an essential part of this plan.

During World War II public and research libraries alike suf-

fered from the Allied bombing raids. State libraries in Kassel,
Stuttgart, Dresden, and Würtemburg were completely or largely
destroyed. Lesser damage was done at Darmstadt, Kiel, Dortmund,
and Düsseldorf. In 31 major municipal libraries, eight out of fourteen million books were destroyed. Smaller public libraries also
suffered, and it is estimated that probably one-third of all public-
library books in Germany were destroyed between 1939 and 1945.
Along with the popular reading matter, which could eventually be
replaced, many irreplaceable manuscripts and unique printed works
were lost.

Since 1945, the story of public libraries in West Germany
has been one of reconstruction and rapid growth. Particularly on
the popular library level there has been a tremendous increase in
service and books available. By 1962 there were over 10,000
peoples' libraries containing together over 15,000,000 books and
circulating about 50,000,000 volumes per year. However, at the
same time there were over 600,000,000 volumes borrowed from
commercial lending libraries, indicating that the public libraries
are still far from meeting the public demand for popular reading
material. Church libraries for congregational use have also been
popular, and there are nearly 11,000 of those, including both Catholic and Protestant. In each German state (Land) there are central
library agencies to coordinate the work of the public circulating libraries, and in addition they are promoting publicly supported libraries in factories, mines, hospitals, prisons, and even in large
stores. The United States Information Service libraries established
in Germany since 1945 have encouraged the development of the
American-English type of public library service, but there is still
a strong division between the public and research libraries, even
to the extent of having separate library associations and separate
programs for the training of librarians. The American Memorial
Library in West Berlin, opened in 1954, has served as an example
of American public library service and standards for all to see.

In East Germany, the library situation has developed somewhat differently. As in all Soviet dominated countries, the emphasis on library service has been high, and Leipzig continues to be a

strong library and bibliographic center. However, books and libraries are strongly controlled. All public libraries are under the control of the Ministry of Culture, and a Central Bureau for Scholarly Literature controls all access to non-Communist publications. Under the pretense of removing pro-Nazi books from the public libraries after 1945, a general housecleaning of all books unacceptable to the Communist commanders was made, and thousands of volumes were destroyed or confiscated. In their place Russian and pro-Communist works were substituted, and their reading was made practically compulsory. Throughout East Germany the books and libraries were considered a definite part of the propaganda war. This meant that although there was more reading matter available to the average citizen than ever before, it was controlled reading matter, and the reader had little choice. Since there was little or no freedom of speech or press, the librarian became at the same time a victim and a tool of the propaganda machine.

By the mid-twentieth century the Russians were probably the most library-minded people in the world, if their library statistics can be believed. However, this has not always the case. As of 1500, Russia was not far removed from its period of Mongol control and was still deep in medieval feudalism, far behind even eastern Europe in cultural progress. Russia had experienced neither a Renaissance nor a Reformation and was easily 200 years behind Western Europe in general development as of 1800. Public libraries in the modern sense of the word were unknown until late in the nineteenth century, and even church and monastery libraries were few and far between. Odessa had a municipal library founded in 1837, while there was one in Kazan in 1865, in Kiev by 1866, and in Kharkov by 1886. Some society libraries, semipublic in nature, were also opened in the larger cities, while in rural areas public schools by the 1890's were maintaining small collections of books for adult readers. The library at Kazan, for example, was supported by a private organization, although it was open as a municipal reference library until the 1920's, when it became the basis for the national library of the Tatar Republic. In 1880 the Russian Government statistics reported 145 public libraries through-

out the nation, containing together almost a million volumes.   By
1905, the figure reported had increased to 5,000 free public libraries in Russia, but it was noted that many of them had very few
books, some as little as 50 volumes.   By 1915 there were reported
to be 800 public libraries in Russia large enough to be in charge
of a full-time "librarian," with more than 20,000 smaller book collections scattered throughout the nation.   The municipal library in
Odessa at this time had some 200,000 volumes, while that at Kiev
had over 600,000.   Hence, the idea of public library service in
Russia is not wholly a Communist one, but neither was censorship
and state control.   Both of these enemies of free libraries were
strongly present under the rule of the Czars, and freedom of speech
and press were only a little more present before 1917 than afterwards.

        Since the Russian Revolution the printed word has become a
much-used tool and weapon in Soviet Russie.   Books by the millions are poured through libraries by the thousands to readers,
who by all reports are eager to read and do read heavily.   This library movement was off to a good start even by 1920.   Madame
L. Haffkin-Hamburger, who had struggled long before the Revolution for library service for the Russian people, continued to work
for libraries under the Soviets, and Madame Lenin (Nedezhda
Krupskaya) also encouraged and sponsored libraries.   By the time
Soviet control was definitely established, libraries were growing by
leaps and bounds, both in numbers and size.   State libraries were
established in the capitals of the various Soviet Republics in the
1920's.   For example, the state library of Turkmenistan in Ashka-
bad was organized in 1925, grew to over 150,000 volumes by 1934,
and to nearly a half-million by 1960.   Books in Russian public libraries increased from about 10,000,000 before the war to over
125,000,000 in 1934, while the number of readers in the same period jumped from 120,000 to 15,000,000.   To encourage and improve
libraries -- and control them -- library departments were established in each of the Soviet Republics, and library sections in the
regional and provincial departments of education.   Besides the regular public libraries, there were libraries in factories and on

farms.   Hundreds of reading rooms were established for army personnel and for construction workers on railroads and other major
projects.   Of libraries of all types -- public, school, and special
-- there were nearly 200,000 in Russia in 1934, with some 272
million volumes in them.   This averages out to one library for approximately every 1,200 people in Russia, but that average library
would have contained only about 1,400 volumes.   Also it should be
noted that most of these books were in Russia proper rather than
in the other satellite republics.

World War II caused immense damage to libraries in the
areas overrun by the Nazi armies and also in the major cities affected by air raids, particularly Moscow and Leningrad.   Book
losses amounted to millions of volumes, and many library buildings
were destroyed.   Since 1945, however, the public libraries have
made a tremendous comeback, and new library buildings, many of
them immense in size, have sprung up in the once-ravaged cities.
The war also brought new types of libraries especially designed to
aid the millions of war veterans -- hospital libraries, veterans' society libraries, vocational libraries, and libraries for the blind.
The war also brought a realization of the value of technical and
scientific libraries, and the greatest growth since 1945 has come
in the spread of scientific literature on the public, academic, and
research levels.

As of the 1960's, all Russian libraries are organized into
basic library networks controlled from Moscow.   Three of the most
important of these networks are the public, or "mass," libraries,
the scientific and technical libraries, and the university libraries.
The mass libraries are directed by the Ministry of Culture of the
U.S.S.R., and at a lower level under the departments of culture in
the various Soviet Republics.   Besides the state, or republic libraries, many of which have millions of volumes, there are also
large regional libraries, city libraries, district libraries, and rural libraries.   Beyond these are the trade union libraries, collective farm libraries, and public children's libraries.   For the public libraries the established aims are threefold: to propagate the
Marxist-Leninist philosophy, to disseminate the government and

Communist party news and propaganda, and to improve the material
and cultural level of the people so that they can become better Soviet citizens.   All public libraries are limited in accessions to books
published in Russia or officially approved for Russian use.   Some
foreign literature, particularly technical, is available in translation,
but only a few of the larger research libraries are permitted to obtain actual books from foreign countries.   Book collections must
frequently be "weeded," not for worn-out books, but for books containing undesirable information.   In 1950, for example, a government decree ordered the discarding of books including obsolete
technical and agricultural titles; political, economic, and Communist party literature published prior to 1938; and legal, war, and
defense literature prior to 1941.

As of 1960 there were reported to be about 400,000 libraries
of all kinds in the Soviet Union.   Of these some 145,000 were municipal collections, 120,000 were rural, and the remainder were
academic and special.   Altogether they held over a billion and a
half volumes, but such magnificent statistics require at least a
small amount of interpretation.   Many of the so-called "libraries"
are little more than a few shelves of books in a village community
hall or in a factory workers' lounge.   Also, the large number of
volumes often results from multiple copies of the favorite Communist writings, particularly those of Lenin and Marx.   Some of the
larger public libraries have literally hundreds of copies of the individual works of those Communist leaders.   However, even grant-
ing the duplication and some exaggeration, it must be admitted that
the library picture in Soviet Russia sets an example for serious
consideration by the rest of the world.

Elsewhere in the Soviet-dominated world, the library pattern is much the same, but library development has been for the
most part on a slower and smaller scale than in Russia.   In Poland, for example, the eighteenth-century nobles began to collect
private libraries, many of which became large and valuable.   Some
of them eventually became parts of public collections, but the dis-
memberment of Poland in the 1790's set back cultural development,
and for more than a century the Polish people were minorities in

Russia, Germany, and Austria. Most of the large Polish cities
did develop municipal libraries of a sort in the late nineteenth century, although they were more scholarly than popular. Danzig's
public library, for example, grew out of a collection originally given
to the people of the city by the Marquis Giovanni Oria in 1596. It
grew slowly until the nineteenth century, but by 1939 it contained
some 250,000 volumes.

Even before the end of World War I, a Polish Library Association was formed, and after 1918 public libraries were greatly encouraged by the new government of free Poland. By 1939 there
were 25,000 library outlets in Poland, but these included schools
and small public library stations. A modern public library was established in Warsaw as early as 1907, and this had grown by 1957
to a collection of 420,000 volumes, with branch libraries, lending
stations, collections for children, and even one for the blind. The
coming of the German invasion in 1939 brought great destruction
with it. Library buildings were destroyed, library personnel captured and put into concentration camps, library books burned,
stolen, or sealed up in closed collections. With little to begin with,
a new start was made after 1945, and tremendous growth has come
since that time. By 1946 a new library law was enacted establishing a nationwide library system. There were to be main libraries
in the large cities, branches in the suburbs and smaller towns,
reading rooms in villages and factories, and delivery stations in
rural areas. By 1960, much of this plan was in action. In Cracow, for example, there was a main library of several hundred
thousand volumes, plus 15 branches including one exclusively for
children, and over 100 delivery points in schools, factories, and
recreation centers. In rural areas there are reading circles and
clubs to encourage reading, and workers' libraries are placed wherever large groups are employed. To supplement the public libraries there are also workers' libraries sponsored by trade unions.
There were nearly a thousand of these in Poland in 1960, with their
contents including popular, political, and technical literature. In
that same year there were 30,000 public library outlets in Poland,
not counting 27,000 rural delivery stations and 22,000 school li-

braries.   Poland nevertheless still had only eight-tenths of a book per capita in its public libraries.

In Bulgaria and Rumania there was even less in the way of public libraries before the twentieth century.   About 1860 public reading clubs were started in Bulgaria as a part of the general resistance movement to Turkish domination, and after independence was achieved in 1878, some of these grew into small public libraries.   The largest public libraries before 1900 were those in Sofia and Philippopoli, with about 25,000 volumes each.   Down to World War II there was relatively little library progress in Bulgaria, with those libraries in the larger cities being mainly reference collections.   After 1945, however, the Communist emphasis on libraries took hold, and rapid library progress has been reported.   At a national conference of Bulgarian librarians in 1948 it was decided that the aim of libraries in Bulgaria thenceforth was to be the Communist education of the masses.   Public libraries are all supported and controlled by the government, with the national library in Sofia as the bibliographic center.   As of 1950 there were 17 regional library centers and about 5,000 reading rooms and library stations in the nation as a whole.

In Rumania modern library history begins in 1831 with the establishment of a public library in Bucharest.   Progressive library legislation was included in the general reform laws passed in 1864, but library development was slow until after 1900.   From then until 1945 public libraries were centered in the few larger cities, and even these followed the European form of reference rather than circulating collections.   Since 1945 a network of some 40,000 library outlets has been organized, with the Library of the Rumanian Peoples Republic in Burcharest as its center.   In addition to public libraries, branches, and stations, there are rural library clubs, trade union libraries, school libraries, and youth organization libraries.   A separate system of scientific and technical libraries allows the public libraries to concentrate largely on popular reading and political indoctrination.

Czechoslovakia and Hungary, being culturally closer to Western Europe, had more contact with the concept of public libraries but were more familiar with the German research library rather than the circulating collection. A public library began in Prague in 1831 and one in Budapest in 1895. After both countries became independent in 1918, public libraries were encouraged by library laws, and particularly in Czechoslovakia there was much progress. Both countries suffered from Nazi occupation and censorship during World War II, and both countries succumbed to Communist regimes after 1945. In Czechoslovakia by 1960 there were over 60,000 library outlets of all types, all supervised by a national library network. Bookmobiles and package libraries are employed to reach remote areas, and considerable use is made of volunteer workers in all the smaller libraries. In both Hungary and Czechoslovakia research libraries have been thrown open for circulation, and the demands have placed heavy burdens upon the relatively small staffs of the larger libraries. Hungary's library law of 1952 has created a similar library network in that country, under the control of the Ministry of Popular Education. Church-related libraries have in most cases been turned over to public institutions, adding many valuable rare books and manuscripts. Thus in both countries better organization and many new library outlets have improved the library service, but librarians are considered to be "educators of the masses" and their libraries are designed to fit into the official indoctrination program.

In southern Europe, the library pattern in Yugoslavia is similar to that in Hungary and Rumania, although its five states and three different languages make it more of a small version of Soviet Russia. President Tito became acquainted with the value of books in the small collections carefully hoarded by his anti-Nazi guerrilla fighters in World War II and has encouraged the development of public library service. Since 1945 each of the five Yugoslav states has developed a centralized system of public libraries, and although they are growing rapidly, they find it difficult to keep up with the demand. In Greece there is a national library in Athens and public libraries in Salonika and a few larger towns, but rural and village library service has been slow in developing.

Austria and Switzerland follow more closely the German

pattern of library service, and their public libraries are usually of
the reference type.   Public circulating libraries are beginning to
make their appearance, however, and many cities have both types.
In Austria modern public library service began in the 1860's when
small circulating collections were made available in schools and
churches.   Vienna had its first free circulating library in 1887,
and by 1900 it had 17 branches.   Since 1920 library progress has
been steady, with public circulating collections in every district
and larger central libraries with major reference works in the
larger towns.   In Linz, for example, there were a main library
and 7 branches in 1938, but only 5 per cent of the city's population were registered library borrowers.   Switzerland's public libraries, which include some of the oldest in Europe, are well organized along canton lines, with due emphasis being placed upon
the language spoken in each part of the country.   Central libraries,
branches, and stations serve every canton, district, and commune,
so there was an average of one library outlet for every 1,000 persons in 1960.   The larger cities have several types of public libraries.   Bern, for example, has a national library, a municipal
reference library, and a popular circulating library.   Cooperating
closely with the public libraries of Switzerland are a variety of society, special, and professional libraries of all types.

Italian libraries are, of course, a story of their own.   The
great Renaissance libraries, private and public, led the way for all
European libraries into the modern era, but unfortunately library
progress slowed considerably in Italy after the sixteenth century
and did not keep up with northern Europe.   Many of the large private collections ended up in libraries open to the public, but they
were more often museums of books rather than public libraries.
In the late nineteenth century, as the new nation of Italy was created out of several minor states, large public libraries were begun
in the larger cities.   Suppressed monasteries were sources for
books, and a law was passed in 1867 making it mandatory for the
municipalities to house and make available all confiscated books.
As a result, hundreds of public collections were created, many
small and some quite large, but their contents were of more in-

terest to the scholar than to the general public. Even in the 1920's
many of these collections were housed in wings of public buildings
or in rented upstairs rooms over stores or offices. As late as the
1930's, advocates of popular libraries in Italy were pleading for
"libraries on the ground floor" where new books could be easily
reached and invitingly displayed. Under Mussolini, the libraries
were incorporated into the national socialist system, but as far as
the general effect on the reading public was concerned, not much
was accomplished. A national adult education movement took the
lead in advocating public libraries in Italy in the 1930's, and as a
result some 3,000 small collections were placed in reading rooms,
school offices, labor union halls, and similar locations for the use
of relatively limited groups.

Some libraries were damaged during World War II in Italy,
especially in Naples, and other libraries sent their rarest books to
the Vatican for protection; but on the whole Italian libraries came
out of the war in good physical condition, as compared with those
of Germany, Poland, or western Russia. Since World War II there
has again been made a serious effort to give the Italian people real
public library service. In the absence of public libraries in small
towns and villages, particularly in the south of Italy, "reading
units" have been distributed since 1952 by the Directorate General
of Popular Education. These collections of books are placed in
schools under the direction of teachers, but they are really designed for the use of older children and adults. There are also
"loan units," or book boxes of 40 to 50 books each, placed in social
centers, cultural clubs, and smaller schools. One of the first modern circulating libraries was opened in Turin in 1960. The eight
"national libraries" are of course public reference libraries and provide excellent service in this respect, and there are also 14 other
special public research libraries, such as the Biblioteca Laurenzi-
ana in Florence. The 12 public university libraries are also open
for general reference use, but Italy still lacks anything like adequate public library service.

In Spain and Portugal, public libraries are even less advanced than those in Italy. As a matter of fact, it has been esti-

mated that there were more books available in public libraries per
literate reader in Moslem Spain in 900 than in Christian Spain in
1900.   Down to that date little effort was made to provide public library service, although the national library and the university libraries were important centers of research and contained many bibliographic treasures.   Oporto in Portugal has a municipal library
dating from 1833, but it was largely a reference collection, as was
a similar institution established in Barcelona, Spain, in 1841.   The
latter library also served a university.   A public library was
founded in Santander in the early years of the twentieth century, but
it also did not circulate books.   In 1911 Madrid opened several
small public reading rooms and circulating libraries, with three to
ten thousand volumes in each, and a similar system began in Barcelona in 1915.   In 1931 a school law in Spain called for the establishment of libraries for adults in public schools, and a library
commission was set up in 1934 to provide funds for public libraries
that could match the government funds with library quarters and
personnel.   Still, in 1935 only 150 of 5,000 Spanish municipalities
were offering anything like public library service, although some
3,000 schools had small collections available for adults.   The Spanish Civil War, 1936-39, did considerable damage to libraries, especially in Madrid, but both Spain and Portugal were spared from
the damages of World War II.   Since 1945 both nations have made
some progress, and Madrid and Barcelona in particular have made
strong advances in providing public library service, but there is
still a great need for books, libraries, and librarians.

In northern Europe, Belgium and the Netherlands have libraries that resemble those in both England and Germany.   Libraries are particularly well advanced in the Netherlands, and Belgium is fast approaching that position.   Like Germany, both Belgium and Holland had important research libraries belonging to the
cities during the seventeenth and eighteenth centuries.   However,
they were not circulating libraries and in many cases were hardly
even open to the general public.   Amsterdam's municipal library,
for example, dates from 1578 while one in Antwerp was founded in
1609.   In the latter half of the nineteenth century popular libraries

were established in the larger cities, but they were more often
used by children than adults and were open only a few hours a day.
Their bookstocks were usually only a few thousand volumes. Belgian libraries suffered much in both World Wars, and rebuilding after them was slow and difficult. The public library at Dender-
monde, for example, was founded in 1850 and contained about
28,000 volumes when it was destroyed in 1914 by the German armies. It was later rebuilt. Seriously damaged again in 1940, it
had only about 5,500 volumes in 1949. Modern public library history began in Belgium with the passage of the Destrée Library Law
in 1921, which authorized government aid for the establishment and
maintenance of public libraries in each commune. Under this stim-
ulation over 2,000 commune libraries had been established by 1926,
with a total of a half-million volumes in all. Before World War II
began these libraries contained nearly 3,000,000 volumes, but still
one out of four communes in Belgium was without library service.

In the Netherlands the library picture is much the same as
that in Belgium, except that modern public libraries there date
from about 1900 instead of 1920. The public library of Dordrecht,
for example, was founded in 1899 and by the 1920's had about
50,000 volumes, with branches in surrounding communities and deposits in the city elementary schools. After 1920, the Dutch public libraries turned to open-stack, circulating libraries and patterned themselves after the American and British library systems.
The city of Rotterdam suffered some library losses in World War
II, as did some of the smaller cities, but since 1945 much progress
has been made in new buildings and additional library services, particularly to children, hospitals, and special groups.

Dr. H. E. Greve, librarian of the public library at The
Hague from 1909 to 1949, may be said to be the leader in the
modern public library movement in the Netherlands. His library
has led the way in public services at all times. Dutch libraries
differ to some extent from public libraries in other countries in
that a small fee is charged for all books taken from the library,
although there is no charge for using the books in the building. Also, along with the public libraries that are nondenominational, there

are other public libraries supported by the Roman Catholic Church
and still others supported by Protestants.   These church-related
libraries receive some public support, and indeed almost all public
libraries in the Netherlands were originally founded by private
groups, and some are still so administered.   Despite this diversity,
there is much cooperation among Dutch libraries.   In addition to
the city libraries, with their branches and special collections, there
is also a national library service for providing books to small villages and rural areas.   All in all, Dutch libraries are still not
perfect, but they do reach virtually every citizen in the nation who
wants library service.   In 1962 there were in Holland some 200
public libraries with over 4,500,000 volumes available for use, and
the only discouraging note was that the number of registered borrowers still represented only a small percentage of the total population.

The libraries of the Scandinavian countries are last for consideration not as a matter of accident or even of geography.   They
may well be considered almost in a separate category because their
public libraries are probably the best in Europe.   The reason for
this lies partly in the relatively compact population of the countries,
but also in the manner in which the Scandinavian peoples approach
the problem of libraries and the enthusiasm with which they have
advanced library service in the last century.

In Denmark modern public libraries date from the 1880's
when Andreas Schack Steenberg began a campaign for public libraries operated along American lines.   A municipal free library
was established in Frederiksberg in 1887, and other public libraries
followed so that by 1909 there were some 50 public libraries in the
country with about 700 branches and stations.   A central public library that was established in Aarhus in 1902 had about 200,000 volumes by 1910, and this library came to operate as a central clearinghouse on public library matters and as an advisor for small public libraries elsewhere in Denmark.   In 1905 an association for promoting public library service was formed, and this group did much
to sponsor and develop library service in villages and rural areas.
Libraries in Denmark fortunately suffered little in the two World

Wars, and in the 1920's and 1930's much reorganization and centralization in public library service took place. Since 1945, Denmark's library service has expanded to the point where every citizen now has local library service from library, book truck, or
mail; through a well-developed union catalog and inter-library loan
service, he also has access to virtually every book in Denmark.
Library service to children, hospitals, and adult education groups
is also extensively promoted in modern Denmark.

    Norway's modern public libraries also began in the nine-
teenth century -- in many cases, with small private reading societies and lending libraries. Later, parish libraries were organized,
often supported by private means and administered by the local
clergy. A few Norwegian public libraries date from the late eighteenth century. The Deichmann Library in Oslo, for example, was
founded in 1780 as a free library. In 1898 it was reorganized
along modern lines by Haakon Nyhuus who had received library
training in the United States. A public library was opened in Aren-
dal in 1832, and one in Bergen in 1874. In 1901 a national commission to study the use and needs of public libraries resulted in
the appointment of a national library inspector and in the passage
in 1905 of a public library law. By 1910 there were some 800 public library outlets in Norway, mostly small village libraries with
only a few larger ones in the major towns. Traveling book-boxes
were also available for fishermen and workmen in the more sparse-
ly populated areas, as well as some 3,000 small collections for
children in the public schools. By 1935 there were 1,298 state-
supported public libraries in Norway, with 74 of them in towns and
the others in villages and rural areas. In World War II there was
some loss to libraries, and the public library in Oslo was occupied as a barracks by German troops during the early days of the
invasion; but aside from censorship, the Norwegian libraries suffered relatively little from the war. Since 1945, Norway has made
much progress in new library buildings, centralized library service,
and new services added to its already fine library organization.

    There were some public libraries or at least publicly owned
book collections in Sweden prior to 1800, but neither these nor a

movement for public library service in the 1830's achieved much
in the way of public circulating libraries. In the 1840's tnere was
government aid for small public collections in the schools, and
privately sponsored libraries were also opened to the public subject
to inspection by district school inspectors. The 1850's brought the
establishment of small public libraries similar to those in England,
and more of the privately sponsored or society libraries. Some industries, particularly in lumbering areas, provided small popular
libraries for their employees. By 1900, Sweden had some 7,500
library outlets in schools and public collections, and central county
libraries were being formed to supervise the many small libraries.
Grants of government funds for the support of public libraries as
such came in 1905, while the first modern children's library was
established in 1911. By 1926, over 1,100 libraries were receiving
government aid, and from four headquarter-libraries in Stockholm,
Lund, Gothenburg, and Lulea, traveling libraries were sent out to
any part of the nation without local libraries. Reorganization and
centralization of library service proceeded in the 1920's and 1930's,
and since World War II, Sweden's libraries are considered among
the best in the world. Malmo, for example, might be considered
as a typical large city and its library as fairly representative of
the larger public libraries. There is a main library that serves
as the central library for the county, a local library for the city,
and a headquarters-library for a region of nine counties. There
are 10 branches within the city, with special collections for children and the blind. Full use is made of audio-visual aids, with
the circulation of films, records, and tapes and the use of educational radio and television. Sweden has one rather unique feature
in its public library set-up, and tnis is a series of five public libraries supported almost entirely from The Dickson Foundation,
created by a Scottish lumberman, Robert Dickson, who made a fortune in Swedish lumber in the nineteenth century.

Two small countries usually included in the Scandinavian
area are Iceland and Finland. The former had village library reading circles and the beginning of town libraries in the early nineteenth century. The State Library in Reykjavik, founded in 1818,

had over 125,000 volumes in 1930, and the municipal library in the same city serves as the main circulating library for the entire country. There is also a public reference library and a government sponsored but privately supported children's library. Libraries in Finland developed somewhat as those in Sweden, with strong public libraries in the capital, Helsinki, and in the port city of Abo. With its native language, Finnish, made secondary first by Swedish and then by Russian control, Finland's libraries have long suffered from the necessity of providing literature in several languages. Many of its public buildings in the major cities were damaged in the twin wars against Russia and Germany in 1940-45. Since the war, however, with characteristic Finnish industry, rebuilding of schools and libraries has proceeded rapidly, and today there are over 3,000 libraries, including branches and lending stations, serving the Finnish people. Probably nowhere in the world are books more read and appreciated than in modern Finland.

In short, public library service in Europe since 1500 has been largely a story of four centuries of indifference, followed by a single century of library progress. Europe's publicly owned libraries have long contained treasures of literature and history that cannot be duplicated anywhere else in the world, but these libraries have been poorly housed, supported, and used. On the other hand, public circulating libraries were developed by private groups, commercial or benevolent; by religious groups; and by reading societies, only to be taken over in the late nineteenth century by the governments or at least partially supported by government funds. The philosophy that the only worthwhile libraries are research libraries has handicapped the development of popular circulating collections. Users of public libraries are often handicapped by fees, short hours of service, poorly organized collections, and limited staffs. The result has been that the percentage of library users is often small. However, despite the variety of types of public libraries available in the various parts of Europe and the disparity between their services, the over-all picture is one of great progress. Experimentation in many phases of library service is being made. The Anglo-American form of public library is not necessarily the best, and it is quite possible that out of the efforts of European libraries may come a new form of public library service that is even better.

Additional Readings

(Material available on the development of the public libraries of modern Europe is plentiful. In addition to the following books, which are representative, the periodical literature on the subject is voluminous.)

Anderson, John
    History of the Linen Hall Library, Belfast. Belfast, 1889.

Birmingham, England. Public Library.
    Notes on the history of the Birmingham Public Libraries, 1861-1961. Birmingham, 1962. 26 p.

Bostwick, Arthur E.
    Popular libraries of the world. Chicago, 1933. 316 p.

Brown, Samuel
    Some account of itinerating libraries and their founder. Edinburgh, 1868. ix, 115 p.

Busse, Gisela von
    West German library developments since 1945. Washington, 1962. 82 p.

Carnell, E. J.
    County libraries: retrospect and forecast. London, 1938. 260 p.

Credland, W. R.
    Manchester public free libraries: a history and description . . . Manchester, England, 1899. x, 283 p.

Diaz y Perez, N.
    Las bibliotecas de España en sus relaciones con la educacion popular . . . Madrid, 1885. 217 p.

Doecker, R.
    Das Spanische Bibliothekswesen. Leipzig, 1928. 62 p.

Dufresne, Hélene
    Érudition et esprit public au XVIIIe siècle: le bibliothécaire Hubert-Pascal Ameilhon (1730-1811). Paris, 1962. 614 p.
    (Good on effect of French Revolution on libraries in France.)

Foltz, Karl
    Geschichte der Salzberger Bibliotheken. Wien, 1877. 119 p.

Frauenfelder, Reinhard
    Geschichte der Stadtbibliothek Schaffhausen . . . 1636-1936.
        Schaffhausen, 1936.

Gariel, Hyacinthe
    La Bibliotheque de Grenoble, 1772-1878.   Paris,   1878.

Gass, Joseph
    Strassburg's Bibliotheken: ein Rück- und Überblick auf
        Entwickelung und Bestand.   Strassburg, 1902.   viii,   82 p.

Gautier, Jean
    Nos bibliothèques publiques.   Paris, 1903.

Geisser, Alb.
    Deve Torino avere una biblioteca pubblica circolante?   Turin,
        1893.   117 p.

Goldmann, Karlheinz
    Geschichte der Stadtbibliothek Nürnberg.   Nürnberg, 1957.
        131 p.

Great Britain.   Parliament.
    Report from a select committee on public libraries.   London,
        1849.   317 p.

    Report on public libraries in England and Wales.   London,
        1927.   356 p.

Greenwood, Thomas
    Public libraries, a history of the movement in England. London,
        1890.   xx, 586 p.

Greve, H. E.
    Geschiedenis der Leeszaalbeweging in Nederland.   The Hague,
        1933.

Grycz, Jozef
    Les bibliotheques polonies.   Warsaw, 1937.

Hamlyn, Hilda M.
    Eighteenth century circulating libraries in England.   The Li-
        brary, London, 1947.   5th series, v. 1 (1946-47), pp. 197-
        222.

Harrison, Kenneth C.
    Libraries in Scandinavia.   Grafton, 1961.   248 p.

Henriot, Gabriel
    Des livres pour tous.   Paris, 1943.   262 p.

Hugelmann, Hans
    Die Volksbücherei.   Stuttgart, 1952.   280 p.

Irwin, Raymond
  The National Library Service. London, Grafton, 1947. x, 96 p.

Italy. Direzione generale delle accademie e biblioteche.
  La riconstruzione delle biblioteche italiane dopo la guerra 1940-45.
  Rome, 1947-53. 2 vols.

Jira, Jaroslav
  Legal basis and development of communal public libraries in the
  Czechoslovak Republic from 1918 to 1945. Washington, 1956.
  xii, 256 p.

Keysser, Adolf
  Die Stadtbibliothek in Köln; Beiträge zu ihrer Geschichte.
  Cologne, 1886. viii, 109 p.

Kildal, Arne
  Norske Folkeboksamlinger. Oslo, 1949. 303 p.

Kirkegaard, Preben
  The public libraries in Denmark. Copenhagen, 1950. 103 p.

McColvin, L. R.
  The chance to read: public libraries in the world today.
  London, 1956. 284 p.

  The public library system of Great Britain. London, 1942.
  218 p.

Mason, Thomas
  The free libraries of Scotland. Glasgow, 1880. 32 p.

Meister, Albert
  Cultura popolare e funzione delle biblioteche rurali. Ivrea,
  1955. 111 p.

Minto, John
  A history of the public library movement in Great Britain and
  Ireland. London, 1932. 366 p.

Mollica, Carmela
  Le biblioteche popolair italiane nelle' ottocento. Rome, 1935.
  64 p.

Morel, Eugène
  Bibliothèques: essai sur le développment des bibliothèques
  publiques et de la librarie dans les deux mondes. Paris,
  1909. 2 vols.

Netherlands Library Association
  Libraries in the Netherlands. The Hague, 1962. 60 p.

Neveux, P. Louis
  Richesses des bibliothèques municipales de France. Paris,

1932. 32 p.

Nielsen, H.
Folkebibliotekernes forgaengere: oplysning, almue, og borger-
bibltoteker fra 1770-erne til 1834. Copenhagen, 1960.
677 p.

Ogle, J. J.
The free library: its history and present condition. London,
1897. xx, 344 p.

Oldman, C. B.
English libraries, 1800-1850. London, 1957. 78 p.

Pecheur, Louis V.
Histoire des bibliothèques publiques du Département de l'Aisne
. . . Soissons, 1884. 144 p.

Pelisson, Maurice
Les bibliothèques populaires à l'étranger et en France. Paris,
1906. 220 p.

Placzek, Herbert
Die sowjetische Massenbibliothek. Leipzig, 1954. 294 p.

Recht, Pierre
Les bibliotheques publiques en Belgique. . . Brussels, 1928.

Reyer, Eduard
Entwicklung und Organization der Volksbibliotheken. Leipzig,
1893. 119 p.

Riess, Jiri
Libraries in Czechoslovakia. Prague, 1945.

Rojnio, Matko
Yugoslav libraries. Zagreb, 1954. 61 p.

Ruggles, Melville J.
Soviet libraries and librarianship. Chicago, 1962. x, 147 p.

Rumania. Ministry of Culture.
The libraries in the Rumanian People's Republic. Bucharest,
1961. 67 p.

Schultze, Ernst
Freie öffentliche Bibliotheken, Volksbibliotheken und Lesehallen.
Stettin, 1900. xx, 362 p.

Steenberg, A. S.
Folkesbogsamlinger, deres historie og indretning. Copenhagen,
1900. vi, 176 p.

Stephens, George A.
    Three centuries of a city library: an historical and descriptive
        account of the Norwich Public Library . . . Norwich,
        England, 1917.   86 p.

Tobolka, Zdenek V.
    Bibliothèques publiques de la République Tcheco-slovaque.
        Paris, 1924.   10 p.

Varjas, Bela
    The development of librarianship in Hungary, 1945-1955.   Buda-
        pest, 1956.   58 p.

Vauclin, V. E.
    Anciennes bibliothèques normandes, 1689-1731.   Bernay, 1888.
        36 p.

Voisin, Auguste
    Documents pour servir a l'histoire des bibliothèques en Bel-
        gique . . . Ghent, 1840.   xvii, 350 p.

Wellard, James Howard
    The public library comes of age.   London, Grafton, 1940. viii,
        205 p.

13.

Special Libraries in Modern Europe

So far three types of libraries in modern Europe have been considered -- the national libraries, the university libraries, and the public libraries. Although each of these is in a way a special library, its holdings are general in subject content, and its reading public is broad if not universal. There are other libraries, however, that are limited in subject content or in types of users, or both, and these have come to be designated by the term "special libraries." Although the term is usually used in a more restricted sense, for the purpose of this discussion it will be broadened to include religious libraries and those in public schools.

Although the monastery and cathedral libraries were all-important before 1500, they were already coming to be overshadowed by other types of libraries. It is difficult to say just when the university libraries replaced the monastery and cathedral collections as pre-eminent sources of literary materials, but it is safe to say that it was before 1500. After that date the cultural competitors of the university libraries were the public and national libraries, although they were slow in catching up, much less competing. Both monastery libraries and cathedral libraries survived after 1500, of course, and in some cases still survive. However, they ceased to be the important centers of learning that they were during the Middle Ages, and in most cases their treasures passed on to other libraries or were lost by the nineteenth century. The date when the monastic collections were closed or dispersed varies in different countries. In parts of Germany it came during the early days of the Reformation in the sixteenth century; elsewhere during the Thirty Years' War in the seventeenth. In England it came during the 1540's when Henry VIII closed the monasteries and scattered the libraries. In France and Italy many libraries were confiscated when the Jesuits were driven out in the seventeenth cen-

tury and again in the eighteenth. The French Revolution, of
course, closed many monastery and religious libraries in France in
the 1790's, and the ensuing wars in Europe resulted in the loss and
dispersal of religious libraries in other countries. Italy saw a final
dispersal of most of its monastic libraries in 1875 when 1,700 collections were confiscated. Some 650 of them were turned over to
libraries already in existence, while the remainder were handed
over to local authorities to serve as bases for new public libraries.
By 1900 the great majority of the monastic collections had been
dispersed, and their contents were saved, if at all, in public or
university collections.

In the late nineteenth century the Vatican Library experienced
a rebirth and renovation, and its great masses of books and manuscripts were arranged and organized; the books at least were made
available to the public. Under Pope Leo XIII a reading room was

After its re-creation in the fifteenth century, the Vatican Library experienced further growth in the sixteenth century and in
1588 moved into a magnificent new building erected by Pope Sixtus
V. He also added to its bookstock with various gifts, and in 1600
it was further enlarged with the library of Fulvio Orsini, a most
valuable collection. Pope Paul V (1605-21) divided the papal library
into archives, manuscript, and book collections, and added two
large halls to hold the increased number of books. The Palatine
Library, a gift of Maximilian I, Duke of Bavaria, was added in
1622, and later came the large and valuable manuscript collection
formerly belonging to Queen Christina of Sweden. Important gifts
followed each other with regularity in the seventeenth and eighteenth
centuries, and in treasures the Vatican Library became one of the
most important in Europe. During the French Revolution, however,
it was the Vatican's turn to suffer, and 500 of its choicest manuscripts were taken by the victorious French to the libraries of Paris. Fortunately, most of these were restored in 1815. More gifts
followed in the nineteenth century, with the major one being the library of Cardinal Angelo Mai, a collection of almost 40,000 volumes amassed over a lifetime and containing histories and records
of Christianity from all over the world.

opened in 1888, and a public reference collection was made available. New collections continued to pour in, and the beautiful halls and rooms soon became crowded and difficult to work in. By 1900 the library contained over 400,000 volumes, with some 40,000 manuscripts and nearly 4,000 incunabula. After 1920 a new reorganization was made, and American librarians were invited to act as consultants on modernizing the collection. The Carnegie Corporation in 1926 sent Dr. William Warner Bishop to survey the Vatican Library and make recommendations for its future growth and development. Pius XI was then Pope, and as a former librarian he was intensely interested in the suggested reforms. A new cataloging system was adopted, modern book stacks were installed, new quarters were added, and in general the whole purpose of the institution was directed toward making it not only usable but used. In December, 1931, a tragedy occurred when a section of roof over a reference room collapsed, destroying about a thousand volumes and damaging many others. This, however, was only a temporary setback, and rebuilding and enlarging continued. During World War II library treasures from other Italian collections were taken into the Vatican for safekeeping. Since the War, the Vatican Library has taken its place as one of the greatest libraries in the world. Scholars from everywhere make use of its treasures, and the services of the library and its staff aid not only other Roman Catholic libraries, but libraries in general in virtually every country on the globe. Many of its rarest possessions have been made available in facsimile or photographic form, and bibliographies of its collections are available to scholars everywhere. Its nearly one million volumes make it one of the great bibliographic centers of the Western World.

Elsewhere in Italy the special libraries are varied and numerous. Each of the universities has around it a number of institutes and special faculty libraries that are essentially special libraries in their respective subject fields. They vary in size from a few hundred to twenty thousand or more. In addition, there are the libraries of the technical institutes not connected with the universities. The library of the Polytechnic Institute of Milan, for

example, was founded in 1863 and has a specialized library of some
75,000 volumes. In Rome there are several important special libraries of considerable size. The Library of the International Institute of Agriculture contains over 300,000 volumes, with files of
3,000 agricultural and related periodicals. Founded in 1905, it
went into a new building in 1933. It is organized along the lines of
American technical libraries and serves not only its own organization, but also agricultural scientists throughout Italy. Its bibliographies and inter-library loan service are available around the world.
A somewhat smaller special library is the Biblioteca Romana formed
in 1930 to be the historical library for the city of Rome, specializing in Roman history -- political, social, and economic. It also
maintains a union catalog of all such materials located anywhere in
Italy. Most of the departments of the Italian government have head-
quarters-libraries in Rome, and some of them have reached considerable size and importance. The Library of the Ministry of Agriculture and Forestry has over a half-million volumes.

School libraries in Italy are largely a twentieth-century development, and although government financial support is available,
they still lag behind those in England and America. This is due in
part to a lack of trained school librarians, and partly to the continued emphasis on textbook teaching rather than individual study and
reading, particularly on the lower grade levels. However, since
the 1930's, and particularly since 1945, the new emphasis on public education has brought an increased interest in school library
work, and the current library scene is improving.

Special libraries in France are similar to those in Italy, although more numerous. Beginning with those of Paris, it can be
noted that some of the most important ones are connected with or
part of the Bibliothèque Nationale or the University of Paris libraries. The great national law and medical libraries, for example,
are part of the University library, while the Mazarine Library is
a part of the Bibliothèque Nationale. The Bibliothèque de l'Arsénal,
formed in the eighteenth century, is, despite its name, a remarkable library of French literature, containing over a half-million volumes with thousands of rare literary manuscripts. Open to the pub-

lic since 1900, it is also a part of the Bibliothèque Nationale today.   The Catholic Institute of Paris has a theological library of
nearly a half-million volumes, dating from 1875.   The various technical schools and institutes of Paris also have their own libraries,
ranging from the general to the very specialized, and from the National Institute of Aeronautics to the National School of Veterinary
Science.   In addition to these are the many libraries of the French
government departments in Paris, some of them quite large and important, others small and used only by departmental employees.
Aside from these there are such special libraries as those of the
Musée et Bibliothèque de la Guerre, which aims at collecting all
available printed material on the two World Wars.   At the other ex-
treme there is the Bibliothèque de l'Heure Joyeuse, a children's
library founded in the 1930's as something of a noncirculating,
model juvenile collection.

In other parts of France there are technical libraries in the
various public institutes and in the technical schools of the universities.   There are in a few of the larger cities business libraries
that are a cross between municipal reference libraries and Chamber of Commerce publicity collections.   The French Army has
maintained service libraries since the days of the French Revolution, and each post and headquarters has a library or libraries,
sometimes both technical and popular, and sometimes in three divisions -- for officers, noncommissioned officers, and privates.
The French public schools have also had libraries of a sort since
the French Revolution, but they were for many years small, out of
date, and of little use to the students.   In Paris an improved
school library system was established in 1862, and by 1880 there
were 440 school libraries in the city, averaging about 100 volumes
each.   In more recent years French schools, particularly the secondary schools, are paying more attention to library service and
are providing not only books and periodicals but audio-visual in-
structional materials as well.   Shortages of school librarians or
teachers trained in library work continue to limit the number of
school libraries that can provide effective service.   Rural areas
and small towns are still lagging behind the larger urban areas in

library service, and France will continue to be slow in the development of libraries until more funds are made available.

Some of the most important special libraries in the world are to be found in England. London contains libraries on just about every possible specialization, many of them large and filled with rare and valuable works. The British Museum Library itself is composed of many special collections, such as the Harleian Collection of Manuscripts, or the Sloane or Cottonian libraries, and of course the library of King George III. Its newspaper library is probably the largest single collection of newspapers in the world. The various Royal Societies all have libraries in their specialties, such as the Royal Society of Medicine, the Royal College of Surgeons, and the Royal Economic Society. The London School of Economics has a library of political science that is particularly strong in municipal history and government throughout the British Empire. The Public Record Office is the official archives of Britain, and its treasures include Parliamentary records, state papers, and treaties going back for hundreds of years. The Patent Office Library is only one of many government libraries in each phase of government operations, ranging from agriculture to foreign service. Among the oldest special libraries in London are those of the various law schools known as Gray's Inn, The Inner Temple, and Lincoln's Inn. The latter, founded in 1497, is the largest law library in London and one of the largest in the world. The Science Museum Library and the Victoria and Albert Art Museum Library are among the best in their fields, while the India Office Library has one of the greatest collections known on the history and culture of India. The Royal College of Music Library specializes in English music and has the original scores of many English and other composers, while the National Library for the Blind takes a lead in providing talking books and books in Braille for blind readers all over the British Isles. A noted special library in Scotland is the Signet Library in Edinburgh, founded as a law and theology library in 1580. Although it is largely a law library in the 1950's - with over 150,000 volumes -- it also has strong collections in history and theology. Elsewhere in England and Scotland there are special collections in several of the college and university libraries and also in some of the larger public libraries. Since the 1920's, commercial and industrial libraries have been established in the larger cities. Each of these tends to specialize in the business needs of its particular area, as in the Leeds Commercial and Technical Library that builds its collection to serve the textile industries.

The cathedrals of England and Wales still maintain libraries, although they are largely theological and historical materials for the use of the clergy. In many cases their contents are very valuable, including surviving books and manuscripts from medieval monastery collections. The Cathedral at Durham has one of the largest such libraries, numbering well over 25,000 volumes. There are several notable English Catholic libraries, such as those at the Oratory at South Kensington, established in 1849, and at the Catholic Cathedral of Westminster. The libraries of the Cathedrals of York and Canterbury are among the richest in rare books and manuscripts, but there are a number of parish churches scattered throughout England that have small but valuable collections in theology and history.

England has been fortunate in the creation of endowed libraries, some specialized, some of rare books, and others of a general public nature. One of the largest of these is the John Rylands Library at Manchester, founded in the 1890's by Mrs. John Rylands in memory of her husband. Its special holdings include rare Bibles and early printed books, and its collection of over 125,000 volumes includes 2,500 incunabula. A famous endowed theological library is the Dr. Williams Library, founded by the will of a Presbyterian minister and opened in 1729 in London. It was moved into a new building in 1873, and its 50,000 volumes are strong in Presbyterian history and theology, but also include material on other denominations and religions. Many public libraries in English and Scottish cities stem from endowed collections formed in the nineteenth century and taken over later with public support.

School library history in England is a comparatively recent development, although many of the private schools have had libraries since the seventeenth century. Shrewsbury School library,

as a matter of fact, dates from the late 1500's, and its original
philosophy of library service could be considered quite modern.
Included in the materials to be provided in the library were books,
maps, spheres, instruments of astronomy, and "all other things per-
taining to learning." An apprentice's school in London, the Merchant Taylors' School, founded in 1561, also made provisions for a
library from its beginning. Other private schools had libraries,
but for the most part they were of a reference nature, and the
average student's reading was either from textbooks or from books
that he had purchased himself.

English public school libraries for the most part came into
existence after the passage of the Public School laws in the 1870's,
although real working school libraries did not develop until the
twentieth century. Today the average English school is well supplied with books, although there is probably more dependence upon
public library service for children than in the United States. Also,
there are less "frills" associated with school libraries than in
American schools, but the reading matter is standard, and apparently the use made of school libraries is greater per pupil than
in most American ones. A group of visiting American librarians
in the 1930's found, for example, that the quality of books and the
interest in books and reading was very high in English school libraries, although library quarters often left much to be desired.
Since 1945, English school libraries have turned heavily to audio-
visual and other aids to learning, and the concept of the school library as an educational materials center is being widely accepted.

Germany is another European country that is well supplied
with special libraries. Berlin alone had over 200 special libraries
before 1939. These of course included government office libraries,
special libraries of universities and institutes, and libraries of scientific societies. Governmental libraries were strong even before
World War I, with the library of the Reichstag (Parliament) having
over 175,000 volumes; that of the Patent Office, 118,000 volumes;
that of the Foreign Office over 100,000 volumes; and that of the
Census Office, nearly 200,000. The German Army was also well
supplied with technical libraries, with the major one being at the

headquarters in Berlin.   These were disbanded by the Treaty of
Versailles in 1919 but were reformed in the 1920's and became
very important during the Hitler era.   All in all, Germany had in
1924 over 275 research libraries with total holdings of over
34,000,000 volumes.   Eighty-four of them contained over 100,000
volumes each, thus making Germany one of the greatest sources of
research information in the Western World.

Elsewhere in Germany, the former royal or ducal libraries
of the various states that existed before the unification of Germany
form a particular type of "special" library.   Each is a special library on the history and culture of its particular area.   Throughout Germany there are the technical libraries of the Hochschule, or
colleges and institutes, and of course hundreds of special libraries
connected with the various universities.   The larger cities also developed commercial libraries, such as that in Leipzig, which had
nearly 100,000 volumes in 1936.   Leipzig also had the famous
Peters Music Library with about 30,000 volumes.   All told, Germany in the twentieth century has been fairly well supplied with
special libraries, ranging from the small departmental library in
the universities to the million-volume state reference library.

School libraries in Germany, that is, the libraries of the
lower schools corresponding to American elementary and high
schools, have been very slow in developing.   Emphasis on the textbook and lecture have prevented the growth of usable school libraries down to the mid-twentieth century, and where there have
been libraries in the schools they have largely been small collections of old books rather than living, working libraries.   Since
World War II, however, the influence of American school libraries,
particularly the libraries in the schools for children of Americans
stationed there, has led to an increased interest in the possibilities
of school library service and to wide experimentation in this field.

Some special German libraries that have emerged since
World War II include the American Library in Berlin, the International Youth Library in Munich, and a library at Hanover that contains a book collection, a translation center, and a bureau of documentation to give a complete research service.   The new German

National Library at Marburg is also a post-war development, and
in the sense that it is a bibliographic center it too is a special library.   The German research libraries are coming to cooperate
very closely on both regional and national levels, not only in inter-
library loans and union catalogs, ·but also in the selection and acquisition of special subjects and materials.   Some libraries concentrate on special geographic areas in order to assure complete coverage of literature on all parts of the world.   This means that
somewhere in a German research library there can be found books
or information on almost any subject and from almost any place on
earth.

In Russia the special library is a vital part of the complete
library picture of that library-minded nation.   In addition to the
national, public, and university libraries already discussed, Russia
and its various federated republics share a widespread system of
technical libraries.   These are concentrated in the library network
of the Academy of Sciences of the U.S.S.R.   The Academy library
alone has over 7,500,000 items, and its activities are closely tied
to those of the various institutes, academies, museums, and other
technical libraries in all parts of the Soviet Union.   In addition
there is a science academy in most of the other republics, and
each of these has a library with books in the major languages of
the specific republic as well as in Russian.   Russian technical libraries usually contain much foreign technical and scientific literature, either in the original or in Russian translation or digest.

Another type of special library in Russia is the trade union
library.   This serves both as a technical or sociological library on
trade union history and programs, but also in the lower reaches,
as popular libraries for the workers.   The system is headed up by
the Gorki Reference Library of the All-Union Central Council of
Trade Unions in Moscow.   This serves labor specialists and students rather than the general public.   In addition, it assists in the
work of trade union libraries all over the Union by training workers,
providing bibliographies and booklists, and by publishing material in
the trade union field.

In Moscow there is a series of technical libraries embracing

almost every conceivable field of interest. Some of these include
the Geographical Society, the Botanical Institute, the Institutes of
Physiology, Ethnography, Linguistics, History, and Russian Literature, The All-Union Library of Foreign Literature, the Central
Polytechnic Library, the All-Union Patent and Technical Library,
and the State Central Medical Library. In the capitals of the other
Soviet states there are similar professional and technical libraries,
although on a more limited scale. Many of the technical libraries
in the other parts of the Union are quite large, as for example the
Pushkin Science Library in Yakutsk, which has over a million
items. Throughout the Soviet Union access to these technical and
scientific libraries is available to all serious students.

The Russian Army libraries form a network all their own,
and the total number of books involved is tremendous. Actually,
library service began for the Red Army troops during the Revolution, when package libraries by the hundreds were sent to the Communist troops in training camps and even on the front lines. The
libraries for the troops became more permanent after the establishment of the Soviet Union, and they continued to grow in size and
usefulness until the mid-thirties when there were over 16,000,000
volumes in the various army libraries. The military headquarters
library in 1941 was a seventeen-story building in Moscow, containing over a million volumes. These libraries proved their worth
during World War II both for technical and morale purposes, and
since the war they have continued to grow and expand.

Public school libraries in Russia are under the jurisdiction
of the National Ministry of Education, which controls libraries in
elementary and secondary schools and in teacher-training institutions. Russian school libraries and textbooks are of course carefully controlled as to content; not only are the books themselves
carefully censored and written for full propaganda effect, but the
libraries are remarkably alike in all parts of the Union and in all
schools of the same grade level. Despite this fact, they are still
well used, and in many areas where schools are crowded or under-
staffed, the few books available are often not enough to meet the
needs of all the pupils. With their school libraries aided by the

children's collections in the available public, or mass, libraries,
the Russian child is not only aware of books but has used them
widely long before he has reached the equivalent of the American
high school age.   In the secondary schools, the libraries are more
practical, and the library reading becomes a necessary adjunct to
course work.   At this stage, the student has reached a point where
his concentration on sciences, foreign languages, and Communist
theory makes it almost impossible for him to have time for leisure
reading; so popular literature, available on a small scale in the
lower school libraries, tends to disappear on the secondary school
level.   Whatever the library contents, technical or popular, the
books are still designed to produce the same end -- the well-
trained and well-indoctrinated Soviet citizen.   Certainly no country
on earth makes as much use of the printed page, in all its forms,
and with all its adjuncts, as does the Soviet educational system.

In other Soviet-dominated countries of eastern Europe, the
pattern of special libraries follows somewhat the Russian system,
although it is tempered by local customs and situations and modi-
fied to some extent by Western library methods.   Special libraries
in general fall into four main classes: government departmental
libraries, scientific and technical libraries, military libraries, and
school libraries.   Theological libraries of all types have either
been closed or have been restricted considerably in their activities.
Some examples of special libraries in these countries include the
Central Education Library in Lodz and the library of the Medical
Society of Warsaw, both in Poland.   The latter was founded as
early as 1820, and had about 75,000 volumes in 1939, while the
former began only after World War I and reached 20,000 volumes
in its first two decades.   Both suffered considerable losses in
World War II but have come back strongly since 1945.   Both serve
personnel in their respective professions, in person or by mail,
throughout Poland.   Another Polish special library of note is that
of the Polish Society of Friends of Science, founded in 1802, and
still existing as one of the most important technical libraries in the
nation.

In Czechoslovakia a Central Technical Library heads up and

coordinates a system of technical libraries, providing catalog cards
and bibliographic services in technical fields for all the libraries
in the country. A similar function is performed by the Central Law
Library, also located in Prague. In Bucharest the library of the
Rumanian Academy of Science is the largest technical library, but
there are other smaller, specialized libraries in the capital, and
an Institute of Technical Documentation to provide special research
services as needed. Hungary has had since 1952 a system of research libraries separate and distinct from its public or mass libraries. Yugoslavia's technical libraries are for the most part
connected with either governmental departments in the capital or
with the universities and institutes of the five constituent states.

School libraries in eastern Europe have been patterned on
those of the Soviet Union since 1945, and although their numbers
have increased, the size of the collections and their contents leave
much to be desired by Western standards. Poland reported in
1954 some 26,000 school libraries, averaging about 1,000 volumes
each. This is still short of the goal of one book per student in
the lower grades and three per student in the secondary schools,
but it is twice the number available just ten years ago. Hungary
reported some 6,400 school libraries, averaging about 500 volumes
each; Rumania about 15,000 with less than 400 each; while Yugoslavia reported 21,000 schools with book collections of less than
200 each on an average. With these small collections and with
teacher-librarians of little or no library training, the amount of
school library service available to most pupils is very limited.
According to library statistics in each country, however, the school
libraries are well used, and this is confirmed by reports of visiting librarians from other countries.

Spain and Portugal lag far behind the rest of western Europe
in special and school libraries. The Library of the National Academy of History in Madrid, founded in 1758, contains over 30,000
volumes, almost totally on the history of Spain and neighboring
countries. The Library of San Lorenzo de la Escorial, founded in
1565, is also a most valuable historical collection, with some
40,000 volumes and several thousand manuscripts. Both Spain and

Portugal have valuable national archives, although much of the most important material is not arranged for easy usage. In technical libraries, Spain has such noted collections as the Library of the Faculty of Medicine in Madrid, the library of the Astronomical Observatory at Cadiz, and that of the National Conservatory of Music in Madrid. Portugal has similar institutions in the libraries of its Academy of Sciences in Lisbon, its Faculty of Medicine in Porto, and its Faculty of Sciences at the University of Lisbon. The Archives of the Indies at Seville is one of the most valuable sources of information on the history of the Spanish conquest and settlement of Central and South America. School library service has been slow in development in both Spain and Portugal, although in recent years more interest has been taken by the educational ministries of the two governments, and some progress is being made. In 1954 Spain reported only 260 school libraries in the nation, and almost all of them in secondary schools. Also, most of them are in the larger cities, and outside of Madrid and Barcelona school library service is practically nonexistent in the American sense of the term.

In central Europe, Austria and Switzerland resemble Germany and France in the development of their special libraries. Both have government departmental libraries, university and institute special collections, and rare book collections. In Austria governmental departmental libraries began as early as 1848, and by 1900 there were four major ones, with that of the Ministry of the Interior being the largest. In that same year there were some 165 different libraries in Vienna alone, most of them special collections of one type or other. Some of the larger professional libraries in Vienna include those of the National Society of Medicine, the Zoological-Botanical Society, the Geological Association, and the Archaeological Institute. Austria is one of the few countries where monastery libraries of importance have survived into the twentieth century. Those of the Benedictine Monastery at St. Paul, the Cistercian Monastery at Heiligenkreuz, and the Monastery of St. Peter at Salzburg are particularly noteworthy.

In Switzerland two libraries, the State Library at Bern and

the City Library at Lucerne, cooperate in maintaining historical collections on Switzerland, with the former taking modern Swiss history and the latter concentrating on Swiss history prior to 1850. Switzerland also has several international libraries, including what was formerly known as the Library of the League of Nations in Geneva. Before World War II, tnis library had over a quarter-million volumes. The International Labor Office library is also in Geneva. The Polish Museum at Rapperswil has a library of almost 100,000 volumes devoted to Polish history and culture. In both Austria and Switzerland, school libraries follow the German pattern and are not well developed according to American standards.

In Belgium and the Netherlands there are a wide variety of special libraries. As elsewhere there are special collections associated with public and university libraries, and the governmental libraries are notable for their history and size. For example, the library of the Belgian Ministry of War in Brussels has over 100,000 volumes, and that of the Ministry of Colonies is almost as large. The library of the Royal Conservatory of Music in Brussels was founded in 1832 and contains over 20,000 volumes of music and drama. The Plantin-Moretus Museum in Antwerp, founded in 1640, contains a library of some 20,000 printed works and 15,000 manuscripts relating to the Plantin family and the development of printing in the fifteenth and sixteenth centuries. In the Netherlands, the Society for the Literature of the Netherlands, founded in 1766 at Leiden, is one of the most important literature collections in Europe. Connected since 1877 with the library of the University of Leiden, it contains some 2,000 manuscripts and over 100,000 volumes, almost entirely relating to Dutch literature and literary history. In Rotterdam there is an interesting private library, the Leeskabinet, which offers its members the advantages of a club, a restaurant, and a library. Its 100,000 volumes are both popular and technical and even include children's books. Amsterdam has had a noted music library since 1937, when the music division of the public library joined with the library of the Society for the Advancement of Music to form the Amsterdam United Music Library. Many of the special libraries in Belgium and Holland cooperate in

the general inter-library lending programs so that their holdings
are available to library users throughout their countries.

Belgian and Dutch school libraries are not well developed
and in most cases nonexistent.   In some towns the public libraries
render direct service to the schools, as in Deventer, Holland,
where collections of books are rotated among the 20 public schools
at the rate of 1.5 books per student at a time.   In other towns,
the children use the public collections directly, with no deposits
made to the schools.   Central school libraries as such are virtually unknown.

A fairly large number of religious libraries round out the
special library picture in the Netherlands.   The most important library of Roman Catholic literature is that of the Collegium Maxi-
mum of the Jesuits at Maastricht, which has over 200,000 volumes.
In addition there are some 20 monastic and seminary libraries of
over 30,000 volumes each, and some 70 smaller ones.   Their
holdings are largely theological, but many of them contain manuscripts and early printed books of considerable value.   An Association for Seminary and Monastic Libraries ties together the various
Catholic libraries and their librarians, and also aids in training
workers for the libraries as well.   In recent years the Association
has encouraged the compilation of a union catalog of the holdings of
all member libraries, and has also experimented with the printing
of catalog cards in a type of centralized cataloging.

Scandinavian countries are as well known for their special
libraries as for their public and university collections.   Moreover,
library service to children is well developed, although it is done
more through public libraries than through school libraries except
in Sweden.   In that country, since 1919, schools have administered
their own libraries by law, and some feel that library service has
suffered through this arrangement, since many school libraries are
of necessity small, and being permanent collections they do not
benefit from rotating deposits.   Sweden in 1954 reported some
1,600 school libraries averaging about 500 volumes each.   Norway,
on the other hand, reported some 5,400 school collections, but
these are largely deposits from public libraries, and although they

may number only a hundred or so volumes at a time, by rotation
each school has access to a much larger number of books in the
average school year.   Denmark, where schools also depend largely
on public libraries for books, has a system of folk schools, or
adult education centers, which sometimes have large and well-used
libraries.   The library of the high school for adult education at
Askov, for example, has over 30,000 volumes and dates back to
the 1840's.

One special library in Denmark is of particular interest to
Americans.   This is the Emigrants' Archive, a library that specializes in books and manuscripts relating to the migration of Danish people, and of Scandinavians in general, to the United States
and Canada.   It includes thousands of manuscripts, particularly letters from emigrants, and some 25,000 books relating to emigra-
tion.   Also in Denmark there are several special government libraries, such as the National Zoological Museum Library with its
50,000 volumes; the Institute of Botany Library with its 40,000 volumes, and others for such specialized fields as statistics, social
work, life insurance, military history, and industrial arts, as well
as more general but still special collections in the fields of agriculture, commerce, history, and art.   Many special collections are
a part of, or connected with, the Danish Royal Library, the University of Copenhagen Library, or the Aarhus State and University
Library.   Not all Danish special libraries are modern developments,
as can be seen by the Royal Horticultural Library in Copenhagen,
originally founded in 1752.

In Norway, the Bergen Museum Library serves as the technical library for the western provinces.   It specializes in natural
sciences and technology, but also has books on history, geography,
and archaeology.   From about 60,000 volumes in 1913 it had grown
to over a quarter-million by 1960.   The Scientific Society Library
in Trondheim is a similar institution, and serves the northern
provinces of Norway through both direct service and inter-library
loans.   There is a special library for the fishing and whaling industry at Sandefjord in Norway, while another interesting special
collection is that of the Nobel Institute in Oslo.   In the govern-

mental offices in Oslo the usual libraries can be found, including
particularly those of the Parliament, the Foreign Affairs Office, the
Patent Office, and the Army General Staff. Each of these contains
over 50,000 volumes and serves the general public to some extent
as well as meeting the needs of its particular department.

Several of Sweden's major special libraries date back to the
eighteenth century. Among these are the library of the Royal Academy of Sciences, founded in 1789; the State Historical Museum Library in Stockholm, begun in 1786; and the Library of the Botanical
Gardens, founded in 1791. The University Library in Stockholm
has strong divisional libraries in the humanities, social sciences,
natural sciences, and law, each of which is a generalized-special-
ized collection. The Chalmers Institute of Technology in Goteborg
had about 150,000 volumes in its technical library in 1960, while
the library of the Royal Institute of Technology in Stockholm was
somewhat larger. Various other technical schools in forestry, commerce, dentistry, medicine, and law are well supplied with libraries. Each of the Scandinavian countries has done much toward
providing libraries for hospitals and other public institutions in the
recent years, and also special library services for the blind. Much
is provided in the way of special services for and by the public libraries, and they are supplemented extensively by numerous special
and technical collections.

The Scandinavian countries have carried the idea of library
cooperation farther than most countries in that they have a formal
plan of international, inter-library cooperation on the special and
research library level. This plan, known as the Scandia plan, is
based on voluntary cooperation between university, college, and
special libraries in Denmark, Finland, Norway, and Sweden. The
cooperation is largely in the form of concentration in research collections, with specialization by country and particular libraries in
subject, area, and language fields. Duplication in rare, little
used, and expensive research materials is thus avoided, and by
means of inter-library loans and photoduplication, anything in any
Scandinavian library is readily available to any other library in the
four countries.

In Europe as a whole, the special libraries meet special
needs and supplement the services of more general collections.
Their progress has been as varied as their origins and purposes,
but collectively they add millions of volumes to the total library
holdings. Their role in the cultural development of modern Europe
can scarcely be underestimated.

Additional Readings

(There is much on European special libraries in the works on university and public libraries, and also in the general library histories. There is also much material in periodical and pamphlet
form, and in a variety of books, as indicated by the following selections.)

Adriani, Gert
    Die Klosterbibliotheken des Spätbarock in Österreich und Süd-
        deutschland . . . Graz, 1935. 108 p.

Arberry, Arthur J.
    The library of the India Office: a historical sketch.
    London, 1938. 108 p.

Barrajo, E. M.
    The Guildhall Library, its history and present position.
    London, 1908.

Botfield, Beriah
    Notes on cathedral libraries of England. London, 1849. 527 p.

Burkett, E. J.
    Special libraries and information services in the United Kingdom.
        London, 1961. 200 p.

Carnegie United Kingdom Trust
    Libraries in secondary schools. Edinburgh, 1936. xvi, 86 p.

Christ, Karl
    Die Bibliothek des Klosters Fulda im 16st Jahrhundert.
        Leipzig, 1933. xiv, 343 p.

Coates, Thomas
    Report on the state of literary, scientific and mechanics' insti-
        tutions in England . . . London, 1851. 117 p.

Donat, L.
    Studi e ricerche nella Biblioteca e negli Archivi Vaticani.
        Vatican City, 1959. 361 p.

Douthwaite, W. R.
Gray's Inn: its history and associations. London, 1886. 283 p.

Dziatzko, Carl
Entwicklung und gegenwärtiger Stand der wissenschaftlichen
Bibliotheken Deutschlands . . . Leipzig, 1893. 55 p.

Favier, Justin
Coup d'oeil sur les bibliothèques des couvents du district de
Nancy pendant la Révolution. Nancy, 1883. 60 p.

Grothusen, Klaus-Detlev
Die Entwicklung der wissenschaftlichen Bibliotheken Jugoslaviens
seit 1945. Cologne, 1958. 176 p.

Grulich, Otto
Geschichte der Bibliothek und Naturaliensammlung der Kaiser
Leopoldinisch-Carolinischen Deutschen Akademie der Natur-
forscher. Halle, 1894. ix, 300 p.

Hamlin, Talbot F.
Some European architectural libraries: their methods, equipment and administration. New York, 1939. xviii, 110 p.

Hennig, G. A.
Zehn Jahre Bibliotheksarbeit: Geschichte einer Arbeiter-biblio-
thek in Leipzig. Leipzig, 1908. 39 p.

Institut Internationale d'Agriculture.
Bibliothèques agricoles dans le monde et bibliothèques
specialisées dans les sujets se rapportant à l'agriculture.
Rome, 1939. xx, 311 p.

Jessen, Peter
Eine öffentlichen Kunstbibliothek in Berlin.
Berlin, 1921. 28 p.

Kricker, Gottfried
Medizinische Bibliotheken in Köln. Berlin, 1938. 57 p.

Kunze, Horst
Aus der Arbeit der wissenschaftlichen Bibliotheken in der
Deutschen Demokratischen Republik. Leipzig, 1955. viii,
253 p.

Lamb, Joseph P.
Commercial and technical libraries. London, 1955. 315 p.

League of Nations
The League of Nations Library. Geneva, 1938. 45 p.

Leyh, Georg
Die deutschen wissenschaftlichen Bibliotheken nach dem Krieg.

Tübingen, 1947. 217 p.

Morazzoni, Giuseppe
L'Ambrosiana nel terzo centenario di Federico Borromeo.
Milan, 1932. 139 p.

Mueller, Hugo
Behordenbibliotheken. Berlin, 1925. 259 p.

Nicholson, Albert
The Chetham Hospital and Library . . . Manchester, 1910.
xi, 120 p.

Rees, Gwendolyn
Libraries for children, a history and a bibliography.
London, 1924. 260 p.

Rumania. Academy of Sciences.
La bibliothèque de l'Académie de la République Populaire
Roumaine. Bucharest, 1955. 64 p.

Sayers, W. C. B.
The children's library . . . London, 1911. 224 p.

School Library Association
School libraries today. London, 1950.

Spratt, H. Phillip
Libraries for scientific research in Europe and America.
London, 1936. 227 p.

Thornton, John L.
Medical books, libraries and collectors. London, 1949.
xviii, 293 p.

Scientific books, libraries and collectors. London, 1954. x,
288 p.

Tisserand, L. M.
La première bibliothèque de l'Hôtel Ville de Paris, 1760-1797.
Paris, 1873. 128 p.

Tisserant, Eugène
The Vatican Library. Jersey City, 1929. 31 p.

Tricht, V.
La bibliothèque des écrivains de la Compagnie de Jesus et le
Père Augustin de Backer. Louvain, 1876. 298 p.

Vatican Library
Libraries guests of the Vatican during the Second World War.
Vatican City, 1945. 70 p.

Venice.   Biblioteca Marciana.
   Biblioteca Marciana nella sua nuova sede.   Venice, 1906.   117 p.

Vogts, H.
   Hospital St. Nicolaus zu Cues.   Leipzig, 1927.   56 p.
      (Includes a history of the Cusanus Library, founded 1464)

14.

Private Libraries in Modern Europe

The libraries discussed heretofore have been in one way or another public libraries. Either they have been publicly owned or open to the public, with or without restrictions. However, the purely private library is also a part of library history and must be considered, if for no other reason than that it often ends up in a public collection. The private collector with means at his disposal often has a better chance to build up a well-rounded library or a definitive subject collection than does a public library. With no "public" to worry about, the private library can be built to a point nearing perfection and maintained at that point without fear of loss or wear. Unfortunately, the death of a particular book collector often results in the sale or dispersal of his library; only rarely does a family maintain an ancestral book collection through several generations. When the private library is dispersed it may be given or sold to a public library, or it may find its way into the hands of other collectors. Eventually, however, many of the finest private libraries have been obtained and preserved intact in public hands.

While the medieval book collector was most often a member of the nobility or the clergy, many of the great collectors since 1500 have been wealthy merchants or professional men. However, book collecting is not a monopoly of any group, and people from all walks of life have been ardent bibliophiles. The development of printing undoubtedly broadened the field of book collecting and added many neophytes to the art. With the lower cost of the printed book, virtually every educated man was in a position to collect a small library, and indeed most of the writers and thinkers of the period did so. At least part of the stimulus for book collecting came with the Renaissance as it spread northward from Italy, and although it may be said that modern learning began with the books in public libraries, it certainly spread and flourished through the

249

ownership and use of private collections.

The Italian book collectors of the fourteenth and fifteenth centuries had their counterparts after 1500, but not quite to such an important extent. In 1521 Giulio dei Medici, afterward Pope Clement VII, gave to Florence the books that his ancestors had collected and commissioned Michelangelo to build a library for them. It was completed as the Laurentian Library in 1571, in a typically long, narrow building, 34 by 152 feet. On each side of the interior there was a row of 44 desks, each containing 20 to 30 chained books, with a list of them posted on the end. In the next century, another Florentian, Antonio Magliabecchi, collected books with such a mania that he filled room after room with them until he had amassed over 30,000 volumes. At his death in 1714 his library was bequeathed to the city of Florence, where after a century and a half as a separate institution, it was in 1862 joined with other libraries to form the basis of the National Library there. At Milan Cardinal Federigo Borromeo (1564-1631) began collecting books as a boy, and in his later and wealthier years he sometimes bought whole libraries at once. When he died he also had over 30,000 books, many extremely rare, and some 15,000 manuscripts. His library was partially opened to the public in its own building in 1609 as the Biblioteca Ambrosiana, and it remains one of the finest of Italy's rare libraries.

The National Library of Naples was similarly founded in 1804 on the basis of a private library collected in the eighteenth century by Cardinal Seripando, while the collections of the Ducal House of Savoy served in 1723 as a basis for a university library that eventually became the National Library of Turin. One of the private libraries that Borromeo purchased was that of Gian Vincenzio Pinelli (1535-1601). Pinelli was one of the early merchant-collectors, and his library was strong in early Italian printing. Cardinal Jerome Aleandro spent his lifetime collecting a library that he bequeathed to the Monastery of Santa Maria del Orto, near Venice, from which it was later taken to be joined with the Library of St. Mark. Another private library that became a part of the St. Marks Collection was that of Melchior Guilandini, received in 1589.

In 1600, Fulvio Orsini (1529-1600) bequeathed his library to the Vatican in Rome, thereby almost doubling the size of that famous collection.   These magnificent donations were followed by many others during the seventeenth and eighteenth centuries.   In 1621 Cardinal Bellarmino bequeathed his library to the Jesuits' College in Rome.   In 1630, Bartholomew Selvatico bequeathed his library to Padua University.   Luigi Marsigli, collector of Greek, Arabic, Turkish, and Persian manuscripts, gave his library to Bologna University early in the eighteenth century.   In 1675 Cardinal F. M. Brancaccia founded the Brancaccian Library in Naples with books collected by himself and his family.   In 1695 another library was added to St. Marks in Venice, this time from books collected by J. Contarini.   In 1701, Girolamo Casanate gave his library to the city of Rome, to be opened to the public as the Biblioteca Casanatense. In 1734, the library of Giulio Guistiniani was added to St. Marks. In 1758 Pope Benedict XIV bequeathed his library to the University of Bologna, and in 1799 the library of J. B. Branca was acquired by the Ambrosian Library in Milan.

Thus, we see that for a period of some 400 years the Italian nobility, clergy, and merchant classes took a great interest in the building up of personal and family libraries.   Many of these were of course dispersed upon the death of the collector, but others, of which a few examples have been given, were fortunately given to public collections.   In fact, most of the larger reference libraries of Italy owe their origin to such private libraries.   It is not difficult to see that in the final analysis it was the private book collector who developed the great Italian libraries, even more than the church, the universities, or the government.   Too much credit cannot be given to these hardy bibliophiles for the treasures they gathered together and preserved throughout those turbulent years.

After the Italians came the French as great book collectors and molders of libraries in the sixteenth and seventeenth centuries. Most of the great libraries of Paris had their beginnings in private collections.   The great library of Ste. Geneviève, for example, goes back to a private library collected in the seventeenth century by C. M. LeTellier, Archbishop of Rheims, who collected some

7,000 volumes through dealers in England, France, Holland, Italy, and Germany. In 1624 Cardinal de Rochefoucauld acquired the Le-Tellier Library, and with it founded a collection later opened to the public as the Bibliothèque Ste. Geneviève. In a similar manner in the eighteenth century, a library collected by the Marquis de Paulmy was acquired by the Count d'Artois to form the basis of the Bibliothèque de l'Arsenal in Paris.

One of the greatest French private libraries was that collected by the Cardinal Mazarin in the seventeenth century. While the Cardinal was busy with political and religious duties, his library was largely collected by his librarian, Gabriel Naudé, although the library already contained some 5,000 volumes when Naudé was employed. In a little over one year, in 1646-47, Naudé purchased more than 14,000 volumes for Mazarin from collectors and dealers all over western Europe. Despite the political troubles faced by Mazarin in his later life, his collection numbered over 45,000 volumes in 1760, and with it he founded the library of the Collège Mazarin, destined to become one of the most famous libraries in Paris. Jacques Auguste de Thou (1553-1617) was also a famous collector, amassing over 8,000 books and 1,000 manuscripts, with some of the most exquisite printings and finest bindings of any private library. In the field of bindings, however, the library of Jean Grolier (1479-1565) was outstanding. His bindings were in fine leathers, gold-tooled in geometric designs. His library was sold and widely scattered in the seventeenth century, but at least 400 Grolier bindings are known to have survived into the twentieth century. Two other famous collectors of the seveteenth century were Nicolas Claude de Peiresc, who specialized in Coptic manuscripts, and Gilbert Gaulmin, whose 557 Oriental manuscripts were sold to the Bibliothèque Nationale in 1667.

In 1662, the library of Raphael Trichet du Fresne was purchased for the Royal library by Prime Minister Colbert, who himself amassed a private library almost as large as the King's. His library at his death in 1683 contained over 40,000 volumes and 13,000 manuscripts. The Colbert library continued to grow in the hands of his immediate descendants, but in 1725 it began to be sold and dispersed. Fortunately, the larger portion of it was purchased in 1732 and added to the Royal Library. In 1663 another collection, that of Philip de Bethune, was added to the Royal Library, bringing in some 2,000 valuable medieval manuscripts and several thousand printed works. Cardinal Richelieu also collected a notable library of his own, and this went for a time to the College of the Sorbonne, but it was scattered during the French Revolution.

In the eighteenth century, the number of important collectors was fewer, but at least one of them built up one of the largest private libraries ever formed. This was Duke Louis de la Lavalliere, who began his collecting activities in 1738. He bought widely in many fields, including rare books, fine bindings, manuscripts, and sometimes whole collections of items. At his death in 1784 the library numbered over 100,000 items, and although it was divided up and sold, the more important volumes ended up in the Bibliothèque de l'Arsenal in Paris. Men were not the only collectors of books in France, however. When Margaret of Navarre died in 1524, her library contained 355 books in 6 large bookcases. Anne de Beaujeu, daughter of Louis XI, left a library of 314 volumes on 11 desks at her death in 1523. In 1599 Catherine de Medici's library, including many rare manuscripts in Greek and Latin, went to the French Royal Library. Even her secretary, Thomas Mahieu, was a noted book collector, famous for his collection of fine bindings. All in all, the French collector thrived for more than three centuries, and his activities are reflected in the many rare and valuable collections still present in French libraries.

Unfortunately the French Revolution, beginning in 1789, marked the end for some of France's finest private libraries. Books owned by the nobility and many of the clergy were seized and sent to collection centers in various parts of France. Some of them were sent to the great public collections in Paris, others were scattered among the cities and towns for municipal libraries, and still others were destroyed or sold to other countries. When Napoleon came into power after the Revolution, he favored the development of the French national library, but he also had a private library of his own. Napoleon carried with him, even on his military

travels, a small library encased in several oak book-boxes. He
once ordered a "perfect library" of some 3,000 volumes of the best
of French literature and history to be printed and bound especially
for him, but apparently the cost was a little too much even for an
Emperor, and his plan was never put into effect. After Napoleon
the French never quite regained their rank as great book collectors,
and the day of the great private libraries seems to have passed.
Indeed, some of them that had survived the Revolution, such as
those of the Duke de Talleyrand and the Duke d'Abrantes, were carried to England for sale in 1816. One nineteenth-century collector
worthy of mention, however, was the Count de la Bedoyère, who
collected in England and France nearly 75,000 volumes on the
French Revolution alone. His library fortunately came to the Bibliothèque Nationale after his death. Another Frenchman, Jacques
Charles Brunet, was not so much a collector as a bibliographer,
but his Manuel de Libraire became a standard tool for other collectors. First published in 1810, this bibliography went those in-
several editions and remains today the guidebook for all those in -
terested in incunabula and other rare books in French and Latin.
Still another nineteenth-century French collector, Charles Nodier,
stressed the importance of collecting books and printing of all kinds
to illustrate the history of the art, rather than merely the rarer
items. Although the large collections became rarer, the small private library became a national custom for middle-class Frenchmen
in the nineteenth century. Almost all professional men and many
in the business world maintained small home libraries of anywhere
from a dozen to a few hundred volumes. In fact, it is quite possible that the lack of interest in popular and school libraries stems
from the fact that so many French families prefer to buy their
books rather than to borrow them.

From the seventeenth through the nineteenth centuries, the
English took over the honors as Europe's most ardent book collectors. During this period, while the British Empire was literally
encircling the globe, wealthy merchants and nobility plus many of
the clergy proceeded to amass collections of books and manuscripts
representing virtually every subject and country known. The list of

British private libraries is almost endless, but a few of the most important, either for size or value or for later roles in the development of research libraries, are worthy of mention.

One of the early sixteenth-century collectors was John Leland, who spent a large part of his life collecting manuscripts from church and monastery libraries, presumably on behalf of the King but apparently largely for himself. Unfortunately, his library did not remain intact, but many items from it are preserved today in the Bodleian Library and the British Museum. Another great sixteenth-century bibliophile was Matthew Parker (1504-75), Archbishop of Canterbury. His library, also including many manuscripts rescued from the monasteries, eventually ended up in the library of Corpus Christi College at Cambridge. The historian William Camden (1551-1623) left a large library of books and manuscripts, with his books going to Westminster Abbey and the manuscripts to Sir Robert Cotton. A great family library was begun about 1600 by Sir Thomas Egerton, and further enlarged by his son, the Earl of Bridgewater. This collection, considerably increased in size by various descendants, remained intact throughout the nineteenth century and was finally sold to the Huntington Library in California in 1917. England also had its collectors of fine bindings, as evidenced in the work of Thomas Wotton, the late sixteenth-century nobleman who is sometimes known as the English Grolier.

Not the least interesting of the English book collectors of the sixteenth and seventeenth centuries were the students at Oxford and Cambridge. Although no records were kept of the great majority of student libraries, the wills of those students who died while at the universities have been preserved, and from them we know the general nature of student collections. For example, William Dayrell, who died at Oxford in 1577, left a collection of some 30 volumes, including works of Aristotle, Erasmus, Roger Ascham, Thomas Elyot, and other classical and medieval writers. Other student wills indicate that most of the books owned were texts or related to their courses, but there were also books on more popular subjects. Particularly noticeable are volumes suitable for the personal needs of young English gentlemen, such as etiquette, hunt-

ing, agriculture, and the law of estates. Many of the student libraries indicated a wide interest in political theory, including
Machiavelli's Prince and More's Utopia. Protestant theology was
much in evidence in the works of Calvin, Zwingli, Melancthon, and
the like. One of these student libraries had over 300 volumes,
and several included more than 100. Some of the professors also
built up notable libraries; for example, John Grocyn (1444-1519),
who taught Greek and left a large classical library. Another professor, John Selden (1584-1654) taught Oriental languages and left
a library of books in Persian, Turkish, and Chinese to the Bodleian.

In the seventeenth century the great era of English private
libraries reached a high point, and about the same time they began
to be given to the public libraries, particularly those of colleges
and universities. Sir Thomas Bodley (1545-1613), founder of the
Bodleian Library at Oxford, was a collector and gave his collection
of some 1,300 manuscripts to the library he founded. The Bodleian
also benefited from the gifts of the libraries of William, Earl of
Pembroke (1629), Archbishop William Laud (1645), and Sir Kenelm
Digby (1634). These, added to previous holdings, gave the Bodleian no less than 9,000 valuable manuscripts by 1700. Sir Robert
Bruce Cotton (1571-1631) collected about a thousand volumes of
bound manuscripts that, after many vicissitudes, ended up as the
Cottonian Collection in the British Museum. George Thomason
(1600-66) collected an immense library on the Commonwealth period
of English history, concentrating on books, pamphlets, broadsides,
and other printed material about the period from 1641 to 1660.
This collection was kept intact, and a century later it was purchased for the British Museum. Bound in chronological order, it
now forms the collection known as the "King's Tracts." Samuel
Pepys (1633-1703), the diarist, left a library including many valuable early English printings to the library of Magdalene College,
Cambridge, where it is still preserved in its original bookcases.
Some indication of the number of important private libraries can be
obtained from a contemporary directory of British libraries. Edward Bernard in 1697 compiled a Catalogi librorum manuscriptorum
Angliae et Hiberniae, listing the major library resources of England

and Ireland, and nearly half of them were private libraries. Virtually every notable library in England owes its beginning or its major collections to gifts or purchases of private libraries.

In the eighteenth century the nobility of England were particularly prominent in the field of book collecting. They were the first to expend really large sums of money in the collection of books, and some of their collections reached enormous size, considering the amount of printing to that date. Robert Harley, one of Queen Anne's ministers, began collecting in 1705, and in a few years he had a collection of 40,000 printed volumes and 6,000 manuscripts. John Moore (1646-1714), Bishop of Norwich, collected over 30,000 volumes and 1,800 manuscripts, the majority of which were later bought by King George I and presented to the Cambridge University Library. Charles Spencer, Earl of Sunderland (1674-1722) had a library that contained over 20,000 volumes, particularly strong in English incunabula. This fine collection remained intact for over a century and a half, but it was finally sold just before 1900. Smaller but more valuable, since it was almost entirely incunabula, was the library of Thomas, Earl of Pembroke (1686-1735). It too was not dispersed until the early twentieth century. Of all these early eighteenth-century English noblemen's libraries, the only one to be preserved into the twentieth century was that of Thomas Coke, Earl of Leicester. Greatly augmented by Thomas William Coke (1754-1842), it is still maintained at the family estate at Holkham and is one of the most important private libraries still in existence in England.

Possibly the greatest of the eighteenth-century English bibliophiles was Thomas Rawlinson (1681-1725), who collected a library of nearly 200,000 volumes, many of them very rare. Sixteen sales between 1721 and 1734 were necessary to dispose of the entire library. Some of the more valuable printed works and most of the manuscripts were eventually given to the Bodleian Library by their various purchasers. The Bodleian also received in 1735 the library of books and manuscripts collected by the historian Thomas Tanner (1674-1735). Sir Hans Sloane, a physician, accumulated over 50,000 books and 4,000 manuscripts that he in-

structed his executors to sell to the British Government. This
was, of course, an important part in the founding of the British
Museum. Two other physicians, Dr. Anthony Askew (1722-72) and
Dr. William Hunter (1718-83) were better known for their libraries
than for their medicine. The former specialized in editions of the
Greek classics, while the latter directed his collecting toward works
on medicine and natural science. Askew's library was sold at auction; but Hunter's, along with his collection of coins, went to the
University of Glasgow. Dr. Samuel Johnson's private library, so
strong in English language and literature, was sold at auction in
1785 in 650 lots. In fine bindings, one of the most magnificent collections was made by Joseph Smith (1682-1770), at one time British
consul in Venice. His library was sold to King George III and
eventually went into the British Museum. Smith later collected still
another library that was sold at auction in 1773.

Though most of the eighteenth-century English collectors were
interested in incunabula and sixteenth-century printings of major
European presses, some turned to English literature and especially
to Shakespeare. The actor David Garrick (1717-79) brought together an excellent library of drama and stage history, including
much Shakespeareana, which he bequeathed to the British Museum.
Charles Jennens (1700-73), a Shakespeare scholar, collected many
early editions of his works, and some of Jennens's choicest items,
after passing through many hands, have come down to the Folger
Shakespeare Library in Washington. Probably the best Shakespeare
collection of the eighteenth century was rounded up by Edward Ca-
pell (1713-81) who edited a ten-volume edition of Shakespeare in
1768 and whose library was given in 1779 to Trinity College, Cambridge. Edmund Malone (1741-1812) was apparently the first collector to compile a complete set of Shakespeare folios, including
the unique first edition, first printing of Venus and Adonis of 1593.
The rarest items of Malone's library was given by his brother to
the Bodleian Library, but the remainder was sold at auction.

In the nineteenth century the value of rare books had reached
such high levels that the scholar was almost priced out of the picture and the nobility and men of wealth again emerged as the most

important book collectors. George John, Lord Spencer, (1758-1834)
was one of the most ambitious of these. He had inherited a fairly
good library, especially strong in Elizabethan imprints. Over a
period of some 30 years, he bought thousands of volumes, including
many entire libraries. Thomas F. Dibdin, the bibliographer, was
employed by Spencer in buying, organizing, and cataloging his collection, and in time it became probably the greatest private library
ever amassed by one man. It included hundreds of incunabula, two
editions of the Gutenberg Bible, hundreds of other rare Bibles,
psalters, block-books, books printed on vellum, and more rare
works in general than almost any of the great libraries of Europe.
The library remained on the Spencer estate at Althorp until 1892
when it was bought for L250,000 by Mrs. John Rylands and presented to the city of Manchester as a memorial to her husband.
Today it there constitutes the heart of the John Rylands Library, one
of the truly great research libraries of the modern world.

Another nineteenth-century British nobleman, William Caven-
dish, Duke of Devonshire (1790-1858), built upon a family library
dating back to the seventeenth century to form at Chatsworth a great
private library that has been kept intact. Devonshire was able to
profit from many of the dispersal sales of the great eighteenth-century private libraries. In 1816, another noble library, that of
Richard, Viscount Fitzwilliam (1745-1816), was given to Cambridge,
along with an art collection and a sum of money to endow the Fitzwilliam Museum there. John, Duke of Roxburghe (1740-1804), was
another nobleman who built up a family book collection into a great
private library. His collection of incunabula and of French, Italian,
and English literature was unequalled in his day. When this collection was sold, it was divided into more than 10,000 lots, with the
Duke of Devonshire and Lord Spencer being among the greatest
buyers. Roxburghe's collection of some 1,300 broadside ballads
eventually reached the British Museum.

Others of the nineteenth-century British collectors are noted
for the quality rather than the quantity of their holdings. William
Beckford (1759-1840) was one of these. He collected books for
more than a half century, and unlike the collectors of early printing

and incunabula, he specialized in illustrations, odd works, and fine
printing.   In addition to books, he and his son-in-law, the Duke of
Hamilton (1767-1852), brought together a most valuable collection of
manuscripts that was sold in 1882 to the Royal Prussian Library in
Berlin.   One collector with a wide range of interests was Richard
Heber (1773-1833).   He often purchased multiple copies of the same
work, and his library, although strong in many fields, including
Latin, Italian, French, and Spanish literature, was so broad in
coverage that it could be said to have included a bit of everything
in Western European history and culture.   He may have had over
200,000 volumes at the time of his death, scattered in several locations in England.   His books were sold at several auctions after
1834, but many of them were purchased by William Henry Miller
(1789-1848) and remained in the Miller family until the 1920's.
Some of the more valuable Americana in the Heber collection eventually came to the Huntington Library, while other rare works in
theology, law, science, travel, and literature were acquired by the
British Museum.

Thomas Grenville (1755-1846) was an English collector who
preferred perfection to quantity.   His library totaled not more than
20,000 volumes, but in quality it was unsurpassed.   His fine books
included almost every subject, but he specialized in early Americana, incunabula, and classics.   His library was bequeathed to the
British Museum where it has been kept as a special collection.
Another collector of quality, Sir George Holford (1860-1926), built
on his father's library to form a collection of rare printings that
was not dispersed until long after his death, when many of the
rarest volumes went to the Pierpont Morgan Library in New York
City.   In the field of manuscript collecting, the name of Sir Thomas
Phillipps (1792-1872) stands out.   He began his collecting about
1820, and from many trips on the continent he gathered literally
thousands of rare manuscripts, sometimes individually, sometimes
in lots of several hundreds.   In subject content his manuscripts
were classical and medieval, historical, theological, legal, and
literary in almost all European languages.   Many of them originally came from the declining monasteries.   In all, he amassed the

amazing total of 60,000 manuscripts, dating from the tenth century
on and constituting probably the greatest collection of manuscripts
ever compiled.   Beginning in 1886, some of these manuscripts were
sold, most going to large libraries or archives in Europe and America, but as late as 1930 there were still some 20,000 of them at
the family home, Cheltenham, the property of Phillipp's grandson,
T. Fitzroy Fenwick.   Another great collector of manuscripts was
the Earl of Ashburnham (1797-1878).   He usually bought whole collections at a time, as for example the Guglielmo Libri collection of
1,900 manuscripts, purchased in 1847.   Ashburnham built up an immense library, but it was broken up and sold in various lots before
1900.

Two other late nineteenth-century English private libraries
are worthy of note.   These are the collections of J. O. Halliwell
(1820-89) and Henry Huth (1815-78).   Halliwell began collecting
about 1840 and on several occasions brought together small but well-
selected libraries that he sold at a profit.   His major collection
centered around Shakespeare and Elizabethan literature, although at
times he collected in many other fields.   In later years Halliwell
gave widely from his holdings to libraries both in England and America, but he still held an immense collection at his death.   His library was afterward sold, with most of the Shakespeare material
ending up in the Folger Shakespeare Library in Washington.   Henry
Huth was also a long-time collector and a careful bibliographer as
well.   His interests were wide but almost exclusively for the rare
and beautiful.   His son, Alfred H. Huth (1850-1910) continued to
build up the collection after his death.   The Huth Library, with the
exception of some 50 of the rarer works bequeathed to the British
Museum, was sold over a period of some 10 years and brought in
over Ł300,000, probably the most ever realized from the sale of a
single collection.

It can easily be seen that book collecting and the building of
private libraries was an important part of the English cultural scene
for several centuries.   Aided and abetted by booksellers, these book
lovers provided a remarkable service in collecting, binding, and
preserving many of the most valuable books in the Western World

until the public and research libraries were advanced enough to
handle them. Without their services, many important and rare
books and manuscripts would have been irretrievably lost, and our
cultural history would have suffered accordingly. With these private libraries, the Shakespeare folios, the incunabula, and thousands of other rare works have been ably retained, so that today
they are available for the study and enjoyment of millions of people.

Next to the English, the Germans were probably the most
active in the modern book collecting field, although the germs of
bibliomania touched all parts of Europe at various times. As already noted, most of the great state and national libraries of Germany began as private libraries of the various rulers. For example, the Bavarian National Library at Munich began with the library of Albert V, Duke of Bavaria (1550-79). August of Saxony
in 1556 began a collection that, moved to Dresden in 1650, eventually became the Royal Library of Saxony. Johann Albrecht, Duke
of Mecklenburg (1525-76), possessed a private library notable not
for its size but for its wide variety of contents, which included history, theology, law, science, philosophy, and literature in both
Latin and German. Other Germans gave their private libraries as
the beginnings of municipal reference libraries and university collections. In 1516 Ulrich Krafft gave his books to the town of Ulm
for public use. In 1763, Christian Theophilus Buder willed his library to the University of Jena. The library of Johann Fredrich
von Uffenbach was given in 1769 to the University of Göttingen.
The fate of other early German libraries is unknown; most of them
were dispersed after the death of the collector. Willibald Pirk-
heimer of sixteenth-century Nuremberg was a humanist and book
collector who was reputed to have owned a complete set of the
Greek printings of Aldus Manutius. Konrad Peutinger of Augsburg
in the same century collected both manuscripts and books, classic
and contemporary. His library of 2,100 volumes was not large by
later standards but notable for his era. Johannes Reuchlin's library was rich in Greek and Hebrew texts, while another sixteenth-
century library, that of Beatus Rhenanus of Schlettstadt, concentrated on Latin. Hans Sachs in the seventeenth century collected

in science and pseudoscience, a somewhat original collection for that period. Though it is difficult to generalize, it would seem that many if not most of the German nobility and wealthy middle class of the sixteenth to eighteenth century had at least small private libraries, and some of them are known to have reached the size of several thousand volumes.

Like the English, the Germans also produced several great family libraries that remained intact over several generations. The Fugger family library stands out in this category. Ulrich Fugger (1526-84), merchant of Augsburg in southern Germany, added to a collection already begun by his father and grandfather. His descendants continued to enlarge the collection, and eventually parts of it went to three major libraries, the Austrian National Library, the Bavarian National Library, and the Palatine Library at Heidelberg. Otto Heinrich, Elector Palatine of Heidelberg, and his successors had built up one of the most important libraries in Germany. With much of Ulrich Fugger's library added, it was a prime target for military conquest, and in the military wars of the early seventeenth century it was captured by Maximilian, Duke of Bavaria. Maximilian in turn gave it to Pope Gregory XV, and it was carried in triumph to its permanent home in the Vatican Library.

In some of the smaller German states the libraries of the rulers remained in private hands or at least became only semipublic. The library of the Counts of Hesse-Rotenburg came into the ownership of the Prince of Retibor and Corvey in 1820. It consisted of almost 65,000 volumes housed in 15 palace rooms in large cabinets. It had its own librarian in the nineteenth century and a catalog was completed about 1850, but it was little used until the 1930's when it was finally opened to the public. The Ducal Library of Gotha was established by Duke Ernest the Pious in the seventeenth century. It was opened to the public in the nineteenth century and contained about 190,000 volumes by 1900. The Ducal Library of Wolfenbüttel was established by Duke Julius in the sixteenth century, and by 1900 it had nearly 300,000 volumes and was open for public reference use. The library at Oels, built up over many years by the Dukes of Brunswick, was in the 1880's given to the Royal Saxon Li-

brary at Dresden. It contained about 25,000 volumes, many very
rare, plus several hundred manuscripts. Besides the formal libraries, many German rulers had "private" libraries for their own
use. For example, Frederick the Great of Prussia was a book collector in his own right and had large libraries at his palaces in
Sans-Souci and Potsdam. He even carried a small library with him
on his military campaigns.

Many important German private libraries eventually came to
rest in the Prussian Royal Library. In the nineteenth century the
libraries of Count Mejan, with some 14,000 volumes, and Baron
Beusebach, with some 36,000 volumes, were purchased, as were
also those of H. J. von Diez (17,000 volumes) and C. A. Rudolphi
(15,000 volumes). The musical libraries of Ludwig Tieck and
James Meyerbeer were also obtained by the Prussian Royal Library.
Two of the largest private libraries in Germany, however, went to
the Royal Library at Dresden. These were the libraries of Count
Heinrich von Bruehl, with 64,000 volumes, and Count Buenau, with
about 40,000 volumes.

However, not all of the German private libraries remained
in Germany. Several of the largest were acquired by American libraries, including the Americana collection of the historian Leopold
von Ranke, which was acquired for the Syracuse University Library
by Charles W. Bennet. Carl Otto von Kienbusch's 5,000-volume
library of German literature, very strong on Goethe, was secured
by Princeton University Library. The library of Johannes Vahler
of Vienna and Berlin, largely Greek and Latin classics, was bought
by the University of Illinois Library in 1913, while Northwestern
University Library acquired the library of Johann Schulze, also
classical, in 1900.

Elsewhere in Europe, book collecting was not quite as important as in the countries already discussed, but there were still
a number of large libraries brought together, particularly by the
nobility. In eighteenth-century Holland such libraries as those of
Daniel Wyttenbach (1746-1820), a professor of Greek and Latin at
the University of Leyden, and Jacob Krighout, another classics
professor, are worthy of note. Wyttenbach's collection numbered

only some 4,000 volumes, but it was well selected and ranged from medieval manuscripts to modern printing. Krighout's library was more general, but included rare items and sold in 1770 for 20,000 guilders. Hieronymi de Wilhelm, another Dutch collector, concentrated on Dutch and German literature and built up an outstanding library in these fields, only to have it dispersed in a sale after his death.

In Poland, Count Joseph Andrew Zaluski (1702-73) spent much of his life collecting books and manuscripts. At his death the library of almost 400,000 items, including 20,000 manuscripts, was willed to the nation to form the basis for a national library. This was, of course, the library taken in 1795 by the Russians to become the foundation of the Russian Imperial Library in St. Petersburg. The eighteenth century was a great one for Polish private libraries, and many members of the nobility collected libraries in German, French, Polish, Russian and other European languages, staffed them with scholarly librarians, and used them for their own research or subsidized other scholars who used them. Many of these collections were scattered in the wars of the 1790's, but even in a divided country, the Poles continued to collect books in the nineteenth century. These collections often were given to town or school libraries in the later years as a part of a general movement toward the preservation of Polish culture and nationality under German, Austrian, and Russian domination.

In Russia before the Revolution, the noble families usually possessed libraries, some of them quite large. These collections often contained more books in French or German than in Russian. The library of Count Gregory Stroganov is representative of these. Numbering about 8,000 volumes, it was presented by his son to the University of Tomsk in 1880. During the Russian Revolution most of these private libraries were scattered or destroyed, with the more valuable volumes going to the early Soviet public and university libraries. Many other volumes were destroyed as being anti-Communist in content. Since the Revolution, the ownership of private libraries is discouraged and is practically impossible for most people. However, most students and teachers manage to possess

a few choice volumes, and undoubtedly some of the party leaders
and government officials have sizable personal collections.

President Jan Masaryk of Czechoslovakia built up a library
of nearly 100,000 volumes in the 1920's, with major emphasis on
the history and literature of the peoples of his new nation.   In 1932
he gave this library to his country to be used as a national reference library.   In 1802 the library of Count Franz Szechenyi was
given to the nation to form the basis for the Hungarian National Library at Budapest.   By 1900 it had 400,000 printed volumes plus
16,000 manuscripts, strong in Hungarica.   Count Teleki de Szek had
collected a library of over 60,000 volumes when he died in 1822,
and part of this collection went to found a public library in the town
of Maros-Vasarhely.

In Spain, the great Escorial Library, founded by Phillip II
as virtually a national reference library, was itself made up almost
entirely of private libraries and collections.   Don Diego de Mendoza
presented his private library to the Escorial in 1576.   Ten years
later it acquired the library of Antonio Agustin, Archbishop of Tar-
ragona, a collection on the history of the church in Spain that had
taken over forty years to compile.   On the other hand, the famous
collection of manuscripts brought together by the Duke of Ozuna
went to the Spanish National Library at Madrid after that library
was founded in 1711.   The Swiss have long been noted for their private libraries from the earliest days of printing to the present.   A
noted library long in the hands of the Amerbach family of Basel was
inherited by Basilius Iselin, who sold it to the University of Basel
in 1674.   It was strong in the classics, theology, and history of the
ancient world, and had been cataloged for the Amerbachs by Conrad
Pfister.   A modern Swiss collector, Martin Bodmer of Colligny,
near Geneva, has since 1920 built up a library of manuscripts, incunabula, and first editions that rivals the Huntington Library in
California.   In the early nineteenth century a similar fine collection
was built up by Charles van Hulthem, curator of the University at
Ghent and member of the Belgian Academy at Brussels.   He spent
almost 50 years and virtually all of his salary and private fortune
in the purchase, repair, and binding of his books.   In subject mat-

ter his library centered on the history and literature of the Low Countries but also contained many other subjects. In 1837, some 60,000 books and 1,000 manuscripts from his magnificent collection became a part of the Belgian National Library then in the process of establishment.

In the Scandinavian countries private libraries have also played an important part in library history. Denmark's Royal Library, for example, has gained much from private collections, including those of Tycho Brahe and Otho de Thott. The latter, who died in 1785, left his country a library of over 100,000 volumes, including 4,000 manuscripts and about the same number of incunabula. Christian Reitzer, the Count of Danneskjold, also gave his library of 8,000 volumes to the national collection. Another large Danish private library was that of Jorgen Seefeldt, containing over 25,000 volumes, strong in Old Norse and Icelandic history and manuscripts. This library, however, went to the Royal Library of Sweden, where much of it was lost in the fire of 1697. A Danish seventeenth-century woman collector, Anne Gjoe, built up a library of Danish history and literature. She left it to a relative, Karen Brahe, who added to it many volumes of German literature and history and then presented it to a convent in Odensee. Remnants of it still remain in the regional church archives at Odensee, where it forms one of the few seventeenth-century libraries that is still relatively intact.

Magnus Gabriel de la Gardie, Swedish chancellor in the seventeenth century, built up his library both by purchase and by spoils of war captured in Germany and central Europe. His library ended up with the books going to the University of Uppsala and the manuscripts to the Royal Swedish Archives. In eighteenth-century Sweden, Carl Gustaf Tessin was a bibliophile and collector in the French manner, binding his rare volumes in the finest tooled leathers. Unfortunately, his library was later sold and scattered. Carl Gustaf Warmholtz in the same century concentrated on books relating to Swedish history and wrote a definitive history of Sweden before willing his books to the Royal Library. In the later seventeenth century the library of Queen Christina, which had been collected by both the Queen and her father, Gustavus Adolphus, was taken to Rome by the abdicating Queen and later willed to the Library of the Vatican.

Norway never developed as many private libraries as did Denmark and Sweden, probably because it lacked the wealthy nobility of those countries. However, the eighteenth-century library of Gerhard Schøning should be mentioned. It was strong in Norse history and literature, and it eventually came to rest in the Scientific Academy Library in Trondheim. Carl Deichman collected a library of a general nature that he presented in 1780 to the city of Oslo, where it forms the basis of the present municipal library. His father before him had given a library to the city of Copenhagen in 1732.

The debt owed by society in general to private collectors of books and manuscripts can hardly be overestimated. Although their ranges of interest are often narrow and their holdings are for years removed from the public view, the end results of their collecting are usually to the benefit of all mankind. Whether donated or sold as a unit to a public or university library, or split up and resold to other collectors, the books have been preserved where otherwise they might have been lost or destroyed. Moreover, they are often kept in far better condition in private libraries than they would have been in public ones. Without the prodigious efforts and costly collecting, and even the personal vanity of the book collector, many of our most valuable literary treasures would have been lost. Rather than condemn the book collector for removing books from circulation, we should thank them for preserving those books for future use.

Additional Readings

(Material on modern European private libraries is also extensive. In addition to the wealth of material in book and periodical form, the numerous book sales and auction catalogs are to be consulted. Biographies of eminent persons often give information on their libraries, and so also do discussions of estates and homes long associated with important people.)

Babeau, Albert
   Le château de Palis et sa bibliothèque.   Troyes, 1879. 16 p.

Bartholin, Thomas
   On the burning of his library . . .   ed. by C. D. O'Malley.
   Lawrence, Kansas, 1961. viii, 101 p.

Berrier, Theodore
   Histoire et déscription de la Bibliothèque Mazarine.   Paris,
   1883. 24 p.

Bertoni, Giulio
   La Bibliotheca Estense di tempi de Duca Ercole I.   Turin,
   1903. 307 p.

Bortolan, Dom
   La Biblioteca Bertoliana di Vicenza.   Vicenza, 1892. 223 p.

Crawford, Earl of
   Alexander Lindsay, 25th Earl of Crawford, and the 'Bibliotheca
   Lindesiana.' New York, 1957. 21 p.

Doucet, Roger
   Les bibliothèques parisiennes au XVIe siècle.   Paris, 1956.
   174 p.

Elton, C. I.
   The great book collectors.   London, 1893.

Fiske, Willard
   Book collections in Iceland.   Copenhagen, 1903.

Galindo Romeo, Pascual
   La biblioteca de Benedicto XIII (Don Pedro de Luna).
   Zaragossa, 1930.

Goodhugh, William
   The English gentleman's library manual . . .   London, 1827.
   392 p.

Gregori, Luigi de
   La Biblioteca Casanatense.   Rome, 1940.

Guerriera, G.
   Il fondo Farnesiano.   Naples, 1941. 56 p.
      (History of the library of Cardinal Alexandro Farnese,
      dating from 1534, now in the National Library at Naples.)

Guppy, Henry
   The John Rylands Library, Manchester, 1899-1924.
   Manchester, 1924. 144 p.

Hedeler, Georg
  List of private libraries.   Leipzig, 1898.   2 vols.

Heinemann, Otto von
  Die herzöglichen Bibliothek zu Wolfenbüttel . . .
      Wolfenbüttel, 1878.   48 p.

Hodges, John C.
  The library of William Congreve.   New York, 1955.   116 p.

Jayne, Sears
  Library catalogues of the English renaissance.   Berkeley, 1956.
      226 p.

Jones, Stephen Kay
  Dr. Williams and his library.   Cambridge, 1948.   35 p.

Juntke, Friedrich
  Geschichte der von Wallenrödtschen Bibliothek.   Leipzig, 1927.
      156 p.

Keynes, G. L.
  The library of Sir Edward Gibbon.   1950.

Krieger, Bogdan
  Frederick the Great and his books.   New York, 1913.   24 p.

Lacroix, Paul
  La bibliothèque de Jules Janin.   Paris, 1877.   52 p.

Lawler, John
  Book auctions in England in the seventeenth century.   London,
      1899.   xliv, 241 p.

Leslie, Shane
  The Percy library.   London, 1934.   14 p.

Lewis, Wilmarth Sheldon
  Horace Walpole's library.   New York, 1958.   x, 74 p.

Mason, Thomas
  Public and private libraries of Glasgow.   Glasgow, 1885.   448 p.

Mortimer, Jean E.
  The library catalog of Anthony Higgin, Dean of Ripon, 1608-
      1624.   Leeds, 1962.   75 p.

Munby, A. N. L.
  The formation of the Phillipps Library up to the year 1840.
      Cambridge, 1954.   xi, 177 p.

  The dispersal of the Phillipps Library.   Cambridge, 1961.   xi,
      203 p.

Nielsen, L.
  Danske privatbiblioteker gennem tiderne. Copenhagen, 1946.
    261 p.

Nolhac, Pierre
  La bibliothèque de Fulvio Orsini. Paris, 1887. xvii, 489 p.

Quaritch, Bernard
  Contributions toward a dictionary of English book-collectors as
    also of some foreign collectors whose libraries were incor-
    porated in English collections. London, 1892-1921. 14 parts.

Ricci, Seymour de
  English collectors of books and manuscripts, 1539-1930 . . .
    Cambridge, 1930. ix, 203 p.

Sallander, Hans
  Bibliotheca Walleriana, the books illustrating the history of medi-
    cine and science collected by Dr. Erik Waller . . .
    Stockholm, 1955. 2 v.

Santi, L.
  The Piccolomini Library in the Cathedral of Sienna. 1951. 32 p.

Schutz, Alexander H.
  Vernacular books in Parisian private libraries of the sixteenth
    century according to the notarial inventories. Chapel Hill,
    1955. 88 p.

Solms, Ernst-Otto
  Die Laubacher Bibliothek. Laubach, 1957. 32 p.

Van Even, E.
  Notice sur la bibliothèque de Charles de Croy, Duc d'Aerschot.
    Brussels, 1852. 33 p.

Williams, H.
  Dean Swift's library. Cambridge, 1932.

15

Colonial American Libraries

In the English colonies in America from 1607 to 1776, the book was an important cultural implement, but one that was not usually present in quantities. Colonial libraries, whether college, semipublic, or private, were few and far between, but they were nevertheless present almost from the beginning, and their influence was noticeable. The tasks involved in developing a new society in a wilderness occupied much of the energies of the early settlers in America, but as soon as that society became relatively stable, books became more important and a few small libraries began to appear. None of these colonial libraries reached a large size, but the sum total of them indicates a wide interest in literature and a degree of culture far beyond the frontier. Considering the time and place, their very existence is noteworthy, and in these small collections we see the beginnings of library history in the United States.

Small private libraries existed from the very beginning in the Pilgrim and Puritan colonies in Massachusetts. Of the Pilgrims, the Rev. William Brewster left a library of over 400 volumes when he died in 1643, with many of them obtained after he came to the New World. Governor William Bradford owned some 80 volumes, while the Plymouth minister Ralph Partridge had almost as many books, and even Miles Standish owned some 50 volumes. Most of these books were of course religious in nature, but there was also much history, some travel and political science, a very little literature and classics, and a few practical works such as those on agriculture and military science owned by Standish. Governor Bradford's library contained some works in French, while William Brewster owned some volumes in Latin and a Hebrew grammar.

Among the Puritans on Massachusetts Bay, the ministers and doctors usually had small private libraries, ranging from a

dozen or so to several hundred volumes. For example, Thomas
Jenner, who came to New England as a minister in 1635, left a library of 200 volumes in 1650, almost all religious in nature.   In
the same year Thomas Weld's ministerial library of 195 volumes
was sold to another preacher, John Eliot.   Samuel Brackenbury, a
young physician who died in 1678, left a small library including
works on chemistry and medicine.   John Alcock, who died in 1676,
left a library of over 100 volumes, but only about half of them were
medical in nature, while the others were religious, classics, and
some recent literature including Cervantes' Don Quixote in English
translation.   The Rev. Benjamin Bunker in 1669 left about 80 volumes in religious works, while his contemporary, the Rev. Jonathan Mitchell, left about 180 in the same field, 74 volumes of classics, and 11 of science, mostly medicine.   The Rev. John Brock
in 1668 left about 360 volumes, including a wide range of subjects
besides religion.   Other college graduates of the period also usually
left at least a few books in their wills, but this was also true of
many merchants, farmers, skilled craftsmen, and fishermen.   Generally speaking, the smaller the number of books owned, the more
religious their nature; the owner of the single volume usually possessed a Bible.

The largest library in mid-seventeenth century New England
was probably that of Governor John Winthrop, Jr., of Connecticut.
As early as 1640 this collection numbered over 1,000 volumes, and
after his death in 1676, it was preserved and enlarged by his son
and grandson.   Remnants of the collection given to the New York
Society Library in the nineteenth century indicate that it was cosmo-
politan in nature, with books in Latin, French, Dutch, Italian,
Greek, and Spanish as well as English, and on subjects as varied
as religion, history, travel, philosophy, law, and literature. There
were a number of grammars and dictionaries in several languages.
In the later seventeenth century, the largest library in New England
was probably that of Cotton Mather, the author and minister.   His
father, Increase Mather, had owned some 675 volumes in 1664, but
many of them were burned in a fire in 1676.   Cotton Mather's library contained about 2,500 volumes by 1700 and before his death

reached some 4,000 volumes. Both of these libraries contained
largely theological works, but there were also many volumes of history, geography, and philosophy, with a few volumes of science.
Works of fiction, poetry, and drama were conspicuous by their absence, but the son's collection included one intriguing title: The
Woman's Advocate, or, Fifteen Real Comforts of Matrimony. One
other private library of seventeenth-century New England is worthy
of mention, not so much because of its size, as because of its wide
variety of contents. This was the library of Samuel Lee, a Rhode
Island minister, whose books were sold in Boston in 1691. The
collection included over 1,000 volumes, and the books as usual
ranged from classics through philosophy and theology, but there
were also over 100 volumes in medicine and science and several
hundred others in history, geography, mathematics, astrology, law,
and general textbooks. All told, the libraries of the earliest New
Englanders indicate a wide range of interests and not merely the
strong concentration on religion usually reported.

Seventeenth-century Virginia also had its private libraries,
although they were usually smaller than those mentioned in New England. Government officials, lawyers, and large planters were the
most likely possessors of libraries in this colony, but surviving
wills show that blacksmiths, carpenters, and ship captains also
owned books. Ralph Wormeley, Secretary of the Colony, left a library of 375 titles, quite general in nature. William Fitzhugh's
library room, which he called his "Study of Books," contained works
on history and medicine as well as law. James Love, a former
ships surgeon, left in his will a "cedar chest full of books." Thomas Cocke in 1691 left a library of over 100 volumes, including much
history. Colonel William Moseley left books in English, Dutch,
French, and Latin. Some women left libraries, although the collections may have been those of their husbands. Mrs. Sara Willoughby
left a library in 1673 that was largely religious in nature, but included Aesop's Fables and a do-it-yourself title: Directions for
Planting Mulberry Trees. In one county, Lower Norfolk, and in one
fifty-year period, over 100 owners of books left wills, some of
them mentioning only a few titles while others ran into hundreds of

volumes.   One writer estimates that there must have been a thousand book collections worthy of being called private libraries in seventeenth-century Virginia.   Subjects included in the libraries range from theology to farming and from the classics to current handbooks.   They indicate a high degree of literacy among at least a part of the population, but it must be pointed out that in spite of all this half of the men and two-thirds of the women in the colony could not read or write.

Though actually smaller than some of the private libraries, the early college libraries were probably more important and more generally used.   Harvard College's library of the seventeenth century definitely illustrates this point.   In 1638 John Harvard gave the college some 380 books and a small cash endowment, a gift so important at the time that the college took the name of the donor. Other gifts of books to Harvard followed, including one of 40 volumes from Governor John Winthrop in 1642, but the college library grew only slowly.   Its holdings were largely theological, since the college of that day was mainly a training school for Puritan ministers.   Even in 1723, when the first library catalog was printed, there were only 3,500 volumes in the Harvard collection, and two-thirds of these were religious.   Of the remaining thousand volumes or so, history and geography took up about half, with other titles in the classics, science, and languages, in that order.   Only about 50 volumes consisted of literature written during the Renaissance or later.

In 1764, when Harvard College was more than a century and a quarter old, the library contained less than 5,000 volumes, and in that year it was burned with almost a total loss of its book collection.   After this tragedy, friends of the college came to its aid, and the Massachusetts Legislature voted Ł2,000 to replace the burned building.   In addition, a popular subscription raised almost another Ł1,000 and many gifts of money and books were received, so that by 1775 the library was back to its former size.   Something of the nature of the colonial college library can be gathered from the rules of the Harvard Library in 1765.   The librarian was required to keep the library room open and heated only on Wednesdays. Among the students, only juniors and seniors could take books from the library, but they could keep one book at a time out for as much as six weeks. The books were divided into two collections, the great library and the smaller library, with the smaller library being designed particularly for the use of the undergraduate students, with only about 30 per cent of its titles in theology.

Yale College also began with a collection of books. The 11 ministers who organized a society for the formation of a college in New Haven in 1700 each gave books, and in the next decade other donations increased the collection to several hundred volumes. In 1714, a group of English gentlemen, including Sir Isaac Newton, made a gift of 800 volumes to Yale through the good offices of Jeremiah Dummer, then the agent of Connecticut in London. In 1717, the Rev. Elihu Yale, for whom the college was named, gave 300 books to its library, and in 1733, the Rev. George Berkeley of London sent a gift of a thousand volumes, including many valuable folios. In 1742, the Yale library contained some 2,500 volumes, and the college president, Dr. Thomas Clap, reorganized and cataloged the collection with the aid of a tutor. He divided the library into sections, roughly according to size, and numbered each book in each section, giving to each a fixed location. Next, he drew up three catalogs, or booklists: one alphabetically by author, one arranged as the books on the shelf, and a third by subjects under some 25 headings. In the next quarter century some 1,400 volumes were added. Dr. Clap's interest in the library aided considerably, but it must be admitted that he censored the collection considerably as he built it up. By 1765, Yale's more than 4,000 volumes were still largely theological, although there were many volumes on history, classics, philosophy, and mathematics. There was not much literature or science, however, few books printed in America, and in fact few titles published after 1725.

It is of interest to note that a college and a college library were planned for the new colony of Virginia as early as 1620. A collection of books was sent by friends in England to the proposed "Henrico Indian College," but the Indian uprising of 1622 put an end to the plans, and Virginia did not acquire a college until William and Mary was founded in 1693. The President of this college, the Rev. James Blair together with Mungo Ingles, Headmaster of the lower school, gathered together a few books for the use of the teachers and students before 1700, but there were only a few hundred books before 1705. In that year a fire destroyed much of the college library, and in the succeeding years it grew only slowly and then by gifts. Some of the major acquisitions included about 200 books given by Governor Francis Nicholson in 1742, and a good portion of the private library of the Rev. Blair after his death in 1743. Even so, it is doubtful that the library contained over 2,000 volumes before the Revolution. The "keepers" of the library were usually ushers or clerks in the colonial period, and the library was open only a few hours per week. No books circulated, and apparently it was used chiefly by the faculty. Most of the contents were theological, with a smattering of classics and history but very little modern literature.

Among other colonial colleges, the library of King's College (later Columbia University in New York) was formed in 1757, largely on a gift from the Rev. Bristowe of London. Oxford University Library sent a gift of duplicates from its collection, and several British noblemen made gifts of books to the King's College Library. Unfortunately, during the Revolution this collection was virtually destroyed when the British soldiers used it as quarters for a military hospital. Dartmouth's college library began in 1770 with a few books brought in by Eleazar Wheelock who founded the college as a school for Indians. The University of Pennsylvania (then the Academy) had its library beginnings in 1750. It was small and poor in everything but classics until after 1800, and the college students depended more on the subscription libraries of Philadelphia for their reading matter. The library of the College of New Jersey (later Princeton University) also began about 1750 but had only some 1,200 volumes as late as 1764. These books were almost entirely composed of gifts by friends of the college. A gift of 474 volumes from Governor Jonathan Belcher of New Jersey almost doubled the collection in 1757. Rhode Island College (later Brown University in Providence) began about 1764 but had only 250 volumes in 1772. Before the Revolution began, however, its size had doubled with gifts from the Rev. John Gill of London and others. Fortunately, the early students at this college had access to the volumes in the Providence Library Company, founded in 1753. It is interesting to note that shortly after the Revolution, the King of France, Louis XVI, probably influenced by the Marquis de Lafayette, made gifts of several hundred volumes each to the colleges at Williamsburg, Virginia, and Philadelphia.

Probably the first attempt at a public library in the colonies came in 1656 when Captain Robert Keayne, a merchant of Boston, willed his book collection to the town for a public library, on condition that the town build a suitable building to house them. Boston at least partially met this condition, building a Town House with a room for the books, but it is doubtful that they were used to any great extent. A catalog was made in 1702, a few other books were added, and the collection met its end in a fire in 1747. New Haven began a small town library in 1659 with books formerly belonging to Governor Eaton, but this collection of only a hundred books or so aroused so little interest that it was finally sold to a minister in 1689. Many New England churches, especially after 1700, provided small libraries of religious works for public use. The King's Chapel Library in Boston, for example, was founded in 1698 with books given by the Bishop of London, and the First Church in Milford, Connecticut, established a small parishioners library in 1745.

The Rev. Thomas Bray, the English religious leader who had sponsored parish libraries in England, also encouraged and promoted the establishment of semipublic church libraries in the American colonies. This was done largely through the Society for the Propagation of the Gospel in Foreign Parts, an English missionary organization. Libraries were established around 1700 and later from Charleston, South Carolina, to Boston. Usually less than a hundred volumes each, these parish libraries were largely religious and were designed for the use of the ministers, except for a few inspirational books intended for the general public. The Province of Maryland received the majority of these parish libraries, and in the course of a decade some 30 parishes there obtained collections

of books varying from a dozen to 300 or more. Anne Arundel
County received at least two deposits of the Bray library books --
one in 1698 for the use of the ministers and another in 1703 for the
general public. At Annapolis there was a public library maintained
by the provincial government in the State House from 1697 to 1704,
when it was burned. The surviving books were united with the library of a school and survived into the twentieth century as a
prized collection of the St. John's College library.

Other parish libraries stemming from the activities of Bray
and his associates were formed in New York, Pennsylvania, North
Carolina, and South Carolina. A collection of books sent to Bath,
North Carolina, in 1700 numbered 166 bound volumes for the use
of the ministers and some 800 books and pamphlets for the use of
the general public. Oddly enough, the books for the use of the ministers were more general in nature than those for the use of the
public, since the latter were almost entirely theological or inspirational. A Bray library sent to Charleston led to the passage of a
legislative act in 1700, possibly the first library law passed in the
American colonies. This act placed a minister in charge of the library and gave detailed instructions as to its use, but it did open
the use of the books to "any inhabitant" of the colony. A similar
act "for securing the Parochial Libraries of this Province" was
passed in Maryland in 1704. With such an auspicious beginning, it
would have seemed logical for the parish libraries to grow and
eventually become active public services, but such was not the case.
No provisions were made for adding new books, and after the death
of the Rev. Bray, interest in parish libraries declined and most of
them disappeared. A few books originally in the parish libraries
have survived in public or church collections, and they serve as a
reminder of a library venture that came almost two centuries before
the public was ready for it.

Probably the most successful means of making books available for a general reading public came in the eighteenth century
with the establishment of subscription libraries. Benjamin Franklin
is usually given credit for establishing the first American subscription library in Philadelphia in 1731, and it followed in general the

pattern already popular in England and Scotland. Franklin and a
small group of friends formed the Philadelphia Library Company,
and some 50 members paid two pounds each for memberships, with
ten shillings yearly for dues. Franklin sent to England for books,
and on his later visits to Europe he personally selected and sent
back many more volumes for the library. At first the books were
kept in the home of one of the members, Robert Grace, but in 1740
they were removed to a room in the Pennsylvania State House, a
public building later known as Independence Hall. Following the success of this subscription library, others were formed in Philadelphia, but by 1773 at least three of them had joined the original one
and the resulting collection was moved to the second floor of the
Carpenters' Hall. These subscription libraries were mainly for the
use of members, but some of them were open at certain hours for
the reference use of the general public. During the Revolution and
the later Constitutional Convention, the Philadelphia Library Company made its books available to the founding fathers, and in fact it
served as the national library of the infant nation. In 1789 it moved
into a building of its own, and it has survived into the twentieth
century as an important part of the city's library system.

Other colonial towns soon followed the lead of Philadelphia in
establishing subscription libraries. There were four in Connecticut
before 1740 and about 50 in all of New England before 1780. Some
of them were merely voluntary associations or book clubs, but usually they took the form of a legal corporation chartered by the provincial government. The Redwood Library in Newport, Rhode Island, was one of the more fortunate of these early libraries. It
was operated by the Redwood Library Company chartered by the
provincial assembly in 1747. In 1750 it moved into its own quarters,
probably the first public library building erected in the English colonies. This library was fortunate in having a librarian from 1755
in the person of Dr. Ezra Stiles, a minister in Newport who devoted a few hours of his time each week to keeping the library in
return for the privilege of using the books. In Charleston, South
Carolina, a library society was formed in 1748, but due to opposi-
tion from the governor, it was not chartered until 1755. Despite

wars and fire, this collection has survived, and throughout its long
existence it has served its city as a valuable and valued cultural
asset.   Another surviving colonial library is that of the New York
Society Library, founded in 1754.   Several small collections of publicly owned volumes, including some of those sent by the Society for
the Propagation of the Gospel, were added to the Society Library at
the time of its founding.   By 1773 it contained over 1,500 books,
but it was largely destroyed during the Revolution and reorganized
as a subscription library in 1788.

Subscription libraries were also formed in several smaller
towns during the late colonial period.   In Pennsylvania there were
such libraries in Hatboro (just north of Philadelphia), Chester, and
Lancaster.   The latter, named the Juliana Library in honor of
Thomas Penn's wife, was formed in 1770 and eked out a meager existence for some 60 years until it was finally sold to pay the personal debts of its last librarian.   In South Carolina, the Winyaw In-
digo Society of Georgetown, a charitable organization, formed a library about 1755, but little is known of its later history, although
the Society itself was active until the 1850's.   Strictly speaking, the
subscription library was a private or special library, but it was
generally available to any interested reader who could afford the
relatively small membership fee.   It was sometimes open for brief
hours for public use, and it usually contained local and other provincial newspapers as well as a few periodicals from England and
possibly other European countries.   Its bookstock consisted of the
books that its members wanted to read.   Sometimes they were theology and the classics; at other times more contemporary literature
and political works were included.   Franklin's first library, for
example, contained a number of works on philosophy, history, and
science, while that of the Charleston Library Society included more
literature, both classical and contemporary.   Ordinarily the collection was in charge of some member who devoted a small amount of
time to it, or perhaps to an interested nonmember who received the
use of the collection by caring for it a few hours each week.   Only
rarely was there a paid librarian, but there was usually a strong
core of members who were interested in building up the library,

and often the bookstock came to include many valuable items through their collecting activities. All things considered, the subscription library was the nearest thing to public library service that was available during the colonial period.

In the eighteenth century the private library became more common, particularly among professional people, government officials, and large plantation owners in the South. In New England there were such noted private libraries as that of Thomas Prince, a Boston Minister whose avocation was the study of New England history. He formed an important library of books and manuscripts related to New England and deposited them in the Old South Church in Boston before his death in 1758. These books later became the property of the Boston Public Library. In Newport, Rhode Island, the minister and lawyer Abraham Redwood built up a private library that later formed the nucleus around which the Redwood Library was formed in 1745. In the middle colonies, John Sharp of New York built up a large collection of books and gave it in 1713 to the city for public use. It was largely theological, and there is little record of its use until it became a part of the New York Society Library in 1754. The Rev. Alexander Innes left a sizable collection of books at his death in 1713, and these were donated to the Anglican churches of New Jersey and New York. Samuel Johnson, an early president of King's College in New York, built his library around English literature, the classics, and history. One of the finest private libraries in New Jersey was that of Richard Stockton, a signer of the Declaration of Independence. Because of his patriotic activities, he was a marked man for the British and his home and library were destroyed in 1777.

Probably the most important private library of the middle colonies was that of James Logan of Philadelphia. This gentleman, who had served as chief justice and as lieutenant governor of Pennsylvania, collected more than 3,000 volumes before his death in 1751. His library was strong in mathematics, astronomy, and science in general, but it also included many of the classics and works of ancient history. A building was erected to house his library, and it was opened for public use, with books circulating outside the building "under certain circumstances." The Loganian Library eventually became a part of the Philadelphia Library Company and added considerably to the importance of that collection. Thomas Chalkley, also of Philadelphia, gathered a small library on the history and doctrines of the Quakers; in 1742 he donated it to help form the Friends' Library, which was to become the most important library of that religious group in America.

In the South the largest private library of the colonial period was that of William Byrd of Westover, Virginia. Byrd's father had built up a large estate and had started to collect books, but it was the son who, before his death in 1740, enlarged the library to more than 4,000 volumes. The Byrd Library is interesting because of its contents and its contrast with the New England ministerial collections. Byrd was a planter, lawyer, and public official as well as a writer, and his library reflected the cultural level and interests of the well-to-do planter. Almost a fourth of the collection was made up of works of history, with another fourth in classical literature and about 10 per cent each in English literature, law, and science. There were a number of volumes in French and Latin, but theology was represented only by a few works of the Church Fathers and some volumes on the Church of England. The remainder of the collection was made up of philosophy, travel, and practical handbooks of value to the planter and his family. Although the Byrd family library was probably the largest in Virginia, there were a number of other planters who had libraries numbering into the hundreds of volumes. Colonel Robert Carter in 1774 had a library of some 700 well-selected volumes that included classics, law, history, travel, science, and philosophy. Carter's library was also notable for his selection of contemporary literature, including fiction, poetry, and drama. Another Carter, John Carter II, owned a plantation library that was strong in both religion and medicine. Other examples of eighteenth-century Virginia private libraries are not difficult to find and lists of the contents of a number of them have survived. The contents of the libraries of Ralph Wormeley, Richard Lee, Edmund Berkeley, John Waller, David Black, as well as others, have been published in the William and Mary Quarterly His-

torical Magazine. In addition to works of obvious literary value,
these libraries contained volumes on farming, surveying, architecture, and law, as well as books on etiquette and gentlemanly conduct.

In both North and South Carolina there were several private
libraries of note, though none equaled those of Byrd, Logan, or the
Mathers. One of the North Carolina libraries might well be called
the Governor's Library, since it was begun by Governor Robert
Eden (1673-1722); the collection was passed on by his daughter to
her husband, Governor Gabriel Johnston (d. 1752), and later to her
nephew, Governor Samuel Johnston (1733-1816). This was a distinguished collection including strong sections of biography, travel,
and history, as well as books on medicine, economics, literature,
and law. The library remained in the Johnston family well into the
nineteenth century, and by 1865 was estimated to contain over 4,500
volumes, although it was considerably smaller than that during the
colonial period. Other colonial North Carolinians who had fairly
large private collections were Edward Moseley, Colonel James
Innes, John Hodgson, James Iredell, John Eustace, and David Mil-
ner.

In South Carolina, plantation libraries were customary but
not usually large in size. Henry Laurens, merchant and planter,
developed a large family library that he augmented with books personally selected on his trips to Europe. Governor James Glen, in
office from 1743 to 1756, made a collection of works on history,
particularly those relating to South Carolina, and used them as a
basis for his short history of the colony that he published on his return to England. A little later a Presbyterian minister, Alexander
Hewat, did much the same thing. While in a pastorate in Charleston he collected books and manuscripts relating to the history of the
colony, and then used them to write a two-volume history in 1779.
John M'Kenzie, a Charleston lawyer, collected books on a wide variety of subjects and presented them in 1771 to the Charleston Library Society. Other South Carolina planters whose libraries remained in the same families for several generations included the
Izards, the Middletons, and the Rutledges.

Many of the colonial leaders, whether in business, church, or government, had small but well-used collections of books in their homes, and the men who led the colonies into the Revolution were obviously well-read. Their speeches and writings abound with allusions to authors both classical and contemporary, and most of these works were undoubtedly in their own private libraries. Among those leaders known to have had sizable private book collections were John Hancock and John Adams of Massachusetts, the Livingstones of New York, the Pinkneys and Carrolls of Maryland, Jefferson and Madison in Virginia, John Rutledge and the Pinckneys of South Carolina, and many others. Jefferson's first library was burned in 1770, and although he mourned its loss, he noted that it was composed of replacable law books and textbooks. He immediately began to rebuild, however, and by 1783 his library totaled over 2,500 volumes. George Washington was also a book collector and delighted in fine bindings, having many books bound to his own design by a Philadelphia binder. His library is noteworthy because of his interest in essays, drama, and fiction, as well as in the more serious works common in his day. After his marriage to the widow Martha Custis, his purchases of books from London contained works that were obviously selected for his wife and stepchildren. William Hooper, one of North Carolina's signers of the Declaration of Independence, was a Harvard graduate and owned a large library that was destroyed by the Tories in 1782. Even on the frontier, or at least far from the coast, there were private libraries that were more than merely a handful of law books. The library of Waightstill Avery (1745-1821), lawyer in Mecklenburg County, North Carolina, contained, besides his law books, many titles in the classics, history, and politics. When his first library was destroyed by the British in 1780, he accumulated another even larger. Another library destroyed by the British was that of the Rev. David Caldwell, of Guilford County, North Carolina, also an area of near-frontier in the late colonial period. From their speeches and writings it is obvious that most of the colonial leaders were well-versed in the Bible, the classics, and contemporary politics, and even those who did not collect books must have had access to them from some source.

One possible means of acquiring reading matter without buying it was the rental or circulating library that became available in
the towns after about 1760. Maintained usually by printshops or
bookstores, these libraries made available rental books for a small
fee, either for a book at a time or for a number of books over a
given period of time. Possibly the first of these "circulating libraries" was opened by William Rind in Annapolis, Maryland, in
1762. He proposed to allow his customers the use of two books at
a time for an annual fee of 27 shillings. His venture was unsuccessful and it was discontinued in 1764. However, the idea caught
on and by about 1765 there were rental collections in Boston, Philadelphia, New York, and Charleston. One in Boston, begun by John
Mein, was particularly ambitious and published a catalog of some
1, 200 titles available for rent at the rate of 28 shillings a year for
all that one could read, one volume at a time. Unfortunately, Mein
was a Loyalist, and as the Revolution approached he was forced to
leave the city. In New York, Samuel Loudon's circulating library
offered some 2, 000 titles to discriminating readers in the early
1770's, and some of his most popular volumes were poetry. The
circulating library achieved its greatest success in the years after
the Revolution, but it did have its beginning in the colonial era, and
it undoubtedly added to the reading matter available, especially for
the working classes. It should be noted that the main business of
the bookstores was the selling of books, and only a few of them established circulating libraries. By the late colonial period, bookstores were common in the larger towns. Philadelphia, for example,
had about 25 in the period from 1765 to 1775, although probably not
all at once. Their basic bookstock included primers, textbooks,
prayer books and dictionaries, with the local laws and almanacs
being regular standbys. Aside from this, the average buyer could
find sermons, current political tracts, and some literature, but the
heavier works found in most private libraries were probably ordered
from England. The New England bookstore would be a little more
heavily religious in content than those in Philadelphia or Charleston.

A variation on the subscription library was the social library that became popular in New England especially after 1760. The Social Library of Salem, Massachusetts, was formed in 1760 with 32 shares at 5 guineas each. It was apparently never very large and consisted of relatively popular literature for the day, with about 800 titles listed in its catalog of 1809. The Leominster, Massachusetts, Social Library was begun in 1763, and it was even smaller, although it survived for half a century. The Social Library at Hingham, Massachusetts, formed in 1773, reached a total of 1,750 volumes and lasted well into the nineteenth century.

In general, the average colonial American was not a literary man, although surprisingly large numbers of his contemporaries did own books. Those who emerged as political and social leaders usually owned small but well-selected libraries. It is quite probable that a larger percentage of the educated Americans owned libraries in 1770 than in 1960. It has been estimated that Philadelphia had as many libraries and bookstores in 1760 as any European city of comparable size. Moreover, the leaders of the colonial era not only owned books but read them, and with considerable taste. From their private libraries and from the bookstores of the coastal towns or their merchants in England, they had access to almost any book available for sale in Europe at that time. That they made effective use of them is evidenced in the Declaration of Independence, the Constitution of the United States, and the numerous journals, diaries, and books that have come down to us from the colonial era.

Additional Readings

(Printed material on libraries in the American colonies is available, but scattered. Serious studies are available in several phases of the subject, and more pertinent theses and dissertations are appearing each year. Periodical literature is also fairly generous, and such indexes as Library Literature and Writings on American History will lead the serious student to many worthwhile items.)

Anonymous.
    A catalog of the collection of books of Thomas Prince.
        Boston, 1870.

Bolton, C. K.
    American library history. Chicago, 1911. 13 p.

Proprietary and subscription libraries. Chicago, 1912. 10 p.

Byrd, William
The writings of Col. William Byrd of Westover . . . New York,
1901. 461 p. (The appendix contains a catalog of the books
in the Byrd Library at Westover.)

Cannon, Carl L.
American book collectors and collecting from colonial times to
the present. New York, 1941. 391 p.

Christ Church, Boston.
The parochial library of the eighteenth century in Christ
Church . . . Boston, 1917. 85 p.

Conner, Martha
Outline of the history of the development of the American public
library. Chicago, 1931. 179 p.

Eaton, F. Thelma
Contributions to American library history. Champaign, Ill.,
1961. 277 p.

Gray, Austin K.
Benjamin Franklin's library. New York, 1936. 80 p.

Keep, Austin B.
History of the New York Society Library, with an introductory
chapter on libraries in colonial New York. New York,
1908. 607 pl

Lehmann-Haupt, Hellmut
The book in America: a history of the making and selling of
books in the United States. New York, 1939. 453 p.
(This edition has a chapter on early American libraries.)

Keys, Thomas E.
"The colonial library and the development of sectional differences," Library Quarterly, VII (1938), 373-390.

Miller, Perry
The New England mind: the seventeenth century. New York,
1939. xi, 528 p.

Monaghan, Frank
This was New York: the nation's capital in 1789. Garden City,
1943. xi, 308 p. (Includes about 20 pages on the early use
of the New York Society Library.)

Morison, Samuel E.
The Puritan Pronaos: studies in the intellectual life of New
England in the seventeenth century. New York, 1936.
288 p.

Pennington, Edgar L.
The beginnings of the library in Charles Town, South Carolina.
Worcester, Mass., 1935.   31 p.

Philadelphia Library Company.
A catalogue of the Library Company of Philadelphia, 1764.
(Facsimile ed., Philadelphia, 1956.   55 p.)

Potter, A. C.
The library of Harvard University.   Cambridge, Mass., 1934.
4th ed. 186 p.

Predeek, Albert
A history of libraries in Great Britain and North America,
translated by Lawrence S. Thompson.   Chicago, 1947. x,
178 p.   (Original German edition in the Handbuch der
Bibliothekswissenschaft, III, 855-975, 1940).

Roberts, A. S.
Two centuries of the Redwood Library and Athenaeum, 1747-
1947.   Newport, 1948.   58 p.

Rosenbach, A. S. W.
"The libraries of the Presidents," in pp. 130-167 of his Book
Hunter's Holiday.   Cambridge, 1936.

Shera, Jesse H.
Foundations of the public library.   Chicago, 1949.   308 p.

Shores, Louis
Origins of the American college library, 1638-1800.
New York, 1935.   290 p.

Steiner, Bernard C., ed.
Rev. Thomas Bray: his life and selected works relating to
Maryland.   Baltimore, 1901.   252 p.

Thompson, C. Seymour
Evolution of the American public library, 1653-1876.   Washington, 1952.   287 p.

Tuttle, Julius H.
The libraries of the Mathers.   Worcester, 1910.   90 p.

U.S. Bureau of Education.
Public libraries in the United States of America, their history,
condition and management.   Washington, G.P.O., 1876.
1187 p.

Whitney, Henry M.
The development of public libraries within the bounds of the Old
New Haven Colony.   New Haven, 1904. 16 p.

Wright, Thomas G.
   Literary culture in early New England, 1620-1730.   New Haven,
      1920.   322 p.

16

College and University Libraries in the
United States

The few college libraries formed during the colonial period were subjected to varied losses during the Revolution, and in fact higher education in general was set back seriously by the conflict leading to Independence. Still another decade of uncertainty was to follow the Peace of Paris in 1783, but by the 1790's there was a definite improvement in colleges and college libraries and even a few new colleges were begun. Growth was slow, however, for most college libraries until after 1850, and the colonial tradition of the library open only a few hours a week, with close restrictions on the use of books, was hard to outgrow. Not until after the Civil War, and indeed not until the late nineteenth century, did modern libraries really begin to develop in the nation's colleges and universities.

Though forced to move from Cambridge to Concord during the early part of the Revolution, Harvard College saved its library and even added to it with funds allocated by the new state legislature and with books confiscated from fleeing Loyalists. It revived during the 1780's, and by 1790, with 12,000 volumes, it had taken the place that it was to keep as the nation's pre-eminent academic library. The printed catalog of the year shows a still-strong emphasis on theology, but an increased interest in English literature and more titles by eighteenth-century writers. History, travel, and philosophy were strongly in evidence, but there was very little in the field of science. Periodicals, with the exception of the Gentleman's Magazine, were almost entirely absent. By 1827, Harvard's library totaled 25,000 volumes, and by 1840, when it was moved into a building of its own, there were 40,000 volumes exclusive of pamphlets. The building was a bequest of former Massachusetts Governor Christopher Gore (1758-1829), and although

291

it was constructed with the expectation that it would meet the needs
of the college for a century, it was outgrown in less than 25 years.
By 1856, there were 70,000 books and 30,000 pamphlets, while in
1866 there were 114,000 books and 95,000 pamphlets.   Much of
this growth came through gifts, and a number of important ones are
worth mentioning.   In 1818 the library acquired the American history collection of the German historian C. D. Ebeling, totaling
about 3,000 volumes relating to America, and including nearly
10,000 maps and charts, the most complete cartographic collection
on America then in existence.   Thomas Palmer gave a collection
of 1,200 volumes, mostly in English literature, in 1820.   The oriental library of Henry Ware Wales, former professor of Sanskrit,
was also acquired.   Two presidents of the United States, John
Adams and John Quincy Adams, both gave portions of their libraries to Harvard, while Senator Charles Sumner, over a long
period of time, gave some 1,300 volumes, 15,000 pamphlets (many
very rare), and some 250 valuable maps.   Dr. James Walker, a
former president of the college, left his library of 2,400 volumes.
All told, between 1780 and 1840 alone, more than 1,000 noteworthy
gifts of books were received, not counting the many gifts and bequests of funds for endowment or for direct purchases of books.

    Besides its main college library, the ante-bellum period al-
so saw the establishment of several special libraries on the Harvard campus.   The Law School Library had its beginning in 1817,
also with a gift from Mr. Gore -- his law library.   Many other
gifts were added, and in 1863, this collection alone totaled 13,000
volumes.   The Divinity School Library dates from 1825, and by
1863, this collection, augmented by some 4,000 volumes from the
religious library of Professor Gottfried Lücke of Göttingen, also
totaled over 13,000 volumes.   The Library of the Phillips Astronomical Observatory began in 1847, and before the Civil War there
were also libraries in the Museum of Comparative Zoology and the
Lawrence Scientific School.   There were besides the student society
libraries, such as those of the Procellian Club, the Hasty Pudding
Club, the Christian Brethren, and St. Paul's Society.

    At Yale the growth of the library was slow but steady, with

numerous gifts of funds and books. In 1808 the main library had 4,700 volumes; in 1835, 10,000 volumes; in 1850, 21,000 volumes; and in 1870, 55,000 volumes. Here also there were several special libraries, including the Law School Library founded in 1845 and the Theological Seminary Library. Two student society libraries, the Linonian and the Brothers in Unity libraries, were actually begun before the Revolution. The Linonian in 1860 had 12,000 volumes, while the Brothers in Unity was somewhat smaller. The two were united in 1872 and placed under the supervision of the general library committee. By 1876 the combined bookstocks of all the libraries on the campus totaled nearly 115,000 volumes. The Yale Library had moved into a new building in 1846, after having been housed previousiy in rooms or wings of several college buildings.

Other New England colleges were formed in the half-century after the Revolution, and in general they followed a familiar pattern. The gift of a small collection of books started off the college library, while later gifts of endowment funds and books added to it, and somewhat reluctantly about the middle of the nineteenth century some support came from the college authorities, a regular librarian was appointed, and the collection began to be used rather than stored. The library of Trinity College, Hartford, was founded in 1824, and after the gift of the library of ex-President Nathaniel Wheaton and the incorporation of the student society libraries in 1870, it still had only 15,000 volumes. Wesleyan University in Middletown, Connecticut, began its library in 1833, based on the collection of Thomas Chapman of Camden, New Jersey. In 1868 Isaac Rich of Boston gave funds for a library building, and a few years later this building housed 26,000 volumes, an excellent collection in the 1870's. Bowdoin College Library in Brunswick, Maine, began with the college, but received its real start in 1811 with the gift of some 4,000 volumes from James Bowdoin. Bowdoin College was particularly fortunate in gifts during its first half-century, and its library reached 18,000 volumes by the 1870's. Amherst College Library began with a single case of books in 1821, but with gifts of books from friends and subscription drives among

the alumni, the library grew to some 30,000 by 1875. By that year
Amherst was fortunate in having as assistant librarian a young man
named Melvil Dewey, who was recataloging the library with what
he called the decimal system of classification. Tufts College library began in 1854 with a total of 1,500 volumes received from
many sources. In 1865 the library of its first president, Hosea
Ballou, was purchased, and with this and other gifts and purchases,
the library in 1875 included about 16,000 volumes. In that year
Tufts reported that its library was being cataloged with a card catalog, a process still new enough to be proudly noted. In 1800 the
Dartmouth College Library numbered only 3,000 volumes, and at
one time it was reduced to selling rare volumes in order to purchase new and more usable ones. After its student society libraries were added, the Dartmouth Library reached nearly 47,000
volumes by 1875. Brown University began its post-Revolutionary
existence with a library that consisted of some 500 old, moth-eaten
and mildewed volumes that had been stored during the war. With
several major gifts of books and funds from the Brown family, along
with others from alumni and friends, it reached some 45,000 volumes by 1860, housed in the Doric architecture of Manning Hall.

In the Middle Atlantic States, the University of Pennsylvania
Library was one of the foremost in the ante-bellum era. Beginning
its post-Revolutionary period with a gift of books from the King of
France, a series of fairly large gift collections of books increased
its holdings steadily until by 1860 it had some 20,000 volumes.
There were also medical and law libraries on the campus as well
as two student society collections. Other college libraries in Pennsylvania before 1850 included Dickinson College in Carlisle, founded
in 1783; Lafayette College in Easton and Haverford College in Haverford, both founded in 1832. Student society libraries in each of
these colleges added several thousand volumes to the books available for student use. In New York, Columbia College library developed with a relatively small central collection and several department libraries. With the gifts of the private libraries of several of its presidents, and of such notable New Yorkers as Supreme
Court Chief Justice John Jay, the central library totaled some

18, 000 volumes by 1860, while the collections of the School of
Mines, the Law School, and the Botanical Garden brought the total
up to some 31, 000 volumes by 1875. Hamilton College in Clinton,
New York, began in 1812 with the books of a former academy library, but its growth was very slow before the Civil War. In 1860,
the books of two society libraries were added to the main library,
and the gift of two large private collections in 1865 brought the total
to about 20, 000 volumes. The library occupied a separate building
of its own after 1872. Elsewhere in New York State, the Union
College in Schenectady, founded in 1795, had a library of 20, 000
books by 1875; the College of the City of New York, founded 1850,
had 20, 000; and the University of Rochester, also founded in 1850,
had only 12, 000 volumes.

In the South Atlantic States, the colonial college of William
and Mary was joined after the Revolution by the state colleges of
North Carolina, South Carolina, and Georgia. In Williamsburg, the
college that had provided colonial Virginia with both political and intellectual leadership suffered a decline after the Revolution and grew
only slowly. During the Civil War its library was again almost destroyed, and in 1875 it had only about 5, 000 volumes. After 1825
the new University of Virginia in many ways replaced William and
Mary, and its library, as planned by Thomas Jefferson, became one
of the finest in the South. Jefferson personally selected the first
consignment of books for the University library and spent the last
year of his life (1825-26) working with them. He died soon after
the University was formally opened, but his effect on the institution
was long felt. President James Madison also gave the University of
Virginia Library a large gift, including some 2, 500 volumes and
$1, 500 in cash. Another large donation came in 1838 when Chris-
tian Bohn of Richmond gave the Library about 4, 000 books and
1, 500 engravings. By 1875 the University of Virginia Library had
over 40, 000 volumes. It had been housed almost from the beginning
in the Rotunda Building, also designed by Jefferson and one of the
most handsome college structures in the nation. The University
and its library were most fortunate in escaping the ravages of the
Civil War, while much of the remainder of Virginia was almost a

constant battlefield.

Washington College, founded in 1796 and destined to become
Washington and Lee University, was not so fortunate as the University of Virginia.   Instead, both it and its neighbor, Virginia Military Institute, had most of their library books destroyed or stolen
during the War.   Afterwards, the gifts of several large collections
helped these libraries to reorganize.   In particular, Washington
College received 4,000 volumes, largely classical, from the library
of N. P. Howard of Richmond.   Washington College's two literary
societies also had about 2,500 volumes each in 1875, so that the
total book resources available there were about 16,000 volumes.
Two other ante-bellum Virginia college libraries were those of
Randolph-Macon, founded in 1834, and with 10,000 volumes in 1870;
and Roanoke College in Salem, founded in 1853, and with 14,000
volumes after the Civil War.

North Carolina's University library at Chapel Hill began in
1795 with a small collection including 14 volumes donated by the
Governor of the State, William R. Davie.   Other donations followed, and in the 1820's the president of the University sent to England to purchase almost a thousand volumes for the library, along
with apparatus for a chemistry laboratory.   In 1850 the library
moved into a separate building, constructed in the form of a Greek
temple, and at that time it numbered about 7,000 books.   Like
many other Southern colleges, it suffered during the Civil War and
was closed for several years during Reconstruction.   By 1875, however, it had reopened, and with the purchase of some 2,000 volumes of the scientific library of Professor Elisha Mitchell, it then
numbered about 10,000 volumes, with an additional 4,000 available
in the two student society libraries.   The library of the University
of South Carolina at Columbia began shortly after the founding of
the University in 1805.   Though most gifts to the library were relatively small, the State did give more support that most contemporary publicly owned college libraries received, and the book collection grew steadily.   Relatively untouched until the very last days of
the Civil War, South Carolina's university library survived the
burning of Columbia and in the 1870's owned over 25,000 volumes,

including many rare works. In its own building after 1841, the main college library was supplemented by a student society library of 1,250 volumes. Elsewhere in the Carolinas, there were only two other ante-bellum colleges of note: Charleston College in South Carolina with about 8,000 volumes, and Trinity College in North Carolina with about 11,000 volumes in main and society collections by 1875.

The second quarter of the nineteenth century saw a number of colleges established in the Ohio and Mississippi Valleys, although for the most part their libraries were not as large as their east coast neighbors. Northwestern University in Evanston, Illinois, began in 1856 with a purchase of a 3,000 volume library and added to this in 1869 a larger collection purchased from Germany. Other gifts and purchases brought the university library to about 30,000 volumes in 1875, with an additional 3,000 in the theological library. The University of Michigan at Ann Arbor was founded in 1841 and had about 27,500 volumes by 1875. Its major accession came in the donation of another German library, that of Dr. Heinrich Rau of Heidelberg, purchased and presented to the university by Philo Parsons of Detroit, and containing about 4,000 books and 6,000 pamphlets. St. Louis University Library began in 1829, and by 1875 had 17,000 volumes, with an additional 8,000 in the student society libraries. The University of Indiana Library began in 1829 with a collection of books purchased by the first president. Gifts were few and far between on the Indiana frontier, but small appropriations were occasionally available, and state and federal documents helped fill the shelves. The first catalog was printed in 1842, and a fire destroyed most of the library's 5,000 volumes in 1854. By 1875 there were still only about 5,000 volumes, but there was also a law library and two student society libraries. Marietta College, in Ohio, founded in 1835, raised some $8,000 in subscriptions from friends and alumni in 1850 to add to the college library, and by 1870 had some 15,000 books with another 10,000 in the society libraries. Beloit College and the University of Wisconsin, started in 1848 and 1849 respectively, had about 10,000 volumes each in the early 1870's. The University of Missouri, founded in

1841, bought no books before 1849, and the library did not begin to
grow until after 1870. Both the University of Illinois and the University of Minnesota had just begun by the 1870's. On the whole,
there were few major college libraries west of the Appalachians before the Civil War. Those that did exist usually followed the Eastern college libraries in nature and operations, except that they
tended to be somewhat more liberal in student use than some of
their older Eastern brethren.

The typical college library prior to the Civil War was small
in size, usually under 25,000 volumes, and was made up almost
entirely of gifts, with little direct financial support from the college
administration. Open to students only a few hours per day or even
per week, its bookstock consisted almost entirely of old books,
reference works, and standard editions. Little attempt was made
to keep the library attractive or inviting to students, and in fact
the student was not expected to use it much. If the collection was
housed in a separate building, that structure was usually classic in
design and little fitted for library needs. The librarian or keeper
of the books was usually a younger faculty member, assigned the
library duties in addition to a full teaching load. He was often little
interested in the library and entirely inexperienced in library management; so he considered it an added burden rather than an op-
portunity to serve the students and his fellow faculty members.
Student reading was of necessity confined to textbooks, other personally owned books, and books from the student society libraries,
of which there were usually one or more on each campus. These
student libraries, although usually managed by a student worker,
were more suited to the immediate library needs of the student
body and really served more as the college library than did the official book collection. Since the student societies were usually in
competition -- they often resembled the medieval student "nations"
in that they represented different areas or parts of a State -- their
libraries were often well selected and frequently augmented by student and alumni gifts. In point of usefulness, and sometimes in
actual number of volumes, they were often superior to the general
college library.

After the Civil War, higher education in the United States advanced at a more rapid pace, with several trends that definitely affected college and university library service.   One of the most important of these was the trend in state-owned institutions of higher education, especially in the agricultural and engineering fields.   The Morrill Act of 1862, providing federal aid to such vocational colleges, greatly affected this move, and by 1875 most of the states had one or more such "land-grant" colleges either in operation or planned.   State universities and teachers colleges also began to prosper, particularly after 1880.   Some of the older colleges and a few of the newer state institutions definitely became "universities" with graduate work and several professional schools on each campus.   Finally, the liberal arts college held its own in the midst of the newer institutions, and many more of them were established. In each type of higher institution, the library situation varied from college to college, but there were also definite trends in each group, and a few generalizations can be made.   The land-grant college libraries, for example, usually grew slowly, concentrating on the technical, professional, and government publications in their teaching fields, collecting journals and monographs but often neglecting the general reading needs and interests of their students.   The teachers' colleges also failed to emphasize the library for many years, and the one-woman library, with the publications of the U.S. Office of Education prominently displayed, became more the rule than the exception.   On the other hand, the university that was beginning to offer graduate work early realized the importance of the library and began to build up huge collections of research materials, sometimes buying whole libraries from collectors and professors and aiming at complete coverage of all material relating to the fields in which degrees were offered.   One fault or virtue, depending upon the viewpoint, of university libraries in this period was the proliferation of departmental libraries and special collections. Following the European precedent, many professorial collections became departmental libraries, often with valuable but little used contents.   Since their contents were usually poorly cataloged if at all, and unavailable through a main or union catalog, they were practi-

cally nonexistent for the majority of the university students and
faculty.   Among the liberal arts colleges, a few libraries came to
life in the late nineteenth century, but most of them tended to follow in the ways of an earlier period.   Lack of financial support,
untrained librarians, mausoleum-like atmospheres, and poorly cataloged collections all combined to make the library less than it
should have been on most liberal arts campuses.

The effect of the Civil War and Reconstruction periods, particularly on the colleges of the South, is worthy of note.   Besides
the destruction already mentioned in Virginia, at least two other
major college libraries were virtually destroyed during the War.
These were the university libraries of Louisiana and Alabama.
Louisiana's university library had scarcely been established when
the War began and had only about 2,000 volumes, but in 1864 when
the town was captured by the Union forces, the books were hauled
away as spoils of war.   Similarly, when in the spring of 1865 Union
troops marched into Tuscaloosa, Alabama, the University there was
burned and all of the 8,000 library books not in circulation were
destroyed.   Elsewhere in the South most of the colleges were closed
for longer or shorter periods between 1860 and 1875, and books often suffered more from neglect than from military action.   A number of smaller colleges simply never survived the War; they closed
for lack of students during the War and were never able to get back
into operation afterward.   In the long run, the major effect of the
War on Southern college libraries was the half-century of financial
neglect that came after 1865.   With state governments still paying
for War and Reconstruction debts, little attention was paid to public education, and the public colleges struggled along largely on student tuitions.   Another long-range effect was that many fine private
libraries, which would probably have ended up in public collections,
were destroyed or scattered during the War.   One positive result
came during Reconstruction and later in the establishment of colleges for Negroes in the South, both by private philanthropy and by
state and federal government in cooperation under the Morrill Act.
In either case they had to begin as little more than high schools,
but in several cases they had by 1900 become respectable colleges.

The growth of college and university libraries west of the Mississippi after 1850 was particularly encouraging, both in numbers and size.   As an example, 17 colleges were established in Iowa between 1848 and 1873, and their libraries in 1875 ranged from 300 to 7,000 volumes in size.   In California, during roughly the same period, 9 colleges were begun, and by 1875 their libraries ranged from 600 to 12,000 volumes, with the larger being that of the university at Berkeley.   This university was not only fortunate in having generous state support for its library, but also in receiving several large donations of books in its early days.   The library of F. L. A. Pioche of San Francisco, a thousand volumes of literature and art, was acquired, along with some 3,000 volumes of scientific literature from the library of Dr. Francis Lieber.   The other Far Western States began their state university libraries in the latter half of the nineteenth century, ranging from the University of Washington founded in 1861, to Oregon State in 1868, University of Colorado in 1877, and the University of Wyoming in 1887. Each of these universities began with a definite emphasis on library service, and growth was more rapid than in the college libraries founded earlier in the East.   By 1900 most of these collections were well past the 25,000 mark and on their way to becoming modern university libraries.   By the mid-1930's these libraries were ranging in bookstock from Wyoming's 85,000 to the University of Washington's 325,000, and the University of California at Berkeley was approaching a million volumes.

Back East, Harvard's University Library, plus the other collections on its campus, totaled over 225,000 volumes by 1875 and over 560,000 by 1900.   By 1925 it had reached nearly 2,500,000, and by 1940, nearly 4 million volumes were crowded into its varied libraries.   In 1900, Harvard's main library was still in Gore Hall, but in 1915 it moved into the new Widener Library, a building that was supposed to meet the university's needs for a half-century at least.   By 1930, however, it was filled to overflowing, and the Widener Library has been supplemented by the Houghton Library for rare books and manuscripts and the Lamont Library for undergraduate use.   Beyond these there were some 70 departmental and as-

sociated libraries, many of them almost definitive in their subject
coverage, plus hundreds of thousands of books in storage.

Among other university libraries, Yale had some 78,000 volumes in 1875, with an additional 25,000 pamphlets, while at the end
of the century its collections reached nearly 300,000 volumes.
Princeton University moved its library into a new building in 1873
and gave its bookstock as 151,000 in 1900. The University of
Pennsylvania had 182,000 volumes at the turn of the century, while
Columbia had reached a quarter-million in all of its collections,
and Brown University's library was about half as large. Other college libraries in the Northeast were smaller except for Cornell University with well over 200,000 volumes in 1900. Dartmouth had
only 90,000 volumes; Amherst, 72,000; Rutgers, 41,000; and in
Washington, D.C., Georgetown had 88,000. In the Southern States,
the universities of Virginia and North Carolina had about 50,000 and
30,000 volumes respectively, while Vanderbilt University had 32,000
and the University of Texas, 34,000. In the Middle West, the new
University of Chicago, founded in 1892, had taken a commanding
lead in bookstock by 1900, with nearly 300,000 volumes to make it
one of the major libraries of the nation. In that same year the
University of Illinois had only 42,000 volumes and the University of
Missouri, 34,000; but the universities of Michigan and Minnesota
had forged ahead with 145,000 and 65,000 respectively. Total numbers of volumes do not, of course, tell the whole story of library
development in the colleges and universities of this era. The approach to library service on the campuses was changing rapidly,
with longer hours, better catalogs, and more efficient library service for students and faculty. The development of the Indiana University Library in the latter quarter of the nineteenth century may be
typical of many other university libraries. In 1875 the library of
about 10,000 volumes was poorly cataloged and open only a few
hours a week. In 1880 the first full-time librarian was employed,
and despite a disastrous fire in 1883, a card catalog was prepared,
new books purchased, and three additional library staff members
were needed by 1888. In 1891 the library moved into a new building, Maxwell Hall, with a large reading and reference room. In

addition to a law library, other departmental libraries appeared in the 1890's. Additional staff members, student assistants, and a reserves reading room gave the library a twentieth-century air by 1900, and the library budget in that year was 20 times what it had been in 1875.

Throughout the country the university libraries in the early part of the new century continued to grow more and more rapidly, with bookstocks expanding far beyond the capacity of old buildings and new buildings soon being filled to capacity. On larger campuses, departmental libraries grew rapidly in size and numbers, although in a few cases there was a tendency to return all books to a centralized collection. There was a constant striving, with varying success, to keep bookstocks, buildings, and staffs in line with the growing numbers of students and faculty. Gradually the college library ceased being a museum and became an active part of the academic program. Newer teaching methods called for more student use of the library, more faculty interest in book selection, and of course for larger expenditures for books. The seminar method of teaching especially called for greater emphasis on the use and proximity of books. Growing graduate schools demanded rare and expensive books and periodicals for research. Above all, the increasing size of libraries meant that books and materials had to be better organized and arranged, so that in many cases whole libraries had to be recataloged with new classification systems employed. Fortunately, this was also a period of library philanthropy, when most of the major universities and many of the minor ones received substantial gifts in money, buildings, and books. The Carnegie Corporation in particular gave money for buildings on literally hundreds of campuses. Later in the century the same institution provided funds for library schools, surveys, recataloging projects, and publications.

The 1920's saw a number of university libraries in the South and West beginning to compete in size and importance with the older ones in the Northeast. The universities of Virginia, North Carolina, Florida, and Texas, along with those of the private universities of Duke, Tulane, Emory, and Vanderbilt began to attract at-

tention as major research centers. Similarly, the libraries of liberal arts colleges, teachers' colleges, technical and agricultural institutions took on more importance, and although not equal in size
to those of the universities, they increased their significance in
their own fields. On many campuses there was a conflict between
those who wanted departmental libraries and those who wanted everything in a central collection, and as new buildings were constructed,
the latter often won out. Each type of organization had its own good
and weak points, but the departmental systems, by choice or necessity, remained in vogue in the larger institutions as a general rule.
As the donations of books and funds for library purposes became
smaller in comparison to needs, many libraries turned to the formation of Friends of the Library groups, where many could make small
gifts to take the place of the few large ones formerly received.
The coming of the depression in the 1930's hit the college and university libraries, and staffs and budgets were curtailed. Plans for
expansion and improvements, for new buildings and larger staffs,
were often shelved indefinitely. Federal Government assistance and
relief workers from the Works Progress Administration and the National Youth Administration brought temporary relief to many libraries, and useful projects in binding, cataloging, indexing, and
sometimes even buildings, were carried forward. The W. P. A. public records projects in particular provided outstanding research materials in their indexes and abstracts of public records on the local,
state, and federal levels.

In order to extend the services that their strained budgets
could not provide, college and university libraries sought for new
methods of performing old tasks and more efficient methods of providing more and better services. Various new methods of book
charging and circulation control were introduced in the 1930's, with
some of them being widely adopted and others soon disappearing.
As book acquisitions far exceeded stack space, ideas for reducing
the size of book forms were investigated, and from these experiments came a wide variety of microforms as means of storing
large quantities of graphic materials in a small space. Microfilms
and microcards in particular became widely used, and newspapers,

periodicals, and government publications were soon reproduced in these forms. Cooperative acquisition programs, especially in the matter of foreign publications, were tried and some of them adopted. Duke University, North Carolina, and Tulane, for example, co-operated in the acquisition of Latin American materials, with each specializing in one or more of the countries south of the border. On a larger scale, the Farmington plan, uniting many of the major research libraries of the nation, assured complete coverage in the acquisition of foreign newspapers and governmental publications. Union catalogs and inter-library loans furthered this cooperation, and photo-mechanical means of reproducing printed materials made possible the acquisition of copies of rare materials at a reasonable cost.

Before the college and university libraries had recovered from the effects of the depression, World War II came on the scene with all its problems. Colleges and universities were called upon to supply the special training needed for soldiers and specialists in a national war, and their libraries felt the strain. Funds were usu-ally plentiful, but staff members were scarce and the demands for books and services for the new programs, the newly organized aca-demic departments, and the war information centers severely taxed the abilities of even the largest libraries. Under the pressure of need, however, new methods were employed, new tools were de-veloped, thousands of new workers were introduced to the library field, and the end of the War saw the nation's college and univer-sity libraries stronger than ever. Not only were their bookstocks larger but their position on the campus was stronger. The trite expression that "The library is the heart of the college" became nearer the truth than ever, and from one end of the nation to the other, college and university administrators pressed for more funds, bigger buildings, and larger staffs for their libraries. The thou-sands of war veterans flooding the campuses after 1945 made these library needs more meaningful, and library progress was rapid if not spectacular. Both graduate and undergraduate enrollments rose to new heights, and the presence of the older veterans on the cam-pus made all students more serious in their work. Capacity use

was made of all library facilities, and once again the libraries
faced a crisis with more demands for their services than facilities
to fill them.   By the 1950's, most college and university libraries
were undergoing building programs, either in the form of new buildings or annexes.   Once again departmental libraries flourished on
many campuses for lack of space in the main library, and storage
facilities for little used materials became a necessity.   Most of the
new library buildings were constructed in the newer forms of modu-
lar arrangement, with open shelves and subject divisional plans.

With Harvard in the lead with more than 6 million volumes,
some 20 other university collections passed the million volume level
by the 1950's, and the end to library expansion seemed nowhere in
sight.   The university library collection of a half-million volumes
became almost a norm, with the largest institutions having library
budgets of over a million dollars annually, and staffs of well over
a hundred members.   On the other end of the college scale, dozens
of junior colleges became four-year institutions after World War II,
and literally scores of new junior, or "community," colleges were
established.   Some states, like Florida, established new universities,
beginning with campuses designed for thousands of students from the
start and with multiple departments and even graduate schools.
Thanks to microforms and widely reprinted source materials, it was
possible to begin these institutions with reasonably adequate library
facilities when the funds were available.

However, there were still many college and smaller university libraries that were far from adequate for the needs of their
faculties and students.   Among these were some of the newer colleges, small church-supported institutions, Negro colleges and institutions in the economically poorer areas.   Colleges in the South
were particularly noted for their less-than-adequate library facilities, but meager collections and small staffs were not restricted to
any particular area.   Regional accrediting agencies, such as the
Southern Association of Colleges and Secondary Schools, have done
much to improve library conditions in colleges and universities
through their library standards.   As late as 1950, however, it was
still true that almost two-thirds of the colleges in the Southeastern

States failed to meet Southern Association standards in one or more points.

While the smaller colleges were having trouble getting enough books to meet demands and standards, the larger universities were having difficulties finding space to house all the books they were acquiring. As bookstocks reached unmanageable proportions, they turned to various types of storage plans. Some found storage on their own campuses or in rented buildings nearby, while others made full use of microfilming and discarding. In two areas, however, the storage problem was met by the formation of cooperative inter-library storage centers, jointly owned and controlled by several universities. The New England Deposit Library in Boston is maintained by the major libraries of that area, including Harvard and the Massachusetts Institute of Technology. In it are deposited newspapers, runs of periodicals, sets of little-used works, state and foreign documents, and miscellaneous ephemeral material. In most cases this material is not duplicated in any of the member libraries but is available to any of them. Duplicates are not usually kept in the storage centers either, but are sold or exchanged. The other major storage library, the Midwest Inter-Library Center at Chicago, is the result of cooperation among a dozen or so Middle Western university libraries. It was formed in 1951 and has a capacity of over 2 million volumes. This center functions much the same as that in New England, but it also has the task of acquiring certain types of little-used materials itself, thus relieving its constituent libraries of that necessity. Another approach to the same problem has come through the complication of union catalogs of the research holdings of many libraries in the same area. These of course provide excellent tools for reference and inter-library loan services, but they also serve as an acquisition aid. Expensive, rare, or bulky volumes are often not purchased by individual libraries when they are found through union catalogs to be already available in a neighboring collection.

It is difficult to generalize on the academic library in the United States in the twentieth century, due to the wide range of collections in college and university libraries. From Harvard's 6 mil-

lion volumes, with its numerous departmental and special collections, its staff of hundreds, and its budget of millions, down to the
one-librarian, one-room junior college library of 1,500 books is
too great a step to encompass in sweeping statements. Still, it is
safe to say that in the majority of academic libraries, the demand
is greater than the supply, whether that demand be for books, for
staff, or for space. In the 1960's, students and faculty are making
greater demands on their libraries than ever before. Wherever the
college librarian turns he is met with demands for more and better
services, and he is trying to meet those demands. Whether the
solutions to his problems lie simply in more money, more space,
more books and more staff, or in new developments such as micro-
facilities, automation, and cooperation, or in some entirely new
concept of bringing student and knowledge together, the librarian is
trying and to a degree succeeding in meeting those demands.

Additional Readings

(In addition to the titles listed below and similar works, there is a
wealth of information on American college and university library
history to be found in the histories of the institutions themselves.
Almost every college history has a chapter on the library or libraries, and if not such information is usually available through the
index. Annual reports of the colleges and of state departments of
education are useful for statistics of college and university library
growth.)

Bach, Harry
    Bibliographical essay on the history of scholarly libraries in the
        United States, 1800 to the present. Urbana, 1959. 24 p.

Bidlack, Russell E.
    The nucleus of a library: a study of the book collection of the
        University of Minnesota, 1837-1845. Ann Arbor, 1960.
        106 p.

Bishop, William W.
    The Carnegie Corporation and college libraries, 1929-1939.
        New York, 1939. 66 p.

Blegen, Theodore C.
    Book collecting and scholarship. Minneapolis, 1954. 67 p.

Breedlove, Joseph P.
    Duke University Library, 1840-1940. Durham, 1955. 81 p.

Brough, Kenneth J.
Scholar's workshop: evolving conceptions of library service. Urbana, 1953. 197 p.

Brown, Ralph M.
History of the Virginia Polytechnic Institute Library, 1872-1928. Blacksburg, 1929. 33 p.

Butler, Pierce, ed.
Librarians, scholars and booksellers at mid-century. Chicago, 1953. 107 p.

Carlson, William H.
The development and financial support of seven western and northwestern university libraries. Berkeley, Calif., 1958.

Clemons, Harry
The University of Virginia Library, 1825-1950 . . . Charlottesville, 1954. xxii, 231 p.

Danton, J. Periam
Book selection and collections: a comparison of German and American university libraries. New York, 1963. 204 p.

Downs, R. B.
Resources of southern libraries: a survey of facilities for research. Chicago, 1938. 370 p.

Erickson, E. Walfred
College and university library surveys, 1938-1952. Chicago, 1961. 115 p.

Galbraith, Charles B.
Sketches of Ohio libraries. Columbus, 1902.

Harrar, Helen Joanne
Cooperative storage warehouses. New Brunswick, 1962. 209 p.

Jefferson, Thomas
Jefferson's ideas on a university library, ed. by Elizabeth Cometti. Charlottesville, 1950. 49 p.

Kroll, Morton, ed.
College, university and special libraries of the Pacific Northwest. Seattle, 1961. x, 310 p.

Longhead, Flora H. A.
The libraries of California . . . San Francisco, 1878. 304 p.

Lowell, Mildred H.
College and university library consolidations. Eugene, Oregon, 1942. vii, 136 p.

Lundy, Frank A.
The divisional plan library: origins and development, present meaning and future potential. Kent, Ohio, 1959. 8 p.

Marshall, John David, ed.
An American library history reader. Hamden, Conn., 1961. 464 p.

Metcalf, Keyes D.
The Hampshire Inter-Library Center. South Hadley, Mass., 1957. 31 p.
A report on Harvard University Library . . . Cambridge, 1955. 131 p.

Miller, Durand R.
Carnegie grants for library buildings, 1890-1917. New York, 1943. 40 p.

Oklahoma Library Commission.
Oklahoma Libraries, 1900-1937: a history and handbook. Oklahoma City, 1937. 273 p.

Potter, Alfred C.
Librarians of Harvard College, 1667-1887. Cambridge, 1897. 47 p.
The library of Harvard University: descriptive and historical notes. Cambridge, 1934. 186 p.

Rhees, William J.
Manual of public libraries, institutions and societies in the United States . . . Philadelphia, 1859. 687 p.

Rider, Fremont
Compact book storage: some suggestions toward a new methodology . . . New York, 1949. 90 p.
The scholar and the future of the research library . . . New York, 1944. xiii, 236 p.

Roberts, Ethel D.
A brief history of the Wellesley College Library. Wellesley, Mass., 1936. 46 p.

Rothstein, Samuel
The development of reference services through academic traditions, public library practice, and special librarianship. Chicago, 1955. ix, 124 p.

Rush, N. O.
History of college libraries in Maine. Worcester, Mass., 1946. 53 p.

Severence, Henry O.
   History of the library, University of Missouri. Columbia, Mo.,
      1928. 98 p.

Sharp, Katharine L.
   Illinois libraries. Urbana, Illinois, 1907-1908. 2 v.

Starrett, Agnes
   The Darlington Memorial Library of the University of Pittsburgh.
      Pittsburgh, 1938. 28 p.

Texas Library Association.
   Handbook of Texas libraries. 4th ed. Houston, 1935. 161 p.

Williams, Edwin E.
   The Farmington plan handbook. Bloomington, Ind., 1953. 170 p.

Wilson, Louis R.
   The library of the first state university: a review of its past
      and a look at its future. Chapel Hill, 1960. 40 p.

17

Public Libraries in the United States

The generation following the American Revolution saw little in the way of public library service available in the new United States. Even the subscription libraries and rental circulating libraries found it hard going until the 1790's when business began to improve a little. Publicly supported free circulating libraries were virtually unknown until after 1850, but in the form of social libraries, proprietary and subscription libraries and their variations, there was some type of relatively inexpensive reading available in the larger towns, especially after 1800.

Some of the colonial social libraries survived the Revolution. The Philadelphia Library Company, the Redwood Library in Newport, the New York Society Library, and the Charleston Library Society can be mentioned as among the more important ones. Many more were added, however, after 1790, and it has been estimated that over 500 were organized in New England alone between 1790 and 1815, and almost another 500 before 1850. Many of these lasted only a short time, of course, but enough of them did survive so that for the average reader they provided most of the reading matter down to about 1875. In its simplest form the social library was a subscription library, containing popular reading available to anyone who cared to pay the small fee. In other forms it served a more restricted clientele and built its book collection along more specific lines. Besides the general social libraries that served readers in a town or area, there were also lyceum libraries, mercantile libraries, mechanics' libraries, apprentices' libraries, Young Men's Christian Association Libraries, and even factory workers' libraries. After 1800 the social library spread into the smaller towns, to the middle West, and to a lesser degree into the South. In the North and East almost every town had at least one social library, and the larger towns usually had several. In book numbers, these collections ranged from a few hundred to several thousand in a few exceptional cases. Some completely excluded fiction, while others included up to half of their book stock in this increasingly popular form of reading. Science, economics, agriculture, sociology, and law made up only a small percentage of titles in most social libraries, but literature, travel, history, and religion were usually well represented. Many libraries maintained public reading rooms and added the latest English and American periodicals to their holdings of books and pamphlets.

The organization of the social library was usually very simple. In the smaller ones there was little or no attempt at arrangement or classification, but in the larger collections books were usually divided by larger subjects or even by locally developed systems of classification. Catalogs ranged from none through simple manuscript accession records to printed alphabetical or classed lists. Housing for the collection might be in a public building, a member's home or business, or in the case of larger collections, in a separate rented or owned building. One of the most interesting of the subscription libraries flourished on a houseboat on the Erie Canal. This "Book Boat" flourished for about a generation after 1830, plying the canal from Albany to Buffalo about once each month. Tying up to a wharf for a few days at a time, it would rent its literature, varying from religion to joke books, at 2 cents an hour or 10 cents a day. The more permanently located collections usually were open only a few hours per day and sometimes only a day or so per week. An attendant, voluntary or paid, charged books and checked on their return in the smaller collections, while the larger libraries had more or less full-time "librarians." As early as 1793 a pamphlet had been written to advise the book selectors for social libraries on the best methods of obtaining books, and the best books to be chosen. This was the Selected Catalogue of Some of the Most Esteemed Publications in the English Language Proper to Form a Social Library, written by Thaddeus Mason Harris, a young man who had served for a short time as librarian at Harvard. His booklet was one of the earliest American works on book selection, and as such it is interesting. He divided all books into three classes: memory, reason, and imagination. The first

class included all phases of history, biography, and travel; the second, science, philosophy, and religion; and the third, poetry, drama, fiction, and art. In all he recommended only 81 titles, but
these were well selected for the time and purpose. Ordinarily, the
smaller social libraries bought only a few new books each year, but
collectively they made up a major book market, so that book publishers and dealers soon came to offer them special discounts to
secure their trade.

The mercantile library, popular in the larger cities, began
primarily as an educational effort designed to improve the status of
the clerical workers in the stores, warehouses, and shops. They
were often encouraged and even partly financed by the business interests, but their primary appeal was to the ambitious young worker
who could afford the small fees. They were similar to the "mechanics" libraries' established in England in the late eighteenth century, but unlike them they tended in time to broaden the range of
reading matter on their shelves and become more like a general
subscription library than a vocational collection. The two earliest
mercantile libraries were those of New York and Boston, both established in 1820. The Philadelphia Mercantile Library began the
next year, while by the 1830's the movement had reached Baltimore,
Detroit, and Cincinnati. Other similar institutions were known as
Young Men's Institutes, Young Men's Associations, Mechanics' Institutes, and Apprentices' Libraries, and many of them in time became important libraries of many thousands of volumes. The New
York Mercantile Library, for example, had over 150,000 volumes
by 1875, while that at Philadelphia had about 125,000. These libraries were often associated with other educational features, such
as adult education classes, public lecture programs, recreation
rooms, and even gymnasiums. The educational and cultural effect
of these libraries is difficult to assess, but undoubtedly they must
have served a valuable purpose because of their widespread and long-
continued operation. Throughout most of the nineteenth century they
and similar institutions provided the best library service available
in their respective areas, and they did not give way until long after
the beginning of the free public library movement.

After 1850 the library service for young men was augmented by the libraries of the Young Men's Christian Association. Organized in Boston in 1851, this morally motivated organization spread rapidly across the nation, having over 180 local chapters, or associations, by 1875. Most of these local groups conducted reading rooms or libraries and circulated books to the members. Since membership fees were rather small, the YMCA libraries reached a potentially larger clientele than even the mercantile libraries, but the religious overtones served to limit the number served. Actually, although the moral improvement of the young man was a primary motive of the book collection, and the study of the Bible was a central theme, the libraries soon came to include much general reading matter. The reading rooms were always free to the general public, and newspapers and periodicals always available, as well as general reading and reference works. One popular feature of the YMCA libraries was that they were open Sunday afternoons and evening when other libraries were closed. The YMCA library in New York reached 10,000 volumes by 1875, but most of the others were much smaller.

The social library in its various forms spread westward not long behind the general flow of settlers. In Athens County, Ohio, a settlement in 1803 established a library partially paid for by coonskins sent back East for sale. Hence it has become known as the "Coonskin Library," although its formal title was the Western Library Association. It began with a collection of 61 volumes and flourished for about 30 years before a period of decline set in. The remaining books were finally disposed of about the time of the Civil War. Lexington, Kentucky, had a library organized as early as 1795, with many books ordered from England. It was chartered in 1800 with the title of "The Lexington, Georgetown and Danville Library Association." It absorbed the Lexington Juvenile Library in 1810, indicating a children's subscription library before that date, and had some 8,000 volumes listed in its catalog published in 1821. There is reported to have been a subscription library in Vincennes, Indiana, in 1806, and St. Louis had one by 1811. Cincinnati had an active circulating library in 1814, and Detroit in 1817. Chicago had a Sunday School Library in 1832, a Lyceum Library in 1834, and a Young Men's Association Library by 1841, among others. If newspaper notices can be believed, there were a variety of "reading rooms" in almost every midwestern town, with St. Louis boasting at different times of one in a hotel, one in a newspaper office, and a combined "Reading Room and Punch House" that must have been very popular. The New Harmony, Indiana, Working Men's Institute Library of 1847 consisted of about 1,000 volumes, of which 250 titles were of history, 105 of science, 95 of fiction, and 60 of sociology, but only 12 were of poetry and 7 on religious topics. In all, there were more than 160 social libraries chartered in Ohio before 1850, and though there were considerably fewer in Indiana, Illinois, and Michigan, the coverage in those states was fairly general for the larger towns.

In the South the Charleston Library Association remained a successful subscription library, having about 4,500 volumes in 1808 and about 18,000 by 1850. It was not alone, however, since there were other library societies in Charleston and about 30 in other parts of South Carolina for longer or shorter periods of time before 1850. One particularly worthy of notice was the Georgetown Library Society, formed by a group of planters in that coastal South Carolina town in 1800. It never grew large in size, but it was well used, and as a combination of a popular library and an agricultural collection it existed until the Civil War. It is interesting to note that a local printer was librarian for a time and did much to insure the library's success. In Baltimore a Library Company was formed in 1795 with 59 members; shares sold at $30 each and there was an annual fee of $4. By 1800 it had 345 members and 3,300 volumes in rented quarters on Holliday Street. It flourished for a while, but a number of similar libraries sprang up and competition became strong. In 1854 its remaining collection was deposited with the Maryland Historical Society. Among the other social libraries of Baltimore was the Mercantile Library Association that began in 1839 and had over 30,000 volumes in 1875. Alexandria, Virginia, had a subscription library, founded by George Wise and others in 1798. In a catalog published in 1856 it listed 4,481 volumes, but it declined during and after the Civil War.   New Orleans, according to an 1820 directory, contained a Library Society, a Law Library, a subscription reading room, and a "free library at the Presbyterian Church." The Library Society Collection was burned in 1828, but reopened later as a Commercial Library that by 1837 had over 5,000 volumes.   Library fortunes in the Crescent City were variable, however, for by 1857 the scene there included a State Library, a Merchants' Reading Room, a Young Men's Association Library, and a Public School Lyceum and Society Library.   The latter was a subscription library, but it was directed particularly toward young people and in a roundabout way was an ancestor of the present New Orleans Public Library.   Elsewhere in the South there were subscription libraries at various times before 1850 in Natchez, Mississippi; Mobile, Alabama; Savannah and Augusta, Georgia; Wilmington and New Bern, North Carolina; Nashville and Knoxville, Tennessee; and in several towns in Virginia.   In Augusta the Young Men's Library Association began its collection in 1848, but it soon gathered several thousand volumes and provided service to its members for well over a half-century.   A Library Company was chartered in Knoxville in 1817 with 48 charter members at $5 each, but it was apparently not very successful.   Otherwise in the South, the scarcity of large towns kept down the number of opportunities for social libraries, and library development along with education in general was greatly retarded.

The purely commercial circulating library also increased in numbers after the Revolution, but its cultural importance was negligible when compared to the social libraries.   For one thing, it was restricted, as was the bookstore of which it was usually a part, to the larger towns.   It depended upon a reading public slightly different from that of the social library -- more on the casual reader than on the serious one.   It was usually small, but in a few cases of old, established stores, it sometimes reached several thousand volumes.   Caritat's Circulating Library in New York City, opened in 1797, had several thousand volumes in its catalog of 1804, including more than a thousand titles of fiction.   Even more than the social library, the circulating library reflected popular reading

tastes, but unfortunately there are few surviving records of the
bookstocks of those commercial ventures, much less any counts of
actual circulation. Suffice to say that they were less important
than the social library in the ultimate creation of public libraries,
but they did provide a needed public service. They may rightly be
considered more the ancestor of the public library pay collection
than that of the twentieth-century drugstore rental shelf.

If we define the public library as being a book collection that
is publicly supported, publicly controlled, and for general free public use, then there were very few public libraries in the United
States before 1850. However, the few that approached this definition were important and deserve recognition. In Salisbury, Connecticut, a collection of books donated in 1803 by Caleb Bingham was
preserved and made available by the town as the Bingham Library
for Youth. It survived to become a part of the modern Scoville
Memorial Library. In Lexington, Massachusetts, in 1827, the town
meeting voted to purchase a library for the youth of the town and to
employ a librarian to manage it. The collection was deposited in
the town church, but so small was the public support that it went
out of existence in 1839. In Castine, Maine, a social library
founded in 1801 became the property of the town about 1827 and
continued to operate as a free public library. Other examples of
small collections, more or less publicly owned and supported, can
be found especially in New England, but the town usually considered
to be the pioneer in permanent public library service was Peterborough, New Hampshire. There, in 1833, it was decided by the
town meeting that a part of the State Literary Fund, usually applied to the support of schools, should be used for the purchase of
books for a free public library. Other donations added to the size
of the book collection, and it was kept for public use in the store
that housed the local post office, with the postmaster acting as librarian. By 1837, the collection numbered 465 titles made up
largely of religion, history, and biography. The Peterborough Public Library provided a prototype for the future public libraries of
the nation. Only in the late 1840's was there a definite movement
toward public libraries, as in the case of Orange, Massachusetts,

which in 1846 voted $100 to establish a free town library.

It was the passage of state laws enabling the local governmental units to levy taxes for the support of public libraries that really began the modern public library movement. New Hampshire took the lead in 1849 with a law authorizing towns to appropriate money for the establishment and maintenance of public libraries. In 1851, Massachusetts passed a similar law, to be followed by Maine in 1854, and after the Civil War by several other New England and Middle Western States. Furthermore, it was the establishment of a public library in Boston that gave the public library movement a solid foundation. There had been talk of a public library in Boston for several years, and in 1847 Mayor Josiah Quincy, with a conditional offer of $5,000 for books, induced the city council to urge the passage of a library tax. In 1848 the necessary legislative action was obtained for such a tax in the city of Boston, and by 1852 local plans for a public library were underway. Various gifts aided the new library to prepare for its official opening in 1854. Mayor John P. Bigelow gave $1,000, and Edward Everett gave a valuable collection of United States documents along with other books to total more than 1,000 volumes. Joshua Bates gave an endowment of $50,000, the proceeds from which were to be used for the purchase of books. Later on, he gave a large collection of reference works, which together with other volumes were made available to the public in 1861 in the main reference room, or Upper Hall. Numerous other gifts followed, including the Prince Library, collected before 1758, the Bowditch library of mathematics and science, and the George Ticknor library of Spanish history and literature. Such a growing library warranted the management of an experienced librarian, and to this end Charles Coffin Jewett, who had made a name for himself as librarian of the Smithsonian Library in Washington and as author of a study on the library situation in the United States, came to Boston in 1857 to head the new library. His selection was an excellent one, and under his direction the library grew rapidly in size and use. In 1858 the Boston Public Library moved into its own building, and in the same year a printed catalog of the popular library, or Lower Hall, was issued. The reference library, or Upper Hall, had a separate printed catalog, and the total number of volumes in both collections at this time approached 100,000. By 1877 the library contained nearly 300,000 volumes, was circulating over a million volumes per year, had several branches in operation, and was easily the most important public library in the nation.

In contrast to Boston, New York City did not develop a free public library until nearly the end of the nineteenth century. Thanks to the generosity of the Astor family, it had already enjoyed the use of a public reference library since 1848. In that year the will of John Jacob Astor provided funds for a free reference library for the city, including the cost of books, building, and equipment. Later his son and grandson added other gifts to form one of the most important libraries in the nation. The Astor Library was opened for use in 1854 with 80,000 volumes, largely the results of buying expeditions made by the first librarian, Dr. Joseph C. Cogswell. By 1875 it contained some 150,000 valuable works, none of which, according to the librarian, could be classed as "light or ephemeral." Another private collection of great importance in New York City was the Lenox Library, collected and endowed by James Lenox. It was particularly strong in American history and Shakespearean literature, and opened for public reference use in 1870. Although it lacked a public circulating library, New York was well supplied with private and semipublic collections, including the New York Society Library, the New York Historical Society Library, the Mercantile Library, and the Apprentices' Library, to name only a few. These, together with numerous smaller professional, society, and commercial circulating libraries, made it one of the book centers of the nation. About 1880 the New York City Free Circulating Library, a private philanthropy, began operating. By 1895 it had 11 branches and did provide some degree of public library service. None of these institutions were free public libraries, however, and New York City was essentially without such service until after 1895.

In 1886 Samuel Tilden left the bulk of his estate, including his own library of some 20,000 volumes, to the Tilden Trust, with the power to found a free public library in New York City. When

the Tilden funds became available in the 1890's, the city officials
of New York decided to combine all their libraries into one centrally controlled system.   This was done in 1895 with the creation of
the New York Public Library.   Dr. John Shaw Billings, former librarian of the Army Medical Library, was its first director.   At
first there was no central library, with the Tilden collection housed
in the Astor building and the Lenox Library remaining in its own
building.   This situation was remedied after 1901 when Andrew Carnegie donated $5,200,000 to the city of New York for the erection
of 65 branch libraries, and these were completed in a few years.
In 1911, the city completed a central library building, long wanted
and long awaited, and this is the building known as the New York
Public Library.   It is a public reference library, housing the Lenox,
Astor, Tilden, and other research collections, and is one of the
truly great libraries of the world.   By 1913 the New York Public
Library system already contained more than 2 million volumes, and
in 1960 there were over 4 million books in the main library alone.
Brooklyn's public library began in a similar consolidation of several
smaller collections in 1897, while the third large public library system in greater New York City, the Queens Borough Public Library,
grew out of the Long Island City Library begun in 1896.

        Three other public libraries in various parts of the country
will illustrate the methods by which the larger cities acquired their
public library systems.   St. Louis had a Library Society as early
as 1824, but its development was uneven, with some good years and
some bad, until the books were finally sold in 1839 to the St. Louis
Lyceum, which in turn passed the library on to the Mercantile Library Association.   This group, which had begun a library in 1846,
moved the combined collection into a building of its own in 1854,
with over a thousand members and 12,000 books.   By 1875 it had
over 42,000 volumes and was on the whole a most successful subscription library, destined to last well into the twentieth century.
The Mercantile Library, however, was not only a subscription library, but it was also restricted by its subject field to only one
segment of the general reading public.   Hence, there was a strong
demand for a more-available public library, and this was answered

in 1865 with the creation of the St. Louis Public School Library.
The title was misleading in at least two ways -- it was not strictly
public since a fee was charged, and it was not a school library,
although most of its clientele was derived from teachers and students.   In 1868 the library became more public when it moved into
a city-owned building, and several smaller libraries were purchased
or received as gifts.   By 1875 it contained nearly 40,000 volumes
and had nearly 6,000 paid members.   In 1874 the library was
opened to nonmembers for reading and reference, but only members
could take books from the building.   By 1884 the word School was
dropped from the title, and in the next 10 years the membership
fees were dropped, and a free public library was well under way.
After remaining in the Board of Education building from 1893 to
1909 and in rented quarters from 1909 to 1912, the St. Louis Public Library moved into its first central building, a Carnegie structure, in 1912.   In 1929 it had some 750,000 volumes and 17
branches, and by 1960, 1,200,000 volumes and 22 branches, making
it one of the major municipal libraries in the nation.   In addition to
the city library, St. Louis County has its own library, organized
around several suburban collections in 1946 and serving 465,000
people in 1962 with a collection of 435,000 volumes.

        New Orleans has a library history as varied as that of St.
Louis, with a number of institutions serving as ancestors of the
present Public Library.   As early as 1805 the Territorial Legislature had authorized a public library in New Orleans, and in the
same year a Library Society was chartered there, but nothing came
from either venture.   The surviving books from the Library Society of the 1820's and the Commercial Library of the 1830's came
into the hands of the philanthropist, Alvarez Fisk, and was opened
to the public as the Fisk Free Library in 1849.   This was a free
reference collection, not a circulating library.   In 1896 the Fisk
Free Library and the Public School and Lyceum Society Library
were combined to form the New Orleans Public Library, and in
1908 it moved into a new building.   By 1929 this library had some
250,000 volumes and 5 branches, while by 1960, in a new modern
building it reported over a half-million volumes, 11 branches, and

2 bookmobiles. In 1889 another privately owned but publicly available reference collection was opened as the Howard Memorial Library, a memorial to Charles T. Howard by his daughter, Annie. This library was later joined with the Tulane University Library to form the Howard-Tilton Memorial Library.

On the west coast, the Los Angeles Public Library illustrates the development of a public library in a rapidly growing metropolis. The Los Angeles Library Association was formed in 1872, with life memberships at $50 and yearly dues at $5. Four rented rooms housed the collection at first. In 1889 it moved into the City Hall and with some city aid became a municipal agency, but dues were still charged for two more years. By 1895 it had 42,000 volumes, and by 1901 its first branch was opened. In 1906 and again in 1914 the library headquarters moved, first into rented quarters, and then into the Metropolitan Office Building. Not until 1926 did the central library have a building of its own, and by that time it had 44 branches and 76 deposit stations with nearly a million volumes in all. By 1962, Los Angeles had one of the world's largest public libraries, with 2,765,000 volumes serving some 2,500,000 people. It had 6 regional library units, plus 53 branches, 4 special libraries and 4 bookmobiles. In 1957, a $6,400,000 building program enabled the city to build 28 new branch buildings, some in new areas and some consolidations of earlier, smaller collections. To supplement the library service outside the Los Angeles city limits, there is the Los Angeles County Library system, which serves the unincorporated and rural areas, 39 different muncipalities, and over 2 million people. It has 93 service outlets and 8 bookmobiles, with 8 regional headquarters and nearly 1,785,000 volumes to serve them. The two Los Angeles systems together form a truly amazing library service, which in terms of materials available and service rendered to the public can hardly be surpassed anywhere else in the world. Yet even with these superb facilities, Los Angeles is growing so fast that its library services cannot keep up with its library needs.

Getting back to the development of public library service in general, the school district library should be mentioned. This early

service was publicly owned and controlled, and although usually
housed in schools, it was intended to be used largely by adults.
This type of library apparently originated in New York State, but it
spread widely throughout New England and the Middle West.   New
York's Legislature passed an act in 1835 that made it permissible
for school districts to levy taxes for school libraries.   This law
brought little response, but a second one passed in 1838, which provided state funds to match local levies for books, was more successful, and in three years more than 400,000 books were placed
in the schools of New York State.   This idea grew until by 1850
there were nearly a million and a half volumes in the state school
libraries.   However, without proper staff and quarters, many of the
books were lost or allowed to deteriorate.   The interest in the libraries was high at first but soon declined, and state laws were
passed allowing the library funds to be spent for school equipment
or even for teachers' salaries.   The school district library plan in
Massachusetts dates from a law passed in 1837, and 2,084 libraries
were reported in that state by 1850.   In all, they contained only
about 100,000 volumes, or an average of about 50 books per collection, and here again the movement was a failure.   Connecticut followed Massachusetts in 1839, and Rhode Island in 1840.   In these
states the idea was somewhat more successful in the long run.
Several Middle Western States, including Michigan, Indiana, and
Ohio, made arrangement for school district libraries before 1850,
but in general they were not very successful.

      The school district libraries were usually small, and their
contents consisted of textbooks, general works, and a smattering of
inspirational literature.   The majority of the books were above the
reading level and beyond the interests of all but the most advanced
students, and though they were theoretically available to the adults
of the community, they were not too widely used.   Several publishing
firms took advantage of the school district library laws and compiled sets of works, poorly selected, printed and bound, but sold
on commission through local representatives.   These sets often
took up the entire funds available, and their drab appearance and
dry contents did little to promote the public library idea.   For lack

of quarters in the schools themselves, the library books were often
stored in the homes of teachers or school board members, and an
investigation of the New York school district libraries in the 1850's
found many of the books molding in closets, cellars, and attics.
The school district library movement was premature, poorly supported, and consequently unsuccessful, but it did serve to establish
the precedent of public support for library service, and in this respect paved the way for genuine public libraries at a later date.

Probably the most numerous and the least appreciated of all
the semipublic libraries of the nineteenth century were the Sunday
School libraries. Practically every church, particularly in the
North and West, designated a small collection of books as the Sunday School library. Sometimes books of a general nature were included, but usually the contents were religious or inspirational.
Where other sources of reading matter were not available, they
were probably well used, but in time many of them came to include
works of such maudlin sentimentality that their use declined. The
term Sunday School book came to be used as a term of derision
when other types of literature became more available. In the larger
cities, several churches of the same denomination were sometimes
able to combine their efforts and provide a larger collection of
books, complete with a library room and the services of a part-
time keeper, but these libraries were more for the use of ministers
and church-workers than for the average member or his children.
Again the Sunday School library must be considered an effort in the
right direction, but as a forerunner of the true public library it was
a failure.

Something of a cross between a public library and a special
library was the railroad library of the late nineteenth century.
There seem to have been at least three different types, or phases,
of the railroad library. First was the popular library for railroad
crews and employees; second, a popular library for use of railroad
passengers; and third, a technical library for the use of railroad
employees. The Baltimore and Ohio Railroad, for example, maintained a circulating library in Baltimore from 1881 to 1931 for its
employees. Some contents were technical, but most volumes were

simply for popular reading. This library was sold when its usefulness was ended by public libraries and popularly priced books, but
in 1944 the company organized a technical research library. The
Seaboard Air Line had a popular library in Jacksonville, Florida,
which was turned over to the public library in that city in 1922.
The Atchison, Topeka and Santa Fe Railroad had a library with deposits on each long-run train for the use of the passengers. Other
railroads made similar efforts to provide reading matter for their
employees and customers, but the system had virtually disappeared
by the 1920's.

The greatest progress in American public libraries has come
since 1900 with the impetus of the Carnegie building funds and the
general increased effect of public education. Andrew Carnegie, an
immigrant from Scotland who made millions in the steel industry,
began in the late nineteenth century to direct his philanthropy toward the erection of library buildings for public and college libraries. As early as 1881 he began to encourage the construction
of free public libraries with a gift of a library to the Pittsburgh
area where his steelworkers lived. After this he began to offer library buildings to any municipality that would form and guarantee
to support a public library, and by 1920 he had provided financial
aid toward the construction of no less than 2,500 library buildings
in the United States, Canada, and Great Britain. It is true that in
some cases the libraries begun in substantial buildings never ful-
filled their promise and were poorly stocked and staffed, but in
most cases the libraries, once begun, were kept up over the years,
and the provided at least a moderate amount of library service for
millions of people.

Besides Carnegie, other benefactors aided libraries, and in
the first decades of the twentieth century public libraries were well
established in all the nation's larger towns and cities, and in many
smaller ones as well, although quality and quantity of service varied
from town to town. The subscription libraries continued to decline,
and most of them either went out of operation entirely or merged
with the newer public libraries. This was not always easily accomplished, however, as for example in Philadelphia. There was

a move in that city to merge the strong Mercantile Library into the Philadelphia Free Library as early as 1900, but it was not until 1944 that it was finally accomplished. Public libraries that were firmly established began offering new services with the new century, and such innovations as children's rooms, open stacks, and public card catalogs became more and more common. A few larger libraries were finding it necessary to establish many branches, and in rural areas various ideas were tried out in attempts to bring library service to residents outside the towns. Van Wert County, Ohio, began a successful rural library service, complete with a book van, in 1897, and both Hamilton County, Ohio, and Washington County, Maryland, began some rural library service before 1900. After that date county-wide library service became more popular, although it was not until the 1930's that it became widespread. Another significant step in the promotion of public library service came with the establishment of State Library Commissions. The first of these was established in Massachusetts in 1890, and by 1900 sixteen other states had formed similar bodies for the aid and support of public libraries. For the most part these agencies merely encouraged the establishment of public libraries, advised their personnel, and provided a central clearinghouse for library and book information. In some states, however, particularly in Massachusetts, direct state aid to public libraries was a part of the early state library commission laws and duties. In other states, the library commission or the state library was empowered by law to provide library service by mail to citizens of areas in the state without local library service.

The U.S. Office of Education, taking stock in 1913 of the nation's libraries, proudly reported 3,062 free public circulating libraries of over 1,000 volumes each. It is interesting to note, though, that the great majority of these were in the Northeast and Middle West, while in the South and West public libraries were still few and far between. Soon after this date the coming of World War I slowed down the development of public library service somewhat, but it did bring about another event in American library history that was to have a lasting effect. This was the formation of

libraries for the use of servicemen in camps, on ships, and overseas. Over $1,600,000 was raised by public subscription to fi-
nance this venture, and its direction was placed in the capable
hands of the American Library Association and the American Red
Cross. With the A. L. A. -A. R. C. books thus purchased or donated
by libraries and individuals, 47 major camp libraries staffed by
trained librarians were set up at training bases and overseas headquarters. In addition to these, 261 smaller libraries and over
2,500 supply points, deposits of 50 to 100 books each, were placed
at smaller posts, on board ships, and at Red Cross canteens.
These books were well used, and there can be little doubt that many
soldiers and sailors who were thus introduced to library service
during their military careers came home with an increased interest
in reading and libraries. At any rate, the return of peace and relative prosperity in the 1920's saw many smaller towns opening their
first public libraries, while others extended their services to rural
areas, acquired new buildings, or explored new fields of library
service. Library extension in particular came into its own during
the postwar decade, and library commissions were active. Public
funds for library service remained small, however, and large areas
of the nation remained without library service, while many other
towns and areas were inadequately serviced with untrained staffs
and pitifully small book collections.

    With the development of public libraries in the Southern
States, which came largely after 1900, an interesting social phe-
nomenon occurred in the library service, or lack of it, for the
Negro population. Negro schools had lagged behind those for white
children since Reconstruction days, and when public libraries began
to be erected, they were almost always limited to white readers in
all of the Southern States. In a few of the larger and more progressive cities library branches, and occasional completely separate
public libraries, were established for the Negro population. These
tended to be small, poorly equipped and financed, and staffed by un-
trained personnel. In 1910, Jacksonville, Florida, was serving
Negroes from a basement room in the main library, while Louisville, Kentucky, had just opened a colored branch library. In

Houston, Texas, a Colored Library Association sponsored the opening of a colored branch.   In 1913, 14 public libraries in the South
were offering some type of library service to Negro patrons, and
in 1926 this number had reached 45, with some 800,000 Negroes
having libraries available.   In 1935 seventy-seven public libraries
in the South were offering service through separate facilities to
some 1,500,000 Negroes, or approximately 17 per cent of the colored population.   As late as 1947, only 188 out of 597 public libraries in the South offered some type of library service to Negroes,
but the scene was changing and at least a few main libraries were
beginning to be opened to Negro readers.   This change continued
more rapidly in the 1950's and 1960's, with the complete desegra-
gation of public library service throughout the South.

   In 1926 the American Library Association published a serious study of the libraries of the nation in its Survey of Libraries
in the United States.   It was mainly a factual summary, but it emphasized the fact that library service was still far from what it
should have been.   Over 3,000 libraries of 5,000 volumes or more
were queried as to administration, staff, services, and facilities,
and a wide variety of replies were received.   The survey made few
recommendations as to how the services could be improved, but it
did serve as a solid basis on which to plan for the future, and had
it not been for the depression years that followed, it would have
quite probably inaugurated a period of definite library progress.

   The depression years that began in 1929 at first brought se-
vere difficulties for public libraries.   Budgets were reduced and
services were curtailed.   Branches were closed in many cases, and
bookmobiles discontinued, or services to children reduced.   But the
depression also brought with it new demands for library service
from the unemployed who desired to improve their chances for jobs
or from those who simply wanted popular reading matter for their
enforced leisure.   After 1933 the federal government entered the library scene with the Works Progress Administration, which aided
local libraries in many ways.   Library workers, both skilled and
unskilled, became available under the W.P.A. and National Youth
Administration programs, and funds were also made available for

new buildings.   Eventually statewide W. P. A. library programs were
set up to demonstrate public library service where there had previously been none, and many of these "demonstration libraries" became permanent.   New books were purchased, old ones mended,
and bookmobiles were made available to many new areas.   Library
extension services throughout the country were given new strength,
and more people became public library conscious than ever before.
Another federal agency, the Tennessee Valley Authority, began a
regional library experiment in the seven states touched by the Tennessee River, and brought public library service to many countries
that had hitherto had none.   All in all, 1939 found 3,000,000 more
Americans with library service thanks to these efforts, but there
was still nearly one-third of the nation with no library service at
all.   Only 400 counties, about one in eight, in all the United States
offered county-wide library service in 1940.   A third federal agency
with library interests came in 1936 with the establishment of the Library Services Division in the U. S. Office of Education.   This gave
the nation a central clearinghouse for library planning and statistics
gathering, and a source of information and guidance for all types of
libraries.   State aid for local public libraries also gained ground in
some states during the 1930's, and this added considerably to the
improved library scene.

The effects of the depression years, both favorable and un-
favorable, can be seen in the U. S. Office of Education's public library statistics for 1938-39.   Bookstocks and circulation were up,
but staffs were still too small and budgets considerably stretched
to meet the demands.   Statistically, there were 6,880 public libraries reporting in that year, and their bookstocks totaled more
than 104 million volumes.   Some 24 million borrowers had taken
home over 400 million volumes, and 7 million new books had been
added to public library shelves during that one year.   The Northeastern and Middle Western States still had the largest number of
libraries, but the Far West was rapidly catching up, and the remainder of the nation was also increasing its library services at a
steady rate.   The South lagged most noticeably in this respect, but
its larger cities were developing stronger libraries and rural library

services were expanding.

Between the depression years and the mid-twentieth century came the long years of World War II. Unlike World War I, however, this conflict did not greatly hamper the development of public library service in the United States and if anything tended to encourage it. There were shortages of personnel in most libraries, and in some war-industry areas the rapid growth in population tended to outstrip available library service. Generally speaking, however, public libraries expanded their services and went far beyond the usual supplying of educational and recreational material for reading. In maintaining public morale, in serving business and industry, and in the broad fields of adult education and public information, the wartime services of libraries can hardly be overestimated. Without exaggeration it can be said that America's public libraries more than proved their worth to the nation during the trying days of World War II.

After the war, the public libraries saw a rapid return to normal conditions and then a progressive surge ahead with new branches, new buildings, and new services offered to the public. New problems arose with television and the millions of inexpensive, paperback books that flooded the market. Postwar shifts in population added thousands of patrons to some libraries and subtracted them from others. Two groups in particular, those under 21 and those over 65, increased out of proportion to the remainder of the population, and they provided both a problem and a challenge to library service. Libraries have faced these problems and for the most part are stronger for having met them. Television has been welcomed as an ally and even as a tool for library service, with book reviews and book talks reaching additional thousands of people. Book titles mentioned even casually on a national television program bring thousands of requests for the book to booksellers and libraries. The paperback popular reading, available at low cost, relieves the public library of part of its task in supplying purely entertainment reading, but the better paperbacks, either rebound or not, have been used to stretch library budgets, and in many cases where the format and print is attractive, they have found thousands of new readers for old favorites or for new titles in serious fields. The population changes have been met with improved services to children, special departments for teen-agers and also for those over 65. The demands of high school students for the research services of public libraries have often raised serious problems for the under-staffed public libraries, but here again, cooperation between public and school libraries have often increased the value of both.

One great development in the 1950's in the field of public library service came with the passage in 1956 of the Library Services Act by the Congress. This act provides for federal government aid to library extension in rural areas and in towns of 10,000 or less population. In its first 2 years of service it resulted in improved library service in rural areas of 46 states and served as a stimulus for greater effort toward library service on the part of state and local government. Though not directly associated with federal aid to libraries, the same period has seen a great improvement in library service to Negroes, particularly in the South. In 1964, the Public Library Services Act was considerably broadened and strengthened.

Despite these advances, there were in 1963 still over 18 million Americans without access to public library services, and over 110 million Americans still had only inadequate service available. These were the citizens served by libraries where the books were too few or too old, where funds were insufficient to provide the necessary services, and where the staffs were too small or un-trained in library skills. The ideal of library service for all was there, but the implementation was lacking. Tremendous progress had been made in only a little more than a half-century, but there was still a long way to go to realize the goal of adequate library service for all Americans.

Additional Reading

(The material on the history of public libraries in the United States is relatively plentiful, although definitive studies are few. In addition to periodical material, there are library school theses on many of the public libraries, and often there are also locally printed library histories. Failing these, most public libraries have manuscript histories, or reports and board minutes from which such a history can be readily compiled. The following bibliography is more representative than definitive.)

Adams, Herbert B.
   Public libraries and popular education. Albany, N.Y., 1900.
      xlix, 271 p.

American Library Association
   A national plan for public library service. Chicago, 1948.
      168 p.
   A survey of libraries in the United States. Chicago, 1926-27.
      4 vols.

Antrim, Saida B.
   The county library. Van Wert, Ohio, 1914. 306 p.
      (Largely on the history of this "pioneer county library")

Apponyi, Flora H.
   The libraries of California. San Francisco, 1878. 304 p.

Barker, Tommie Dora
   Libraries of the South: a report on developments, 1930-1935.
      Chicago, 1936. 215 p.

Bidlack, Russell E.
   The city library of Detroit: Michigan's first public library,
      1817-1837. Ann Arbor, 1955. 33 p.

Bostwick, A. E.
   The American public library. New York, 1910. 394 p.

Brandt, Beverly S.
   The Alexandria, Virginia, Library: its history, present facili-
      ties and future program. Alexandria, 1951. vii, 93 p.

Butler, Pierce, ed.
   Books and libraries in wartime. Chicago, 1945. 159 p.

Case, Harry L.
   Municipal libraries in Texas. Austin, 1937. 89 p.

Cincinnati. Public Library.
   A decade of service, 1930-1940. Cincinnati, 1941. 175 p.

Cole, George W.
   Early library development in New York State. New York, 1927.
      19 p.

Compton, Charles H.
   Twenty-five crucial years of the St. Louis Public Library.
      St. Louis, 1953. 204 p.

Connecticut. Committee on Libraries.
A study of library services in Connecticut. New Haven, 1962.

Conner, Martha
Outline of the history of the development of the American public
library. Chicago, 1931. 179 p.

Daniel, Hawthorne
Public libraries for everyone. . . Garden City, 1961. 192 p.

Detroit. Public Library
A brief historical summary. Detroit, 1887.

Ditzion, Sidney
Arsenals of a democratic culture: a social history of the American public library movement in New England and the middle
states from 1850 to 1900. Chicago, 1947. 263 p.

Eddy, Harriet G.
County free library organizing in California, 1909-1918: personal recollections. Berkeley, 1955. 113 p.

Enoch Pratt Free Library, Baltimore.
The reorganization of a large public library: ten year report . . .
1926-1935. Baltimore, 1937. 167 p.

Fair, Ethel M.
Countrywide library service: a compilation of articles on service organized by counties and larger units. Chicago, 1934.
208 p.

Fleming, Jiles Barry
199 years of Augusta's library: a chronology. Athens, Ga.,
1949. x, 85 p.

Fletcher, William I.
Public libraries in America. Boston, 1894. 160 p.

Georgia. Library Commission.
Ten years of library progress in Georgia. Atlanta, 1931. 60 p.

Githens, Alfred M.
Program for the public libraries of New York City. New York,
1945. 141 p.

Gleason, Eliza Atkins
The Southern Negro and the public library. Chicago, 1941.
xvi, 218 p.

Goldberg, Arthur
The Buffalo Public Library, 1836-1936. Buffalo, 1937. 156 p.

Green, Samuel S.
    The public library movement in the United States, 1853-1893.
        Boston, 1913.   viii, 336 p.

Harris, Thaddeus M.
    A selected catalogue of some of the most esteemed publications
        in the English language proper to form a social library, with
        an introduction upon choice of books.   Boston, 1793.

Henry, William E.
    Municipal and institutional libraries of Indiana.   Indianapolis,
        1904.   166 p.

Humble, Marion
    Rural America reads: a study of rural library service.   New
        York, 1938.   101 p.

Jewett, Charles C.
    Notices of public libraries in the United States of America.
        Washington, 1851.   207 p.

Jockel, Carlton B.
    Library extension: problems and solutions.   Chicago, 1946.
        260 p.

Johnson, Alvin
    The public library: a people's university.   New York, 1938.
        85 p.

Kidder, N. T.
    The first sixty years of the Milton Public Library, 1870-1931.
        Milton, Mass., 1932. 166 p.

Koch, Theodore W.
    A book of Carnegie libraries.   New York, 1917. 226 p.

    War libraries and allied subjects.   New York, 1919.   300 p.

Kroll, Morton, ed.
    Libraries and librarians of the Pacific Northwest.   Seattle,
        1960.   x, 271 p.

Leigh, Robert D.
    Governor's study of public and school libraries in the State of
        Hawaii.   Honolulu, 1960.   iv, 83 p.

    The public library in the United States.   New York, 1950. 273 p.

Lester, Robert M.
    Forty years of Carnegie giving . . .   New York, 1941. xi, 186p.

    Libraries and lotteries: a history of the Louisville Free Public
        Library.   Cynthiana, Ky., 1944.   300 p.

Long, Harriet G.
    Rich the treasure: a public library service to children. Chicago, 1953. 78 p.

Lovett, R. W.
    From social library to public: a century of library service in Beverly, Massachusetts. Beverly, 1952.

Lydenberg, Harry M.
    History of the New York Public Library. New York, 1923. 643 p.

Maryland. State Planning Commission.
    The Free Public library in Maryland. Baltimore, 1944. ix, 118 p.

Minneapolis. Public Library.
    Fifty years of service, 1889-1939. Minneapolis, 1939. 60 p.

Mohrhardt, Charles M.
    The Springfield City Library Association, 1857-1950 . . . Springfield, Massachusetts, 1950. 110 p.

New Orleans. Library Club.
    The libraries of New Orleans. New Orleans, 1945. 44 p.

Norton, Elizabeth S.
    Sketch of the Transylvania Library, 1783-1919. Lexington, Ky., 1919. 15 p.

Oregon. State Library.
    Public libraries in Oregon. 1963.

Pardee, Helen L.
    A story of the Akron Public Library, 1834-1942. Akron, 1943. 52 p.

Peterborough, New Hampshire. Public Library.
    The town library of Peterborough, established April 9, 1833. Peterborough, 1903. 27 p.

Peters, Orpha M.
    The Gary Public Library, 1907-1944. Gary, Indiana, 1945. 56 p.

Raddin, George G., Jr.
    An early New York Library of fiction, 1804. New York, 1940. 113 p. (On H. Caritat's Circulating Library.)

Rhee, William J.
    A manual of public libraries, institutes and societies in the United States . . . Philadelphia, 1859. 687 p.

Rossell, Beatrice S.
Public libraries in the life of the nation. Chicago, 1943. 116 p.

Sandoe, Mildred W.
County library primer. New York, 1942. 221 p.
(Includes some history of county libraries in Ohio.)

Schenck, Gretchen K.
County and regional library development. Chicago, 1954. 272 p.

Sharp, Henry A.
Libraries and librarianship in America. London, 1936 191 p.

Spencer, Gwladys
The Chicago Public Library, origins and backgrounds. Chicago, 1943. 473 p.

Stanford, Edward B.
Library extension under the W. P. A. Chicago, 1944. xiii, 284 p.

Stearns, Lutie Eugenia
Traveling libraries in Wisconsin. Madison, 1910. 41 p.

Suggett, Laura S.
The beginning and the end of the best library service in the world. San Francisco, 1924. 89 p.

Titcomb, Mary L.
The Washington County Free Library, 1901-1951. Hagerstown, Maryland, 1951. 52 p.

Torry, Jesse, Jr.
The intellectual torch; developing an original, economical and expeditious plan for the universal dissemination of knowledge and virtue by means of free public libraries . . . Ballston Spa, N.Y., 1817. 36 p.

Utley, George B.
The Librarians' Conference of 1853: a chapter in American library history. Chicago, 1951. 188 p.

Wadlin, Horace G.
The Public Library of the City of Boston. Boston, 1911. 256 p.

Whitehill, Walter Muir
Boston Public Library: a centennial history. Cambridge, 1956. 274 p.

Wilson, F. Allan
The Nahant Public Library . . . a history ... Nahant, Mass., 1895. 40 p.

Wilson, Louis R.
    County library service in the South, a study of the Rosenwald
      County Library Demonstration. Chicago, 1935. 259 p.

18

School Libraries in the United States

School library service in the United States has something of a dual origin. One ancestor is undoubtedly the library of the nineteenth century academy, while another is the service for children that grew up in the public libraries later on. Whatever its origin, library service for children was very meager before 1900, but some beginnings can be traced back to the early 1800's. One factor in library service to children was of course the scarcity of children's books, of which there were very few until the mid-nineteenth century. Learning and reading for children had previously been confined to textbooks or to adult books. Hence, the delay in establishing children's libraries was at least partially due to the lack of children's books.

There were several academies established before 1800, but little is known of their libraries, except for those that later grew into colleges. The Boston Latin School, for example, is supposed to have been founded in 1635, but nothing is known of a library for the school until the nineteenth century. There was definitely a library in the school as early as 1844, but there was no trained librarian until 1926. In 1804 Rumford Academy was chartered in Virginia, with legislative authority to promote a lottery to raise funds for its library. In St. Louis, an Academy founded in 1818 boasted of a library in its first advertisements. Abbott Academy at Andover, Massachusetts, was established in 1829 and had a well-organized library by 1842. This academy is of particular interest because it was for girls only. The academy movement was rather general by 1825, strong in the North and Middle West, weaker in the South and Southwest. In Ohio there were no less than 171 academies and institutes founded between 1803 and 1850. Little is known of their libraries in most cases, but from the remains of libraries that have survived, it is apparent that they were for the most part

gift collections, poorly selected and little used. However, it should
also be noted that many of the teachers in the academies had good
private libraries of their own, and in some of the stronger academies the student literary societies had fairly active libraries.

Aside from the academies, there were also a few public libraries offering books particularly for children in the early nineteenth century. The library founded by Caleb Bingham at Salisbury,
Connecticut, in 1803, was specifically designated for children from
9 to 16 years of age, although it seems to have been used generally by adults as well. In 1804 Dr. Jessey Torrey started a library
for young people in connection with the New Lebanon, New York,
Library Society. Some of the subscription libraries contained books
for children, and there is evidence of a Children's Library Society
in Louisville, Kentucky, in 1810. The West Cambridge, Massachusetts, Juvenile Library was started in 1835, and it was opened a
few hours each Saturday. Three books per family could be taken
out for 30 days. Two types of general public libraries already mentioned, the apprentices' libraries and the Sunday School libraries,
served children to some extent. The apprentices' libraries were
usually available to boys over 11 or 12, while the Sunday School libraries tried to win juvenile readers with syrupy stories of unbe-
lievably good little boys and girls. Circulating rental libraries also contained some titles of interest to older children, but in general books available to children before the Civil War in public collections were extremely scarce.

Whereas the school district libraries established before 1850
were more for adults than children (and hence have already been
discussed under the heading of public libraries), those established
after that date tended to be more directly for the school children
In California, for example, where library laws of 1854 and 1866 established state aid to school libraries, the emphasis was on libraries for school children and teachers. People who were not
pupils or teachers could use these libraries upon the payment of a
fee, but the response to this offer was apparently not very large.
By 1875 some 20 states had passed laws providing for some type of
library in the schools, but for the most part they were not success-

ful either as school libraries or as public libraries.

Actually it was not until after 1900 that school libraries in
the modern sense of the term became fairly general.   Before this
there was a period of experimentation in the provision of library
service for children from the public libraries.   In some cases, the
public libraries or their branches were located in the vicinity of
schools, and opened for school use by groups during school hours
and by individual children afterward.   In other cases, public libraries simply supplied books to the schools in deposits, either by
classrooms or in central collections.   In a few cases the public library or a branch was actually located in a school building, serving
both school and public from that point.   By 1900 there was a con-
troversy between those who favored public library service to schools
and those who favored independent school libraries.   In 1896 the
National Education Association formed a Library Section that was interested in bringing library service to school children by some
method.   In 1898 in its national conference this group was divided,
with strong voices raised in favor of both types of library service.
By 1899, however, the majority seemed to favor independent school
libraries, and particularly there was a demand for classroom libraries selected according to the reading level and interests of each
grade.   The discussion over the two methods of reaching school
children was lively in both school and library circles for another
decade, but by 1910 the concept of the independent school library
had become widely adopted.   Although in some cities and counties
the link between public and school libraries has been successfully
maintained, the trend for the most part has been toward separate
library systems for the public schools.

New York State began to establish school libraries in the high
schools in the 1890's, particularly in the larger cities.   By 1900,
some of these high schools had trained librarians, thanks to the efforts of Melvil Dewey and his library school at Albany and to the
training course for librarians at Pratt Institute in Brooklyn.   Erasmus Hall High School in Brooklyn had a trained librarian in 1900,
and Brooklyn Girls High in 1903.   Morris High School in New York
City obtained its first trained librarian in 1905, and in the same

year there were high school librarians in Albany and Rochester.
Central High School in Washington, D. C., had its trained librarian
in 1898, and in Los Angeles the first trained high school librarian
was employed in 1903. New York and New Jersey in the East,
Michigan and Minnesota in the Middle West, and California and Oregon in the West took the lead in the establishment of high school libraries and in the employment of full-time librarians for them.
Elsewhere in the nation, the development of independent school libraries was rather spotty, but by 1915 most of the larger high
schools did have something in the way of a central library, although
often inadequate.

One reason for the trend toward the independent school library
as distinct from the public library school deposit can be found in
the newer methods of teaching adopted after 1900. As early as the
1880's the idea of learning to read for the pleasure of reading was
impressed on the school system, and the importance of having good
books available at all times was of course realized. After 1900,
the presence of a central school library was stressed in the newer
theories of the child-centered school, where the child was educated
not for a profession but for a well-rounded, meaningful life. Such
educational programs as the platoon school, which varied the pupil's
day into a work, play, study routine; or the Winnetka plan, which
emphasized the individual abilities of each pupil, called for free
and frequent use of library materials, and hence for the permanent
independent school library. These newer methods called for a library in the school, but there was still the question of whether to
have a single, central library for the whole school or to have individual classroom libraries. The elementary schools that had libraries usually preferred the classroom collections, but the secondary schools for the most part preferred the central library. By
1913 the U. S. Office of Education could report that there were approximately 10, 000 public school libraries in the nation, but only
about 250 of them contained over 3, 000 volumes. The others were
characterized as having their contents out of date, or for being too
small, poorly housed, unclassified and uncataloged, and sometimes
as being completely unavailable for use. Obviously there was still

a long way to go in school library service, even though a few cities
did already have excellent school library systems. Detroit, Spo-
kane, and Washington, D. C. were cited in the report as examples
of the better school library systems.

The idea of the school library as the laboratory for the social sciences and humanities and as the laboratory annex for the sciences was catching on, however. In 1915, the "new high school library" was being described as a large, airy, well-lighted room,
cheery and inviting, with books readily available for all grades and
all subjects taught in the school. There was to be a "librarian's
office and work-room" next to the library room. Something antici-
pating the audio-visual program of later years was described in the
listing of lantern slides, pictures, post cards, and "Victrola records" as suitable adjuncts to the book and magazine contents of the
library, and a clipping file was heartily recommended. This type
of library and library service was described as "dynamic" in contrast to the old "static" library that merely preserved collections of
books that were largely text or out-of-date books. It was admitted
that libraries of this type were few and far between, but they were
held up as ideals for all schools to anticipate.

After 1920 this "ideal" school library became more common,
and new developments in the field of school library service came
rapidly. Demand for school librarians far exceeded the supply,
and teacher-librarians became the answer to the school library
staff needs. Other national organizations besides the N. E. A. and
the A.L.A. became interested in the development and use of school
libraries. The National Council of Teachers of English created a
permanent committee on the use of school libraries, while the Department of Elementary School Principals concerned itself with
standards for elementary school libraries. Regional accrediting associations took an interest in the school library situation, and
standards for school libraries were adopted. Surveys of school library conditions by towns, cities, and states brought out the
strengths and weaknesses of already existing libraries and pointed
the way for future expansion of school library service. These surveys culminated in a national secondary school library survey con-

ducted in 1932 for the U.S. Office of Education by Dr. B. Lamar
Johnson.

School libraries progressed steadily in the 1920's, and most
of the new school buildings of the decade provided special quarters
for library service.   In 1922, when a large bond issue was passed
for the construction of new schools in Los Angeles, library quarters
were planned in each building, and committees of librarians were
invited to help plan these quarters.   In New York State, a Regents'
ruling in 1925 made compulsory the keeping of a library in every
school of over 50 pupils.   In 1928 this was enlarged to rule that all
high schools had to have approved libraries if their graduates were
to be admitted to the state-controlled universities and colleges, and
every high school with over 100 pupils had to have a certified
school librarian.   In Texas, a state-wide study in 1923 showed the
weakness in and need for school libraries in the state, and inaugurated a period of improvement in this respect.   However, in 1926
four Southern States reported libraries in a total of 928 high
schools, but the average number of books in them was less than
500.

Aid and advice from outside sources were available to help
the school administrators in planning school libraries after 1920.
Many states, for example, created the office of school library su-
pervisor to encourage and supervise the development of school libraries.   Cities and towns followed this lead and hired library specialists who advised school librarians in the larger schools or
teachers and teacher-librarians in the smaller ones.   On the national level a school library specialist was appointed in the U.S. Office
of Education.

With the growth of school systems in the more populated
areas, the necessity for centralized purchasing and processing of
school library materials became obvious, and many cities established such centers.   Los Angeles began centralized purchasing and
cataloging in 1927 for its high schools, some special schools, and
a junior college.   Centralized cataloging was also tried in Seattle,
and other of the nation's larger cities adopted the idea in the
1930's.   The advantages were not only the obvious ones in economy,

but also in freeing the librarians for more time to work with students and teachers rather than in processing duties.

Charitable foundations, such as the General Education Board and the Rosenwald Fund, provided financial aid to school library demonstration projects in various parts of the nation, particularly in those areas where school library service had lagged. In 1929 the Rosenwald Fund provided aid for 11 county library systems to demonstrate public library service to rural schools. The Carnegie Corporation's aid to library schools also furthered the training of school librarians and the improvement of school libraries. Books and pamphlets to aid the school librarian, whether new or experienced, were published by the American Library Association, by the U. S. Office of Education, and by the various state library commissions and school library supervisors. State aid for the purchase of school library books and materials became available in some areas in the 1930's, but many parts of the nation were still without good school libraries. The depression years hit school budgets particularly hard, and new books for the libraries were often simply not available. For example, the State of Tennessee in 1936 reported that 80 per cent of its high schools had no funds for library books. Fortunately this situation was remedied to some extent in 1937 with the appropriation of small allotments of funds for library books to be purchased from an approved state list. School librarians were hard to find even when funds were available, and Kansas reported only 31 full-time trained school librarians in the state in 1938.

The depression years did bring about a reappraisal of the public library--school library relationship, and cooperation between the two systems took on several forms. In some cases there was a single library system, including a public library in the county seat with rotating book deposits in all the schools. There were many advantages to this including lower administration costs, lower operating costs, and the advantage of having to supply only one set of children's books for both school and public library use. In other systems, the school libraries were permanent collections, but they were bought and processed by the central public library. Either way brought obvious benefits but also some disadvantages, such as in the slowness of obtaining new books, lack of participation by the teachers in book selections, and lack of trained school librarians to give the necessary library service along with the books. Where professional libraries for teachers could be incorporated into the public school library system, the advantages were even greater, and this feature has proved even more popular than direct public library service to the children.

Since World War II school libraries have expanded rapidly, both in numbers and in types of services. In recent years the public school library has expanded far beyond the medium of books and into the field of audio-visual aids and other nongraphic but informative materials. In fact, the school library is becoming the school-teaching materials center, supplying any and all learning needs of the teacher and pupil, whether books, slides, films, filmstrips, maps, charts, pictures, pamphlets, records, tapes, or even three-dimensional models. A large high school library of 1960 might well include a suite of several rooms, consisting of open-shelf reading rooms, reference rooms, browsing room, conference room, storage room and work rooms. It might have an audio-visual room adjacent where projection equipment, record players, radios and television sets, tape records, and teaching machines were available. Its field of service would be broad; its annual budget could run into 20 or 30 thousand dollars, its staff into two or more professional plus clerical and mechanical help, and its collection could include 10,000 or more books, plus several thousand other items. This of course was not the average school library, but it was not an unusual one. The American Library Association's school library standards called for 1 full-time trained librarian for every 250 students in a school, and 1 clerical worker for every 500 students. Unfortunately few school libraries could meet those standards in 1960.

One other bright aspect of the school library scene in the 1950's and 1960's was the increasing number of elementary school libraries. Long the stepchild of the school library world, the elementary school library was finally coming to be realized as an important part of the elementary school picture. Increased emphasis

on individual effort on the part of the pupil and on learning by doing rather than memorizing textbooks meant that a wider variety of
materials entered into the daily elementary school teaching and
learning experience. The classroom library, long favored by many
elementary school teachers, gave way to the centralized elementary
school library, and the trained elementary school librarian took her
place as a part of the teaching team. Both elementary and high
school librarians have generally taken as a part of their duties the
teaching of the students to use books and libraries. This wider
concept of the use of materials as a subject in itself has greatly
enhanced the value to the school of both the school library and the
school librarian.

The overall picture in 1960 still had a few dark spots. Ten
per cent of the nation's high schools were still without central libraries, and many more were without full-time trained librarians.
Almost two-thirds of the nation's elementary schools were still without centralized collections. Many of the schools with libraries had
only inadequate ones, and the shortage of school librarians was still
acute. But the school library picture was much better in 1960 than
in 1950, and the rate of improvement was increasing. The school
library had won its place as a part of the formal educational scene,
and the only limitations on its services were material ones. Given
more school librarians and more funds for materials, the future of
school librarianship was virtually unlimited.

Additional Readings

(Material in book form on the history of school libraries in the
United States is relatively scarce, but in the form of periodical
articles, official reports, and unpublished theses there is a fair
amount of source material available. In addition to Library Literature and the periodical indexes, the reports of state and federal education and library agencies should be consulted, especially the library statistics published by the U.S. Office of Education and its
predecessors.)

Aldrich, Frederic D.
    The school library in Ohio. New York, 1959. vi, 237 p.

American Library Association.
  School libraries for today and tomorrow, functions and standards.
    Chicago, 1945. 43 p.

Cecil, Henry L.
  School library service in the United States. New York, 1940.
    334 p.

Cundiff, Ruby Ethel
  School libraries in the South. Nashville, 1936. 45 p.

Galloway, Louise
  The historical development and present status of public high
    school libraries in Kentucky. Frankfort, 1952. 121 p.

Henne, Frances, ed.
  Youth, communication and libraries. Chicago, 1949. xi, 233 p.

Johnson, B. Lamar
  The secondary-school library. Washington, 1933. 109 p.

Johnson, Clifton
  Old time schools and school books. New York, 1904. xxi,
    381 p.

King, William A.
  The elementary school library. New York, 1929. 224 p.

Kroll, Morton, ed.
  Elementary and secondary school libraries of the Pacific North-
    west. Seattle, 1960. x, 330 p.

Logasa, Hannah
  The high school library: its function in education. New York,
    1928. 283 p.

Wilson, Martha, ed.
  Selected articles on school library experience. New York, 1925.
    351 p.

Wood, Katharine H.
  Public and school libraries and the State Board of Education:
    history, statistics. Hartford, Conn., 1951. 32 p.

19.

Government Libraries in the United States

As the national libraries in Europe were among the major
libraries of the world, so in the United States the nation's greatest
library has been a government agency, the Library of Congress.
Originally intended as the reference library for the national legislative body, this institution has had a long and varied history, but
it has emerged in the twentieth century as the national library in
all but name. The Library of Congress is not by any means the
only major library operated by the United States government; besides the federal libraries, there are also the many important ones
belonging to the various states. Altogether, the government libraries
in the United States represent a major portion of the library resources available to the American people.

The history of the Library of Congress virtually begins with
the history of the United States. The new government, from 1776
on, made use of several book collections in New York and Philadelphia, in particular that of the Philadelphia Library Company. Apparently a few books were owned by the Continental Congress, but
no definite move toward an actual library came until after the government moved to Washington, D. C. , in 1800. In this year the
Congress appropriated funds for the purchase of books, and in 1802
a room for the Congressional library was set aside in the new Capitol building. President Thomas Jefferson appointed the first librarian, who also served as Clerk of the House of Representatives.
Little more than a legal reference collection at first, the library
had only about 3,000 volumes by 1814 and had been little used. In
that year, during the war with Great Britain, the Capitol was
burned by the invading army, and the embryo Library of Congress
was destroyed. After the War there was considerable debate as to
how the library should be reconstituted and former President Jefferson solved the problem by offering to sell his excellent private li-

brary to the government.   After much debate, the offer was accepted, and in 1815 the library of some 6,700 volumes was purchased, giving the government a library that was much superior to
the one that had burned.

Mr. George Watterson was appointed Congressional librarian
when the new collection arrived, and temporary quarters were found in
the Post Office Building until 1824 when the library was moved back into the rebuilt Capitol.   By this date Congress was appropriating about
$5,000 per year for the Library, and through purchases, gifts, and
government publications, the book stock was growing steadily.   In 1832
part of the legal works in the Library was removed to form a library
for the Supreme Court but this remained under the jurisdiction of the
Librarian of Congress for the time being.   By 1850, the Library had
reached some 50,000 volumes, second only to Harvard University's library in size.   Once again a fire in the Capitol destroyed much of the
Library in 1851, and only about 20,000 volumes were left intact.   The
Library Hall was reconstructed, however, in what was supposed to be a
fireproof manner, and Congress appropriated $75,000 for book re-
placements.   In the next few years the Library was able to acquire
several large collections that considerably enhanced its value as a
research collection.   Since the acquisition of the Jeffersonian library, the nature of the contents of the Library of Congress had
become more general and less legal, and the addition of the Peter
Force library in 1867 greatly increased the holdings in American
history.   The law library of James Petigru was obtained about the
same time, along with the papers of some of the early Presidents,
including Washington, Adams, and Jefferson.   In 1866, the library
of the Smithsonian Institute, about 40,000 volumes largely in natural science, were transferred to the Library of Congress.   Another
great source of books came in 1870 when the registry of copyright
was placed under the Librarian of Congress, and two copies of each
work printed in the United States came in to the national library.

In 1875, the Library had over 300,000 volumes, and under the capable direction of Ainsworth Rand Spofford, appointed in 1864, it was
taking its place not only as the leading library in the United States,
but also as one of the largest in the world.   It was still housed in

the Capitol building, but it was rapidly overflowing its quarters.

As early as 1871, Dr. Spofford suggested the need for a library building specifically designed for the collection, and in 1874 Congress appointed a committee to look into the possibilities of building a national library structure. But the wheels of government grind slowly, and it was not until 1887 that construction finally began. The building, which was completed in 1897, forms the present main part of the Library, capable of holding nearly 3 million volumes and covering nearly 4 acres. It was equipped with the latest in library equipment for its day, with everything from well-lighted reading rooms and steel stacks to book conveyors and interoffice speaking tubes. Though Librarian Spofford had begun with a staff of 5 in 1864, the new building required a staff of 185 in 1900, with an additional crew of 45 in the copyright office. The old system of classification, an adaptation of Thomas Jefferson's original private library scheme, was far outmoded by the multitudes of new books of the late nineteenth century. To meet this need, a number of classification systems were considered, but in the end a system particularly adapted to the needs of the Library of Congress was developed, and with the "L.C." system the entire library was reclassified and cataloged. As the books were reprocessed, printed catalog cards were produced and made available for purchase to libraries all over the nation. Thus the Library of Congress card distribution program was begun, one of its most valued and appreciated services to the library world.

Though the Library of Congress was still essentially a collection of books designed to aid the Congress and other government officials in the performance of their duties, it had by 1900 come a long way toward becoming the national library. After that date it soon became the nation's largest single library, and under the capable leadership of Dr. Herbert Putnam it extended its influence far beyond the needs of Congress or the confines of Washington, D.C. In the twentieth century its services have gone beyond the printed catalog cards to published bibliographies and other library tools, to the maintenance of a national union catalog, and the sponsorship of a national and international book exchange system. The national

library for the blind centered in the Library of Congress, and
reaching the blind readers throughout the nation through deposit libraries in each state, has become one of the most appreciated extra
services of the Library.   In 1937 the completion of the new National Archives removed many of the public records and manuscript materials from the Library of Congress, and in 1938 the completion
of a new annex served to alleviate the crowded conditions in the
main building.   This new addition more than doubled the space available, but there was still hardly enough room to meet the demands
for book preservation and library service that the growing nation
demanded.

Something of the enormous work done by the Library of Congress can be indicated by the statistics from the Librarian's report
of 1962.   This shows that the Library then contained over
41,000,000 items, including some 12,300,000 books, 17,700,000
manuscripts, 3,000,000 photographs and slides, 2,600,000 maps
and views, and 2,000,000 music scores, plus hundreds of thousands of prints, pictures, recordings, motion picture films, microfilms, and microprints.   A staff of over 1,500 attempted to serve
these collections and to add to them in reasonably orderly fashion
the more than 400,000 new items that arrive each year.   The Law
Library alone contained over a million volumes.   The National
Union Catalog, with its records of the location of 12,500,000 books
in North American libraries, is a most valuable part of the Library,
while the Legislative Reference Service in its functions for the Congress and other government officials provides a service of which
the value would be difficult to assess.   Because of its wide variety
of non-book materials in addition to its millions of printed books,
the Library of Congress is probably the greatest single cultural
center in the world today.

Besides the Library of Congress, the city of Washington and
its immediate vicinity contains more than a hundred other government book collections, many of which are notable libraries in their
own rights.   The State Department Library, for example, had its
beginning in 1789, when that executive department was instructed
by the Congress to collect and preserve the laws of the nation and

of the various states.   These together with the publications of other government agencies formed the beginning of the State Department Library.   By 1825 the Department had added to this core the publications of foreign countries, plus books on history, international law and diplomacy, and political science to a total of more than 3,000 volumes.   Newspapers, both American and foreign, were also collected in the State Department Library, and by 1850 the number of volumes had passed 15,000.   By 1875 there were more than 23,000 volumes, not counting the bound newspapers and pamphlets. Since that time, the subject fields of the collection have narrowed somewhat, so that the concentration tended toward international law and relations, but the size of the library has increased steadily nevertheless.   In 1960 it contained over a half-million volumes, not including thousands of research reports and items in microforms.

The Treasury Department Library was begun in 1803, but it was not of significant size until after the Civil War.   By 1875 it contained about 8,500 volumes and in 1900 only some 12,000.   However, in the twentieth century it too has come to approach the half-million mark in volumes, with materials in the fields of law, economics, and political science.   It is particularly strong in its holdings in finance and taxation.   The Library of the War Department was also small and slow in growing from its founding in 1832 to about 13,000 volumes in 1875.   In the 1960's it had about a quarter-million volumes, largely in military science and law, and an equal number of government documents from the United States and foreign countries.   Overshadowing the Department library, particularly in the nineteenth century, was the Army Medical Library, or as it was originally known, the Library of the Surgeon General's Office.   Under the librarianship of Dr. John Shaw Billings, an army officer, physician, librarian, and scholar, this collection grew from a miscellaneous group of some 1,800 books in 1865 to a well-organized library of 50,000 volumes and more than 60,000 pamphlets in 1880. Dr. Billings made of it one of the major medical libraries of the world, developed a subject card catalog for it, began indexing medical journals, and published a bibliography of medical literature. By 1910 the Army Medical Library had over 100,000 volumes, and

by the 1950's, as the National Library of Medicine, it had passed
the half-million mark, undoubtedly ranking as the finest medical library in the world.

The Department of Agriculture Library was founded in 1860
and had only about 7,000 volumes in 1875, but after 1900 it grew
rapidly so that by 1929 it had over 200,000 volumes. By 1960, as
the National Agricultural Library, it had well over a million volumes, and its contents were particularly strong in all subjects relating to agriculture, including botany, chemistry, forestry, and
geology. One of its strongest points is in its holdings in agricultural periodicals and the publications of societies, institutes, and
governments in agriculture and related fields from all over the
world. The U.S. Office of Education Library began in 1870 and
concentrated on the field of learning in all its phases and from all
parts of the world. In 1929 it contained 135,000 volumes, and in
1960 it formed a major part of the new Department of Health, Education and Welfare Library, with its nearly 750,000 volumes.

Some other government libraries in Washington that were
founded in the nineteenth century include those of the Coast and
Geodetic Survey, founded in 1832; the Naval Observatory, 1845; the
Department of Interior, 1850; the Attorney General's Office, 1853;
and the Post Office Department, 1862. These have, of course,
varied considerably in size over the years due to their different
functions, and today they range in size from the Post Office Department's 50,000 volumes to the Interior Department Library of over
a half-million. One of the more interesting small libraries of
Washington is that in the White House. There has been a library
of sorts there since President Madison's administration, but it was
usually a varied collection, ranging from personal volumes of the
Presidents and their families to legal works for the use of the executive staff. In 1875 it contained about 1,400 volumes and in 1929
only a few more. Since the 1930's there has been a more-or-less
official White House Library of general literature, donated by the
publishers of the United States and selected by a librarian-publisher
committee.

The rapidly increasing number of government agencies that

have come into being in the twentieth century have multiplied the number of government libraries in Washington, and they vary widely in subject and size. The Department of Labor Library is one of the largest of these, containing some 400,000 volumes in 1960, while the Department of Commerce collection is somewhat larger. The Department of the Air Force has only specialized collections for its various offices in Washington, but it controls collections totaling nearly 5 million volumes of both popular and technical literature at its bases all over the world. From the World War I period date such libraries as those of the Federal Reserve System with its 70,000 volumes, and the Federal Trade Commission with some 100,000. From the New Deal era of the 1930's have come such libraries as those of the Federal Housing Administration, the Federal Deposit Insurance Corporation, and the National Labor Relations Board. Literally dozens of smaller and more specialized governmental collections can be found in various parts of Washington and its immediate vicinity. Some of these, as indicative of the variety, would include the Naval Intelligence School Library, with 15,000 volumes; the Selective Service System Library, with 20,000; the Tariff Commission Library, with 93,000; and the Walter Reed Army Hospital Library, with about 50,000 volumes.

Besides the Library of Congress, the United States Senate has its own library of 300,000 volumes, and the House of Representatives has a library of over a half-million. These are largely collections of government documents and state, federal, and foreign laws and court decisions. The Supreme Court also has an excellent collection, with some 200,000 volumes of laws, government documents, and legal periodicals. Finally, it should be pointed out that the Smithsonian Institution, having turned over one library to the Library of Congress, began to develop another and today has one of the finest science libraries in the nation. With more than a million volumes in all, it is particularly strong in anthropology, astronomy, botany, geology, palaeontology, and zoology, as well as industry and engineering.

Not all United States government libraries are in Washington by any means. In fact, there are probably as many if not more

books in government libraries outside the capital city. Some of
them are completely independent libraries, while others are
branches of libraries that have their main collections in Washington.
The military services in particular have libraries in large numbers
outside of Washington. The Military Academy at West Point has a
library that was founded in 1812, with about 20,000 volumes in
1850 and 25,000 in 1875. In 1960 its bookstock totaled about
160,000 volumes, with some 40,000 more in departmental reference
libraries. The Naval Academy Library in Annapolis was organized
in 1845, and by 1875 it had some 18,000 volumes. By 1960 it had
passed 150,000 and was rapidly catching up with the older service
academy. The Coast Guard Academy has a library of some 50,000
volumes at New London, Connecticut, and the new Air Force Academy has a library at Colorado Spring that was passing the hundred thousand mark by 1960.

From the Civil War onward the United States military services attempted to provide library service for all troops, whether in
war or peace. In 1861 the U.S. Military Post Library Association
was founded to provide reading matter for the soldiers in the field,
and although largely voluntary, this move was rather successful.
By 1875 nearly every military post and garrison with a permanent
staff was supplied with a small library, ranging from about 2,500
volumes down to about 50, depending upon the number of troops.
For example, the first library in the newly acquired territory of
Alaska was a garrison collection at Sitka. From benevolent funds,
post petty cash, soldiers' reading clubs, and a little official support these post libraries survived down to the period of World War
I. During the war a renewed effort was made to provide the best
of library service for men in uniform, and from this effort there
was developed a system of permanent government-supported libraries
for all the military and naval services. After 1920 there were libraries with full-time civilian librarians in all posts, camps, and
stations of over 2,500 men, and smaller libraries under special-
service officers at smaller posts. During World War II, a wide
network of military libraries was developed. Wherever servicemen
were stationed -- in training camps, at permanent bases, on naval

vessels, overseas or in hospitals -- there were books available.
At the larger posts, well-stocked and well-staffed libraries of several thousand volumes were maintained, while with the smallest units there were package libraries of 50 or 100 paper backs, considered expendable and passed from man to man until they were worn out.   In 1943 there were over 2,000 post and hospital libraries in the United States alone, employing more than 600 trained librarians and hundreds of service personnel to staff them.   About the same time the United States Navy had over 16,000 library stations serving its various ship and shore units.   To meet the need for inexpensive editions of desirable books, the book publishers produced the Armed Services Editions of popular and serious works that were mass produced and distributed by the thousands.   Since the War, the military library services have continued their important role, providing technical and professional as well as recreational books for all phases of the defense program.

After 1945 another type of overseas government library appeared in the form of the United States Information Libraries sent to the capitals and important cities of virtually every country in the world.   The purpose of these libraries was to serve as America's cultural ambassadors, telling the people of all countries about the United States, its people and culture, and incidentally provide a type of library service that was usually unknown in those countries. The libraries were stocked with informative books, but also with popular and general reading, with magazines, films, and records, and in many cases with children's literature.   They were aimed particularly at the government officials, educators, newsmen, and other influential figures in the countries, but they also served the general public, particularly students.   Though they did not ordinarily circulate books, they did provide generous reading space where possible, and made the collection as inviting as it could be.   Though often criticized at home and abroad, and sometimes damaged in local insurrections and riots, the Information Service libraries have undoubtedly served a purpose in furthering library service, if not necessarily in winning friends for the United States.   As of the 1960's, some of them have been closed, either temporarily or permanently, while others have been turned over to other sponsoring agencies. For example, the U.S.I.S. Library at Tours, France, has been turned over to Stanford University for operation. It was renamed the John F. Kennedy Memorial Library, and its 16,000 volumes will be jointly used by students at the Stanford-Tours Study Center, the University of Poitiers, and the general public.

Other federal government libraries outside of Washington are operated by many agencies. The Veterans' Administration provides libraries in each of the many Veterans' Hospitals scattered throughout the country. The Department of Agriculture has technical and professional libraries at many points in connection with its experimental stations and research posts. The Atomic Energy Commission has libraries at its research bases, such as those at Oak Ridge, Tennessee, and at the Savannah River Authority in South Carolina. The most recent of all the governmental research agencies, the National Aeronautics and Space Administration, is rapidly providing libraries with the highest technical facilities at its bases at Cape Kennedy, Houston, and elsewhere. To obtain some idea of the scope and variety of federal agency libraries outside of Washington, D.C., we might consider those in one state alone, the state of Washington on the west coast. In this one state there were in 1960 five Veterans' Hospital Libraries, two U.S. Air Force Base Libraries, five Army installation libraries, not counting two at the Army Hospital at Tacoma, five Navy installation libraries, one Fish and Wildlife Service library, and one U.S. Penitentiary library. These nineteen libraries were the ones large enough to have professional librarians in charge; they do not include smaller government libraries without full-time librarians.

One government agency that deserves particular note for its library services is the Tennessee Valley Authority. This multi-purposed agency, a product of the New Deal days of the 1930's, was designed to control the Tennessee River as it touched seven states, and to provide flood control, water transportation, and hydroelectric power through a series of dams. Along with its engineering tasks, the T.V.A. was empowered to aid in furthering the economic

and social progress of the valley and its people.   To this end, an
excellent technical library for the Authority's employees was provided at Knoxville, and combined technical and recreational libraries
were developed at each construction site.   Local public and regional
libraries were encouraged and aided by the T. V. A. , especially during the 1930's, and much permanent library progress was made in
the valley.   In 1960, the main T. V. A. library in Knoxville contained some 60, 000 volumes, and branch technical libraries were
still maintained at Chattanooga and Wilson Dam.

In addition to the libraries of the federal government, most
of the states also maintain one or more government libraries.   Even
before the Revolution there were collections of legal works available
in the provincial legislative halls for the use of the officials and
legislators.   Virginia had a small library in the office of its colonial secretary as early as 1661, and at least 50 books survive that
were owned by the colonial government before 1776.   In that year
Thomas Jefferson suggested a bill for a state library for Virginia,
but nothing came of it until 1828 when the various volumes in the
state's offices were collected to form the beginning of a state library.   In 1831 it had 5, 500 volumes, and in 1856, 17, 500.   There
was much damage to the Virginia State Library during the Civil
War, but by 1875 it had grown to 35, 000 volumes.   In 1895 there
came a new building, and in 1903 the first full-time librarian.
Again in 1940 there came another new building, this time to house
a modern collection of 330, 000 volumes, 2 million manuscripts,
and 10, 000 maps.   Pennsylvania's state capitol had a small library
as early as 1777, and New Hampshire also claims a pre-Revolution-
ary legislative library.   The other colonies probably had at least
collections of law books for the use of their officials and legisla-
tures, but it was not until after 1800 that most of the states began
to organize official state libraries.   South Carolina had a legislative
library by 1814, Pennsylvania by 1816, New York and New Hampshire by 1818, and most of the other Eastern states by 1840.   Massachusetts began collecting state documents in 1811, and its state library
was legalized and officially opened in 1826.   Michigan's state library began in 1828, and that of Illinois in 1839, with most of the

other Midwestern and Western States forming libraries by 1850, or in the territories as they were created later.

The early state libraries were usually made up of ·legal works and official state publications for the most part, but there were from the beginning many works of a historical or geographic nature. These acquisitions came largely from gifts, exchanges of state publications with other libraries, and through receipt of Federal documents by acts of Congress. The use of the libraries was ordinarily restricted to state officials, and sometimes even they had to leave deposits if they removed books from the library. Some of the state libraries, however, were for general public use, as that of New York, which was established as "a public library for the use of the government and of the people of the State." Financial support for the early state libraries was usually erratic, and most of them grew only slowly.

In most state government libraries the legal works came to be maintained separately from the other materials, and often state law libraries were established. The state libraries themselves became largely historical and general reference libraries designed primarily for use by state officers, but they were also open to the public. State Supreme Court libraries and legislative reference libraries were other forms of legal libraries belonging to the various states. Where there was a strong historical society library or university library in the state capital, then often the state library became more of a law library than a historical collection. Wisconsin is an example of this type where the strong library of the Wisconsin State Historical Society completely overshadowed the smaller state library. In Illinois, a state library was created in 1839, but in 1842 the law books were removed to form a separate library. The remainder, a rather miscellaneous group, was left under the supervision of the Secretary of State until 1867 when a state library board was appointed.

In the latter part of the nineteenth century, the various state libraries, whether legal or historical or both, continued to improve in size and service, and some of them became really outstanding collections. In size they ranged from the New York State Library with well over 100,000 volumes, down to some of the smaller ones with only 3 or 4 thousand books. Those of the East and Middle West grew most rapidly, and the state libraries of New York and Ohio became particularly well known even outside their state borders. New York's state library provided a home for Melvil Dewey's library school when that institution left Columbia University in 1889.

By 1900 and later many of the state libraries were taking on other functions designed to serve the state as a whole rather than merely the state officials. In Ohio, for example, a state law of 1882 had opened the state library for reference use to all citizens, while in 1896 it began to offer circulation service to any state citizen, with a few special restrictions. By that time the services of the state library included a Legislative Reference Division, a Library Organizing Division, and a Traveling Library Division. The latter two functions were added to state library duties in most of the states by the 1920's. The promotion of public library service, with or without state financial aid, and the distribution of reading material by means of mail service or package libraries to citizens without local library service became accepted state library functions in many states. In others, these duties were performed by State Library Commissions, while in still others the package library service was performed by the extension division libraries of state universities.

In some of the larger states, various state departments, such as agriculture or education, have begun to develop special libraries of their own, exclusive of the state libraries. Other state library functions are found in museums or in various state research agencies. Most states have some form of state archives either so designated or in the form of historical commissions or sometimes merely in the office of the Secretary of State. However designated and under whatever name, these archives constitute a special governmental library and an important part of the state government's library services.

Still a third type of governmental library is located in the United States, and this is of course the international library, par-

ticularly those of the United Nations and its affiliated agencies.
The United Nations headquarters library in New York City is the
Dag Hammarskjold Library, founded in 1947; it already contained
nearly a quarter-million volumes in 1960.   Its contents, in all of
the five official languages of the United Nations plus many others,
are strongly related to international law and relations, plus history
and the social sciences, and an excellent collection of material on
the history of the League of Nations.   The Woodrow Wilson Memorial Library, which is a special collection within the United Nations
Library, is particularly directed toward the history of peace efforts in the modern world.   In Washington there are two other international libraries, those of the International Labor Office and the
International Monetary Fund.   Still other United Nations libraries,
outside of the United States, are those of the United Nations Educational, Scientific and Cultural Organization in Paris; the International Atomic Energy Agency Library in Vienna; and the World
Health Organization Library in Geneva.

Additional Readings

(Material on the history of U. S. government libraries can be found
in the official annual reports, particularly those of the Library of
Congress.   Information on the history of federal departmental libraries, and also of state libraries, is sometimes more difficult
to locate, although information on many of them can be found in the
library journals.)

Bishop, William W. , ed.
    Essays offered to Herbert Putnam.   Washington, 1929. 555 p.
        (Largely on the Library of Congress.)

Bowerman, George F.
    Government department libraries.   Washington, 1919. 11 p.

Cannon, Carl L. , ed.
    Guide to the library facilities for national defense.
        Chicago, 1941.   448 p.

Dixon, Margaret
    The first twenty-five years of the Louisiana State Library.
        Baton Rouge, 1950.   27 p.

Evans, Luther H., ed.
   Federal departmental libraries, a summary report of a survey
      and a conference. Washington, 1963. 150 p.

Hill, David S.
   The libraries of Washington. Chicago, 1936. 162 p.

Jamieson, John
   Books for the army: the Army Library Service in the Second
      World War. New York, 1950. 335 p.

Johnston, W. D.
   History of the Library of Congress. Washington, 1904. 535 p.

Mearns, David C.
   The story up to now: the Library of Congress, 1800-1946.
      Washington, 1947. iii, 226 p.

Morin, Wilfred L.
   State library extension services: a survey of resources and ac-
      tivities of State Library Administrative agencies, 1955-1956.
      Washington, 1960. v, 54 p.

National Association of State Libraries.
   The role of the state library. Chicago, 1955. 5 p.

Salamanca, Lucy
   Fortress of freedom: the story of the Library of Congress.
      Philadelphia, 1942. 445 p.

Temple, Phillips
   Federal services to libraries. Chicago, 1954. 227 p.

U.S. Library of Congress.
   Special report of the Librarian of Congress to the Joint Commit-
      tee on the Library concerning the Historical Library of
      Peter Force, Esq. Washington, 1867.

Washington. State Library Board.
   Report on a survey of the state-supported library activities in
      the state of Washington. Olympia, 1917. 134 p.

Williamson, Roland
   The law library in the Capitol. Washington, 1929. vii, 281 p.

20.

Special Libraries in the United States

Although all libraries are specialized to a certain extent, the special library in the United States is in a category of its own, and as such deserves separate attention. Two types of libraries that might be considered special libraries, those of schools and government agencies, have already been considered. This leaves a large number and a wide variety of libraries that still deserve attention, including some of the most valuable single collections in the country. Where the general collection stops and the specialized collection begins is difficult to delineate exactly, but for the purposes of this chapter the term "special library" can be defined as that library which is restricted in subject matter contained, and usually also restricted in clientele served.

On the whole, special libraries tend to be smaller than general ones, and the average special library would well be considered in the 10,000 volume range rather than the 100,000. Furthermore, the special library usually differs considerably in size and training of staff, in hours of service, general organization, and materials handled. Because of its nature, it can often experiment with new ideas, new methods, new machines, and new services more easily than the older, larger, and more standardized libraries. Thus, it is fortunate for the library profession that special libraries exist, not only for the services that they render, but also for the leadership that they assert in the library world in general.

Special libraries might be divided into two types: those that are independent libraries in themselves, and those that are part of or related to general public or university libraries. Also, they might be looked upon as falling into three other groups: professional, business, and government. Many of the latter type have already been discussed under government libraries, but there are many smaller technical libraries in governmental agencies that are definitely special libraries in the fullest meaning of the term.

364

Historically speaking, it is easy to state that the special library is a development of the twentieth century, since in many respects it is. But on closer observation, the special library can be seen to go back even to colonial days. The early college libraries were heavily theological, and some of the early social libraries were definitely directed toward religion, law, or history. The state libraries usually began as law collections, and the Pennsylvania Hospital Library in Philadelphia, usually considered the oldest medical library in the United States, began in 1763. Five other medical libraries, 2 of them in Philadelphia, were begun before 1800, and by the Civil War there were 23 medical libraries, varying in size from 1 to 10 thousand volumes, in the country, most of them in the Northeast. Historical libraries were also early on the scene, as were the theological collections. Certainly these could be considered as special libraries, and the early mechanics' libraries, apprentices' libraries, and mercantile libraries also tended toward specialization for their respective clients, although of course they also contained much general literature as well. Even the Philadelphia Library Company, as established by Franklin, had its members' vocational interests and advancement in view when its first book orders were placed.

In the field of law libraries some early examples were the Boston Social Law Library, founded in 1804; the Philadelphia Law Association Library in 1802; and the Harvard University Law School Library, 1817. By 1860 there were 35 law libraries of over 2,000 volumes each, mostly in the Northeast. Many of the state libraries, already mentioned in the chapter on government libraries, were largely law collections. County law libraries were also established, some quite early in New York, others by the 1840's in other Northeastern States. In some cases, particularly in Massachusetts, these local law libraries were organized under permissive state laws, while in other states they were largely the results of local law associations. Still another type of law library in the nineteenth century was that of the law school; there were 21 of these before 1875.

Theological libraries, on the other hand, were almost always

associated with colleges and schools of divinity. Apparently the
oldest strictly theological library in the United States was that
founded at St. Mary's Theological Seminary in Baltimore in 1791.
There was also a Presbyterian Theological Seminary in Beaver
County, Pennsylvania, established in 1794. It began with some 800
volumes collected by the Rev. John Anderson. By 1825 some 21
more theological libraries, most of them in seminaries, had been
established, and by 1875 there were over 120. The library of Andover Theological Seminary, Andover, Massachusetts, though larger
than average, is typical of the growth of the theological collection.
The seminary was founded in 1807, opened in 1808 with a small library, and grew slowly with gifts and purchases until by 1875 it
possessed over 34,000 volumes, not including some 12,000 pamphlets. Besides several large gifts, Andover was able to purchase
in 1858 the library of Dr. C. W. Nieder of Berlin, containing some
4,000 rare and valuable works. The seminary library issued a
printed catalog in 1819 and another in 1838, with a supplement in
1849. From 1818 to 1866 it occupied a room in the college chapel,
but in 1866 it moved into a separate building, donated by three Andover citizens. The majority of the theological libraries, however,
were smaller than that at Andover and usually ranged from 2,000
to 15,000 volumes in the nineteenth century. In addition to the
strictly theological collections, it should be pointed out that many of
the early college libraries had strong theological libraries, either
in their main libraries or in departmental collections. Harvard's
Divinity School, for example, began its own library in 1825 and
owned 17,000 volumes by 1875. Small church libraries were fairly
numerous in the mid-nineteenth century, but these were usually
more in the manner of study collections for the ministers than actual libraries. The Sunday School libraries, already considered under public libraries, were as much general as theological, and
were designed more for the church members than for the minister
or theological student.

　　　Historical libraries were relatively numerous, and here
again the sizes varied considerably. The Massachusetts Historical
Society was probably the earliest established, having been organized

in 1791, but it was followed by others in the neighboring states early in the nineteenth century. By 1850 most of the states had historical societies, some of them receiving some financial assistance from their governments, and a number of cities and counties had local historical groups. By 1875 there were some 80 historical society libraries from Maine to California and from Alabama to Wisconsin. In size they varied from a few hundred volumes to the New York Historical Society's 60,000. The Rhode Island Historical Society Library in Providence might be considered typical of these libraries prior to 1875. It was organized in 1822 and had about 150 members, with a $5 admission fee and $3 annual dues. By 1870 it contained some 6,000 bound volumes and about 30,000 pamphlets. The collection was largely on the history of Rhode Island, secondarily on New England, and then on the remainder of the United States. Many of its volumes were obtained by exchange of its publications with similar societies in other states. The Society owned its own building but had no paid employees, and its library was open to members and their guests only, and then for only a few hours per week. Most of the historical society libraries were poorly financed, but their collections often came to contain many valuable volumes, and their publications made notable additions to the published historical literature of the United States. Almost in a class by itself was the Boston Athenaeum Library, a historical collection founded as a subscription library in 1807. Through wise purchases, valuable gifts, and the deposit of several important collections in its midst, the Athenaeum rapidly became one of the most important libraries in the nation. By 1814 it contained over 8,000 volumes, and by 1827 more than 21,000. Moving into a new building in 1849, it had passed the 50,000 mark and ranked along with Harvard and the Library of Congress as the largest libraries in the United States.

Somewhat akin to the historical libraries were the scientific society libraries that developed in the larger cities during the early nineteenth century. The oldest of these was the American Philosophical Society Library, founded in Philadelphia in 1743, as another of the brain-children of Benjamin Franklin. This collection

grew only slowly, but through gifts and wise purchases it acquired
many valuable books in all fields of science and philosophy. By
1875 it contained some 20,000 volumes and about as many pamphlets,
many of them rare association publications received on exchange.
Also in Philadelphia was the Academy of Natural Sciences, founded
in 1812, and by mid-century proclaimed as one of the best in its
field, with about 30,000 volumes and 35,000 pamphlets. The Franklin Institute was founded in the same city in 1824 as a group particularly interested in the physical sciences, and its library was only a little smaller than the other two. In Boston, the American
Academy of Arts and Sciences (founded 1780) and the Boston Society
of Natural History (1831) each had libraries of more than 10,000
volumes by 1875, while the Massachusetts Horticultural Society
(1829) had a library of about 2,500 volumes. In New York there
were such scientific libraries as those of the American Geographical Society, founded in 1852 and with 10,000 volumes in 1875; and
the New York Academy of Sciences, founded in 1818, with only
3,500 volumes at the later date. In 1885, New York City had in all
33 special libraries of note, including 9 medical and hospital libraries, 6 law libraries, 8 scientific libraries, 4 theological libraries, 2 historical libraries, and 1 specializing in insurance.

Although the large cities of the East had the larger and
stronger societies, the scientific society movement was by no means
limited to that area. Chicago had several groups founded after
1860, while St. Louis had a notable Academy of Science begun in
1856. Other cities in the Midwest had similar organizations, but
still others could be found in all parts of the nation. Charleston,
South Carolina, and Topeka, Kansas, supported natural history societies, as did also Saco, Maine, and Davenport, Iowa. In theory
these scientific society libraries were for the use of members only,
but in practice almost any serious student could obtain access to
them. How much use was made of them is debatable, but certainly
the larger of them were well used and undoubtedly provided the material for much serious and valuable study, both by students and
scholars. Several of the societies carried on valuable publication
programs with the results of studies largely made from their own

resources.

Special medical and hospital libraries were fewer and smaller than those in the other subject fields in the nineteenth century, possibly because the literature in the field of medicine was relatively small. In New York City, the New York Hospital Medical Library was begun in 1796, and by 1875 had over 10,000 volumes, while the Academy of Medicine Library, founded in 1846, claimed only 3,000 volumes in 1875. Philadelphia's College of Physicians Library, dating from 1789, had 18,750 books by 1875, and the Pennsylvania Hospital Library had 12,500. Elsewhere in the country the Library of the Surgeon General's Office, already mentioned under government libraries, was the largest medical library, but others were found in medical colleges and societies in virtually every state by 1850. Such institutions as the Medical College of Georgia, the University of Louisiana Medical Department, and the Medical College of Ohio represented the college field, while the medical societies with libraries included the Worcester, Massachusetts, Medical Society, and the Boston Society for Medical Improvement. Each of these had libraries of 5 thousand volumes or more in 1875, as did also the Rhode Island Hospital of Providence, the Cincinnati Hospital, and the Massachusetts General Hospital in Boston. Not to be overlooked are the medical libraries that were part of general collections, such as the 11,000 volumes in the Boston Public Library, or the 5,000 volumes of medicine in the Boston Athenaeum. Again it should be noted that the preponderence of medical libraries were in the Northeast.

By 1875, there were also a few libraries in public institutions such as prisons, reformations, and insane asylums. For the most part they were the result of gifts from charitable individuals and groups, and were cared for by interested inmates. A library in the State Penitentiary at Philadelphia was begun in 1829 by a gift of books, and that at Sing Sing in New York started with a gift of books from Governor William H. Seward in 1840. One prison library, that in Alton, Illinois, began with books donated by the inmates at another prison at Charlestown, Massachusetts, in 1846. By 1867 thirteen prisons reported libraries with an average of about 1,500

volumes each. Sing Sing had the largest at that time with some
4,000 volumes. Some 13 states at that time were appropriating a
few hundred dollars each for the purchase of books for their prison libraries. The reformatory movement for young criminals began in New York in 1825, although most of the similar institutions
in other states came after 1850. In 1875, of 56 reformatories in
the United States, 49 reported libraries ranging from 150 volumes
to 4,000, for an average of about 1,000. Again, the largest was
in New York, this time in the New York City House of Refuge.
Both prisons and reformatories reported heavy use of their books,
and a large percentage of regular readers among their "captive"
audiences. Some received funds from the state, but all relied
heavily on gifts of books and funds, with inmate librarians, to keep
going. The New York State Lunatic Asylum at Utica reported in
1875 a library of some 4,000 volumes, but apparently this was a
technical library for the staff rather than for the inmates.

One other nineteenth-century special library worthy of mention is the newspaper library. This institution tended to take two
forms: the "morgue," a specialized file of clippings of past newspaper issues, topically arranged and forming something of an index
to the paper, and the regular research library of books and other
materials provided for the use of the staff reporters and editors.
The New York Tribune had a research library before 1850, and by
1874 it contained over 5,000 volumes. Its morgue, which was begun in 1860, was largely biographical and designed to provide quick
information on the lives and careers of all important and news-
worthy people in New York and the nation. The New York Herald
had a well-established reference library of some 8,000 volumes in
1870, but its morgue was not begun until later. Two other newspaper libraries established shortly after the Civil War were those
of the Boston Herald and the New York Times. Most newspapers
in larger cities followed suit in the late nineteenth and early twentieth centuries, and the morgue in particular became standard equipment for the average newspaper office. The research library, on
the other hand, was confined to the very largest papers, and for
smaller ones a few standard reference works usually sufficed.

The period after 1875 and before World War I was one of slow growth in the special library field, as in other library areas, but one in which the special library came into its own and was recognized as an institution in itself. Though in types of libraries and fields of service it varied more than those in any other field, it came to be realized that the special library, whether large or small, part of a larger system or not, had something in common, and so in 1909 the Special Library Association was founded. The formation of such a group was first proposed at the Bretton Woods Conference of the American Library Association, when some 45 special library representatives followed the suggestion of John Cotton Dana in joining together. After its formation the Special Libraries Association took a prominent part in promoting the interests of special libraries and in giving leadership and direction to the profession.

After 1910 the number of industrial firms forming special research libraries increased considerably. At first their libraries were largely collections of records and studies made by the firm's specialists, but later they came to include specialized reference materials, technical journals, and general scientific works of value to the particular industry. In the East, some of the early industrial libraries were those of the American Brass Company, the United Gas Improvement Company, and the New York Merchants Association. The industrial libraries were joined by bank and financial house libraries, with Harvey Fisk and Sons, and the National City Bank of New York being among the earliest to form business reference collections for their employees.

The legislative reference library on the state level has been discussed along with the government libraries, but there was a simila: institution on the municipal level in many cities. Baltimore was one of the first cities to form such a library in 1906, and it was followed by Philadelphia, New York, Chicago, and some 10 other cities in the next decade. These libraries combined legal and commercial reference services for municipal employees and businessmen alike. In smaller towns and cities, Chambers of Commerce or other businessmen's associations sometimes provided similar but smaller reference collections for their members.

Among all special libraries, one of the most valuable types
is the endowed reference library, and the United States is fortunate
in having a reasonably large number of them. These libraries are
special in that they are usually limited in subject content, are not
public in either support or general use, and are limited to a relatively restricted clientele of scholars and special students. Two of
these, the Lenox and Astor Libraries, have already been mentioned
in connection with the formation of New York Public Library, but
another most valuable one is the Folger Shakespeare Library in
Washington, D. C. Henry Clay Folger began collecting Shakespeare
as a youth at Amherst College in the late nineteenth century, and
by 1909 his collection was noted as the largest in the United States.
A few years later it was called the largest Shakespearean collection in the world, and before his death he arranged to have it
housed in an appropriate building in Washington, D. C., and eventually opened to research by serious scholars. This library was
opened in 1933, and it contains besides books and pamphlets many
manuscripts, documents, relics, curios, drawings, paintings, prints,
medals, coins, tapestries, playbills, prompt-books, and even furniture and costumes relating to Shakespeare and the times in which
he lived. In 1960, the Folger Library contained over 250,000 volumes, not counting its other prized possessions.

Chicago is fortunate in having two major research libraries,
the Crerar and Newberry libraries. The Newberry Reference Library was founded in 1887 by Walter L. Newberry as a public reference library in the humanities and social sciences. The John
Crerar Library was begun by its namesake in 1895 as a scientific
library to balance and complete the work begun by the Newberry
collection. The Crerar Library in 1960 had approximately a million volumes, while the Newberry Library had over three-quarters
of a million. Since 1960 the Crerar Library has moved into a new
building on the grounds of the Illinois Institute of Technology where
its resources will enhance those of the Institute and yet still be
available as a public reference library. In New York City the
Pierpont Morgan Library is particularly strong in the history of the

book, incunabula, and Americana. On the West Coast the Henry
L. Huntington Library in San Marino, California, is one of the
finest rare books collections in the world. Its 400,000 volumes
and over a million manuscripts make it a scholars' paradise, and
much of the research completed in its resources is published in the
Huntington Library Quarterly. Elsewhere in the nation, there are
several other similar and valuable endowed collections, such as
the Linda Hall Library of science and technology in Kansas City,
and the Lloyd Library and Museum in Cincinnati, also a science
collection. In 1960 the Linda Hall Library had some 225,000 volumes, while the Lloyd Library had 164,000. On the college campuses there are similar valuable collections, such as the Robert
Browning Collection on the Baylor University campus in Waco, Texas, and the William L. Clements Library of American History at
the University of Michigan in Ann Arbor. These libraries and a
few similar ones across the nation are usually open to serious students, and make their resources available by photocopy if not by
inter-library loan to other libraries.

By World War I or later, the university libraries on most
campuses became so large and unwieldy that they began to break
up into many departmental or special college libraries. This trend
had begun in the nineteenth century with the formation of law, divinity, and medical libraries on the campuses, but in the twentieth
century this trend extended to almost all subject fields. A reverse
trend might be noted since World War II toward returning departmental libraries to the central collection when newer and more
adequate facilities were constructed. The special library on the
campus, however, seems to be an established thing, and with the
proliferation of literature in the special fields, there seems to be
no end to them. The University of Michigan, for example, has
some twenty-eight special or departmental collections on its campus, and it is only about average in this respect among the larger
universities. Its special libraries range in subject from architecture to transportation, and from a few thousand in the smaller collections to over a hundred thousand in the business administration
and medical libraries, and over three hundred thousand in the law

library.   Besides these special libraries, moreover, there are also many more special collections in the main university library,
with some of them running into thousands of volumes.   This situation is duplicated, or nearly so, on a hundred other campuses; so
it is obvious that the special library is a definite part of the university library program.

The few industrial research libraries established before
World War I have been followed by literally hundreds of similar es-
tablishments in more recent years.   The technical and scientific
revolution in industry that accompanied and followed World War II
has particularly emphasized the value of research to the industrial
firm, and the company library has come into its own.   The E. I.
du Pont de Nemours & Co. in 1960 had not only 7 technical libraries in its headquarters city of Wilmington, Delaware, but also
branch libraries in Du Pont plants in 13 other cities.   The libraries
in Wilmington ranged in size from a few thousand volumes to over
45,000 in the Central Research Library.   Among the specialties in
the Du Pont libraries are not only such subjects as chemistry,
physics, engineering, business, and manufacturing, but also biology,
bacteriology, biochemistry, and even a legal research library.
Westinghouse Electric Corporation has four libraries in Pittsburgh,
with another in East Pittsburgh.   General Electric Company in
Schenectady has six libraries with branches in eight other cities.
If these are representative of the larger industrial library systems,
then there are hundreds of examples of companies with a single research library.   For example, there are those of the Corning Glass
Works at Corning, New York, with 10,000 volumes; General Tire
and Rubber Company of Akron, Ohio, with 4,500 volumes; the
Libby-Owens-Ford Glass Company of Toledo, with 8,800 volumes;
and the Allied Chemical Corporation of Morristown, New Jersey,
with some 9,000 volumes.   Although the preponderance of special
libraries remains in the East and Middle West, there are also others in all parts of the country.   The Texas Instruments Company of
Dallas has three libraries containing some 9,000 volumes between
them, and the Humble Oil and Refining Company of Houston not only
has a technical research library of 12,000 volumes, but also a law

library, a geological library, a medical library, and an employee
relations library. On the west coast the development of industrial
research libraries has closely followed the movement of industry
to that area, and Los Angeles alone has at least 21 major industrial company libraries, not including those of law, insurance,
banking, and motion-picture firms.

If industry has come to appreciate the research library, the
fields of banking and insurance are no less responsive to the value
of books in the conduct of their business. Banking and insurance
companies were among the earliest to develop special libraries, but
again their widespread use has come only since the 1940's. New
York City is of course a center of such libraries, and those of
Chase Manhattan Bank, Dun and Bradstreet (17,000 volumes), First
National City Bank (40,000), Equitable Life Assurance Society
(36,500), New York Life Insurance Company (25,000), and Standard
and Poor's Corporation (50,000) all bear this out.   Once again,
however, this type of library is not limited to the Northeast, and
such firms as the Prudential Insurance Company of Chicago, the
National Bank of Detroit, the Bank of America in San Francisco,
and the Southwestern Life Insurance Company of Dallas all have research libraries for their employees and clientele. In some cases,
insurance firms and agents join together to support libraries, as in
the case of the Insurance Library Association of Atlanta with its
3,500 volumes, and the Insurance Underwriters Association of the
Pacific Library in San Francisco with its 9,000 volumes.

Newspaper libraries have come far since the early beginnings
in the nineteenth century, and by 1960 there were many ranging
from a few hundred into many thousands of volumes. To point out
only a few, we might mention the New York Times, with its 30,000
volumes not counting its map section with 10,000 maps; its picture
library with 2 million prints and 30,000 cuts ready for immediate
use, and its morgue of 1,600,000 biographical clippings and 70,000
subject entries. In Boston, the Globe Library has 10,000 volumes,
4,000,000 clippings, and 300,000 pictures, while in Chicago the
Tribune has 22,000 volumes, and in Los Angeles the Times has
over 2,000 volumes. Elsewhere the book collections are smaller

in the newspaper libraries, but the collections of clippings and pictures are constantly growing. In recent years, the newspaper library has been joined by the magazine headquarters library. For example, Time magazine has a 41,000 volume library; Newsweek has its 15,000 volumes with 80,000 biographical items and 60,000 subject entries in its information file; McGraw-Hill Publishing Company has a 10,000 volume library for its several publications; and the Curtis Publishing Company in Philadelphia has a 16,000 volume collection. Other magazines, such as McCalls, the Magazine of Wall Street, Popular Science, and Readers' Digest also have libraries at their headquarters offices. This system of research and reference libraries to provide quick and accurate information on persons, places, and events is considered most important in the operation of magazines, particularly for the news weeklies.

Not the least important of modern special libraries are those of national or international organizations. Technical societies, educational associations, labor organizations, and many other types of associations have developed headquarters libraries for the use of their professional staffs, visiting members, and even for the public. Some of these, as for example the Engineering Societies Library of New York with its 180,000 volumes, not only provide a magnificent library, but carry on publishing activities as well. The Engineering Societies Library began the Engineering Index now compiled and published by its own firm. A few others of the many such libraries in New York City alone are the Explorers Club with its 12,500 volume library; the Family Service Association with 1,200 volumes; The Institute of Aeronautical Sciences Library with 12,000 volumes; the International Ladies' Garment Workers' Union Library with 17,000 volumes; the National Association of Manufacturers Library with 17,000 volumes; and the Regional Planning Association Library with 2,500 volumes. Chicago has the National Association of Real Estate Boards Library, and the National Livestock and Meat Board Library, among others. Washington, D. C., has its share of associational and institute libraries, while still others are scattered in almost all of the major cities of the United States.

Hospital libraries and prison libraries have also come into

their own in recent years. Particularly in the hospital field the number and size of libraries have increased considerably since 1945. Both technical libraries for the use of doctors and nurses and popular libraries for the patients have become standard items in the larger hospitals. Chicago, for example, has at least 14 hospital libraries, plus some 10 or more other medical libraries in colleges and association headquarters. The Children's Memorial Hospital has not only a doctors' library and a nurses' library, but a children's library as well. Prison libraries, led by the many excellent libraries in the federal prison system, have grown in importance and now employ professional librarians when they can be obtained. Sing Sing Prison library, in Ossining, New York, had over 10,000 volumes as early as 1929, while San Quentin Prison in California had about 16,000 at the same date. In other correctional institutions, whether reformatories or prisons, the use of the library as an educational and recreational device was common by the 1920's, and in later years its value as an inspirational aid was also realized.

Special libraries in general and more particularly those in the technical and scientific fields were faced in the 1950's with the tremendous task of controlling the vast amounts of information pouring from the presses and processing machines all over the world. Even in the relatively restricted field of certain industrial libraries, the material available for informative use has increased along geometric proportions in recent years, and the special librarian and information specialist has the task of organizing this material for quick and orderly use of the company scientists. Time is money for the industrial concern, and the quicker the information can be retrieved from the books and files, the more valuable it is to the company. Add to the quantity of material available the fact that it comes in many varieties of format, and it is easy to see what a task special librarinship can be. Information in a technical library can be in the usual form of books, periodicals, and films, but it can also be in the form of maps, oil-well logs, meter readings, punched cards, perforated tape, sound-recorded tape, and other shapes, as well as, of course, manuscript, typed, processed, or

filmed reports.   The task of organizing all of this information calls
for new techniques, and the special librarian has risen to the challenge with a variety of devices for information storage and retrieval.   Automation in the library is a definite feature of many
special libraries, and the library world in general is finding that
the special librarian is taking the lead in many respects in breaking
new trails in library service.

Closely allied to or perhaps encompassing the field of special librarianship is the new science of documentation.   Documentation has been defined as "the complex of activities required in the
communication of specialized information including the preparation,
reproduction, collection, analysis, organization and dissemination
. . ." It is generally accepted to mean the storage and retrieval of
technical information, but it can of course be applied to all recorded or preserved knowledge, in which case it would include all
of library service itself.   At any rate, documentation is a term
widely used in discussing the problems of technical and professional
communication in the world today, and as such it is a respected
term in the special library field.   In 1937 the American Documentation Institute was organized, and although concerned strongly with
micro-reproduction in its early years, it has since World War II
extended its field of operations.   Through the journal American
Documentation, it is providing the library world with an excellent
journal of research and interpretation in its field.

The Special Libraries Association continues to be one of the
most effective and productive groups of its kind, and it has in recent years been joined by several other groups in even more re-
strictive library areas.   These include the Music Library Association, the Theater Library Association, the American Association of
Law Libraries, the Medical Library Association, the American
Theological Library Association, and even an Osteopathic Library
Association.   In 1960, a directory of special libraries in the United
States included over 10, 000 collections, some of them with only a
few hundred volumes, but others with over 100, 000, and all serving
special purposes as collectors and disseminaters of information.
Library schools are taking more notice of the needs for special

librarians, and courses designed to train them are being offered.
With a greater demand for men and women to staff the special library positions than there is a supply of library school graduates to fill them, many positions are held by specialists from other fields. In fact, many of the advances in library technology are being made by engineers and communications specialists whose approach to the library field is through the special library. In this alliance of librarianship and technology a revolution is taking place, and there is some doubt as to whether the librarian will grow into an information specialist or whether a new profession will emerge. At any rate, the economic, cultural, and even military value of special libraries to the nation is now fully realized, and the service that they render ranks them high both in the field of libraries and in the wider areas of communication in general.

Additional Readings

(The history of special libraries in the United States is often included in the history of the institutions or associations that they serve. Other information appears in published and unpublished reports, in trade and professional periodicals, and in particular in the publications of the Special Libraries Association.)

Adams, Joseph Q.
    The Folger Shakespeare Memorial Library, a report on progress, 1931-1941. Washington, 1942.   61 p.

Adams, Sherman W.
    Documents and memoranda relating to the origin and present status of the Hartford Library Company . . . Hartford, 1889.   103 p.

Almond, Nina
    Special collections in the Hoover Library on War, Revolution and Peace.   Stanford, Calif. , 1940.   xiv, 111 p.

Bay, J. Christian
    The John Crerar Library, 1895-1944:   an historical report. Chicago, 1945.   ix, 188 p.

Bishop, William W.
    A temple of American history: the William L. Clements Library.   Ann Arbor, 1922.   14 p.

Boston. Athenaeum.
The Athenaeum Centenary: the influence and history of the
Boston Athenaeum from 1807 to 1907 . . . Boston, 1907.
xiii, 236 p.

Bradford, S. C.
Documentation. London, 1948. 156 p.

Crosby, Alexander L.
A half century of power for business, 1904-1954. Newark,
N. J., 1954. ii, 32 p. (On the Newark Business Library.)

Denver. City Club.
The bibliographical center for research, Rocky Mountain Region.
Denver, 1944. 47 p.

Downs, Robert B.
Union catalogs in the United States. Chicago, 1942. 409 p.

Dunglison, Richard
History and condition of the medical libraries of Philadelphia.
Philadelphia, 1871. 46 p.

Dunlap, Leslie W.
American historical societies, 1790-1860. Madison, Wisc.,
1944. ix, 238 p. (Includes information on the society libraries.)

Foss, M. R.
Grosvenor Library and its time. Buffalo, N.Y., 1956. 215 p.

Harrison, Joseph L.
Forbes Library: the half century, 1894-1944. Northampton,
Mass., 1945. 55 p.

Johnston, R. H.
Special libraries. Silver Spring, Md., 1931. 27 p.

Johnston, William D.
Special collections in libraries in the United States. Washington,
1912. 140 p. (U.S. Bureau of Education Bulletin, 1912,
no. 23).

Joskin, Beryl
A history of the Santa Clara Mission Library. Oakland, Calif.,
1961.

Keep, Austin B.
History of the New York Society library. . . New York, 1908.
xvi, 607 p.

Kilgour, Frederick G.
The library of the Medical Institute of Yale College and its catalogue of 1865. New Haven, 1960. 74 p.

King, Marion M.
Books and people: five decades of New York's oldest library. New York, 1954. ix, 372 p. (On New York Society Library.)

King, Stanley
Recollections of the Folger Shakespeare Library, 1927-1948. Ithaca, N.Y., 1950. 44 p.

Lewis, John F.
History of the Apprentices' Library of Philadelphia, 1820-1920. Philadelphia, 1924. vii, 101 p.

Minneapolis. Athenaeum.
Historical sketch of the Athenaeum. Minneapolis, 1876. 18 p.

O'Neal, William B.
Jefferson's fine arts library for the University of Virginia. Charlottesville, 1956. 53 p.

Oklahoma. University Library.
The Harry W. Bass Collection in Business History in the University of Oklahoma Library. Norman, 1956. 76 p.

Perry, J. W.
Documentation and information retrieval . . . Cleveland, 1957. 156 p.

Pierpont Morgan Library, New York.
The Pierpont Morgan Library, a review of the activities, growth and development . . . 1941-1948. New York, 1950. 108 p. (Previous reports covered 1924-29, 1930-35, 1936-40, etc.)

Quincy, Josiah
The history of the Boston Athenaeum . . . Cambridge, Mass., 1851. xii, 263 p.

Roalfe, William R.
The libraries of the legal profession. St. Paul, Minn., 1953. 471 p.

Roberts, Arthur S.
The Redwood Library and Athenaeum. Providence, 1948. 58 p.

Schwerin, Kurt
A guide to the legal collections in Chicago. Chicago, 1955. 148 p.

Shera, Jesse H., ed.
Documentation in action. New York, 1956. 471 p.

Taube, Mortimer
Information storage and retrieval: theory, systems and devices. New York, 1958. 228 p.

United Nations. Library.
The Dag Hammarskjold Library. New York, 1962. 167 p.

Winship, George Parker
The John Carter Brown Library: a history. Providence, 1914. 97 p.

Wroth, Lawrence C.
The first century of the John Carter Brown Library . . . Providence, 1946. vi, 88 p.

The first quarter century of the Pierpont Morgan Library. New York, 1949. 68 p.

Zinsser, William K.
Search and research: the collections and uses of the New York Public Library . . . New York, 1961. 46 p.

21.

Private Libraries in the United States

Not to be ignored in the history of libraries is the development of the privately owned book collection that in size, value, and arrangement warrants the name of library. A collection of books in itself, no matter how large, is not necessarily a library, but when those books are well selected, arranged in some logical order, cataloged or not, but usable by the owner and/or by others, then they constitute a library and deserve a place in the history of libraries. The United States has been fortunate throughout its history in having a large number of citizens who collected and preserved books, and doubly fortunate in that many of those collections have ended up in public libraries.

Many of the private libraries built up in the colonial period suffered considerably during the American Revolution, but by 1800 another generation of library collectors had emerged, and from that time on the private library has been noticeably present upon the American literary scene. The early Presidents all had libraries, and these set the tone and example for other leading figures of the era. George Washington's library has already been mentioned, and our second President, John Adams, also had one of the largest private libraries in the new nation. Though somewhat weak in literature and science, it was comparatively well-rounded for its era and was particularly strong in theology, the classics, and American history. Thomas Jefferson built on a small library inherited from his father in 1757, but a fire in his home in 1770 destroyed this collection. Although he mourned the loss, Jefferson noted that this group of books was largely composed of legal works and texts that could easily be replaced. He immediately began building up another library that numbered 2,640 volumes by 1783 and 6,487 when he sold them to the Library of Congress in 1815. Between 1815 and his death in 1826, he compiled still a third library of nearly a thousand volumes.

President James Madison donated his library of 2,500 volumes to the University of Virginia, while his successor James Monroe left a relatively small library that was kept intact by his descendants. John Quincy Adams gave away many of his books during his lifetime, but still left a library of 8,000 volumes at his death. This library has been preserved by the Adams Memorial Society in Quincy, Massachusetts, although some 750 of the most valuable volumes have been deposited in the Boston Athenaeum. President Andrew Jackson did not have a large library, and many books that he did own were destroyed in a fire that damaged his home in 1834. Martin Van Buren's private library was largely that of a prosperous lawyer, but John Tyler at his home in Virginia had an extensive library, particularly strong in the classics and English literature. Much of his library was destroyed during the Civil War. No other President before Lincoln had much in the way of a private library, except Millard Fillmore who had about 5,000 volumes in all, carefully divided into a law library and a "miscellaneous library." The latter collection was strong in history, travel, and both English and American literature. President Lincoln was a great reader of books, but never held onto many of them. His law library was owned in cooperation with his partner, William H. Herndon, and he also gave to Herndon many nonlegal books that he owned when he became President. Lincoln's first Vice-President, Hannibal Hamlin, was an extensive book collector, and his library was not dispersed until well in the twentieth century. Most of the Presidents after Lincoln had private libraries, none of them particularly remarkable unless Theodore Roosevelt's "big game library" could be so considered. These are for the most part still preserved in the homes of descendants or in memorials. Since President Franklin D. Roosevelt, the custom has developed of placing a former President's private library, together with all his papers and a collection of books relating to his administration and times, in a memorial library supported by private donations. Presidents F. D. Roosevelt, Harry S. Truman, Dwight D. Eisenhower, and J. F. Kennedy have such memorial libraries.

Other American statesmen have also been noteworthy for their private libraries.   Benjamin Franklin is an excellent example of the earlier ones, although his library was of course mainly a product of the colonial period.   There is, however, an interesting description of his library as it existed in 1787, at which time it was described as being housed in a large room, with walls and several alcoves covered with books.   The visitor, Manassah Cutler, estimated that it was at that time the best private library in America.   At his death, an inventory of Franklin's library covered 4,276 volumes, consisting of a wide range of subjects.   It was rather weak on literature but strong on science, and included a few finely printed books as evidence of his lifetime interest in typography.

The first half of the nineteenth century saw the activities of several important book collectors who concentrated on books in the general field of Americana -- history, travel, biography, and literature.   One of the earliest of these was John Allan of New York (1777-1863) who amassed a notable collection of Americana and also collected early illustrated works and examples of early American printing.   His library was sold in 1864 for almost $38,000. John Carter Brown (1797-1874) is one of America's best known book collectors because his library was kept intact and passed on to Brown University in 1900.   Brown's library was enhanced by the fact that as a relatively wealthy man he was able to acquire many rare items and on occasion to acquire whole collections.   It was particularly strong in early Americana, travels and explorations; at the time of its first catalog in 1865, it contained some 5,600 titles, many of course in several volumes.   The Brown Library was later considerably increased by his widow and sons, and has grown considerably larger since becoming the property of the university, so that it is today one of the finest collections of Americana in existence.   Peter Force, editor and historian, began collecting books in the 1820's, and became such an avid collector that he often mortgaged his property in order to add more volumes to his library.   Centering his interest in American history, he collected books, pamphlets, newspapers, periodicals, and manuscripts

until he owned more than 60,000 items in all. In 1867 his heirs
sold this collection to the Library of Congress, thereby more than
doubling that library's holdings in its field. James Lenox (1800-80),
able to retire from business at the age of 40, spent the latter half
of his life building his immense and valuable library. In 1870, con-
vinced that his library was too large for any individual to own, he
gave to the people of the city of New York both his books and his
large collection of paintings, and later a building to house both.
Although he subsequently gave more books and funds for book purchases, his original core library alone contained about 15,000 volumes. Much of his collection was Americana, particularly before
1750, but he also had a large collection of Shakespeareana, English
literature, and Bibles. The Lenox Library, after 1895 a part of
the New York Public Library, has been considerably enlarged over
the years, and by 1960 constituted some 65,000 volumes in the
Rare Book Division. Gardner Drake (1798-1875) was another inde-
fatigable collector of Americana, particularly on the American Indian. At one time his library was reported to contain over 12,000
volumes and approximately 50,000 pamphlets, but he sold part of
it in 1845 to another collector, George Brinley, and the remainder
was dispersed after his death.

By 1850 there were several large private libraries devoted
to Americana, but there were many centered around other subjects
as well. George Ticknor (1791-1871) of Boston collected more
than 3,000 volumes of Spanish history and literature which after
his death went to the Boston Public Library. Caleb Fiske Harris
(1818-81) gathered an immense collection of poetry and drama, with
many very rare items. Fortunately this library ended up in the
Brown University Library in 1884. Charles Francis Adams (1807-
86) owned a library that was general in nature, but strong in American printing in all fields. He virtually made a public library out of
his 17,000 volumes and loaned them widely to his broad circle of
friends. Thomas P. Barton (1803-69) was one of the first American collectors of Shakespeare, and besides a large collection in this
field that went to the Boston Public Library after his death, he also had a general library of some 16,000 volumes. William E. Bur-

ton (1804-60) was another collector of Shakespeare, but he broadened his interests to include all English drama and compiled a library of several thousand volumes in this area. In the field of general history and political science, Andrew Dickson White collected some 30,000 volumes and donated them to Cornell University. One of the largest private collections ever amassed in the United States was that of Hubert Howe Bancroft. With his main interest in the history of the western United States and Mexico, Bancroft collected between 50 and 60 thousand volumes that were purchased from his heirs in 1905 by the University of California Library.

Although these were some of the largest and most valuable private libraries, there were many more smaller ones that were still significant. Dr. John Green of Worcester, Massachusetts, in 1857 willed his private library of 7,000 volumes to the city as a basis for a public library. In 1855 there was published a list of some 40 private libraries in Boston and its vicinity alone. Most of these were in the range of 5 to 10 thousand volumes, and included those of Edward Everett, William H. Prescott, Rufus Choate, Henry W. Longfellow, and Daniel Webster. About the same time a similar list for New York described about 50 major collections in that area. In Philadelphia, Stephen Colwell, lawyer and economist, bequeathed his library of 6,000 volumes on politics and economics to the University of Pennsylvania Library, while in Cincinnati, W. H. Mussey gave his collection of several thousand volumes of history and classics to that city's public library.

Aside from these collections gathered together strictly for the love of books, there were many libraries worthy of that designation but owned for professional purposes by teachers, lawyers, ministers, and doctors. Ministers especially were active in collecting books, and not all of them were theological in content. As early as 1810, for example, the Rev. James Hall gave 60 volumes from his private library to the University of North Carolina, and these volumes included classics and philosophy as well as theology. Other ministers of western North Carolina in the same era left libraries of several score volumes, including history, encyclopedias, law, classics, and political science. In St. Louis, at the time of the Louisiana Purchase (1803), the Catholic Bishop Dubourg owned a library of several thousand volumes, and at least 35 private and professional libraries of over 100 volumes each are mentioned in St. Louis wills dated before 1840. Many of these private libraries eventually ended up as parts of public or college libraries, but many more were sold and dispersed or divided up among descendants.

The latter part of the nineteenth century saw the collection of private libraries in the United States rise almost to the level of a profession in itself. As private wealth became more common, both the true bibliophile and the amateur were able to make large collections, and the cream of many European libraries found its way to America through the activities of book agents and auction sales. Some of the collectors and booklovers formed book clubs such as the Grolier Club of New York, the Franklin Club of St. Louis, and the Roxburghe Club of San Francisco. Among the founders of the Grolier Club was Robert Hoe (1839-1909), undoubtedly one of America's greatest book collectors. He specialized in rare books and fine bindings, and as early as 1896 he had over 8,000 volumes. Between 1903 and 1909 he published 18 volumes of catalogs of his holdings, and when the collection was sold after his death it brought over $2,000,000. A copy of the Gutenberg Bible sold for $50,000 at this sale, the highest price ever paid for a single book up to this time. Fortunately, the Bible and many of the other rarest items in the Hoe sale were obtained by the Morgan and Huntington Libraries.

Probably surpassing even the Hoe collection was the library of rare books and manuscripts collected by the financier John Pierpont Morgan (1837-1913). Morgan began to collect rare items early in life, and by 1900 he had become a collector in the full sense of the word, buying both selectively and in large quantities. With his almost unlimited funds he bought at auctions both in the United States and in Europe, and acquired many of the finest books in the world, often from old English and European family libraries that had existed for centuries but which were being dispersed in the late nineteenth century. Sometimes he bought whole libraries, as in

Private Libraries in the U.S. 389

1899 when he acquired the collection of the London bookseller, James Toovey. At Morgan's death in 1913, the collection contained some 20,000 volumes, and in 1924, when his son opened the library for public reference use, it included over 25,000 volumes, plus hundreds of rare manuscripts, cuneiform tablets, drawings, paintings, prints, medals, and coins -- all housed in a magnificent marble building and preserved with a large endowment. Certainly the Morgan Library is today one of the cultural treasures of the Western World.

On the west coast, the railroad magnate Henry E. Huntington was building up an extensive library beginning about 1890, and in some 30 years he acquired some 175,000 volumes, with extensive collections of manuscripts. The Huntington Library has been described as a "library of libraries" or a "collection of collections," since its owner was able to purchase whole libraries at a time, such as the E. Dwight Church Library of Americana and the British Bridgewater House Library. The Huntington Library is especially strong in incunabula, holding over 5,000 items, but it is also strong in American history, English literature, and other fields. It was opened to research in the early 1920's.

There are several other late nineteenth-century collectors who deserve mention. Beverly Chew (1850-1924) is noted as a collector of American literature and as the third president of the Grolier Club. Having brought together a distinguished library in the American field, he sold this and began collecting English literature. This library was sold to the Huntington Library, and Chew collected still a third library, this time concentrating on the finest bindings, particularly those employing silver and other metals, and this rare group he bequeathed to the Grolier Club. Harry Elkins Widener (1884-1912) was a spectacular collector, bringing together a notable collection of great works in English literature before his early death at 28 in the wreck of the liner _Titanic._ His mother gave his library to Harvard University, along with a building to house the entire university library at that time. Other collectors of the turn of the century era specialized in more narrow subjects, with J. Augustin Daly building up a library on dramatics and playwrights, William C. Prime on editions of the Bible, and Dean Sage on books about fishing. Others concentrated on specific authors, as Luther Livingston on Charles Dickens, and Marshall C. Lefferts on Alexander Pope. Whatever their specialties, these collectors performed a great service for the reading public, not only in preserving books that might otherwise have been lost, but also in most cases by seeing that they reached permanent homes in public libraries, either by gift or by sale.

In the twentieth century the tide of collecting has fortunately continued, although the day of the truly great collector has probably passed. Recent collections have tended to be more specialized and also smaller due to the fact that less money is available for collecting, and fewer of the really valuable books are coming upon the market. Some twentieth-century collections that should be mentioned, however, would include that of William Augustus White, who like Folger concentrated on the Elizabethan era. At his death in 1927 his Shakespearean collection was said to be second only to the Folger Library. In addition, White built up strong collections in two other fields -- William Blake and American drama. His library was scattered somewhat after his death, but much of the best parts of it were acquired by the British Museum and the libraries of Harvard, Princeton, and the University of Chicago. Frederic R. Halsey collected first editions of English and American literature, and some 20,000 volumes of his library were purchased for the Huntington Library in 1915. Samuel W. Pennepacker, once Governor of Pennsylvania, built up a library of books relating to the Penn family, Pennsylvania, and Benjamin Franklin; while in Savannah, Wymberly Jones DeRenne specialized in works relating to Georgia and the Confederacy.

Wilberforce Eames, librarian and bibliographer (1855-1927), found time in his busy life to gather some 2,500 choice volumes, largely on the subject of American Indians. A. E. Newton's private library of over 10,000 volumes was strong in first editions of English literature, particularly William Blake and Samuel Johnson. John Boyd Thacher (1847-1909), mayor of Albany and a notable political reformer, had a variety of collecting interest, including incunabula, the French Revolution, Columbus, and autographs. In the last field he had a complete set of autographs of the signers of the Declaration of Independence. Most of his collection was subsequently obtained by the Library of Congress.

In more specialized fields among modern collectors there can be found such libraries as that of George A. Plimpton, whose interest was textbooks, particularly rare and early mathematics texts. Walter E. Clark of Harvard collected over 1,500 volumes of Sanskrit and Vedic literature, which were later acquired by the University of California Library at Los Angeles. Lucius Wilmerding concentrated on association items, rare books, and fine bindings formerly owned by notable figures; Robert Garrett's collection was in illuminated manuscripts, both European and Oriental. Grenville Kane collected a choice library of early Americana, while W. T. H. Howe built his around association items, autographed presentation copies, and the like. Prominent collectors of single authors would include Robert B. Adam of Buffalo and his library on Samuel Johnson, William E. Elkins' collection on Samuel Goldsmith, and Ellis Ames Ballard who chose Rudyard Kipling for his collecting activities. The rarest of early Americana was the field chosen by Herschel V. Jones, whose library was sold in 1938. From the voyages of Columbus and Vespucius to the diaries of the California gold miners of 1849, Jones possessed many of the rarest items in American history. Jean Hersholt's collection on Hans Christian Andersen, one of the finest private libraries ever gathered on a relatively minor author, has been acquired by the Library of Congress.

Many private libraries exist today as special collections in public or university libraries. New York Public Library has a number of such collections, including the Arents Tobacco Collection, the Arents Collection of Books in Parts, the Berg Collection of 25,000 volumes of English and American literature, the Bernays Collections on Public Relations and Communication, the Gaynor Memorial Collection on Political Science, the Rabinowitz Collection of rare Hebrew books and manuscripts, the James G. Huneker Collection of vocal and instrumental music, the Phelps Stokes Collection of American views, and the David Belasco Collection of theatrical materials. The Cornell University Library at Ithaca contains such collections as the Wason Library on China and Southeast Asia, the Willard Fiske Collections on Dante and Petrarch, the Faust Collection on German-American relations, and the Fiske Icelandic Library. Princeton University Library has the Junius S. Morgan Collection on Virgil. The Horace Furness Collection on Shakespeare is at the University of Pennsylvania Library, and the Library of Wellesley College has a collection of English poetry given by George Herbert Palmer. Further west, the University of Texas has the John H. Wrenn library of English literature, and this same library has more recently acquired the collection of Edward Alexander Parsons, strong in English literature and the history of books. The University of Wisconsin has the George B. Wild Collection of German literature, the Hermann Schlueter Library on European socialism, and the Chester H. Thordarson collection on the history of science. In the same city the Library of the Wisconsin State Historical Society has the former private library of Lyman C. Draper on Western history. The University of California at Los Angeles has the magnificent William Andrews Clark Memorial Library, based on a collection of English literature and other special fields made by a former Senator from California and donated along with building and endowment to the University in 1926. Elsewhere across the nation other such collections can be easily noted; hardly any college or public library of over 100,000 volumes has not benefited at some time or other from the donations or purchases of private collections.

In recent years the library periodicals have carried the news of a number of major collections acquired by American university libraries. Included in these are the 20,000 volumes of medieval and Renaissance literature acquired by the University of Washington from the collection of Allen R. Benham, the library on neurology given by C. J. Herrick to the University of Kansas, and the Ames Library on South Asia acquired by the University of Minnesota. Knox College has secured the personal library of Dr. Clarence H. Haring on South American history and economics, while Yale University Library has obtained a collection of 15,000 phonograph

records from Mr. and Mrs. Laurence C. Witten II.   The Stefans-
son Library on the arctic regions went to Dartmouth College, while
Tulane University has acquired the Felix H. Kuntz Library on the
history of New Orleans.   The University of Virginia Library has
obtained a library of Chinese classics, collected by a former professor at the University of Hongkong; Duke University Library received 17,500 items on the history of Methodism from Dr. Frank
Baker; and the 6,700 volumes on French culture collected by
François Bouvier was obtained by Michigan State University.

Truly the private collector of books belongs in the forefront
of any relation of library history.   The time, money, effort, and
knowledge necessary to build up such outstanding book collections
are seldom present in public or academic libraries, and so without
the private collector we would be without many of our greatest libraries.   It has been said that every great university is but the
lengthened shadow of a great man; so it just as easily may be said
that every great library is usually the results of the efforts of one
-- or a few -- great men and women.   Some of these we like to
think were librarians -- but many of them were pleased to be known
only as collectors of books.

Additional Readings

(There is no comprehensive work on American private libraries as
such, although there are several good works on American book collectors and a number of titles on individual private libraries.   For
additional information on private libraries, one should consult, besides the usual sources, books on collectors, sales catalogs, particularly auction sales, and biographical sources on individuals
thought to have had private libraries.)

Adams, Randolph G.
    Three Americanists. Philadelphia, 1939.   101 p.
    (Essays on Henri Harrisse as a bibliographer, George Brin-
    ley as a collector, and Thomas Jefferson as a librarian.)

    The whys and wherefores of the William L. Clements Library:
    a brief essay on book-collecting as a fine art.   Ann Arbor,
    1925.   32 p.

Bierstadt, O. A.
    The library of Robert Hoe: a contribution to the history of bib-
    liophilism in America. New York, 1895. 236 p.

Boardman, Samuel L.
Descriptive sketches of six private libraries of Bangor, Maine.
Bangor, 1900.   167 p.

Boyd, Julian
The Scheide Library: a summary view of its history . . .
Princeton, 1947.   xv, 172 p.

Cannon, Carl L.
American book collectors and collecting from colonial times to
the present.   New York, 1941.   xi, 391 p.

Clemons, Harry
The home library of the Garnetts of Elmwood.   Charlottesville,
1957.   59 p.

Du Bois, Henry Pène
Four private libraries of New York.   New York, 1892.   119 p.

The library and art collection of Henry Pène Du Bois.
New York, 1887.   xxiv, 487 p.

Farnham, Luther
A glance at private libraries.   Boston, 1855.   79 p.

Gordan, Phyllis W. G.
Fifteenth-century books in the library of Howard Lehman Good-
hart.   Stamford, 1955.   160 p.

Harding, Walter
Thoreau's library.   Charlottesville, 1957.   102 p.

Humphreys, A. L.
The private library.   New York, 1897.   162 p.

McDermott, John Francis
Private libraries in Creole St. Louis.   Baltimore, 1938.   xii,
186 p.

Nolan, Joseph Allen, ed.
The library of George Gordon King.   Newport, R. I. , 1885.   2 v.

Potter, E. S.
Washington, a model in his library and life.   New York, 1895.
xiv, 220 p.

Robinson, F. W.
The private libraries of Philadelphia.   Philadelphia, 1882.   46 p.

Rogers, Horatio
Private libraries of Providence, with a preliminary essay on the
love of books.   Providence, 1878.   iv, 255 p.

Rosenbach, A. S. W.
  The libraries of the Presidents of the United States.
    Worcester, Mass., 1935. 30 p. (Also in pp. 130-167 of
    his Book Hunter's Holiday, Cambridge, Mass., 1936.)

Shaffer, Ellen
  Portrait of a Philadelphia collector: William McIntire Elkins
    (1882-1947). Philadelphia, 1956. 56 p.

Stevens, Henry
  Recollections of James Lenox and the formation of his library.
    New York, 1951. xxxvi, 187 p. (Originally appeared in
    1886.)

Wynne, James
  Private libraries of New York. New York, 1860. viii, 472 p.

22.

The Library's Role in Western Civilization

With the definition of "history" as that period of man's existence since he began to keep records, it is easily seen that libraries are almost as old as history. Indeed, if our knowledge of
when man began to keep records is based entirely upon surviving
records, and if we define a library as any orderly collection of
preserved records, then the library is exactly as old as history.
At any rate, we know that soon after man learned to write and to
put down in graphic form some evidence of his experiences and observations, if not of his thoughts, he began to save those graphic
records for religious, legal, economic, or purely sentimental reasons. For whatever reason, these collections formed an archive or
protolibrary. As we have seen, these libraries have been in existence in the Western World for somewhere close to 5 thousand
years. As man's civilization has progressed, so has his libraries.
Regardless of the format of his books or records, whether clay tablet, papyrus roll, parchment codex, printed book, or microfilm
reel, man has devised a means of arranging, preserving, and using
them. Once arranged, preserved, and used, they became libraries,
and as such they parallel the cultural advance of Western man from
the Nile to the Hudson or from the Euphrates to the Mississippi.

With this knowledge in view, an interesting query develops.
Does man's cultural advances, his general progress upward in the
climb toward modern civilization, come as a product of the knowledge preserved in the form of libraries, or does this cultural advance merely produce libraries as a by-product? A secondary
query along the same lines might well take this form: Are libraries the products of a communal desire for preserving knowledge,
or are they formed largely by individual efforts for the benefit of
the community? Have any people as a majority of the community

ever risen up and demanded libraries, public libraries, free libraries, or library service in general in the same way that, for example, they have opposed tyranny or taxation, or espoused liberty or a new religion? The second query can be answered more easily than the first, and the answer is simple: probably not. But the answer to the second query throws some light on the first, and it is with this in view that we might quickly review the development of libraries in the Western World in the light of our first query: which comes first, the library or cultural progress?

Going back to the ancient Egyptians, it can be argued that the beginning of the library was purely functional. It came about only as and after a written language had been developed, a social structure with a complicated government and religion had developed, and at least a small portion of the population had become literate. The library was functional because it was kept largely to know what had transpired in the past. It was necessary to keep the laws and decrees of former kings, the land ownership records of former generations, the formal rituals of the Church. As the number of these laws, records, and rituals grew beyond a few score, it became necessary to organize them for easy use, to preserve them in a permanent location, and to designate one or more persons to be responsible for their arrangement, preservation, and availability. But once they had been so arranged and preserved, they became a part of the cultural heritage, a steppingstone to further progress. It was no longer necessary for each generation to make the same mistakes, the same experimental approaches to progress, the same solutions for problems. As an individual grows from infancy to adulthood through a learning process, so a society develops from savagery to civilization through the same experiential movement. But just as the individual, without adult guidance, learns only what he experiences himself, so the society without records of past experiences must relearn any progressive developments with each generation. Oral accounts of previous group and societal experiences, of course, are a part of social growth, but the fantasies of legends and myths indicate the unsound basis of oral tradition for substantial growth. In Egypt, the cumulative graphic recordings of social and cultural progress preserved a single culture for nearly 3 thousand years and brought gradual progress despite political and military upheavals.   If no more rapid progress was made it is possible that a reason can be found in the restricted use of the cultural records due to the large percentage of illiteracy during much of Egypt's history.   Generally speaking, the records of past history were available to only a few literate scribes, and the masses of people during most Egyptian eras remained in a cultural rut, living for the most part just as their ancestors had lived, no better or no worse.   Records of past experience, no matter how well kept, have no effect upon the progress of society unless they are used.

In the storehouses of clay tablets of the Babylonians and Assyrians another element enters the story of cultural progress and library development.   The rulers of the Mesopotamian kingdoms, or at least Ashurbanipal if not others, collected libraries with the idea of preserving all that was known to man, not only the records of his experiences and observations, but also the products of his reasoning and imagination -- his philosophies, theologies, and literature.   Records of land ownership or legal acts may be kept of necessity, but philosophy and literature are kept for the love of learning.   True, much of the "literature" preserved by the almost indestructible clay tablets is functional and utilitarian, but there is evidence that there was an effort to preserve all that had been or could reasonably be committed to graphic form, whether business record or epic poem.   If the "book-keepers" of Egypt were largely archivists, those of Assyria came close to being bibliophiles.   Certainly the Assyrians reaped from their libraries the benefits, economic and cultural, of 2 thousand years of Sumerians, Chaldeans, and Babylonians.   Yet even here the great libraries came at the height of a cultural epoch, after a relatively prosperous and semi-urban society had produced wealthy rulers and a prosperous priesthood with great palaces and temples to house and protect their records.   And again we note that only a small minority of the people could read and benefit directly from the knowledge preserved in their libraries.

With the Greeks, the utilitarian function of the library becomes if anything subordinated to the preservation of books for their literary value. The idea of starting a public library so that the correct texts of dramas can be both preserved and readily available is a far cry from the preservation of tax records; yet it is at the same time still utilitarian. In this sense, the early Athenian public library served as a copyright office with the right of legal deposit. And when the Greek master teachers compiled libraries of texts that they read to their students or that they allowed their students to copy, they introduced the educational motive to the function of the library, and the knowledge contained in books was put to use by more and larger groups of people. Of course, the temple libraries of Egypt and Babylonia were also used to teach, but here the function was more the teaching of language or the training of scribes rather than the teaching of literature or philosophy. With the building of the great Alexandrian libraries, still another function for the library appears. Not only were records preserved and literatures collected with the idea of saving everything ever committed to writing, but now there was the task of editing, criticizing, translating, and correcting texts to preserve literary purity and accuracy. Whether the Septuagint was prepared in the Serapeion or not, it could easily have come from such a scholarly institution. With the zeal of the Hellenic scholars and the wealth of the Ptolemies, the libraries at Alexandria approached a completeness never before known, and probably never since. But the libraries and the museum were not all of Alexandria, and Alexandria was not all of the Hellenic world. The thousands of rolls were only a microcosm of learning in a world of ignorance, and this great center of learning was more the result of Alexandrian Greece than the cultural forefather of Rome. Or was it?

For finally with the Romans we begin to see where cumulated cultural resources of societies distant in time or space bring forth the flowering of a new civilization. Certainly the Romans borrowed culturally -- books and teachers and ideas -- from the Greeks and others, whether from Alexandria or Pergamum, Carthage or Syracuse, or directly from Greece itself. When books became spoils of war, and educated slaves came with them, a new

Rome emerged. A literature was begun, a language was formalized, a wealthy, cultured nobility arose -- and a republic became an Empire. What was the debt of Rome to Greece, and how much of that debt was incurred with the rolls of papyrus and parchment and the stolen statues that passed from the eastern Mediterranean to the Italian peninsula? The early libraries of Rome were largely the toys of the wealthy nobility, but this nobility was relatively large, and probably a larger percentage of the citizenry were literate and used those libraries more frequently during the height of Roman culture than ever before in the history of man. Rome had achieved a stable society, strong armies, and wealthy leaders before it acquired large libraries, but from those libraries it developed a strengthened, reinforced, expanded and enlarged culture that was in many respects the sum total of all that had gone before. Even the shadow of Rome and Greece that was Byzantium for a thousand years basked in the glow of the culture that had flowered on the Tiber. Rome reached a height of civilization and culture never before reached by Western man, and its libraries were both a cause and a result of that culture.

Books can preserve ideas, and they can spread them. The lessons taught by an itinerant Hebrew by the name of Jesus - lessons at once both simple and profound - spread a social revolution from one end of the Mediterranean to the other in a little more than a hundred years. Much of the teaching of Christ and his followers was spread by word of mouth, by teachers and preachers speaking to their followers; but with the writing down of the Gospel of Mark and the Epistles of Paul, Christianity adopted the graphic word, and a new dimension was added. The parchment codex carried the story of Christ and the teachings of his followers wherever the Roman legion ruled. From Ethiopia to Ireland, from the Black Sea to the Baltic, a new era was born. Certainly Christianity spread with the book -- The Book -- and though Christians were persecuted by Rome for nearly 300 years, the Empire nevertheless provided them with a relatively peaceful and stable society in which to grow, and in the end Christianity won out. No one can doubt that the heart and strength of Christianity for nearly 2,000 years has been in the written word, and the library, whether of priest or Pope, monastery or cathedral, has been an essential organ of the church from the days of Paul to the present. Did Christianity grow out of the graphically preserved culture of an earlier era? Certainly the culture in which Christianity arose had available the Hebrew literature of a thousand years - the Dead Sea Scrolls confirm this even if we ignore the evidence in the Bible itself - as well as that of the contemporary Greek and Roman civilization. The power of the printed word, and the value of the library, is nowhere better illustrated than in the rise, spread and durability of the Christian religion. Concurrently, it is well to point out that the perseverance and stamina that has enabled the Jewish religion to survive in the face of almost continuous persecution during the same two thousand years stems strongly from the written word that is the Jewish scripture. Surely the Torah and the Talmud have played just as much a part in the survival of Judaism as the Bible has played in the spread of Christianity.

But it was in the Middle Ages that the true value of the book and the library was proven. When barbarians swept over much of the civilized world, and when the sword and flame destroyed all but the remnants of the Roman world, it was in the rolls and codices collected in a few isolated monasteries, or brought into Constantinople by a zealous Christian emperor, that the heritage of both our Christian and classical civilization was preserved. For almost a thousand years these records lay relatively dormant. In Constantinople they were copied, abridged, compended - and little understood. In the Moslem world they were translated and at least the Greek classics were understood and enlarged and fused into a Moslem learning that was to far surpass anything that Western Europe could offer in the Dark Ages. In western Europe, in a thousand monastery cells, monks bent over their desks, copying and recopying old parchments that they barely understood, embellishing them with ornaments, but seldom adding to them or extracting from them any ideas. There were, of course, bright flashes of light in the Dark Ages, light that spread from an Isidore, an Alcuin, a Carolingian renascence, or a brilliant thirteenth century; but on the

whole, the Western World went backward from the fall of Rome to
the Renaissance. During the Middle Ages, the library in the monastery and cathedral, the occasional noble's study, and the early
scholar's room, truly served one of its functions, that of preservation, but its greater function of communicating ideas was little realized. Though many works of the classic era were lost, some
survived and like seed waiting for a fruitful season, they lay dormant and still, awaiting the inquiring mind of the Renaissance, the
mind that would understand them, translate them into action, and
put them to use.

What brought on the Renaissance? Why should a Europe long
locked in a feudal and futile system of ignorance compounded gradually awake and emerge into a "modern era" where ideas ran ramp-
ant -- ideas like humanism, neo-classicism, nationalism, Protestantism, and on down to industrialism, capitalism, and communism?
Was it the Crusades that brought to western Europe new ideas, new
tastes, new methods - and a new look at the classics? Or was it
the economic prosperity, brought on by the revived trade, stimu-
lated by the Crusades and promoted by rising nationalism that led
Europe into a new age? The answer is probably both, not wholely
either, plus other factors less tangible and provable. It is interesting to note, however, that the western Renaissance began in Italy,
never entirely separated from the knowledge of Greek, Moslem, and
Jewish scholars. It was largely from Italy that the Crusaders took
ship for the Holy Land, and it was largely through Italy that their
remnants returned. It was the Italian cities of Venice and Genoa
and Florence that first became merchant metropolises in modern
Europe, and it was their princely and merchant families that encouraged and financed the recovering, translating, copying, and dissemination of the Greek and Latin classics. It was to these cities
and neighboring ones that the manuscripts retrieved from Constantinople and from the monasteries of Greece and Asia Minor came to
enter the private collections and from them the libraries of the
Western World. If the printing press was developed in northern
Europe, it was in Italy that it flowered with the classics, and
from one press alone, that of Aldus Manutius, came more copies

of Aristotle's various works in about 25 years than the world had
known in the previous 2,000. If the printing press brought a revolution in the world of communication, it also brought the library to
the beginning of the modern era. More books meant more libraries, larger libraries, more available information for more
people. The library was finally on the verge of achieving its fullest
purpose -- that of making the heritage of the past fully available to
all the people all the time. But it was still to take nearly four
hundred years before this goal could even be approximately reached.

In modern Europe - since 1500 - the library in its preserva-
tive role has roughly reached its zenith. The great libraries of
Italy, France, Germany, and England have gathered and preserved
virtually every important item in manuscript or print that survived
the Dark Arges or came after them. But on the whole, these libraries have still been available to only a few of the people -- the
collectors, librarians, teachers, a few students and scholars --
and the concept of popular libraries, of mass culture, has been realized only in the twentieth century if at all. Has modern Europe's
culture stemmed from its libraries, or have they resulted from it?
Shakespeare found the sources for his plays in many ways, from
history, folklore, and other writers' works, but in almost every
case he found them in print. Karl Marx's ideas came out of the
British Museum, possibly filtered through a warped mind, but nevertheless his long studies undoubtedly gave form to his theories.
Could well-used popular libraries have prevented the rise of a Hitler? Possibly. Certainly he made use of his brand of librarianship to sell his racist and Nazi theories. Would an educated Russia have adopted communism? Possibly. Certainly no country on
earth has so adopted the book and the library as a means of controlling the minds of the people as has the U.S.S.R. since 1918.
But where did libraries come from before the days of the popular
revolutions? Largely from the efforts of princely collectors, biblio-
philic philanthropists, ecclesiastic scholars, and a few ordinary
book lovers. Only a society that is relatively stable, with at least
a small class that is economically prosperous, can provide the
setting in which libraries can grow. For hundreds of years Europe

has seen the founding and preservation of libraries by the few and for the few. Apparently there was no great demand for library service from the people, nor was there great use of libraries where they were available. But nevertheless they were there, and the leaders of the people - academic, religious, economic, political, scientific - had access to them and made use of them. Modern European culture is, directly or indirectly, a product of its pre-served heritage in graphic form -- in other words of its books and libraries.

If Europe demonstrates the interdependence of libraries and cultural growth in a continuing society, then the English colonies in America well illustrate the value of the written word in the trans-ferral and transformation of a culture from one background to an-other. It was the written word that brought many if not all of the first settlers to America - the explorers' glorified accounts of the New World, the trading company's charters and contracts, or the land promoter's pleadings and promises. Once in the new land, the settler was more often occupied with the plow than the pen; but even if he had only two books, the Bible and the almanac, he re-lied on them and on his leaders who, political or clerical, were never far from the printed word. When the American Revolution came, it was made inevitable by the tyranny of printed laws; in-spired by the printed philosophies of a bygone age; promoted by letter, newspaper and broadside; and fanned into flame by the publi-cation of a single pamphlet - Thomas Paine's Common Sense. The Declaration of Independence drew from a dozen sources, including the composite heritage of the Western World from the Greek de-mocracy, through the Roman republic, the English freedom, the French philosophy, and the colonial American determination to cre-ate a new nation. Behind every significant event in American his-tory there has been a book, a pamphlet, a printed law or treaty, or a written contract. Everywhere one turns in American history the idea preserved in graphic form has shaped events for better or for worse. If colonial America did not develop great libraries, it nevertheless made good use of books, and probably more than any society ever developed before it owed its nature and its very existence to the printed word.

In the nineteenth century, however, the United States did develop great libraries. Slowly but surely over the hundred years, it developed from a frontier nation of a few books to the single most library-minded nation in the world. By 1900 the United States had the most libraries, the largest libraries - with a few exceptions - and certainly the most-used libraries in the world. For a nation founded on books revered the printed word, and as political independence and economic security made it possible, libraries of all types and sizes were formed. Governments, whether state, federal or local, formed libraries; societies formed libraries; schools and colleges formed libraries; and last but not least, business and industry formed libraries. With a few exceptions, all of these libraries were formed for use, not merely for preservation. Books and libraries in the United States came to be meant for the reader -- for educational, recreational, inspirational, and informational use -- and the printed word came to be used in its ultimate form as a means of communication of ideas from one mind to others. The value of the printed word came to be appreciated more than ever before in any time or place. The role of the library as an adjunct to education, as a device for information, as a partner to recreation, as a boon for business, or as a satellite for science has been widely proclaimed, and to a large extent realized. As Western civilization has reached what we like to think is its highest point, the library has come into its own as a key part of that civilization. We still do not have all the libraries and all the books that we feel we need fully to meet the demands of our current culture, but nevertheless we realize that our culture would not and could not have reached its present level without those libraries that we still consider inadequate.

All of which indicates the part that libraries have played in the development of the Western World, but does it answer our main question? The answer at which we have arrived seems to indicate that neither cultural progress nor the library necessarily comes first. Each is at one and the same time to a large extent the cause and result of the other. Cultural progress comes from accumulated experience and knowledge; record of that experience has been best kept in graphic form - in the form of books and libraries. But the preservation of graphically recorded knowledge is not automatic or self-generated. Recorded knowledge does not become a usable library or archive without the conscious effort of some person or people. The accumulation of large collections of graphic materials, and the organization of that material into libraries, seems to depend upon a rather high degree of culture, an advanced civilization -- and one that is relatively peaceful and prosperous. War, pestilence, famine, and ignorance are as much the enemies of books as they are of people. Despite the value of their contents, books and libraries are not indestructible and history provides many examples that in times of great disaster, books are among the first items to be destroyed, whether intentionally or accidentally. Libraries and cultural progress would seem to have an interdependent relationship rather than one of cause and effect.

Another observation on the nature and growth of libraries should be mentioned. Generally speaking, the development of a useful library is more often than not the result of the labors of one man, or a few men, in performing a task that is little appreciated by the majority of their contemporaries. Great popular demand for libraries is almost conspicuous by its absence; great popular support is also usually lacking. Most of the great libraries of the Western World have behind them a history of long neglect, with a constant struggle for funds, for quarters, and for staff. Only in the last century or so have they been generally supported, used, and appreciated. Throughout history their very existence has been the result of the efforts of a few; they have been used intelligently by only a few more. Yet their effect has been universal. Perhaps as the full use of books and libraries becomes realized, then the full benefits of Western civilization will be achieved among all its people.

What of the future of libraries in the Western world? How will the libraries, archives, information and documentation centers be able to cope with the tremendous outpouring of graphic and other recorded materials of the near future - and the distant future? It has been estimated that over half of the graphic materials ever produced has come since 1900; that over half of the scientific research done in the history of man has been done since 1939. With recorded information increasing in geometric proportions, the problems involved in collecting, organizing, and making readily available this mountain of materials on paper, film, disk, and tape seems insurmountable. Perhaps the answer to the problem of "controlling" this informational "wave of the future" lies in electronics and automation. Certainly good minds are at work on this problem. Steps in the right direction have been made with the microfilm and its related forms, with the computer and its electronic allies. Now we seem to be headed toward the micro-microfilm that can reduce the printed page to a little more than pinpoint size. One such extra-reducing camera can reportedly produce a film on which a million pages could be stored in 1 cubic foot, or approximately 3 million average volumes in one 10-foot cube. Add to this reduction in volume the electronic system capable of locating in a few seconds any page wanted in those millions of volumes and reproducing it anywhere in the United States on a television screen, and you have what might be termed the ultimate in library service at present in view.

But somewhere in the midst of this super-mechanization, this Jules Verne world of information storage and retrieval, let us hope that there will always be a place for the ordinary book - and with it the ordinary librarian - the individual who knows books and who finds supreme satisfaction in bringing a book and a reader together. The human element has always been uppermost in the history of books and libraries; let us hope that it always remains that way.

Also in the future the library in its general sense has a tremendous task to perform in human relations, whether on the local, national, or international level. After World War II the United States made a conscious effort to sell the "American way of life" to the rest of the world, and the U.S. Information Service Libraries played a large part in that effort. At present viewing it would seem that this effort has been a failure. Neither our libraries nor our dollars have won us many permanent friends. Perhaps our mistake lay in assuming that what was good for Americans was good for everyone else as well. Perhaps we should accept the fact that other peoples are different and cease trying to mold them into what we think they should be. Communication between peoples in all parts of the world is an established fact and will continue in one way or the other. Instantaneous communication, via television and radio, has reached or soon will reach the point where one voice can conceivably be heard at one time by all the people on earth. This is good, but much of this dynamic communication is what we call "news," seldom subject to serious thought before it is communicated. By accident or intention these electronic means of communication could plunge the world into chaos in seconds. But graphic communication, on the other hand, is a somewhat slower process. It can and must be a more considered process. Whether newspapers, magazines, books, or pictures, the graphic forms of communication must be employed to bring the element of thoughtful contemplation into the consideration of world or local problems. They must be used to bring people together, to teach them to understand each other, to arbitrate and mediate differences, rather than to hurl insults and diatribes. A push-button war can be started in split-seconds; a permanent peace can be achieved only through years of patient effort, of growing appreciation of mutual interests, of education toward an understanding tolerance of other peoples, their cultures, and their problems. Books and libraries will play a most important role in this effort toward world peace and toward arousing the world's people to fighting ignorance, intolerance, disease, and poverty instead of each other. Books and libraries have helped create what we call Western civilization; they can and will help to create a better world.

Additional Readings

(Books relating directly to the role of libraries in the history of Western civilization are extremely few, but books touching the subject in passing are legion. Almost every work on social and cultural history touches on the subject, but many of them do so without mentioning the word "library." The following works, although

varying widely in period and area covered, and in approach to the
subject, are all pertinent to the general topic of the chapter.)

Aelbrouck, André van
    Education populaire et bibliothèques publiques: les conditions
    historiques, sociales et psychologiques de leur evolution.
    Bruxelles, 1956. 182 p.

Artz, Frederick B.
    The mind of the middle ages. New York, 1953. 552 p.

Bailey, Cyril, ed.
    The legacy of Rome. Oxford, 1923. 512 p.

Bolgar, R. R.
    The classical heritage and its beneficiaries. Cambridge, 1954.
    592 p.

Burckhardt, Jakob Christoph
    The civilization of the Renaissance. London, 1929. 526 p.

Butler, Pierce, ed.
    Scholarship and civilization. Chicago, 1944. v, 34 p.

Clapp, Verner
    The future of the research library. Urbana, 1964. 124 p.

DePeyster, Frederic
    The moral and intellectual influence of libraries upon social
    progress. New York, 1866. 96 p.

Gummere, Richard M.
    The American colonial mind and the classical tradition.
    Cambridge, Mass., 1963. 228 p.

Haskins, C. H.
    The Renaissance of the twelfth century. Cambridge, Mass.,
    1927. 437 p. (Reprinted 1957.)

Highet, Gilbert
    The classical tradition: Greek and Roman influences on western
    literature. New York, 1949. 763 p.

Irwin, Raymond
    The heritage of the English library. Amsterdam, 1963. 288 p.

Karstedt, Peter
    Studien zur Soziologie der Bibliothek. Wiesbaden, 1954. 97 p.

Kramm, Heinrich
    Deutsche Bibliotheken unter dem Einfluss von Humanismus und
    Reformation: Ein Beitrag zur deutschen Bildungsgeschichte.
    Leipzig, 1938. 304 p.

Laistner, Max
   The intellectual heritage of the early middle ages; selected
      essays. Ithaca, N.Y., 1957. xvii, 285 p.

Landheer, Bartholomeus
   Social function of libraries. New York, 1957. 287 p.

Learned, William S.
   The American public library and the diffusion of knowledge.
      New York, 1924. 89 p.

Murison, William John
   The public library: its origins, purpose, and significance as a
      social institution. London, 1955. 222 p.

Rose, Ernestine
   The public library in American life. New York, 1954. xviii,
      238 p.

Sandys, John Edwin
   A history of classical scholarship from the sixth century B.C.,
      to the end of the middle ages. Cambridge, 1906-1908. 3 v.

Shera, Jesse H.
   Historians, books and libraries: a survey of historical scholar-
      ship in relation to library resources, organization and serv-
      ices. Cleveland, 1953. 126 p.

Tyregod, Oskar
   Die Kulturfunktion der Bibliothek. The Hague, 1936. 219 p.

Waples, Douglas
   People and print: social aspects of reading in the Depression.
      Chicago, 1937. 228 p.

Wilson, Louis R.
   The geography of reading: a study of the distribution and status
      of libraries in the United States. Chicago, 1938. 481 p.

415

Library bookstock (cont.)
141-2, 149, 152, 153, 155,
159-60, 164, 188, 273-5, 281-
4, 291, 292, 307, 313, 316,
352
Library buildings, 52, 60, 68,
71, 109, 114, 124, 125, 127,
140, 143-4, 150-1, 155, 160-1,
175-6, 190, 280, 282, 291,
293, 295, 296, 298, 302-3,
306, 319, 321, 322, 326,
330-1, 351, 366-7
Library legislation, 197, 200-1,
210-12, 214, 216-7, 219, 279,
319, 324, 340, 365
Library philanthropy, 71, 90,
123, 126, 131, 136, 140, 143,
149, 152, 160, 175, 176, 180,
182, 189, 199, 211, 228, 262,
267, 268, 275-8, 282, 292-5,
300-1, 303-4, 319, 322, 326,
345, 369, 386-8
Library rules and regulations,
102, 112, 113-4, 123-4, 127-8,
144, 275-6, 277, 298, 340, 367
Library standards, 306, 343,
346
Library storage, 307-8
Library training, 190, 378-9
SEE ALSO Librarians
Libri lintei, 64
Linear B script, 45-6
Lincoln, Abraham, 384
Logan, James, 282-3
Los Angeles, Calif., Public Li-
brary, 323
Louvain, Belgium, University
Library, 188
Lucian, 69-70
Lucullus, Lucius, 65, 76
Luther, Martin, 203

Madison, James, 295, 384
Magliabecchi, Antonio, 160, 250
Mai, Cardinal Angelo, 228
Marcellinus, Ammianus, 78
Margaret of York, 134
Martial, 70
Marx, Karl, 403
Mather, Cotton, 273-4
Matthias Corvinus, King of
Hungary, 143, 158
Medici family libraries, 139-40,

250, 253
Mein, John, 286
Michigan. University Library, 373
Micro-materials, 304-6, 308, 353,
407
Midwest Inter-Library Center,
Chicago, 307
Monasticism, 101-5, 108
Mongols, 96
Morel, Eugene, 196
Morgan, John Pierpont, 388-9
Moscow University Library, 182,
184

Napoleon I, Emperor, 253-4
National Central Library, Florence,
160, 250
National Central Library, London,
201-2
National Central Library, Milan,
161
National Central Library, Naples,
250
National Central Library, Rome,
160-1
National Central Library, Turin,
250
National Central Library, Venice,
161
National Education Association,
341, 343
Naudé, Gabriel, 252
Nestorian Christians, 88
New Harmony, Indiana, Working
Men's Institute Library, 316
New Orleans, La., Public Li-
brary, 317, 322-3
New York, N.Y., Public Library,
320-1, 372, 386, 391-2
New York Society Library, 273,
281-2, 312, 320
Newberry Library, Chicago, 372
Nicholas V, Pope, 141
North Carolina. University Li-
brary. 296, 302-3, 305, 387
Novello, Dominico Malatesta, 140,
143-4

Olenin, A.N., 154
Origen, 73
Ostraka, 37, 38, 41
Ovid (Publius Ovidius Naso), 77
Oxford University Library, 84,

416

Tiberius, Emperor, 66-7
Tilden, Samuel, 320
Tischendorf, Constantine, 154-5
Trajan, Emperor, 67
Tyler, John, 384
Tyrannion, 49, 65, 68, 76

United Nations. Library, 362
United States. Department of
Agriculture Library, 354
United States. Department of
State Library, 352-3
United States. Department of
Treasury Library, 353
United States. Department of
War Library, 353
United States. Information Serv-
ice Libraries, 206, 357-8, 407
United States. Library of Con-
gress, 349-52, 367, 386, 391
United States. Library Services
Act of 1956, 332
United States. National Agricul-
tural Library, 354
United States. National Library
of Medicine, 353-4
United States. Office of Educa-
tion Library, 327, 330, 342,
344, 345, 354
United States. Supreme Court Li-
brary, 350
United States. White House Li-
brary, 354
United States. Works Progress
Administration, 304, 329-30
Uppsala, Sweden, University Li-
brary, 189, 267

Varro, Terentius, 66, 69, 76
Vatican Library, Rome, 108-10,
141-2, 144, 228-9, 251, 263,
268
Vespasian, Emperor, 67
Vespasiani da Bisticci, 139-40
Virginia. State Library, 359
Virginia. University Library,
295, 302-3, 384, 393

Washington, George, 285, 350
Washington and Lee University
Library, Lexington, Va., 296
Wax tablets, 16-7, 40
White, William Augustus, 390

Widener, Harry Elkins, 389
William and Mary College Li-
brary, Williamsburg, Va., 277,
295
Williams Library, London, 233
Winthrop, John, 273, 275
Wisconsin. University Library,
392
Wisconsin State Historical So-
ciety Library, Madison, 360,
392
Women as book collectors, 143,
253, 267, 274
Writing, 21, 32, 45-6
Writing materials, 12-8, 40-1,
SEE ALSO Names of particular
writing materials.

Yale University Library, New
Haven, Conn., 276, 292-3, 302,
392
Young Men's Christian Association Libraries, 312, 315

Zaluski family library, 153, 265
Zeno, Emperor, 82
Zenon of Philadelphia, 57